HOUGHTON MIFFLIN
math
CENTRAL

15R2
9)137

HOUGHTON MIFFLIN

Boston • Atlanta • Dallas • Geneva, Illinois • Princeton, New Jersey • Palo Alto

# Authors

## Kindergarten

**Patsy F. Kanter**
Consultant, Teacher, Author
Isidore Newman School
New Orleans, Louisiana

**Janet G. Gillespie**
Title 1 Specialist, Author
Woodlawn Elementary School
Portland, Oregon

## Levels 1–6

**Laurie A. Boswell**
Profile Jr./Sr. High School
Bethlehem, New Hampshire

**Mary Esther Reynosa**
Elementary Mathematics Curriculum Specialist
Edgewood School District
San Antonio, Texas

**Dr. Juanita Copley**
Associate Professor of Education
University of Houston
Houston, Texas

**Dr. Jean M. Shaw**
Professor of Elementary Education
University of Mississippi
University, Mississippi

**Audrey L. Jackson**
Assistant Principal
Parkway School District
St. Louis County, Missouri

**Dr. Lee Stiff**
Associate Professor of Mathematics Education
North Carolina State University
Raleigh, North Carolina

**Edward Manfre**
Mathematics Education Consultant
Albuquerque, New Mexico

**Dr. Charles S. Thompson**
Professor of Mathematics Education
University of Louisville
Louisville, Kentucky

## Consultants and Contributing Authors

**Carole Basile**
University of Houston
Houston, Texas

**Dr. Deborah Ann Chessin**
University of Mississippi
University, Mississippi

**Dr. Karen Karp**
University of Louisville
Louisville, Kentucky

**Cindy Chapman**
Inez Science and Technology
Magnet School
Albuquerque, New Mexico

**Dr. Richard Evans**
Plymouth State College
Plymouth, New Hampshire

**Casilda Pardo**
Armijo Elementary School
Albuquerque, New Mexico

**Dr. Robert Gyles**
Community School District 4
New York, New York

**Caitlin Robinson**
Mitchell Elementary School
Albuquerque, New Mexico

**Acknowledgments** See page 527.

Printed in the U.S.A.

ISBN: 0-395-84742-7

89-VH-03 02 01 00 99

# Contents

# Multiplication and Division Facts  page  118

## 5 Geometry

## CHAPTER 6 · Multiplying by 1-Digit Numbers page 206

# math CENTRAL

# Dividing by 1-Digit Numbers

page 236

# Fractions

page 274

# Addition and Subtraction of Fractions

page 306

# 10  Measurement and Time

page 336

# CHAPTER 11 · Decimals

 **Multiplying by 2-Digit Numbers** page 412

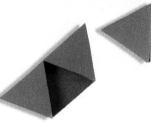

# CHAPTER 13 Dividing by 2-Digit Numbers

page 444

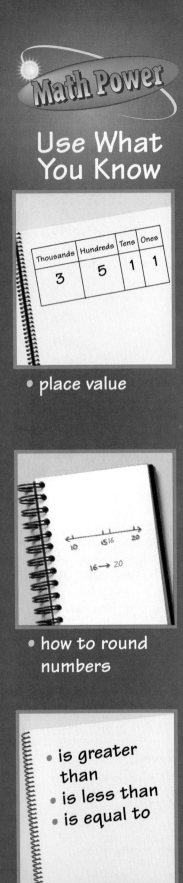

| Thousands | Hundreds | Tens | Ones |
|-----------|----------|------|------|
| 3 | 5 | 1 | 1 |

- place value

- how to round numbers

- is greater than
- is less than
- is equal to

- the vocabulary

## CHAPTER 1

# Place Value

## Try This!

**H**ave you ever wanted to invent something? Use numbers and math ideas to invent a funny number machine.

### What You'll Need

drawing paper, markers

**1** Think of what you want your machine to do. Will it count? Will it estimate? Will it tell place value? Or will it do many things? You decide.

make silly noises for numbers
—what would 167 sound like?

1.

2.

3.

me up in the morning
- all the stars
- bring us popcorn every day

robot

MONDAY 8

POPCORN

Snore Machine

2 5 2 7

Tape Recorder

Pulley

Pulley

2

**2**

Draw a picture of your funny machine. Give the machine a name. Label the different parts. Show how the machine uses numbers or changes them.

Wake Up!

My machine counts snores.

It plays music at 2527 snores.

**3**

Describe how your machine works. Include ideas about numbers in your description.

How did you use math to plan and make your machine?

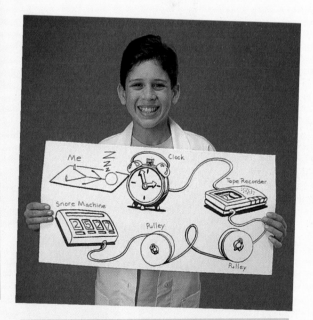

What is an important math idea that your machine shows? Why is it important?

**Ready to Go!**

# Using Tens to Estimate

**C**an you tell how many marbles are in a glass jar without counting them? You can estimate to find a number close to the actual amount. When you **estimate**, you tell about how many.

## Guess How Many!

### Activity

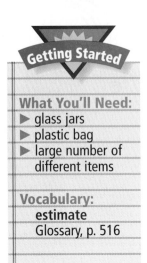

**Getting Started**

**What You'll Need:**
▶ glass jars
▶ plastic bag
▶ large number of different items

**Vocabulary:**
estimate
Glossary, p. 516

- Form a small group.
- Make a chart like the one on page 3.
- Place small items in a clear container.

**1**
Estimate how many items you think are in your container. Record your estimate on your chart.

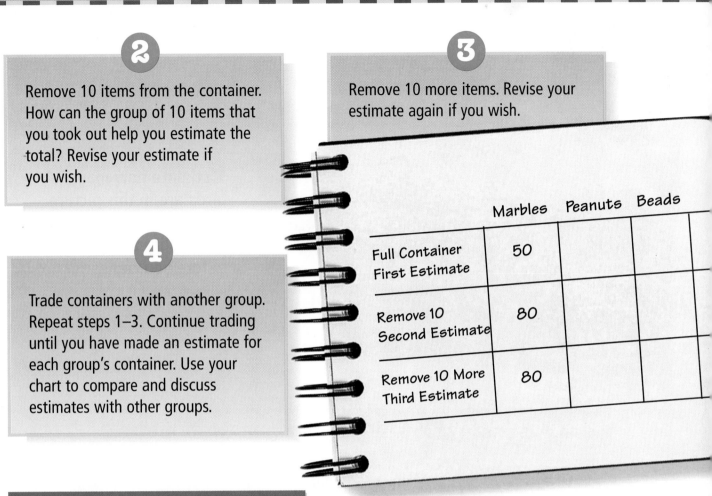

**2** Remove 10 items from the container. How can the group of 10 items that you took out help you estimate the total? Revise your estimate if you wish.

**3** Remove 10 more items. Revise your estimate again if you wish.

**4** Trade containers with another group. Repeat steps 1–3. Continue trading until you have made an estimate for each group's container. Use your chart to compare and discuss estimates with other groups.

| | Marbles | Peanuts | Beads | |
|---|---|---|---|---|
| Full Container First Estimate | 50 | | | |
| Remove 10 Second Estimate | 80 | | | |
| Remove 10 More Third Estimate | 80 | | | |

## Show What You Know!

1. **Critical Thinking** Think about the last items you estimated. Explain how you used the 10 objects you removed to help you estimate the number in the container.

**Use the pictures and captions to choose the best estimate.**

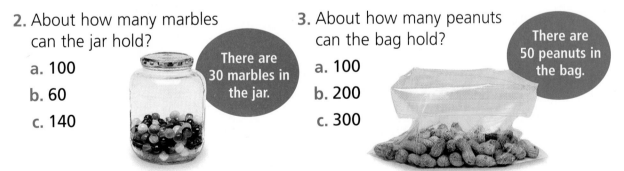

2. About how many marbles can the jar hold?

   There are 30 marbles in the jar.

   a. 100
   b. 60
   c. 140

3. About how many peanuts can the bag hold?

   There are 50 peanuts in the bag.

   a. 100
   b. 200
   c. 300

4. Is it easier to estimate items in a jar or in a plastic bag? Explain.

5. Why are tens and hundreds often used to make estimates?

6. **Write About It** Describe another time when you estimated a number of items.

# Estimating How Many

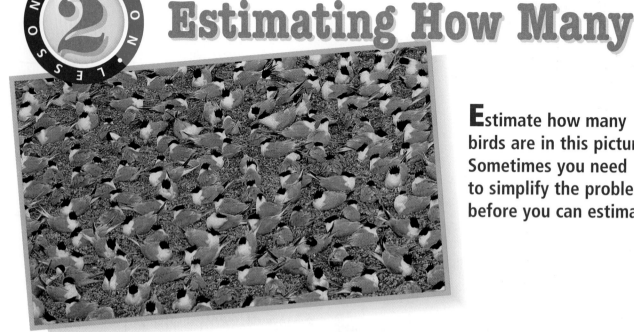

**E**stimate how many birds are in this picture. Sometimes you need to simplify the problem before you can estimate.

## Here's A Way!  Estimate the number of birds.

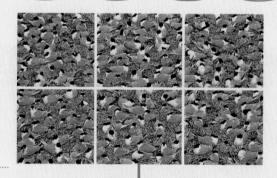

**1** Divide the picture into equal-size parts. How many parts are there?

**2** Estimate the number of birds in one part.

There are about 20 birds in one part.

**3** Use that number as an estimate for each part. Add the parts to find a reasonable estimate for the whole picture.

$$20 + 20 + 20 + 20 + 20 + 20 = 120$$

There are about 120 birds.

## Talk About It!

Describe a situation in which you would choose to estimate rather than count the actual amount. Tell why.

## Show What You Know!

The bar graph below shows some students' estimates of the number of birds in the picture. Look at the bars on the graph and the numbers on the left side. Use the data to answer the question.

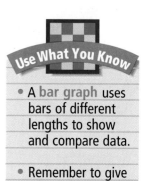

**Use What You Know**

• A **bar graph** uses bars of different lengths to show and compare data.

• Remember to give your graph a title. Label the data.

1. How many estimates are shown on the graph?

2. What is the lowest estimate? the highest estimate?

3. Which student made the closest estimate? How can you tell?

4. What do you think is Mia's estimate? Explain your answer.

5. What do you think is Megan's estimate?

6. Whose estimate is 20 more than the estimate given on page 4?

7. About how much higher is Todd's estimate than Megan's?

**Bird Estimates**

| | Mia | Todd | Josh | Kate | Megan |
|---|---|---|---|---|---|

(Bar graph with vertical axis labeled 0, 20, 40, 60, 80, 100, 120, 140, 160, 180)

## Work It Out!

Use the bar graph above to answer the question.

8. Write a label for the names at the bottom of the bar graph.

9. Write a label for the numbers on the side of the bar graph.

10. **Logical Reasoning** Write at least six facts you can read from the bar graph.

11. **Critical Thinking** How does the bar graph help you understand the different estimates?

12. Look at the chart to the right. Grades 1 through 5 collected newspapers and put them in packs for the Recycling Drive. To show the results in a different way, make a bar graph.

| Grade | Packs of Newspaper |
|---|---|
| 1 | 20 |
| 2 | 50 |
| 3 | 60 |
| 4 | 80 |
| 5 | 50 |

# 3 Mental Math: Using Facts and Patterns

**Y**ou have 9 packages of fruit chews to share with your class. Each package contains 10 pieces. You think you may not have enough to share equally, so you buy 3 more packages. How many fruit chews do you have now?

You can use what you know about basic facts and tens to solve the problem mentally.

## Here's A Way! Use a fact to add tens.

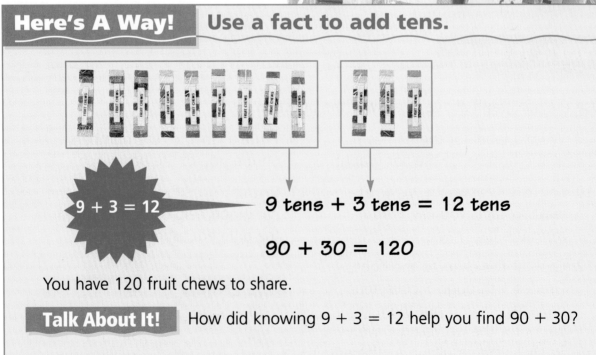

$9 + 3 = 12$

9 tens + 3 tens = 12 tens

$90 + 30 = 120$

You have 120 fruit chews to share.

**Talk About It!** How did knowing $9 + 3 = 12$ help you find $90 + 30$?

## Show What You Know!

Use basic facts and mental math to find the answer.

1. a. $8 + 5 = \blacksquare$      b. $80 + 50 = \blacksquare$      c. $800 + \blacksquare = 1300$

2. a. $7 + 9 = \blacksquare$      b. $70 + \blacksquare = 160$      c. $700 + 900 = \blacksquare$

3. a. $14 - \blacksquare = 8$      b. $140 - 80 = \blacksquare$      c. $1400 - 800 = \blacksquare$

4. **Critical Thinking** Explain why thinking of 1400 as 14 hundreds can help you find $1400 - 800$.

## Work It Out!

Use basic facts and mental math to find the answer.

5. $70 + 40 = \blacksquare$      6. $50 - 40 = \blacksquare$      7. $70 + 40 + 20 = \blacksquare$

8. $170 - 80 = \blacksquare$      9. $300 + 200 = \blacksquare$      10. $1600 - \blacksquare = 800$

11. $120 + 120 = \blacksquare$      12. $500 - 200 = \blacksquare$      13. $\blacksquare - 1200 = 100$

14. Choose pairs of numbers whose sum is 1000.

| 500   200   600   800   500   700   400   300 |

**Functions** Find the numbers to complete the table.

| Number | Number + 300 | Number + 600 | Number − 400 | Number − 200 |
|--------|--------------|--------------|--------------|--------------|
| 800 | 1100 | 1400 | 400 | 600 |
| 700 | 15. ? | 16. ? | 17. ? | 18. ? |
| 900 | 19. ? | 20. ? | 21. ? | 22. ? |
| 500 | 23. ? | 24. ? | 25. ? | 26. ? |

27. **Problem Solving** A supply of 1500 fruit chews was ordered for two school ballgames. If 800 fruit chews were given to fans at the first game, how many were left to give out at the second game? What basic fact can help you solve this problem?

**Calculator** Work with a partner. One partner uses a calculator to find the answer. The other uses mental math. Compare answers.

28. $7000 + 9000 = \blacksquare$      29. $800 - 200 = \blacksquare$      30. $70 + 80 = \blacksquare$

31. $900 - 300 = \blacksquare$      32. $80 - 40 = \blacksquare$      33. $12{,}000 - 4000 = \blacksquare$

**More Practice Set 1.3, p. 472**

# Problem Solving

## Guess and Check

**Y**ou are packing 2 dogsleds for an Arctic journey. The packed sleds weigh the same amount. You need to pack 6 more items. How will you do this and keep the sleds weighing the same?

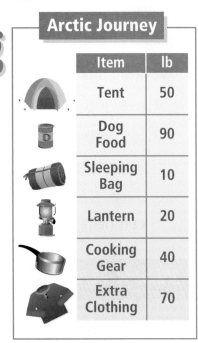

### Arctic Journey

| | Item | lb |
|---|---|---|
| | Tent | 50 |
| | Dog Food | 90 |
| | Sleeping Bag | 10 |
| | Lantern | 20 |
| | Cooking Gear | 40 |
| | Extra Clothing | 70 |

## Here's A Way! Use Guess and Check.

### 1 Understand

- What does the number after each supply tell you?
- Use these numbers to put the supplies into 2 groups that have the same weight.

### 2 Plan

- Which supplies are the heaviest? Start with a guess that uses the heaviest supplies.

### 3 Try It

- What supplies will you add to make the weight equal?

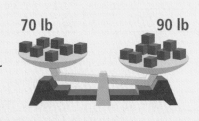
70 lb          90 lb

- What will be your next guess for each sled? How will you make the weights equal again?
- Use Guess and Check until you solve the problem.

### 4 Look Back

- Put the tent, lantern, and clothing in one sled. In the other, put the sleeping bag, cooking gear, and dog food.
- How did checking each guess help you solve the problem?

**Use Guess and Check to solve the problem. Show your work.**

Guess:
2 + 9 + 7 = 18

Check:
18 is less than 20.
18 is not an odd number.

1. Which 3 of these numbers have a sum that is an odd number greater than 20?

| 2 | 5 |
|---|---|
| 6 | |
| 9 | 7 |

2. Which 3 numbers have a sum that is an even number greater than 20?

3. **Critical Thinking** In solving problems 1 and 2, why does it make sense to start by finding the sum?

## Work It Out!

**Use Guess and Check or any strategy to solve the problem.**

4. You have a mystery number. If you double the number and subtract 10, the answer is 50. What is the mystery number?

5. You finish a sled race in fourth place. Your team comes in ahead of 10 other teams. How many teams were in the race? Explain.

6. Suppose you buy 3 pounds of apples and 1 pound of cheese to eat on your Arctic journey. Together, they cost $10.00. If the cheese costs $4.00, how much does a single pound of apples cost?

7. You will be running the dogsled race route shown below. You may choose any route as long as you stop at every checkpoint. In what order should you reach the checkpoints to take the shortest route?

## Share Your Thinking

8. Which problems did you solve by using Guess and Check? Explain.

9. When you used Guess and Check, how did you make your first guess?

# Hundreds and Thousands

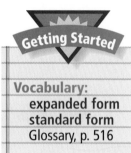

**Getting Started**

**Vocabulary:**
expanded form
standard form
Glossary, p. 516

**Y**ou and your classmates sponsor a walkathon to raise money to help rebuild a senior center that has been damaged by a flood. Together you sign up 1437 people in your community for the walk.

The number 1437 can be written and shown in different ways.

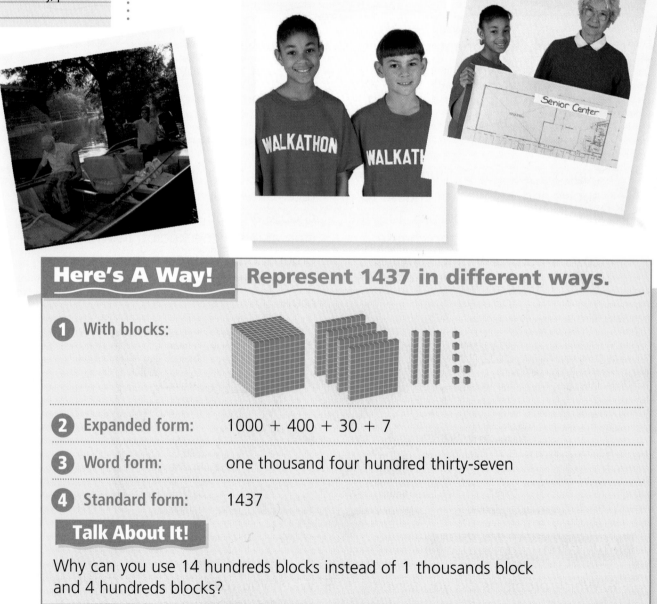

| **Here's A Way!** | **Represent 1437 in different ways.** |

**1** With blocks:

**2** Expanded form:     1000 + 400 + 30 + 7

**3** Word form:     one thousand four hundred thirty-seven

**4** Standard form:     1437

**Talk About It!**

Why can you use 14 hundreds blocks instead of 1 thousands block and 4 hundreds blocks?

Write the number in standard form.

**1.** three thousand six hundred

**2.** two thousand two hundred

**3.** 9000 + 300 + 20 + 4

**4.** 7000 + 200 + 6

Write the number in word form and expanded form.

**5.** 981 **6.** 420 **7.** 1165 **8.** 3009 **9.** 1600 **10.** 2356

Write the three numbers

**11.** after 998. **12.** after 2399. **13.** before 4001. **14.** before 9090.

**15. Critical Thinking** Which form is used most often? Why?

## Work It Out!

**Number Sense** Write the numbers described.

**16.** Write a 4-digit number with 3 in the ones place, 4 in the tens place, and 8 in the thousands place.

**17.** Write a 4-digit number with 2 in the thousands place, 0 in the ones place, and 7 in the hundreds place.

Write the number in two other ways.

**18.** seven hundred eighty-four **19.** 100 + 20 + 3 **20.** 8255 **21.** 6483

**Functions** Complete the chart. Describe any patterns you notice.

### Walkathon Sign-Up

| Schools | Number of Walkers | Number +10 | Number +40 | Number +200 |
|---------|-------------------|------------|------------|-------------|
| School A | 349 | 359 | 389 | 549 |
| School B | 519 | **22.** ? | **23.** ? | **24.** ? |
| School C | 608 | **25.** ? | **26.** ? | **27.** ? |
| School D | 185 | **28.** ? | **29.** ? | **30.** ? |

**31. Problem Solving** If the students at your school signed up 10 more people than 1437 for the walkathon, how many would they have? If they signed up 100 more?

**More Practice Set 1.5, p. 472**

# Number Lines

**Getting Started**

**What You'll Need:**
- ▶ 24-inch piece of string
- ▶ paper clips
- ▶ tape
- ▶ worksheet

**W**hile studying about the Grand Canyon, you learn that the lowest point is about 6000 feet from the rim.

You can show 6000 on a number line.

**Activity**

**1**

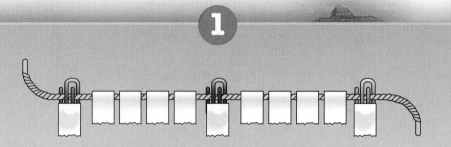

- Get a piece of string about 24 inches long.
- Attach a paper clip near one end of the string.
- Use a ruler. Start at the paper clip and mark 2-inch sections on your string with tape. Mark 10 sections. Put a paper clip at the end of the last section.

**2**

Now you are ready to make a Grand Canyon number line.
- Hold the string vertically.
- Label the paper clip on the top 0 and the paper clip on the bottom 10,000.
- Find the halfway point by folding the string in half so that the paper clips touch.
- Attach a paper clip to mark the halfway point.
- What label should you use for the halfway point?

**3**

Now you are ready to label other points on the number line.

- If 0 stands for the top of the Grand Canyon, which piece of tape stands for the point of 6000 feet? Write *Grand Canyon* on that piece.
- Count by 1000's to label the other pieces of tape.
- Find the following points. Label them *Rock* and *Mule.*
  - a. A rock is on the trail 4000 feet from the canyon's top rim.
  - b. A mule is about 3000 feet from the bottom of the canyon.

0

10,000

## Show What You Know!

**Number Sense** Use your worksheet or draw number lines on a sheet of paper.

1. Counting by 10's, label one number line from 0 to 40. Then find the halfway point. Put a star on it.

**Label the point.**

2. 25    3. 38    4. 19    5. 8    6. 15    7. 12

8. Counting by 100's, label another number line from 100 to 500. Then find the halfway point. Put a star on it.

**Label the point.**

9. 110    10. 250    11. 475    12. 360    13. 150    14. 190

15. **Problem Solving** You are planning to hike to the campgrounds. You know it takes 2 hours to hike halfway there. About how long will it take you to hike the whole distance? Tell your reasoning.

16. **Critical Thinking** At what other time might it be useful to know a halfway point?

# Rounding to the Nearest 10 and 100

**Use What You Know**

Remember that a rounded number is a number expressed to the nearest ten, hundred, thousand, and so on.

**Y**ou and your pen pal plan to visit Space Center Houston. You live 22 miles away. Your pen pal lives 385 miles away.

To tell someone about how far each of you will travel, you do not need exact numbers. You can use rounded numbers instead.

A number line can help you round.

---

## Here's A Way!  Round to the nearest 10 and 100.

**Rounding Tens**

Round 22 to the nearest ten.

Draw a number line from 20 to 30.
Mark the halfway point.
Estimate where 22 is on the number line.

You can see that 22 is closer to 20 than to 30. So, 22 rounds down to 20.

Halfway

22
20      25      30

A number halfway between tens rounds up to the next ten.

**Rounding Hundreds**

Round 385 to the nearest hundred.

Draw a number line from 300 to 400.
Mark the halfway point.
Estimate where 385 is on the number line.

You can see that 385 is closer to 400 than to 300. So, 385 rounds up to 400.

Halfway

385
300      350      400

A number halfway between hundreds rounds up to the next hundred.

**Talk About It!**  How does marking the halfway point help you round?

## Show What You Know!

Draw a number line. Mark the halfway point to help you.

1. Round 78 to the nearest ten.
2. Round 39 to the nearest ten.
3. What number is halfway between 800 and 900?
4. **Critical Thinking** When would you round 83 down? When would you round 83 up?

## Work It Out!

Round to the nearest 10. Use a number line if you need to.

5. 56    6. 72    7. 45    8. 43    9. 57    10. 94

Round to the nearest 100. Use a number line if you need to.

11. 571    12. 650    13. 80    14. 129    15. 358    16. 766

Complete the chart. Fill in the missing numbers.

### Space Cafe's Monthly Orders

| Menu Item | Number Ordered | Round to Nearest Ten | Round to Nearest Hundred |
|---|---|---|---|
| Astro Soup | 379 | 17. ? | 18. ? |
| Spaceburger | 555 | 19. ? | 20. ? |
| Universe Sandwich | 789 | 21. ? | 22. ? |

23. **Critical Thinking** When you estimate how much money you need, is it better to round up or down? Explain why you think so.

## Problem Solving  Using Data

24. Round the distance from Beaumont to Houston to the nearest 10 miles.

25. Is the distance from Dallas to Houston closer to 200 miles or to 300 miles?

26. Which city is closer to Houston, Beaumont or Galveston?

| From | To Houston |
|---|---|
| Beaumont | 79 miles |
| Dallas | 225 miles |
| Galveston | 47 miles |
| San Antonio | 190 miles |

LESSON 8

# Problem Solving
## Choose a Computation Method

**Y**our school is holding a carnival. A friend made this poster to advertise the event. Should you change anything?

### Choose a Computation Method

**Ask Yourself:**

Do I need an exact answer or an estimate?

Should I use a model, paper and pencil, mental math, or a calculator?

What operation should I use?

## You Decide

- Which numbers are rounded? Which numbers are exact?

- What information is each number supposed to give you?

- Should any of the exact numbers be rounded? Should any of the rounded numbers be exact? Why or why not?

School Carnival To
Raise Money for a Piano
Date: October 10
Place: School Parking Lot
Time: About 10:00 A.M.

- 12 booths with games and activities!
- Enough pies and cakes to feed 458 people!
- Goal is to raise $1900.00 for a new piano.

## Work It Out!

**Decide to round or give an exact number. Explain your decision.**

1. Your aunt drives you and a friend to the carnival. To pick up your friend, your aunt needs an address. Would a rounded number help you find the house?

2. You and three friends agree to meet at the carnival entrance at 10:45 A.M. Should you round the time and arrive at 11:00 A.M.?

3. You want to play three $.50 carnival games. You also want to buy a sandwich for $2.59. You have $5.00. Do you need to find the exact total to know if you have enough money?

4. **Create Your Own** Create a poster for a real or pretend event. Use only rounded numbers. Ask a friend to identify the rounded numbers that do not provide enough information.

## Share Your Thinking

5. When does a rounded number give enough information? When do you need an exact number? Give examples.

# Midchapter Review
## for Pages 1–16

## Problem Solving

**Solve. Show your work.** (pages 8, 16)

1. Suppose your Little League team played 15 games this season. The team won 3 more games than it lost. How many games did your team win?

2. Your cousin lives at 2032 W. Adams Street, which is a 42-minute bus trip from your house. If you are giving directions, which number would you round? Which must be exact? Explain your answer.

## Concepts

**What basic facts can help you solve these exercises mentally?** (page 6)

3. $60 + 70 = $ ■    4. $400 + 900 = $ ■    5. $1500 - $ ■ $ = 800$

**Round each number to the nearest hundred.** (page 14)

6. 192    7. 345    8. 850

## Skills

**Use facts to solve.** (page 6)

9. $40 + 60 = $ ■    10. $120 - 50 = $ ■    11. $70 + $ ■ $ = 140$

12. $800 + 900 = $ ■    13. $150 - 60 = $ ■    14. $40 + $ ■ $ = 120$

**Write in standard form and in words.** (page 10)

15. $600 + 90 + 5$    16. $4000 + 800 + 70$    17. $3000 + 200 + 20 + 2$

**Write in expanded form and in words.** (page 10)

18. 235    19. 5280    20. 1767

# Math World

Place value can make hard ideas easy. People use place value all over the world to help them write and understand numbers.

## A World Without Place Value?

What if there were only one number symbol, 1, and no such thing as place value? How would you have to write large numbers?

This girl lives in a city of 200,000 people. To write this number without place value, she would need a piece of paper as long as a football field! What size paper would you need to write the number of people in your town?

## What is a Zero?

Did you know that we didn't always have zeros? To write a number like 1,920,102, people left the thousands and tens columns blank. Sometimes people read the number wrong, because they overlooked the blank spaces. Then around A.D. 870, in India, a symbol that looked like 0 started to appear. It was called sunya (SOON yah), which meant empty.

# Try This! THAI NUMERALS

The Thai (TY) language looks very different from English, but the Thai number system is similar to the one we use. You can write numbers in Thai. Use what you know about our number symbols to help you.

**1** Study the Thai numerals for 1 through 9. Copy the chart onto a piece of paper.

| 0 | 1 | 2 | 3 | 4 |
|---|---|---|---|---|
| ๐ | ๑ | ๒ | ๓ | ๔ |

| 5 | 6 | 7 | 8 | 9 |
|---|---|---|---|---|
| ๕ | ๖ | ๗ | ๘ | ๙ |

**2** Think about how we put our symbols for 1–9 together to make numbers. Look at the Thai symbols for 11, 17, and 19. Then write the missing Thai numbers to complete the chart.

**3** Try writing some greater numbers using Thai numerals. Can you write the number of the last page in this book? How about your street address?

| 10 | ๑๑ 11 | 12 |
|---|---|---|
| 13 | 14 | 15 |
| 16 | ๑๗ 17 | 18 |
| ๑๙ 19 | 20 | |

## Respond

A zero is often a placeholder, but it can also give you important information. Can you think of examples?

Internet:
**Houghton Mifflin Education Place**
Explore the Math Center at
http://www.eduplace.com

19

# Place Value to One Million

**What You'll Need:**
▶ calculator

**Vocabulary:**
**million**
Glossary, p. 516

**D**epending on its size, a hummingbird flaps its wings from 18 to 78 times per second. In one hour of continuous flapping, a hummingbird may beat its wings from 64,800 to 280,800 times.

Numbers can be written and shown in different ways.

| **Here's A Way!** | **Write 280,800 in different ways.** |
|---|---|

**1** Expanded form:     200,000 + 80,000 + 800

**2** Chart form:

| Thousands | | | Ones | | |
|---|---|---|---|---|---|
| Hundreds | Tens | Ones | Hundreds | Tens | Ones |
| 2 | 8 | 0 | 8 | 0 | 0 |

**3** Word form:     two hundred eighty thousand, eight hundred

**4** Standard form:     280,800

**Talk About It!**     If you extended the chart to include millions, how would you label the place values?

Complete the chart. Fill in the missing numbers.

| Wing Beats in One Hour | | |
|---|---|---|
| Standard | Expanded | Word |
| 64,800 | 60,000 + 4,000 + 800 | Sixty-Four Thousand, Eight Hundred |
| 172,789 | 1.    ? | 2.    ? |
| 244,695 | 3.    ? | 4.    ? |

5. **Critical Thinking** Does the greatest place value always have the greatest digit? Explain.

6. **Mental Math** What happens when you add 1 to each of these numbers?
   **a.** 213,609   **b.** 321,599   **c.** 540,999

## Work It Out!

Write the expanded form. Then, write the word form.

7. 247,749    8. 37,982    9. 692,514    10. 99,500    11. 723,620

Write each number in standard and expanded forms.

12. A crow flapping its wings continuously for an hour will flap about twelve thousand, nine hundred sixty times.

13. A mockingbird beats its wings about fifty thousand, four hundred times in an hour.

### Problem Solving

14. **Logical Reasoning** Use the following clues to find the mystery number.
   • I'm a 4-digit number.
   • Three of my digits are even numbers less than 8.
   • My thousands digit is twice my ones digit.
   • My tens digit is odd and is my greatest digit.
   • My hundreds digit is the sum of my thousands digit and my ones digit.

15. **Create Your Own** Choose a mystery number and write clues for it. Then, trade mystery numbers with your partner and solve.

16. **Calculator** Suppose you want to enter 244,583 on your calculator, but the 4 key is broken. List the keys you could press to get 244,583 on your calculator display.

**More Practice Set 1.9, p. 473**

# How Much Is a Million?

**Cooperative Learning Checklist**

☐ Work alone.
☑ Work with a partner.
☐ Work with a group.

**Getting Started**

**What You'll Need:**
▶ a newspaper
▶ calculator
▶ markers
▶ watch or clock

**I**f you read a daily newspaper from front to back, do you think you would read a million words?

## Let's Estimate!

### Activity

- Make a chart like the one at the top of page 23.

- Record your findings.

**Region**

Y, NOVEMBER 13, 1996

**B** Weather B8

**iscounts in reverse**

discontinue
breaks

*100 words*

have saved individual consumers hundreds of dollars in auto insurance premiums.

"It was destined to crumble, it was just a question of when," said Frank Mancini, executive vice president of the Professional Independent Insurance Agents of Massachusetts. "I think the red ink is running pretty strong right now, and discounting is going to come to an end. We'll begin to see it fade in 1997, and by 1998 it will fizzle out."

Safety officials said they are reviewing the firm's 511 other group discounts to see if any others are unprofitable and should be eliminated. Most of the remaining groups are restricted to employees of a particular company or

SAFETY, Page B5

Self Reliance Corp., in bers have flocked to egan offering dis-

announcement hat it wants to may be the cuts that

**Election ripples spr**

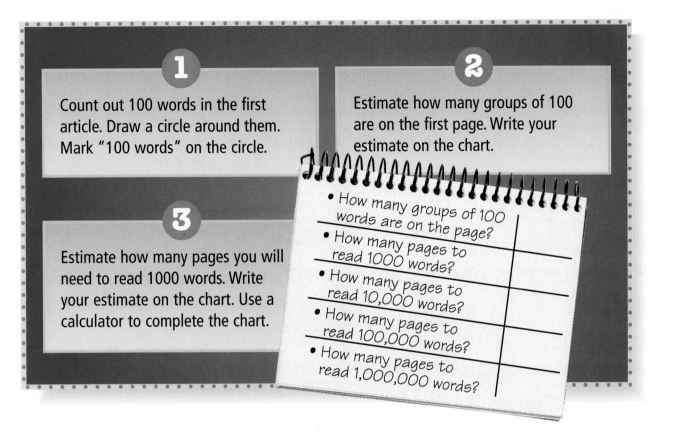

**1** Count out 100 words in the first article. Draw a circle around them. Mark "100 words" on the circle.

**2** Estimate how many groups of 100 are on the first page. Write your estimate on the chart.

**3** Estimate how many pages you will need to read 1000 words. Write your estimate on the chart. Use a calculator to complete the chart.

| | |
|---|---|
| • How many groups of 100 words are on the page? | |
| • How many pages to read 1000 words? | |
| • How many pages to read 10,000 words? | |
| • How many pages to read 100,000 words? | |
| • How many pages to read 1,000,000 words? | |

## Show What You Know!

1. **Critical Thinking** How did your page estimate for 1000 words help you make your estimate for 10,000 words? For 1,000,000 words?

2. Are there a million words to read in your newspaper? If not, how many pages long would a newspaper need to be for you to read a million words?

**Copy the table. Use a calculator and a clock to complete the table.**

3. **Estimation** Estimate how long it will take using the calculator to count to the target number. Record your estimate.

4. **Calculator** Enter 0 + 10 on the calculator. Continue pressing = until you reach the target number of 1000. Record the actual time. Repeat for remaining target numbers.

5. **Patterns** Describe any patterns in the table. Discuss them with your partner.

**Count and Estimate**

| Count By | Target Number | Estimated Time | Actual Time |
|---|---|---|---|
| 10 | 1000 | | |
| 100 | 10,000 | | |
| 1000 | 100,000 | | |

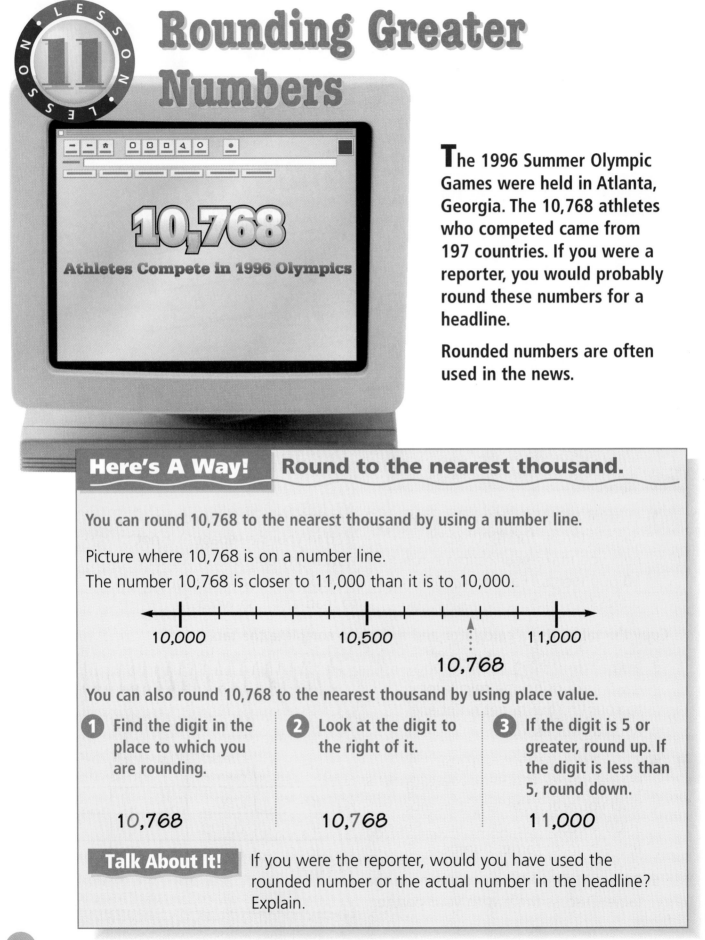

# Rounding Greater Numbers

**10,768**

**Athletes Compete in 1996 Olympics**

**T**he 1996 Summer Olympic Games were held in Atlanta, Georgia. The 10,768 athletes who competed came from 197 countries. If you were a reporter, you would probably round these numbers for a headline.

Rounded numbers are often used in the news.

## Here's A Way! Round to the nearest thousand.

You can round 10,768 to the nearest thousand by using a number line.

Picture where 10,768 is on a number line.
The number 10,768 is closer to 11,000 than it is to 10,000.

10,000      10,500      11,000

10,768

You can also round 10,768 to the nearest thousand by using place value.

**1** Find the digit in the place to which you are rounding.

10,768

**2** Look at the digit to the right of it.

10,768

**3** If the digit is 5 or greater, round up. If the digit is less than 5, round down.

11,000

**Talk About It!** If you were the reporter, would you have used the rounded number or the actual number in the headline? Explain.

Round the number to the nearest hundred. Then round to the nearest thousand. Use the method of rounding you prefer.

**1.** 2719    **2.** 2460    **3.** 1594    **4.** 523    **5.** 1454    **6.** 4720

**7.** 610    **8.** 1024    **9.** 5923    **10.** 923    **11.** 10,144    **12.** 10,890

Use the digits 1, 5, 4, and 8 to write the number.

**13.** A number that rounds to 8200.    **14.** A number that rounds to 9000.

## Work It Out!

Round to the nearest hundred. Then, round to the nearest thousand.

**15.** 1750    **16.** 3045    **17.** 5286    **18.** 6750    **19.** 3427    **20.** 11,299

**21.** 8123    **22.** 5972    **23.** 7540    **24.** 1287    **25.** 982    **26.** 9,969

**27. Critical Thinking** Write a 4-digit number where rounding to the nearest thousand is just as close as rounding to the nearest hundred.

### Problem Solving   Using Data

The following items were sold in one day at a souvenir stand. Use the data in this chart to answer the following questions.

**Olympic Souvenirs**

| Souvenir | Price | Amount Sold | Sales |
|---|---|---|---|
| Olympic T-shirt | $17.50 | 245 | $ 4,287.50 |
| Olympic Cap | $23.90 | 352 | $ 8,412.80 |
| Olympic Pin Set | $39.95 | 526 | $21,013.70 |

**28.** Could you buy one of each of these souvenirs with $50? If not, about how much money would you need?

**29.** About how many items were sold at the souvenir stand?

**30.** Did the souvenir stand make more than $30,000? How can you tell?

**More Practice Set 1.11, p. 473**

# Comparing and Ordering

### Tallest U.S. Buildings

| | |
|---|---|
| Empire State Building | 1250 ft |
| Sears Tower | 1453 ft |
| World Trade Center | 1375 ft |

**W**hich building is the tallest?

You can use what you know about place value to compare the heights of buildings.

Then you can put heights in order from greatest to least.

## Here's A Way!   Compare and order the numbers.

**1** Compare the digits that have the greatest place value.

The thousands digits are the same.

1250
1453
1375

**2** Compare the next place value to the right.

The hundreds digits are different.

1250
1453
1375

Compare 1250 and 1453.      200 < 400    So, 1250 < 1453
Then compare 1453 and 1375.    400 > 300    So, 1453 > 1375

**3** Now put the numbers in order.

Think:  400 > 300 > 200.  Then: 1453 > 1375 > 1250.
The heights are from greatest to least: 1453 ft, 1375 ft, and 1250 ft.

The tallest building is the Sears Tower.

**Talk About It!**   Did you need to look at the tens digit? Explain.

**Algebraic Reasoning** Write >, <, or = to make these statements true.

1. 4315 ● 3280   2. 2938 ● 293   3. 1482 ● 1464   4. 632 ● 689

5. 5218 ● 5182   6. 2005 ● 2050   7. 3449 ● 9775   8. 783 ● 89

9. Write these numbers in order from least to greatest: 1439, 1349, and 1934.

10. Write these numbers in order from greatest to least: 689, 5432, 475, and 5987.

11. **Critical Thinking** When you compare 4-digit numbers, do you need to compare digits in each place? Explain.

## Work It Out!

**Algebraic Reasoning** Write >, <, or = to make these statements true.

12. 597 ● 579   13. 3154 ● 3099  14. 1532 ● 8870  15. 476 ● 1766

16. Write the building heights in order from least to greatest.

### International Buildings

| Country | Building | Height |
|---------|----------|--------|
| Canada | CN Tower | 1815 ft |
| China | Bank of China | 1033 ft |
| Egypt | Great Pyramid | 481 ft |
| France | Eiffel Tower | 1052 ft |

**Write the following numbers in order from greatest to least.**

17. 1033, 513, 1815                18. 451, 1052, 481

**Write a number using 6, 3, 9, and 8. Use each digit once.**

19. least possible number          20. greatest possible number

**Mixed Review**  Add or subtract.

21. 15 − 6 = ■   22. 6 + 5 = ■   23. 12 − 9 = ■   24. 8 + 7 = ■

25. 3 + 8 = ■    26. 16 − 8 = ■   27. 18 − 9 = ■   28. 13 − 5 = ■

**More Practice Set 1.12, p. 474**

27

# Patterns in Money

**S**uppose your fourth-grade class has been saving money to purchase a CD-ROM package that costs $59.50.

Does your class have enough money to buy the CD-ROM?

You can organize bills and coins from the greatest amount to the least amount to count money.

## Here's A Way! Count and write money amounts.

Count the bills and coins from the greatest to the least amounts.

$20  $30  $40  $45  $50  $55  $56

$.25  $.35  $.45  $.50  $.55  $.60  $.61

The class does not have enough money to buy the CD-ROM.

Write fifty-six dollars and sixty-one cents as $56.61.
Use a dollar sign and a decimal point.

### Talk About It!

What counting patterns did you notice? How is counting by $5 like counting by $.05? What other counting patterns with dollars and coins are similar? Explain.

**Write the amount of money.**

1. 2 ten-dollar bills, 1 quarter, 1 dime, 1 nickel, 2 pennies

2. 10 five-dollar bills, 1 quarter, 2 dimes, 2 nickels, 2 pennies

**Patterns** Describe the pattern. Then continue the pattern and write the next three money amounts.

3. $.10, $.15, $.20

4. $.20, $.30, $.40

5. $15, $25, $35

6. $10, $12, $14

7. $2.25, $2.50, $2.75

8. $3.01, $3.02, $3.03

**Draw bills and coins to show these amounts. Find two different ways.**

9. $7.75

10. $18.50

11. $32.10

12. $12.01

13. $52.35

14. **Logical Reasoning** Look at your answers to exercise 13. What are the fewest coins and bills you can use to make $52.35?

## Work It Out!

**Algebraic Reasoning** Write the amount of money described in each statement. Use a dollar sign and a decimal point.

15. one penny less than seventeen dollars

16. ten dollars less than sixty dollars and fifty cents

17. one thousand dollars more than five hundred dollars

### Problem Solving

You have $75.00 to spend on CD-ROM games.

18. Identify two different combinations of CD-ROM games that you could buy with your money.

19. Identify two different combinations of CD-ROM games that would be too expensive to buy with the money you have to spend.

| CD ROM Price List | |
| --- | --- |
| Break the Code | $19.95 |
| Puzzle Word | $39.95 |
| Space Secrets | $26.95 |
| Word Mania | $59.00 |
| Car Rally | $17.50 |

20. **Critical Thinking** What coins can you use to make two dollars and thirty-five cents? What other combinations can you make?

**More Practice Set 1.13, p. 474**

# Problem Solving
## Using Guess and Check and Other Strategies

**F**lorida, Texas, California, and Arizona are states that are known for their orange groves. Together, they grow billions of pounds of oranges each year.

### Problem Solving Process
✓ Understand
✓ Plan
✓ Try It
✓ Look Back

### Choose a Strategy You Have Learned
✓ Guess and Check
  Draw a Picture
  Make a List
  Make a Table
  Act It Out
  Work a Simpler Problem
  Look for a Pattern
  Work Backward

**Y**our younger sister and her friend are selling freshly squeezed orange juice at a stand. You offer to help them. Your job is to replace the glasses that are sold. You know that 12 glasses have been sold for a total of $5.00. How many small glasses and how many large glasses need to be replaced?

- What problem needs to be solved?

- How many sizes of juice are for sale?

- How much does each size cost?

- Decide what strategy you can use to solve the problem. Then solve it.

*Fresh Orange Juice*

50¢  25¢

**Use any strategy to solve the problem. Show your work.**

1. You buy 3 packages of napkins for the juice stand. You use a 20-cents-off coupon. The total price is $1.30. What was the price of each package of napkins without the coupon?

2. Your friend starts a sign like the one shown. She leaves it for you to finish. How many oranges will you have to draw to complete the triangle?

### Orange Juice Sales

|  | Half Gallon | Gallon | Two Gallons |
|---|---|---|---|
| Number of Oranges | 20 | 40 | 80 |
| Number of Glasses | 8 | ? | 32 |
| Money Earned | ? | $8.00 | $16.00 |

3. Copy and complete the table. Then look at the numbers in each column. Do you see a pattern? What does the table tell you about a half-gallon and a gallon?

4. There is $2.60 on the counter. Four coins fall off and $2.00 is left. What coins fell off the counter?

5. A customer has 7 coins worth $.35. What could the coins be?

6. A large glass holds 10 ounces of juice. A small glass holds 5 ounces. Someone wants to buy 30 ounces of orange juice. What are two ways to sell that much juice?

7. Which gives you more juice for 50 cents, 2 small glasses or 1 large glass? Explain.

8. You buy a small or large glass of juice for each member of your family. How many glasses do you buy? What is the total cost?

9. Tell a friend the cost of buying juice for your family. Ask your friend to figure out how many large and small glasses of juice you bought.

### Share Your Thinking

10. Which strategy did you use to solve problem 9? Explain why you chose that strategy to solve the problem.

11. With a partner, find another way to solve problem 9. Then solve the problem using this method.

# LESSON 15

# Making Change

**S**uppose the bill for lunch is $4.22. If a customer gives the cashier $5.00, how much change will the customer get back?

It helps to estimate first and then figure out the exact change by counting on.

## Here's A Way! Count on to make change.

**1** Estimate.
Because the bill was a little more than $4.00, the customer should get a little less than $1.00 in change from $5.00.

**2** Count on to find the exact amount.

Think

| $4.22 | $4.23 | $4.24 | $4.25 | $4.50 | $4.75 | $5.00 |

**3** Here are other ways to show the change.

$5.00 − $4.22 = $.78

| $5.00 | |
|---|---|
| $4.22 | $.78 |

### Talk About It!

Describe how the chart above shows the amount of the bill, the amount the cashier receives, and the change. How is the chart related to the problem?

## Show What You Know!

Use the table to choose a reasonable estimate for the amount of change.

| Cost | Cash Given | Choose an Estimate | | | |
|------|-----------|---|---|---|---|
| $12.88 | $15.00 | 1. | $ 1.50 | $ 2.00 | $ 3.00 |
| $ 4.45 | $10.00 | 2. | $ 5.00 | $ 5.50 | $ 6.00 |
| $10.95 | $20.00 | 3. | $ 9.00 | $ 9.50 | $10.00 |

Write the fewest bills and coins you could receive as change.

4. Cost: $6.58  Cash given: $10.00      5. Cost: $12.01  Cash given: $15.01

6. **Critical Thinking** Why do you think $15.01 was the cash given in exercise 5?

## Work It Out!

Estimate to see if the change is reasonable. Write yes or no.

7. Cost: $1.28  Cash given: $2.00       8. Cost: $5.78  Cash given: $6.78
   Change: $.72                            Change: $1.22

Use your calculator to complete the table.

| Total Cost | Cash Given | | Change | |
|-----------|-----------|---|--------|---|
| $ 4.45 | | $ 5.05 | 9. | ? |
| $11.20 | 10. | ? | $ 3.80 | |
| $15.38 | | $20.00 | 11. | ? |
| $ 5.01 | | $ 6.00 | 12. | ? |

13. **Algebraic Reasoning** How can you find the value for one column in the table when you know the values in the other two columns?

### Problem Solving

14. **Mental Math** How many different ways can you make 50 cents using quarters, dimes, and nickels?

15. **Create Your Own** Create clues for a mystery number of coins. Give your clues to a classmate to solve.

**More Practice Set 1.15, p. 475**

# Money Sense

**A**t the Museum of Science, you spend $2.73 for a package of rubber insects. The cashier gives you 2 pennies and 1 quarter as change from $3. Is that the correct change? What other coins could you have gotten as change?

Once you know the correct amount of change, you can use any coins that make that amount.

## Here's A Way! | Find equivalent amounts.

**1** Use counting on to check that the change is correct.

 +  +

$2.73   $2.74      $2.75      $3.00

The change is correct.
- Can you exchange the pennies for other coins? Can you exchange the quarter?

**2** Find other coins to use for change.

Other coins that have the same money value as a quarter are 2 dimes and 1 nickel.

So, you could have gotten 2 pennies, 1 nickel, and 2 dimes as change.

### Talk About It!

- What other combinations of coins could you have gotten?
- What is the greatest number of coins you could get as change? The least number of coins?

## Show What You Know!

Write the greatest number of quarters you could have in each of the amounts below.

1. $.31   2. $.50   3. $.45   4. $.28   5. $.59

6. $1.00   7. $1.25   8. $2.00   9. $.75   10. $.84

11. **Critical Thinking** What coins would be useful to have in your pocket when you want to exchange them for a dollar bill? Explain your answer.

## Work It Out!

Write the value using the dollar sign and decimal point.

12. two dimes and one nickel

13. two dollars and four nickels

14. five dollars and one nickel

15. three quarters

Write the least number of pennies you could have.

16. $.48   17. $.95   18. $12.17   19. $1.79   20. $8.84

### Problem Solving  Using Data

Give at least two combinations of coins and bills that you would get in change.

21. Purchase one geode; give $10.00 to cashier.

22. Purchase one ant puzzle; give $5.00 to cashier.

23. Purchase one bat video; give $20.00 to cashier.

24. One day the store ran out of one-dollar bills. Someone bought a giant magnifier and paid for it with a $20 bill. What change would the cashier give, using the least possible number of coins and/or bills?

| Welcome to the Gift Shop! | |
| --- | --- |
| Giant Magnifier | $12.95 |
| Ant Puzzle | $ 2.95 |
| Bat Video | $14.95 |
| Geode | $ 6.95 |

More Practice Set 1.16, p. 475

### Math Journal

What are different ways you can put together bills and coins to make five dollars?

# Problem Solving
## Using Strategies

**LESSON 17**

You can read more about Matthew Henson in the pages of *Kids Discover*.

In 1909, Robert Peary, Matthew Henson, and four Inuit left from Greenland and traveled over the ice-covered Arctic Ocean. The U.S. Congress honored them as the first group to reach the North Pole.

Matthew Henson sits on a sled used on the 1909 journey to the North Pole.

**Problem Solving Process**
- ✓ Understand
- ✓ Plan
- ✓ Try It
- ✓ Look Back

**Choose a Strategy You Have Learned**
- ✓ Guess and Check
-   Draw a Picture
-   Make a List
-   Make a Table
-   Act It Out
-   Work a Simpler Problem
-   Look for a Pattern
-   Work Backward

To help Peary and Henson, another team left first to mark a trail. Led by Robert Bartlett, the team went as far as 140 miles from the North Pole. After that point, Peary and Henson were on their own. If their journey to the North Pole totaled 430 miles, how long was Bartlett's journey?

- What is the question you have to answer?
- What is the total number of miles traveled by Peary to the North Pole?
- How many miles from the North Pole did Bartlett's trail end?
- Describe a strategy you can use to solve the problem. Then solve it.

## Work It Out!

**Use any strategy to solve the problem. Show your work.**

1. At the North Pole, the ice drifted and carried the explorers 20 miles in 5 days. Do you walk faster than that? Hint: You can probably walk a mile in less than half an hour.

2. You are at the North Pole. You walk 1 mile south, 1 mile east, and then 1 mile north. About how far will you be from your starting point? Hint: Find a globe. Start at the North Pole and follow this route with your finger.

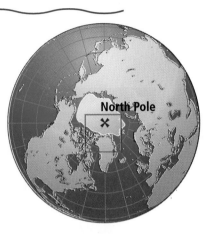

3. You leave your camp at 11:00 A.M. and travel 2 miles every hour. Will you make it to a camp 7 miles away by 3:00 P.M.? Explain.

4. Suppose a sled travels 43 miles a day. How far can the sled travel in 7 days?

5. A team of explorers has 160 pounds of food for 10 dogs. Suppose the dogs each eat 2 pounds of food a day. Will the food last longer than a week? Tell how you found your answer.

6. What if these explorers pick up 5 more dogs after the second day? How many more days will the dog food last them?

7. Find four routes from checkpoint *A* to checkpoint *K* without crossing any cracks in the ice. Use letters to describe your route. Which is the shortest route?

8. **Create Your Own** Make your own map with ice cracks. See if a friend can find the shortest route.

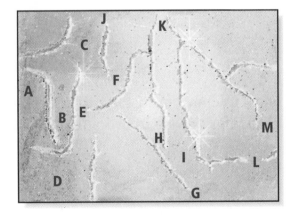

## Share Your Thinking

9. What strategy did you use to solve problem 7? How did it help you to choose the shortest route?

10. Which problem was the most challenging to solve? Why? How did you solve it?

# Chapter 1 Test

## for Pages 1–37

## Problem Solving

**Solve. Show your work.** (pages 8, 30, 36)

1. You have $10. Here are some of the things you might buy with your money.
   a. What 3 items combined will have a total cost between $9 and $10?
   b. Which costs more, 6 packages of Fruit Chews or 2 fair tickets?
   c. What is the greatest number of different items you can buy for less than $10?

| Item | Price |
|------|-------|
| Index Cards | $1.99 |
| Poster | $4.99 |
| Tape | $8.99 |
| Fair Ticket | $3.00 |
| Book | $5.99 |
| Marker | $1.19 |
| Fruit Chews | $0.89 |

## Concepts

**Choose the value of the 8 in each exercise. Write *a*, *b*, *c*, or *d*.** (page 20)

2. 63,800        a. 8          b. 80         c. 800        d. 8000

3. 128,741       a. 800        b. 8000       c. 80,000     d. 800,000

4. 2585          a. 8000       b. 800        c. 80         d. 8

5. 821,074       a. 8000       b. 800        c. 80         d. 800,000

**For the following costs, write the fewest bills and coins you could receive as change from $5. Do not use half-dollars.** (page 32)

6. Cost: $3.18

7. Cost: $1.60

8. Cost: $4.20

**Round the number to the nearest hundred. Write a, b, c, or d.**
(page 14)

9. 549    a. 540    b. 600    c. 500    d. 550

10. 636    a. 700    b. 650    c. 640    d. 600

**Round the number to the nearest thousand. Write a, b, c, or d.** (page 24)

11. 9612    a. 9600    b. 9700    c. 10,000    d. 9620

12. 74,540    a. 74,500    b. 74,000    c. 74,550    d. 75,000

**Compare the numbers. Write > or <.** (page 26)

13. 642 ● 668    14. 1582 ● 1564    15. 2869 ● 286    16. 5838 ● 5862

**Order the numbers from least to greatest.** (page 26)

17. 6435, 752, 3549    18. 984, 9000, 990    19. 1045, 1231, 1248

**Write the value of the amount.** (page 34)

20. 3 quarters

21. 1 quarter and 2 nickels

22. 6 dimes

23. 1 quarter, 4 dimes, and 2 nickels

## Performance Task

(page 7)

| Day | 1 | 2 | 3 | 4 |
|---|---|---|---|---|
| Total Signatures Collected To Date | 15 | 20 | 25 | |

Suppose you have collected 15 signatures to ask the city for a traffic light on your street. If you can get 5 signatures a day, how many more days will it take you to collect 75?

- Explain how you used the table to find the answer to this problem.

**Keep In Mind . . .**
Your work will be evaluated on the following:
☑ A completed table
☑ Clear labels
☑ Correct math pattern
☑ Clear explanation

# Cumulative Review

**Place Value** (Chapter 1)
Write four thousand, three hundred eight in standard form.

**Here's A Way!**

Write the number in expanded form first.
4000 + 300 + 8 = 4308

Standard form

Write the number in standard form.

1. 700 + 80 + 3

2. ten thousand, five hundred sixty-seven

3. two hundred thousand

4. one million, four hundred thirty thousand, six hundred twenty-five

---

**Number Sense** (Chapter 1)
Put 185, 934, and 236 in order from greatest to least.

**Here's A Way!**

To order numbers, start comparing in the greatest place, look to the right and continue.
934, 236, 185

Order from greatest to least.

5. 936, 954, 999       6. 1275, 1246, 1358

7. 860, 4328, 268      8. 43, 4375, 437

Order from least to greatest.

9. 123, 132, 112       10. 1963, 1137, 1482

---

**Mental Math: Using Facts**
(Chapter 1)
Use facts to find 12,000 − 6000.

**Here's A Way!**

You know the basic fact:
12 − 6 = 6.
So, 12,000 − 6000 = 6000.

Use facts to find the missing value.

11. 800 − 300 = ■    12. 400 + 800 = ■

13. 70 + ■ = 140     14. 1100 − ■ = 500

15. Continue the pattern. Write the next four money amounts:
$.40, $.70, $1.00, ■, ■, ■, ■

## Rounding (Chapter 1)

Round 4567 to the nearest thousand.

**Here's A Way!**

Use a number line.

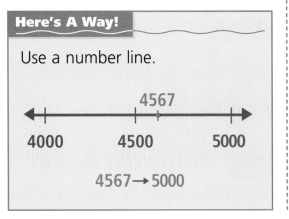

$4567 \rightarrow 5000$

**Round to the nearest ten.**

16. 24      17. 87

**Round to the nearest hundred.**

18. 124      19. 299

**Round to the nearest thousand.**

20. 5643      21. 3099

## Making Change (Chapter 1)

You pay $5.00 for an item that costs $4.39. What is the greatest number of dimes you could get in your change?

**Here's A Way!**

Change from $5.00 is $.61.
**6 dimes = $.60**
You could get 6 dimes.

**Make change. Give two possible combinations of coins or bills.**

22. Cost: $2.75; cash given $3.00

23. Cost: $.42; cash given $1.00

24. Cost: $7.98; cash given $10.00

25. Name a group of coins that is equivalent to 2 quarters.

## Problem Solving

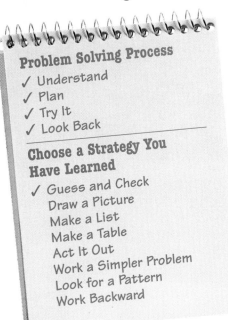

Problem Solving Process
✓ Understand
✓ Plan
✓ Try It
✓ Look Back

Choose a Strategy You Have Learned
✓ Guess and Check
  Draw a Picture
  Make a List
  Make a Table
  Act It Out
  Work a Simpler Problem
  Look for a Pattern
  Work Backward

**Use one of the strategies you know to solve the problem. Show your work.**

26. You double a mystery number and add 2. You get 50. What is the mystery number?

27. Suppose you get a $.50 tip from each home to which you deliver a newspaper. How many homes would you have to deliver to in order to make $20.00 in tips?

INVESTIGATION

# Up to the Sky!

**Geography Connection** **With Your Group**

**L**ook at the map on page 43. This part of California has very high and very low places. Some mountains reach great heights, while the canyons of Death Valley have the lowest points in the United States.

Your class will make a bulletin board display showing and comparing these places.

## 1 Plan It

- In groups, pick four places on the map. Each group chooses different places. Be sure you have places
  - 1000 feet or lower.
  - between 1000 and 9999 feet.
  - 9999 feet or higher.
- Make a list of your places. Order them from lowest to highest.

## 2 Put It Together

- Draw a number line on a strip of paper 30 in. long. Mark one end as zero and the other end as 15,000 feet. Mark the number line to make smaller, equal units. Label them.
- Measure four strips of paper using the number line. Each strip will stand for a place on the map. Cut the strips at the correct heights.

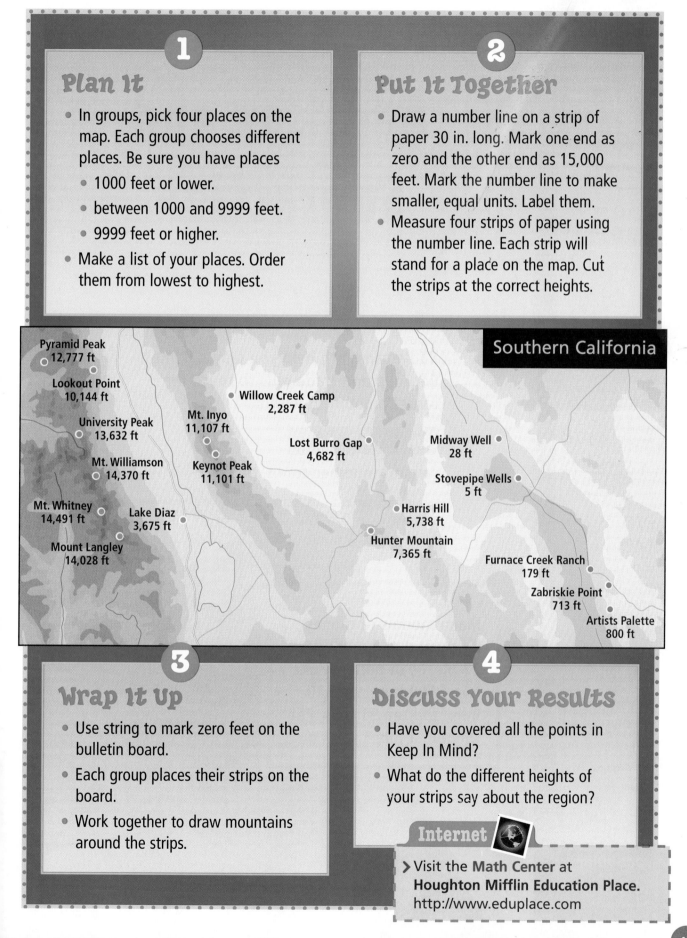

**Southern California**

Pyramid Peak 12,777 ft

Lookout Point 10,144 ft

University Peak 13,632 ft

Mt. Inyo 11,107 ft

Willow Creek Camp 2,287 ft

Lost Burro Gap 4,682 ft

Midway Well 28 ft

Mt. Williamson 14,370 ft

Keynot Peak 11,101 ft

Stovepipe Wells 5 ft

Mt. Whitney 14,491 ft

Lake Diaz 3,675 ft

Harris Hill 5,738 ft

Hunter Mountain 7,365 ft

Mount Langley 14,028 ft

Furnace Creek Ranch 179 ft

Zabriskie Point 713 ft

Artists Palette 800 ft

## 3 Wrap It Up

- Use string to mark zero feet on the bulletin board.
- Each group places their strips on the board.
- Work together to draw mountains around the strips.

## 4 Discuss Your Results

- Have you covered all the points in Keep In Mind?
- What do the different heights of your strips say about the region?

**Internet**

> Visit the **Math Center** at **Houghton Mifflin Education Place.** http://www.eduplace.com

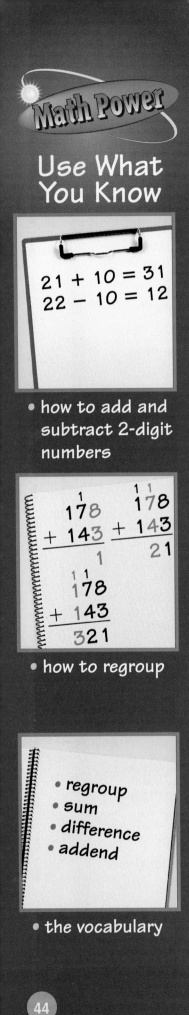

# Addition and Subraction

## Try This!

**H**ow can math help you play a game? Regroup and trade bills to reach the target amount of $200.

### What You'll Need

scissors, number cubes, paper

**1**

Make models of money by cutting and marking 22 pieces of paper. Make two $100 bills, ten $10 bills, and ten $1 bills. Put them in a pile.

---

### Math Power

#### Use What You Know

21 + 10 = 31
22 − 10 = 12

- how to add and subtract 2-digit numbers

$$\begin{array}{r} \overset{1}{1}78 \\ +\ 143 \\ \hline 1 \end{array} \qquad \begin{array}{r} \overset{1\ 1}{1}78 \\ +\ 143 \\ \hline 21 \end{array}$$

$$\begin{array}{r} \overset{1\ 1}{1}78 \\ +\ 143 \\ \hline 321 \end{array}$$

- how to regroup

- regroup
- sum
- difference
- addend

- the vocabulary

## 2

Roll the number cubes to make a 2-digit number. Write it down. Take that many dollars from the pile. If the bills you need are not in the pile, make change with your own money or with the bills in the pile.

## 3

Guess how many rolls it will take you to get $200. Write down your guess. Then write down how many rolls it actually takes you. How close was your guess?

How did you know when you reached $200? Did you count, add, or subtract?

Number of rolls to get to $200

Guess : 22

| Roll Number | Amount |
| --- | --- |
| 1 | 22 |
| 2 | 13 |

How can adding and subtracting numbers help you when you don't have the correct amount of money?

**Ready to Go!**

# Properties and Rules

**U**se what you already know about number patterns to learn about properties and rules for adding and subtracting.

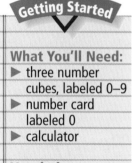

### Getting Started

**What You'll Need:**
▶ three number cubes, labeled 0–9
▶ number card labeled 0
▶ calculator

**Vocabulary:**
order property
grouping property
Glossary, p. 516

### Activity

| Zero in Addition and Subtraction | Order Property |
|---|---|
| 7 + 0 = 7 | 8 + 4 = 12 |
| 7 − 0 = 7 | 4 + 8 = 12 |
| 7 − 7 = 0 | |

| Grouping Property |
|---|
| (3 + 5) + 6 = 14 |
| 3 + (5 + 6) = 14 |

### Zero in Addition and Subtraction

- Place the number card that shows 0 faceup on the table. Roll one cube.

- What is the sum of 0 and the number rolled? What is the difference when you subtract 0 from the number rolled? Record an addition sentence and a subtraction sentence.

- Roll several times. Find sums and differences with zero and the number rolled. Record.

- Write a rule that tells about adding 0.

- Write a rule about subtracting 0.

- What is the difference when you subtract a number from itself? Roll a number. Record a subtraction sentence. Write a rule.

## Order Property of Addition

- Roll two cubes. Find the sum of the numbers. Record.
- Change the order of the addends. Find the sum. Record.
- Repeat the above steps several times. Record.
- Write a rule that tells what happens to a sum when you change the order of the addends.

## Grouping Property of Addition

- Roll three cubes. Use parentheses to group the first two numbers you will add. Use a calculator to find the sum.
  **Example: (2 + 3) + 4 = 9**
- Write the three numbers again. Use parentheses to group different numbers to add first. Use a calculator to find the sum.
  **Example: 2 + (3 + 4) = 9**
- Repeat the above steps several times.
- Write a rule that tells what happens to a sum when you group the addends differently.

## Show What You Know!

**Use the order property. Rewrite the number sentence.**

1. 5 + 7 = 12    2. 8 + 9 = 17    3. 9 + 2 = 11    4. 7 + 6 = 13

**Use the parentheses to help you add the numbers.**

5. (7 + 8) + 1 =16    6. 6 + (2 + 5)    7. 9 + (3 + 0)    8. (6 + 5) + 7

9. 8 + (4 + 1) =13  10. (13 + 4) + 5    11. 15 + (9 + 9)    12. (12 + 11) + 1

**Write About It  Answer each question. Use examples.**

13. Does the rule about subtracting a number from itself apply to a number greater than 10?

14. Does the order property apply to subtraction?

15. Does the grouping property apply to subtraction?

More Practice Set 2.1, p. 476

# Mental Math: Addition and Subtraction

**D**uring a game, you have scored 37 points and your friend has scored 52 points. You score 8 more points. Your friend loses 5 points. What are the new scores?

You can use mental math to find out.

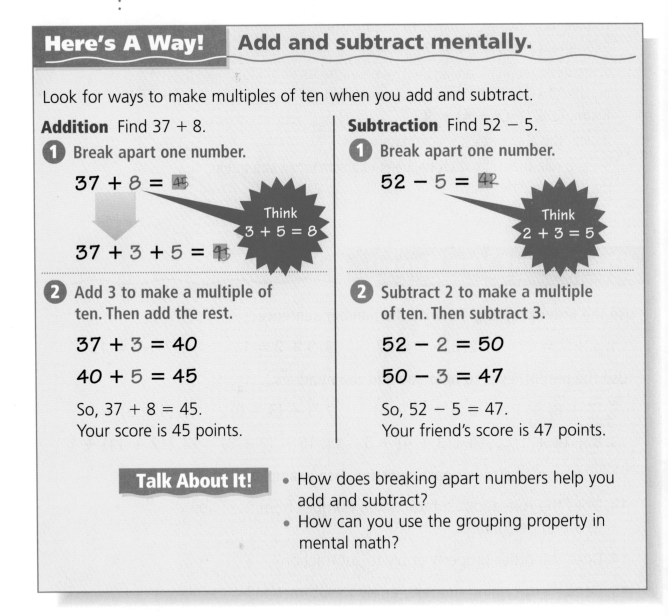

**Here's A Way!** **Add and subtract mentally.**

Look for ways to make multiples of ten when you add and subtract.

**Addition** Find 37 + 8.

① Break apart one number.

37 + 8 = 45

*Think 3 + 5 = 8*

37 + 3 + 5 = 45

② Add 3 to make a multiple of ten. Then add the rest.

37 + 3 = 40

40 + 5 = 45

So, 37 + 8 = 45.
Your score is 45 points.

**Subtraction** Find 52 − 5.

① Break apart one number.

52 − 5 = 47

*Think 2 + 3 = 5*

② Subtract 2 to make a multiple of ten. Then subtract 3.

52 − 2 = 50

50 − 3 = 47

So, 52 − 5 = 47.
Your friend's score is 47 points.

**Talk About It!**
- How does breaking apart numbers help you add and subtract?
- How can you use the grouping property in mental math?

Solve. Explain how you used mental math to find the answer.

1. 33 − 6　　2. 54 − 6　　3. 28 + 5　　4. 67 + 7　　5. 59 + 3

6. 4 + 38　　7. 22 − 3　　8. 85 − 7　　9. 78 + 9　　10. 45 + 7

11. 72 − 8　　12. 56 − 8　　13. 19 + 8　　14. 91 − 4　　15. 44 − 5

## Work It Out!

Find each sum or difference.

16. 49 + 3　　17. 5 + 38　　18. 27 + 4　　19. 7 + 17　　20. 78 + 3

21. 55 + 8　　22. 46 + 8　　23. 25 − 7　　24. 48 − 9　　25. 87 − 9

26. 77 − 9　　27. 12 − 3　　28. 54 − 6　　29. 63 − 4　　30. 35 − 9

Copy and complete each table.

31.

| Add 9 | |
|---|---|
| 58 | 67 |
| 78 | ? |
| 128 | ? |
| 328 | ? |
| 1028 | ? |

32.

| Subtract 6 | |
|---|---|
| 45 | 39 |
| 85 | ? |
| 135 | ? |
| 415 | ? |
| 2125 | ? |

33. **Patterns** Look at the tables you completed in exercises 31 and 32. What patterns do you see in the sums and differences in the tables?

### Problem Solving

34. You are selling T-shirts to raise money for your school. The price for each T-shirt is $13. You need to raise $110. You have already raised $97. How many more shirts do you need to sell?

35. **Create Your Own** Write one addition and one subtraction problem that a friend could use mental math to solve.

**More Practice Set 2.2, p. 476**

# Mental Math Using 5, 50, 500

**Y**ou have to do two chores before playing soccer. One chore takes 25 minutes, and the other takes 35 minutes. How long do you have to do chores before you can play?

Use mental math. The fact that 5 + 5 = 10 can help you add using mental math.

---

## Here's A Way! Find 25 + 35.

**1** Break apart both numbers. Use the fact that 5 + 5 = 10.

Think of 25 as 20 and 5. Think of 35 as 30 and 5.
So, 25 + 35 is the same as 20 + 5 + 30 + 5.

---

**2** Add the multiples of ten.

20 + 30 = 50

Now, add the fives.

5 + 5 = 10

**3** Find the total.

50 + 10 = 60

25 + 35 = 60

**4** Then, answer the question.

You will have to do chores for 60 minutes, or 1 hour, before you can play soccer.

---

**Talk About It!** Can breaking apart help you add numbers in the hundreds? In the thousands? Explain.

## Other Examples

a. 250 + 350 = 600

Think: 200 + 300 and 50 + 50.

b. 2500 + 3500 = 6000

Think: 2000 + 3000 and 500 + 500.

Use mental math to find each sum.

1. 25 + 45
2. 250 + 450
3. 2500 + 4500
4. 305 + 305

5. 1050 + 6050
6. 1500 + 3500
7. 125 + 335
8. 185 + 205

9. Show two ways to find 25 + 45 + 25.

Complete the number sentence.

10. 225 + 25 = 250
11. 350 + 250 = 600
12. 2500 + 3500 = 6000

13. **Algebraic Reasoning** Describe how you completed each number sentence in exercises 10–12.

## Work It Out!

Use mental math to find the sum.

14. 65 + 15
15. 75 + 75
16. 55 + 35
17. 605 + 205

18. 850 + 350
19. 155 + 255
20. 4050 + 2050
21. 7500 + 1500

Find the sum. How can you change the order of the numbers you are adding?

22. 60 + 24 + 40
23. 35 + 80 + 65
24. 450 + 200 + 350

Copy and complete the table. Use mental math.

25.

| ■ | ■ + 25 |
|---|---|
| 35 | 60 |
| 15 | ? |
| 75 | ? |
| 60 | ? |
| ? | 70 |

26.

| ■ | ■ + 150 |
|---|---|
| 450 | 600 |
| 350 | ? |
| 550 | ? |
| 850 | ? |
| ? | 900 |

27. **Write About It** What operation did you use to fill in the last row of the table in exercises 25 and 26?

## Problem Solving

28. Look at the times shown on the notebook. If you start at 2:00 P.M., will you finish all 3 chores by 3:00 P.M.? Explain.

THINGS TO DO TODAY

Wash Dishes          25 minutes
Take Out Garbage   10 minutes
Clean Room           25 minutes

**More Practice Set 2.3, p. 476**

# Problem Solving
## Draw a Picture

**Getting Started**

**What You'll Need:**
► squared paper

**Y**ou are working at an archaeological dig. You need to build a fence around the dig site.

The dig site is 20 feet long by 20 feet wide. You want to build the fence 10 feet from the edge of the dig site. How much fencing will you need?

*These students are digging to find tools and other objects people left behind many years ago.*

## Here's A Way!   Use Draw a Picture.

**1 Understand**

• What is the size and shape of the dig site?
• Exactly where will the fence be?

**2 Plan**

• How might drawing a picture help?
• What will you put in your picture?

**3 Try It**

• On squared paper, draw an outline of the dig site and an outline of the fence.

• Use your picture to figure out the length of the fence along one side of the site. Are all 4 sides equal?

• One side is 40 feet long. Figure out the total length of the fence.

$$40 + 40 + 40 + 40 = 160$$

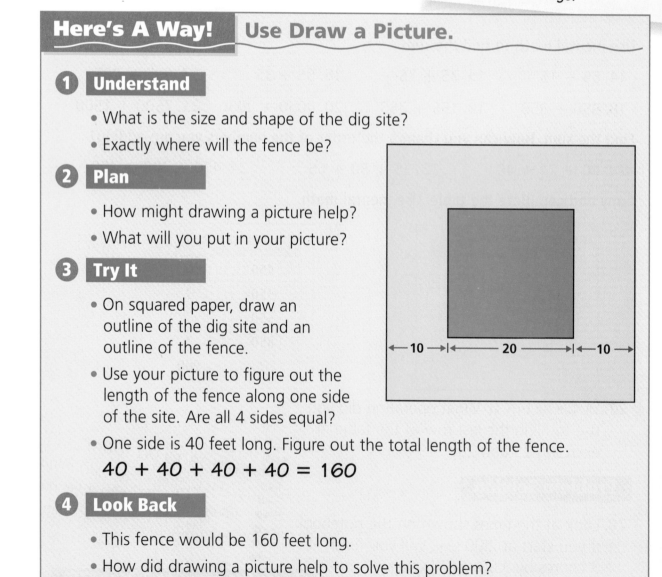

**4 Look Back**

• This fence would be 160 feet long.
• How did drawing a picture help to solve this problem?

**Copy and finish the picture to help you solve the problem.**

**First Side**

1. It takes you 2 hours to build the fence along 1 side of the site. If you start at 9 A.M. and work without stopping, at what time will you finish all 4 sides?

2. **Critical Thinking** Suppose you drew a number line to solve the problem. What would it show? Compare this drawing to the clock.

3. **Create Your Own** Make up a problem that can be solved by drawing a picture. Share your problem with a classmate.

## Work It Out!

**Use Draw a Picture or any other strategy to solve the problem.**

4. An archaeologist is working in the dig site described on page 52. She finds an arrowhead 16 feet from the top side of the site and 5 feet from the left side. What are the distances from the other two sides?

5. The fence around the dig site needs a post in each corner. The rest of the fence needs 1 post every 8 feet along each side. You also need 2 extra posts for a gate. How many posts will you need?

6. A train has 5 cars. Each car is 30 feet long. If the cars are 5 feet apart, how long is the train?

7. Find each pair of mystery numbers.

| Sum | Difference | Mystery Numbers |
|-----|------------|-----------------|
| 12 | 6 | ? and ? |
| 120 | 60 | ? and ? |
| 1200 | 600 | ? and ? |

8. You buy lunch for $1.29. You pay with 8 coins and get a penny in change. What 8 coins did you use?

### Share Your Thinking

9. Did you use a strategy other than Draw a Picture for any of the problems? If so, which problem was it? Which strategy did you use?

10. When you use Draw a Picture to solve a problem, how detailed do you make the picture? What can you leave out? Does it depend on the problem? Explain.

# Estimating Sums

**S**tudents from four schools have a goal to plant 800 trees. Use the chart at the bottom of the page. Have the students reached their goal?

You can use **front-end estimation** and **adjusted estimation** to find the answer.

## Here's A Way!  Estimate the sum.

**1** Add the digits with the greatest place value. These are the front-end digits.

$$
\begin{array}{r}
②47 \\
①68 \\
①25 \\
+③73
\end{array}
\qquad
\begin{array}{r}
2 \text{ hundreds} \\
1 \text{ hundred} \\
1 \text{ hundred} \\
+ 3 \text{ hundreds}
\end{array}
$$

Front-end estimate: 700. Is your front-end estimate close enough to help you solve the problem? Why or why not?

**2** Adjust your estimate. Look for groups of about 100 in the remaining digits.

$$
\begin{array}{r}
24⃝7 \\
16⃝8 \\
12⃝5 \\
+37⃝3
\end{array}
$$

4 tens + 6 tens = 10 tens
So, 47 + 68 is about 100.

2 tens + 7 tens = 9 tens
So, 25 + 73 is about 100.

Adjusted estimate: 700 + 100 + 100 = 900. The students planted about 900 trees.

## Talk About It!  Have you answered the question? If not, what is the answer?

NUMBER OF TREES PLANTED

| | |
|---|---|
| First School | 247 |
| Second School | 168 |
| Third School | 125 |
| Fourth School | 373 |

Make a front-end estimate. Then adjust the estimate.

1.     329
   + 187

2.     126
   + 281

3.    3529
   + 4486

4.    3251
      7425
   + 8225

5.    1473
      5678
   + 2801

Estimate to decide which sum is greater.

6. 306 + 369  or  463 + 119

7. 392 + 284  or  378 + 239

8. 235 + 228  or  278 + 298

9. 523 + 381  or  498 + 497

10. **Critical Thinking** Explain the steps you took to decide which sum was greater in exercises 6–9.

## Work It Out!

Make a front-end estimate. Then adjust your estimate.

11.     543
    + 268

12.     434
        235
    + 134

13.    2846
    + 2159

14.    1618
       2546
    + 3335

15.    8724
       6127
    + 6035

16. **Critical Thinking** Is 485 + 847 + 362 closer to 1000 or to 2000? Explain.

**Algebraic Reasoning** Find a number in the box that makes the number sentence true. Use each number only once.

17. 453 + ● > 800

18. 453 + ● < 800

19. ● + 662 > 1000

20. ● + 662 < 1000

| 289 | 360 |
|-----|-----|
| 309 | 393 |

### Problem Solving  Using Data

Estimate to solve the problem. Explain your answer.

21. The table shows 4 types of trees your school ordered to plant. Did your school order at least 1000 trees?

22. Which two quantities of trees would you need to plant about 500 trees?

23. If the students planted all the trees except the alder trees, would they plant more than or less than 800 trees?

**Kinds of Trees**

| Kind of Tree | Maple | Dogwood | Pine | Alder |
|--------------|-------|---------|------|-------|
| Quantity | 482 | 125 | 365 | 147 |

More Practice Set 2.5, p. 477

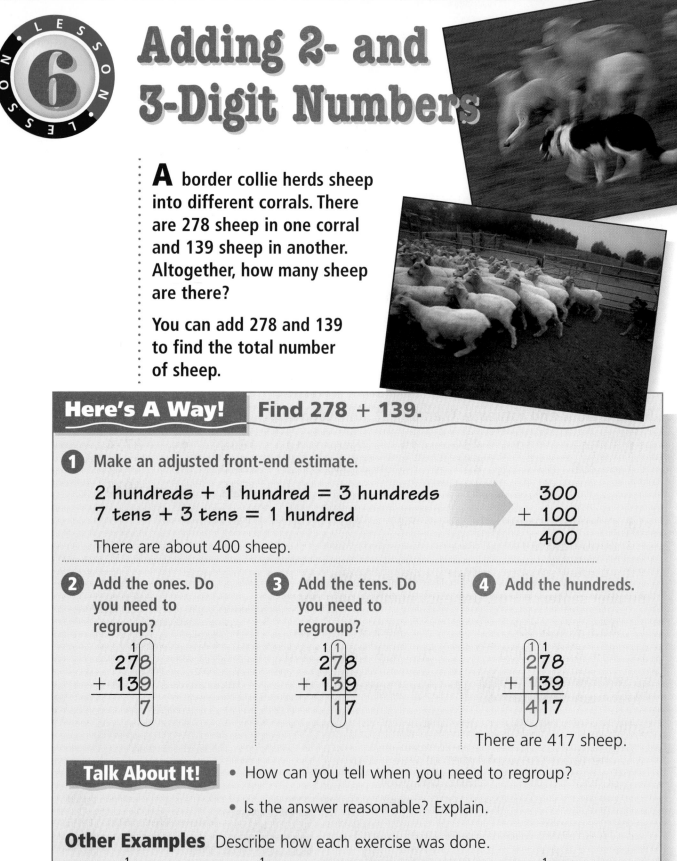

# Adding 2- and 3-Digit Numbers

**A** border collie herds sheep into different corrals. There are 278 sheep in one corral and 139 sheep in another. Altogether, how many sheep are there?

You can add 278 and 139 to find the total number of sheep.

## Here's A Way! Find 278 + 139.

**1** Make an adjusted front-end estimate.

2 hundreds + 1 hundred = 3 hundreds
7 tens + 3 tens = 1 hundred

$$\begin{array}{r} 300 \\ + 100 \\ \hline 400 \end{array}$$

There are about 400 sheep.

**2** Add the ones. Do you need to regroup?

$$\begin{array}{r} {\scriptstyle 1} \\ 278 \\ + 139 \\ \hline 7 \end{array}$$

**3** Add the tens. Do you need to regroup?

$$\begin{array}{r} {\scriptstyle 1}{\scriptstyle 1} \\ 278 \\ + 139 \\ \hline 17 \end{array}$$

**4** Add the hundreds.

$$\begin{array}{r} {\scriptstyle 1}{\scriptstyle 1} \\ 278 \\ + 139 \\ \hline 417 \end{array}$$

There are 417 sheep.

**Talk About It!**
- How can you tell when you need to regroup?
- Is the answer reasonable? Explain.

**Other Examples** Describe how each exercise was done.

a. $\begin{array}{r} {\scriptstyle 1} \\ 408 \\ + 77 \\ \hline 485 \end{array}$

b. $\begin{array}{r} {\scriptstyle 1} \\ 88 \\ + 76 \\ \hline 164 \end{array}$

c. $\begin{array}{r} 135 \\ + 63 \\ \hline 198 \end{array}$

d. $\begin{array}{r} {\scriptstyle 1} \\ 163 \\ + 85 \\ \hline 248 \end{array}$

**Find the sum only for those problems that need regrouping.**

1. 45
   + 37

2. 145
   + 329

3. 237
   + 175

4. 163
   + 25

5. 432
   + 28

6. **Number Sense** When you add two numbers, what is the greatest number of tens you can form by regrouping? Tell how you know.

## Work It Out!

**Find the sum only for those exercises that need regrouping.**

7. 47
   + 69

8. 84
   + 97

9. 26
   + 11

10. 432
    + 27

11. 285
    + 75

12. 555
    + 66

13. 805
    + 107

14. 383
    + 117

15. 324
    + 324

16. 780
    + 780

17. **Algebraic Reasoning** Complete the addition problem shown. How did you find the missing digit?

$$327 + 1\blacksquare 5 = 452$$

## Problem Solving  Using Data

**Use the table to answer the question. Estimate when you can.**

18. A border collie herds sheep into four different corrals. Which two corrals have a total of 740 sheep?

19. In which two corrals is the total number of sheep equal to that of another corral?

20. Name two corrals that together have more than 600 sheep but less than 700. Explain.

### Herding Sheep

| Corral | Number of Sheep |
| --- | --- |
| A | 238 |
| B | 344 |
| C | 396 |
| D | 158 |

**More Practice Set 2.6, p. 477**

### Math Journal

You can add in more than one way. What method do you prefer? Explain why.

# Three or More Addends

**Y**ou are keeping track of the number of tickets sold each hour for a pop concert. You are recording the total numbers on your computer. How many tickets were sold in four hours?

To solve this problem, you can add the number of tickets sold each hour.

## Ticket Sales

| Time | Number of Tickets Sold |
|------|------------------------|
| Hour 1 | 279 |
| Hour 2 | 258 |
| Hour 3 | 336 |
| Hour 4 | 185 |

### Here's A Way!   Find 279 + 258 + 336 + 185.

**1** Add the ones. Regroup if you need to.

```
  2
 279
 258
 336
+185
───
   8
```

**2** Add the tens. Regroup if you need to.

```
 2 2
 279
 258
 336
+185
───
  58
```

**3** Add the hundreds.

```
 2 2
 279
 258
 336
+185
───
1058
```

A total of 1058 tickets were sold in four hours.

### Talk About It!

How can you use an estimate to tell if your answer is reasonable?

**Find the sum.**

1. 135 + 250 + 225

2. 63 + 52 + 47 + 40

3. 315 + 150 + 195

4. 175 + 148 + 85 + 72

5. 237 + 189 + 505 + 197

6. 990 + 150 + 10 + 50

7. **Critical Thinking** Which exercises could you solve by using mental math? What was different about them?

8. **Calculator** A school sold tickets to the school concert every year for four years. The fewest sold in any one year was 1876 tickets. The most was 2672 tickets. What is the greatest number of tickets that could have been sold in the four years? The fewest? Explain.

## Work It Out!

**Find the sum. Circle the sum if you used mental math.**

9. 135 + 206 + 154

10. 1150 + 314 + 25

11. 2056 + 1695 + 181 + 79

12. 1485 + 1260 + 191 + 92

13. 658 + 72 + 20

14. 16 + 14 + 13 + 17 + 15

### Problem Solving   Using Data

**Use mental math when you can to solve the problem.**

15. **Estimation** Were the combined sales of Tuesday and Wednesday higher than sales on Monday?

16. The concert hall can hold 2500 people. As of Thursday has the concert sold out? If not, how many more tickets can be sold?

**Ticket Sales**

| Day | Number of Tickets |
| --- | --- |
| Monday | 1058 |
| Tuesday | 342 |
| Wednesday | 787 |
| Thursday | 120 |

WORLD TOUR

### Mixed Review

**What is the value of the digit in color?**

17. 792

18. 327

19. 5458

20. 4739

21. 73,924

22. 16,348

23. 528,136

24. 971,293

**More Practice Set 2.7, p. 477**

# LESSON 8

# Estimating Sums by Rounding

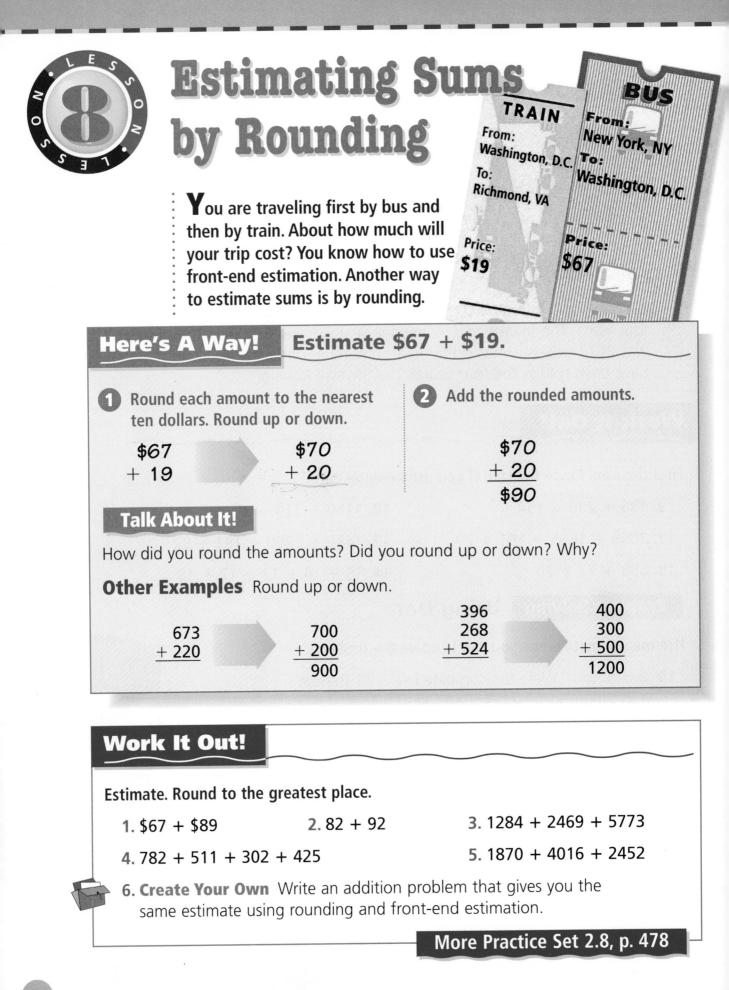

**TRAIN**
From: Washington, D.C.
To: Richmond, VA
Price: **$19**

**BUS**
From: New York, NY
To: Washington, D.C.
Price: **$67**

**Y**ou are traveling first by bus and then by train. About how much will your trip cost? You know how to use front-end estimation. Another way to estimate sums is by rounding.

## Here's A Way!  Estimate $67 + $19.

**1** Round each amount to the nearest ten dollars. Round up or down.

$$\begin{array}{r} \$67 \\ + 19 \end{array} \Rightarrow \begin{array}{r} \$70 \\ + 20 \end{array}$$

**2** Add the rounded amounts.

$$\begin{array}{r} \$70 \\ + 20 \\ \hline \$90 \end{array}$$

### Talk About It!

How did you round the amounts? Did you round up or down? Why?

**Other Examples**  Round up or down.

$$\begin{array}{r} 673 \\ + 220 \end{array} \Rightarrow \begin{array}{r} 700 \\ + 200 \\ \hline 900 \end{array}$$

$$\begin{array}{r} 396 \\ 268 \\ + 524 \end{array} \Rightarrow \begin{array}{r} 400 \\ 300 \\ + 500 \\ \hline 1200 \end{array}$$

## Work It Out!

Estimate. Round to the greatest place.

1. $67 + $89
2. 82 + 92
3. 1284 + 2469 + 5773
4. 782 + 511 + 302 + 425
5. 1870 + 4016 + 2452
6. **Create Your Own** Write an addition problem that gives you the same estimate using rounding and front-end estimation.

**More Practice Set 2.8, p. 478**

# Midchapter Review

## for Pages 44–60

for Pages 44–60

## Problem Solving

**Solve. Show your work.** (pages 52, 68)

1. You plan to use fence posts in each corner and every 6 feet to fence off a section of your backyard. How many fence posts do you need?

6 ft

30 ft

2. Suppose you walk 3 blocks east, then 2 blocks north, and then 4 blocks west. By the shortest path, how many blocks are you from your starting point?

## Concepts

**Make a front-end estimate. Then adjust.** (page 54)

| 3. | 417 | 4. | 180 | 5. | 641 | 6. | 150 |
|---|---|---|---|---|---|---|---|
| | + 271 | | + 135 | | + 249 | | + 750 |

**In which place or places will you need to regroup?** (page 56)

| 7. | 69 | 8. | 86 | 9. | 147 | 10. | 708 |
|---|---|---|---|---|---|---|---|
| | + 54 | | + 64 | | + 285 | | + 435 |

## Skills

**Find the sum or the difference. Show your work.** (pages 48, 56, 58)

11. 44 + 7

12. 63 − 6

13. 74 − 7

14. 26 + 9

15. 27 + 95

16. 163 + 486

17. 872 − 543

18. 16 + 25 + 42

19. 88 + 78 + 95

20. 154 + 165 + 183

# Math World

There are many stories behind number names. Learn about some of them and play a number game.

## "Handy" Numbers to Know

Most groups of people around the world have used their fingers and hands to count things. That is why the names for numbers in some languages today have words that come from words for fingers and hands. For example, the Russian word for 5 is *piat* (PYAHT). This sounds like the Russian word for "outstretched hand" (PYAHST).

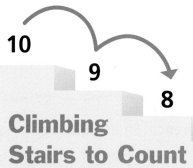

10

9

8

## Climbing Stairs to Count

The Ainu (EYE noo) people live in northern Japan. All of their number words come from the numbers 1, 2, 3, 4, 5, 10, and 20. To make the numbers 6–9, they add and subtract by thinking of a staircase. The Ainu say "1 step down" for 9. How do you think they say 8?

62

Problem 1. 45

Problem 2. 45

$$
\begin{array}{r}
45 \\
+\ 45 \\
\hline
90
\end{array}
$$

# Try This!

A Chinese tale tells about a turtle that was found in the River Lo around 2200 B.C. On the turtle's back was a square. Inside the square were written figures that stood for the numbers 1 through 9. The numbers on the turtle's back added up in an interesting way. Find out how by adding them yourself.

**1** Add the numbers in each of the three rows. What do you get?

**2** Add the numbers in each column. What do you get?

**3** Add the numbers in each of the two diagonals. What do you get?

**4** Fill in the empty squares in each of the three puzzles below. The rows, columns, and diagonals in each puzzle should add up as they did on the turtle.

| 2 | 7 | 6 |
|---|---|---|
| 9 | 5 | 1 |
| 7 | 3 | 8 |

| 6 | 1 | 8 |
|---|---|---|
| 7 | 5 | 3 |
| 2 | 9 | 4 |

| 8 | 3 | 4 |
|---|---|---|
| 1 | 5 | 9 |
| 6 | 7 | 2 |

## Respond

**Base 5 and base 10. . .**
are two number systems you know about. Can you create your own base?

Internet:
**Houghton Mifflin Education Place**
Explore the Math Center at
http://www.eduplace.com

63

# Estimating Differences

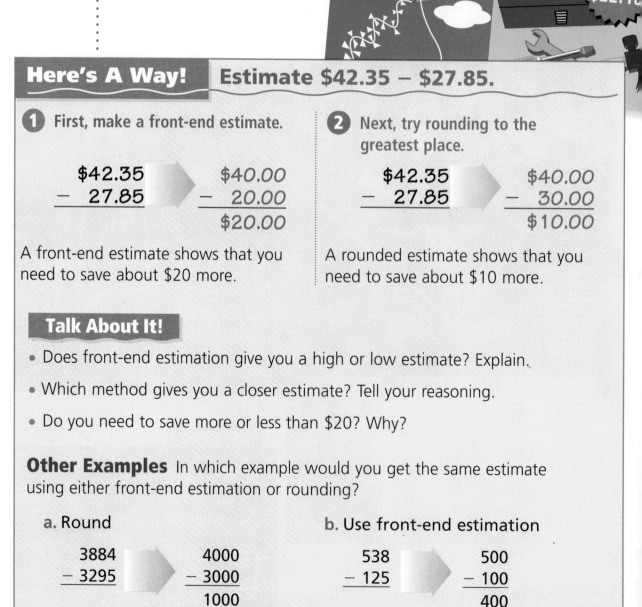

**NOW ON SAL**

$42.35

Model Plane Kit

T REX Model Kit

$14.9

$12.95

$22.45

**Y**ou are saving to buy the dinosaur kit. So far you have $27.85. About how much more do you need to buy it?

You can estimate to help you decide.

## Here's A Way! Estimate $42.35 − $27.85.

**1** First, make a front-end estimate.

$$\begin{array}{r} \$42.35 \\ - \phantom{0}27.85 \end{array} \Rightarrow \begin{array}{r} \$40.00 \\ - \phantom{0}20.00 \\ \hline \$20.00 \end{array}$$

A front-end estimate shows that you need to save about $20 more.

**2** Next, try rounding to the greatest place.

$$\begin{array}{r} \$42.35 \\ - \phantom{0}27.85 \end{array} \Rightarrow \begin{array}{r} \$40.00 \\ - \phantom{0}30.00 \\ \hline \$10.00 \end{array}$$

A rounded estimate shows that you need to save about $10 more.

### Talk About It!

- Does front-end estimation give you a high or low estimate? Explain.

- Which method gives you a closer estimate? Tell your reasoning.

- Do you need to save more or less than $20? Why?

**Other Examples** In which example would you get the same estimate using either front-end estimation or rounding?

**a.** Round

$$\begin{array}{r} 3884 \\ - 3295 \end{array} \Rightarrow \begin{array}{r} 4000 \\ - 3000 \\ \hline 1000 \end{array}$$

**b.** Use front-end estimation

$$\begin{array}{r} 538 \\ - 125 \end{array} \Rightarrow \begin{array}{r} 500 \\ - 100 \\ \hline 400 \end{array}$$

Estimate. Use the method of your choice.

1. 629
   − 285

2. $12.41
   − 10.82

3. 2928
   − 2021

4. 681
   − 275

5. $16.00
   − 9.45

6. **Critical Thinking** In what situations would you use front-end estimation? In what situations would you use rounding?

## Work It Out!

Estimate. Use the method of your choice. Show your work.

7. 972
   − 543

8. $7.27
   − 2.78

9. 94,378
   − 54,481

10. $76.85
    − 28.15

11. 1778
    − 1467

12. 987 − 619

13. 2928 − 2021

14. $32.48 − $22.96

**Number Sense** Decide whether the exercise has a difference between 500 and 700.

15. 825
    − 232

16. 639
    − 225

17. 927
    − 380

18. 698
    − 125

19. 3525
    − 2915

**Algebraic Reasoning** Find a number in the box that makes each number sentence true. Use each number only once.

20. ■ − 256 < 400

21. 325 − ■ < 200

22. 756 − ■ > 400

23. ■ − 372 > 400

| 175 | 310 |
|-----|-----|
| 600 | 792 |

### Problem Solving   Using Data

Use the chart to answer the questions.

24. If you pay $20 for the Greeting Cards kit will you get more than $10 in change? Explain.

25. Which kit is about $10 more than the Stamp Book?

26. Is $45 enough to buy 2 Jewelry kits?

27. **Create Your Own** Write a word problem that uses subtraction. Think of a problem about buying something.

### Craft Price List

| Craft Kit | Price |
|-----------|-------|
| Birdhouse | $ 19.95 |
| Model Ship | $ 12.75 |
| Stamp Book | $ 8.95 |
| Greeting Cards | $ 11.25 |
| Jewelry | $ 24.95 |

**More Practice Set 2.9, p. 478**

# Subtracting Greater Numbers

**P**eople study the places where Native Americans lived hundreds of years ago. Suppose 139 pots are found in one place, and 245 pots are found in another place. How many more pots are found in the second place?

You can use subtraction to find out.

## Here's A Way!  Find 245 − 139.

**1** First, estimate the difference. Use front-end estimation or rounding.

$$245 - 139$$

$$\begin{array}{r} 200 \\ - 100 \\ \hline 100 \end{array}$$  The difference is about 100.

**2** Subtract the ones. Regroup.

$$\begin{array}{r} \overset{3}{\cancel{2}}\overset{15}{4\cancel{5}} \\ -139 \\ \hline 6 \end{array}$$

**3** Subtract the tens.

$$\begin{array}{r} \overset{3}{\cancel{2}}\overset{15}{4\cancel{5}} \\ -139 \\ \hline 06 \end{array}$$

**4** Subtract the hundreds.

$$\begin{array}{r} \overset{3}{\cancel{2}}\overset{15}{4\cancel{5}} \\ -139 \\ \hline 106 \end{array}$$

**5** Check your answer by adding.

$$106 + 139 = 245$$

So 106 more pots are found in the second place.

## Talk About It!

How could you have used your estimate to decide whether your answer is reasonable?

## Show What You Know!

**Find the difference. Circle the answers you find by using mental math.**

| 1. | 2. | 3. | 4. | 5. |
|---|---|---|---|---|
| 88 <br> − 39 | 347 <br> − 125 | 324 <br> − 189 | 749 <br> − 129 | 456 <br> − 338 |

6. **Critical Thinking** How is regrouping in subtraction like regrouping in addition? How is it different? Give examples.

## Work It Out!

**Find the difference.**

| 7. | 8. | 9. | 10. | 11. |
|---|---|---|---|---|
| 76 <br> − 47 | 539 <br> − 126 | 421 <br> − 376 | 518 <br> − 138 | 154,312 <br> − 63,519 |

| 12. | 13. | 14. | 15. | 16. |
|---|---|---|---|---|
| 276 <br> − 87 | 1541 <br> − 1437 | 6421 <br> − 3469 | 91 <br> − 9 | 23,405 <br> − 5219 |

**Algebraic Reasoning** **Estimate. Then use > or < to write a true number sentence.**

17. 95 − 49 ● 20        18. 876 − 491 ● 600        19. 3000 ● 4321 − 2856

20. **Create Your Own** Write a subtraction exercise in which you must regroup tens but not ones.

**Estimate. Then subtract.**

| 21. | 22. | 23. | 24. | 25. | 26. |
|---|---|---|---|---|---|
| 413 <br> − 230 | 413 <br> − 240 | 413 <br> − 250 | 413 <br> − 330 | 413 <br> − 340 | 413 <br> − 350 |

27. **Patterns** Describe the patterns in exercises 21–26. How did the answers for 21 and 24 help you to solve the other exercises?

### Problem Solving

28. A museum has 667 pots on display. It lends 229 pots to one museum and 168 pots to another. How many pots does it still have on display?

29. The price for tickets at a museum is $4 for adults and $2 for children. A family of two adults and four children has $20 for tickets. They also want to buy tickets for their grandmother and grandfather. Will they have enough money?

**More Practice Set 2.10, p. 479**

# Problem Solving

## Using Draw a Picture and Other Strategies

The golden lion tamarin is an endangered animal that lives in the rain forests of Brazil. To help these animals survive, scientists are raising them in zoos. They need to know how quickly the tamarin population can increase.

**Problem Solving Process**
- ✓ Understand
- ✓ Plan
- ✓ Try It
- ✓ Look Back

**Choose a Strategy You Have Learned**
- ✓ Guess and Check
- ✓ Draw a Picture
- Make a List
- Make a Table
- Act It Out
- Work a Simpler Problem
- Look for a Pattern
- Work Backward

Golden lion tamarins live in groups of males and females. In these groups, only one female has babies, and she usually has twins. Suppose scientists are studying a group of 4 tamarins in a zoo. The female in this group has twins every 6 months. This means that the number of tamarins in this group increases in a particular way. Every six months, the group increases by 2 babies. How long will it take this group to increase by 12 tamarins?

- How might a picture help show how the population increases?
- How will you show the number of baby tamarins?
- Can you show how many tamarins there will be at the end of every 6 months?
- Explain a strategy you can use to solve the problem. Then solve it.

**Use any strategy to solve the problem. Show your work.**

1. Suppose the population continues to increase by 2 every 6 months. If none of the tamarins dies, will the zoo have more than 30 tamarins after 10 years? Explain.

2. Suppose one female tamarin has 2 female babies. Those 2 females each have 2 females. Following the same pattern, how many tamarins will there be by the fifth generation?

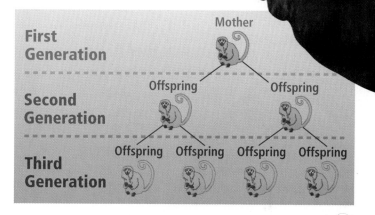

3. Suppose a TV commercial brings more people to visit a zoo. One day, 500 people visit. The next day, 1000 people visit. The third day, 1500 people visit. How many visitors might the zoo have on the fourth day?

4. A scientist must walk from the science lab to the tamarins and then to the birdhouse. What is the shortest route? Explain.

5. Zoo planners want 3 new buildings for movies and classes. First they need to divide the field shown on the map into 3 square lots. What size will each lot be? Find the length of each side.

6. You are at the science lab, and it is 12:30 P.M. You want to go to the snack bar for lunch. You have to be at the birdhouse at 1:00 P.M. It takes you about 1 minute to walk 50 yards. Will you have enough time?

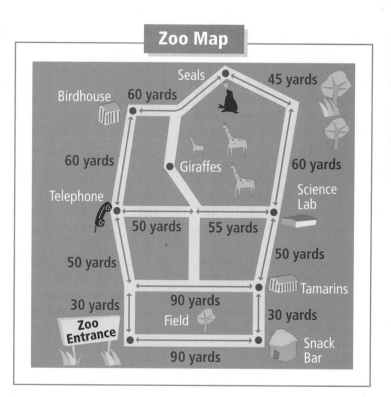

**Zoo Map**

## Share Your Thinking

7. Discuss problem 6 with a classmate. Did you each use a different strategy to solve it? Explain how your strategy helped you.

# Zeros in Subtraction

From the top of Cadillac Mountain, off the coast of Maine, you can be the first person in the United States to see the sunrise.

**Y**ou and your friends are 405 feet from the top of Cadillac Mountain. You climb up another 139 feet. How much farther do you have to go?

You can use subtraction to find out.

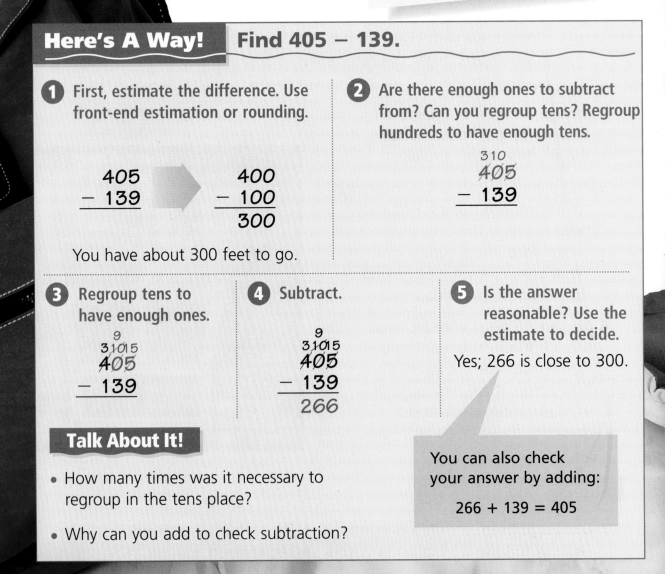

## Here's A Way!  Find 405 − 139.

**1** First, estimate the difference. Use front-end estimation or rounding.

$$
\begin{array}{r} 405 \\ -\ 139 \end{array}
\qquad
\begin{array}{r} 400 \\ -\ 100 \\ \hline 300 \end{array}
$$

You have about 300 feet to go.

**2** Are there enough ones to subtract from? Can you regroup tens? Regroup hundreds to have enough tens.

$$
\begin{array}{r} {}^{3}\cancel{4}{}^{10}\cancel{0}5 \\ -\ 139 \end{array}
$$

**3** Regroup tens to have enough ones.

$$
\begin{array}{r} {}^{3}\cancel{4}{}^{9}\cancel{10}\cancel{0}{}^{15}\cancel{5} \\ -\ 139 \end{array}
$$

**4** Subtract.

$$
\begin{array}{r} {}^{3}\cancel{4}{}^{9}\cancel{10}\cancel{0}{}^{15}\cancel{5} \\ -\ 139 \\ \hline 266 \end{array}
$$

**5** Is the answer reasonable? Use the estimate to decide.

Yes; 266 is close to 300.

You can also check your answer by adding:

$$266 + 139 = 405$$

### Talk About It!

- How many times was it necessary to regroup in the tens place?

- Why can you add to check subtraction?

Solve only those exercises that must be regrouped in the tens place.

1. 401 − 246    2. 328 − 115    3. 822 − 349    4. 687 − 289    5. 742 − 335

**Patterns**  Subtract. Explain how the exercises are alike.

6. 800 − 799    7. 400 − 399    8. 500 − 299    9. 700 − 599    10. 900 − 499

11. **Critical Thinking**  Explain how you can use mental math to subtract exercises 6–10 above.

## Work It Out!

Subtract. Circle the answers you find using mental math.

| 12. | 907 | 13. | 300 | 14. | 387 | 15. | 400 | 16. | 410 |
|-----|-----|-----|-----|-----|-----|-----|-----|-----|-----|
|     | − 532 |   | − 198 |   | − 96 |    | − 275 |   | − 275 |

17. 5691 − 3218    18. 3245 − 203    19. 600 − 299    20. 5250 − 200

21. **Create Your Own**  Write a subtraction exercise in which you must regroup in the tens place and in the hundreds place.

### Problem Solving  Using Data

Use the table to solve the problem.

22. How much more do the boots cost than the tent?

23. If someone paid for the backpack with a $100 bill, how much change would he or she receive?

24. Suppose you have $75 to spend on camping equipment. Which items could you buy?

**Camping Equipment**

| Item | Backpack | Hiking Boots | Compass | Pup Tent | Sleeping Bag |
|------|----------|--------------|---------|----------|--------------|
| Price | $45.00 | $100.00 | $7.00 | $89.00 | $50.00 |

### Mixed Review

Copy and complete. Write > or <.

25. 2351 ■ 251    26. 8720 ■ 8921    27. 6524 ■ 6519    28. 71 ■ 7001

29. Write the value of 7 in each number.  a. 7642   b. 897   c. 6730   d. 6872

**More Practice Set 2.12, p. 479**

# Using Addition and Subtraction

**E**ach year, the drama club puts on a play to raise money for the public library. This year, their goal is to raise $525. The club raises $200 after the first show and $123 after the second show. How much more does the club need to reach its goal?

You can add and then subtract to find out.

## Here's A Way! Add and subtract.

**1** Add the total amount raised in the first two shows.

$$\begin{array}{r} \$200 \\ + \ 123 \\ \hline \$323 \end{array}$$

The drama club has raised $323 so far this year.

**2** Then, subtract this total from $525.

$$\begin{array}{r} \$525 \\ - \ 323 \\ \hline \$202 \end{array}$$

The drama club must raise $202 to reach its goal of $525.

**Talk About It!** Could you have solved this problem another way? Explain why or why not.

## Show What You Know!

Write the answer. Use mental math when you can.

| | | | | |
|---|---|---|---|---|
| **1.** $700 | **2.** $701 | **3.** 8400 | **4.** 8401 | **5.** 8402 |
| − 599 | − 599 | − 3199 | − 3199 | − 3199 |

**6. Patterns** What patterns do you see forming in exercises 1–5?

## Work It Out!

**Write your answer. Circle any answer you get by using mental math.**

7.  9000
    − 500

8.  9000
    − 499

9.  $140
    + 140

10.  4099
    + 4099

11.  3901
    + 3099

12. 5625 − 50

13. 37,202 − 37,201

14. $547 + $423

15. 3362 − 454

16. 7678 − 1245

17. 787 + 986

18. 1250 + 1250

19. 6100 + 2900

20. 12,435 − 12,035

21. **Critical Thinking** Can you use subtraction to check your answer in addition? Explain.

## Problem Solving  Using Data

**Solve the problem. Use a calculator when you need to.**

22. The chart shows the amount of money one school raised for their library over five years. In which years did the school raise more than double the amount they raised in 1995?

23. The school combined money from two years so the library could get a better price on buying more books. After combining the funds, the school had $5051. Which two years were combined?

24. In 1992, the school had raised less than $1000 before the last month of school. Did the school raise more than $2000 during that last month? How can you tell?

25. How much more money would the school have had to raise in 1995 to bring in more money than in 1994?

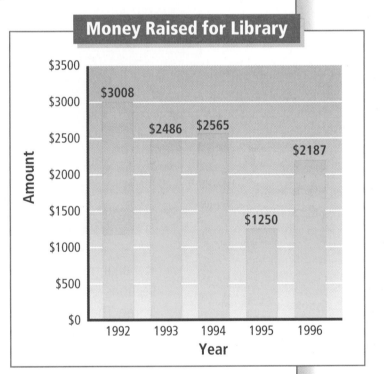

**Money Raised for Library**

**More Practice Set 2.13, p. 480**

# Problem Solving
## Using Strategies

LESSON 14

You can read more about walking sticks in the pages of *Ranger Rick*.

**W**alking sticks are insects that look like twigs. This is how they fool birds and other insects that might eat them.

Suppose you are studying walking sticks in a forest. You need to estimate how many live in a test area 20 feet long and 20 feet wide.

**Problem Solving Process**
✓ Understand
✓ Plan
✓ Try It
✓ Look Back

**Choose a Strategy You Have Learned**
✓ Guess and Check
✓ Draw a Picture
  Make a List
  Make a Table
  Act It Out
  Work a Simpler Problem
  Look for a Pattern
  Work Backward

**W**alking sticks move around on trees. You divide the test area into sections 10 feet long and 10 feet wide. You count 22 walking sticks on 1 tree. There are 4 trees in each section. How will you estimate the total number of walking sticks in the test area?

- How do you estimate the number of walking sticks in each section?

- How many times should you add the number of walking sticks on 1 tree?

- How many times should you add your estimate for each section?

- Explain a strategy that can help solve the problem. Then solve it.

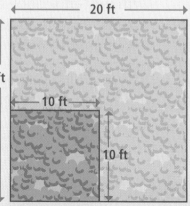

## Work It Out!

**Use any strategy to solve the problem. Show your work.**

1. You count 40 kinds of walking stick insects one day. You count 25 kinds the second day. But 12 of the insects you counted on the second day were the same kind you counted on the first day. How many different kinds of insects did you count?

2. A machine records when a walking stick moves. A needle draws a line up and down each time the insect moves. Study the diagram. Does the walking stick move more in the day or night? Explain.

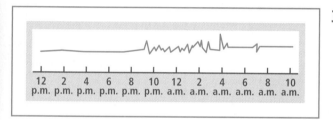

| 12 | 2 | 4 | 6 | 8 | 10 | 12 | 2 | 4 | 6 | 8 | 10 |
|----|----|----|----|----|----|----|----|----|----|----|----|
| p.m. | p.m. | p.m. | p.m. | p.m. | p.m. | a.m. | a.m. | a.m. | a.m. | a.m. | a.m. |

3. Estimate how long the walking stick is most active. About how long does it rest?

4. Walking sticks move very slowly. Suppose you observe one moving 2 inches in 5 seconds. About how long will it take the walking stick to walk 12 inches?

5. A walking stick is moving 2 inches every 5 seconds. It walks for 20 seconds and stops for 10 seconds. Then it walks another 30 seconds. How far has it traveled?

6. A walking stick moves across a table 24 inches in a minute. It walks from the test tube to the pencil. Then it walks in a straight line for exactly 50 seconds before reaching an edge of the table. Which edge has it reached?

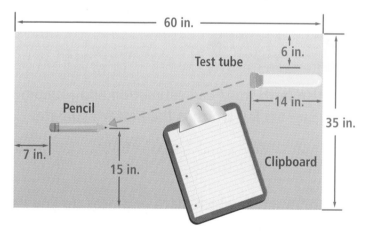

## Share Your Thinking

7. Discuss problem 6 with a classmate. What strategy did you use to solve it? How did this strategy help you?

8. When do you think a scientist might use problem solving strategies? Give an example of a situation and a strategy.

# Chapter 2 Test

## for Pages 44–75

**Test-Taking Tips**
Watch the signs carefully. Should you add or subtract?

## Problem Solving

**Solve. Show your work.** (pages 52, 68, 74)

**1.** To win the championship in the National Basketball Association, a team must defeat four other teams in the playoff series.

| National Basketball Association | | |
|---|---|---|
| Playoff Round | Must Win | Maximum Number of Games in Series |
| First | 3 | 5 |
| Second | 4 | 7 |
| Third | 4 | 7 |
| Final | 4 | 7 |

**a.** To win the championship, how many games must a team win?

**b.** How many playoff games can a team lose and still win the championship?

## Concepts

**Use both front-end estimation and rounding to estimate the answer.** (page 64) **Tell which is the better estimate.**

| **2.** | 78 | **3.** | 645 | **4.** | 175 | **5.** | $31.25 |
|---|---|---|---|---|---|---|---|
| | − 19 | | − 293 | | − 102 | | − 18.95 |

**Subtract. In which place or places do you need to regroup? Show your work.** (pages 66, 70)

| **6.** | 245 | **7.** | 608 | **8.** | 712 | **9.** | 302 |
|---|---|---|---|---|---|---|---|
| | − 137 | | − 424 | | − 556 | | − 245 |

**Write the answer. Use mental math when you can.** (pages 48, 50)

10. 46 + 9        11. 73 − 4        12. 105 + 605        13. 250 + 350

**Estimate. Choose the correct answer.** (pages 56, 58, 66, 70, 72)

14. 537 + 368    a. 895        b. 905        c. 915        d. 925

15. 177 + 95     a. 190        b. 202        c. 252        d. 272

16. 62 − 38      a. 24         b. 34         c. 14         d. 30

17. 256 − 44     a. 202        b. 222        c. 212        d. 210

18. 741 − 346    a. 405        b. 315        c. 375        d. 395

19. 808 + 169    a. 977        b. 967        c. 907        d. 1007

**Add or subtract. Show your work.** (pages 56, 58, 66, 70, 72)

20. $247 + 88   21. 631 − 265   22. 742 − 654   23. $500 − 131   24. 64 27 + 18   25. 132 85 + 116

## Performance Task

(pages 52, 68, 74)

You want to make a wood frame for a painting. It is a square painting that is 10 inches long and 10 inches wide. You want the frame to extend 2 inches from the edge. How much wood will you need?

- How would you show where the frame will go?

- Explain how you decided how much wood you need.

**Keep In Mind . . .**

Your work will be evaluated on the following:

☑ Clear model

☑ Labels with measurements

☑ Accurate math

☑ Reasonable explanation

# Cumulative Review

**Place Value** (Chapter 1)
Write the value of the 2 in 254,904.

**Here's A Way!**

Write the numbers in a place-value chart.

| Thousands | | | Ones | | |
|---|---|---|---|---|---|
| Hundreds | Tens | Ones | Hundreds | Tens | Ones |
| 2 | 5 | 4 | 9 | 0 | 4 |

The value of 2 is 200,000.

Write the digit in the one thousands place. Then write the digit in the tens place.

1. 23,861    2. 980,400    3. 8763

Write the value of the 3.

4. 1,236,572

5. 4,706,030

6. 2,349,617

7. Write a number with 2 in the ones place, 8 in the hundreds place, 4 in the tens place, and 6 in the thousands place.

---

**Using Basic Facts** (Chapter 2)
Find 700 + 400.

**Here's A Way!**

Use basic facts and hundreds.
7 + 4 = 11
7 hundreds + 4 hundreds = 11 hundreds
So, 700 + 400 = 1100.

Find the missing numbers.

8. 5 + 3 = ▥        9. 50 + 30 = ▥

10. 500 + ▥ = 800    11. 17 − 9 = ▥

12. 170 − ▥ = 80     13. 1700 − 900 = ▥

---

**Rounding** (Chapters 1 and 2)
Round 7156 to the nearest thousand.

**Here's A Way!**

Find the thousands place. 7156
Find the digit to its right. 7156
If that digit is 5 or greater, round up. If it is less than 5, round down. **7000**

Round to the nearest thousand.

14. 8752      15. 5372      16. 2500

17. 8997      18. 9495      19. 4731

20. You plan to order a school pin for each student at your school. Would you use a rounded number or an exact number to list the number of students? Explain your answer.

## Comparing and Ordering (Chapter 1)

Put the numbers in order from greatest to least: 5439, 5389, 5539

**Here's A Way!**

Compare numbers in the greatest place, and then in the next greatest place.
**5539, 5439, 5389**

Copy and complete. Use >, <, or = to make the statement true.

**21.** 753 ● 735

**22.** 9533 ● 9533

**23.** 5828 ● 5838

**24.** 6099 ● 7001

**25.** 9111 ● 9138

**26.** 459 ● 459

**27.** What is the largest 4-digit number you can write? What is the smallest 4-digit number you can write?

## Money Sense (Chapter 1)

**Write the amount of money.**

**Here's A Way!**

Organize the bills and coins in groups from greatest to least. Then, count.

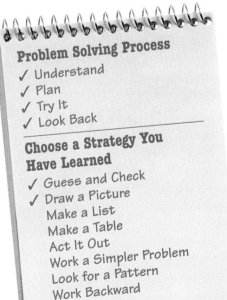

Dimes

Nickels        Pennies

You have $6.46.

Write the amount of money.

**28.** 1 ten-dollar bill, 4 one-dollar bills, 3 quarters, 1 dime, 1 nickel, 3 pennies

**29.** 2 ten-dollar bills, 9 one-dollar bills, 1 quarter, 4 dimes, 2 nickels, 2 pennies

**30.** one twenty-dollar bill, one one-dollar bill, 2 quarters, 2 dimes, 3 nickels, 5 pennies

**What bills and coins do you need to get the amount?**

**31.** $43.67      **32.** $18.32      **33.** $21.55

## Problem Solving

**Problem Solving Process**
- ✓ Understand
- ✓ Plan
- ✓ Try It
- ✓ Look Back

**Choose a Strategy You Have Learned**
- ✓ Guess and Check
- ✓ Draw a Picture
- Make a List
- Make a Table
- Act It Out
- Work a Simpler Problem
- Look for a Pattern
- Work Backward

Use any strategy you have learned to solve the problem. Show your work.

**34.** You want to fill food baskets for 3 senior citizens. You have 4 oranges, 2 apples, 4 pears, and 5 bananas. How will you make each basket have the same number of pieces of fruit?

**35.** If you subtract 10 from the mystery number and then double the result, the answer is 50. What is the mystery number?

INVESTIGATION

# Make it! Mail it!

**Art Connection**  **Your Group's Challenge**

**P**ostage stamps are more than useful—they tell us things too! The stamps on page 81 show famous women throughout history. What theme would you like stamps to show?

Your group will design stamps that will give you the correct amount of postage to send items to different places. Choose a theme, and then design the stamps!

## 1

## Plan It

- Choose a weight from 1 to 10 ounces for your mailing.
- Use the postage chart. Find out how much postage you need to send the same item first-class in the U.S. and then to other countries.

| Weight (ounces) | First-Class U.S. Mail | To Most Other Countries |
|---|---|---|
| 1 | $0.32 | $1.00 |
| 2 | 0.55 | 1.80 |
| 3 | 0.78 | 2.60 |
| 4 | 1.01 | 3.40 |
| 5 | 1.24 | 4.20 |
| 6 | 1.47 | 5.00 |
| 7 | 1.70 | 5.80 |
| 8 | 1.93 | 6.60 |
| 9 | 2.16 | 7.40 |
| 10 | 2.39 | 8.20 |

## 2

## Put It Together

- As a group, choose a theme for the pictures on your stamps. Design stamps in the following amounts:

  1¢, 2¢, 3¢, 4¢, 5¢, 20¢, 23¢, 32¢, 55¢, 78¢, $1, $2, $5

## 3

## Wrap It Up

- Make a chart that shows different groups of stamps that add up to the amount of postage you need. Use at least two different stamps in each group. Remember to make groups for both kinds of mailings.

## 4

## Discuss Your Results

- Have you covered all the points in Keep In Mind?
  - Which stamp value did each group choose the most? What theme did each group use?

**Internet**

> Visit the **Math Center** at **Houghton Mifflin Education Place.**
http://www.eduplace.com

## Math Power

### Use What You Know

- ways to collect data

Number

blue   red

- how to read a bar graph

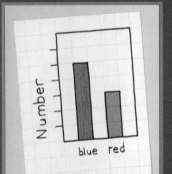

Apples

red   green

There are more red apples than green.

- how to compare data in a graph

# Collecting, Organizing, and Using Data

## Try This!

**W**hich color in a box of cereal do you think you will pick the most?

### What You'll Need

grid paper, crayons or markers, items in different colors such as cubes or cereal, a small bag or box

**①**

Place a handful of cereal in a bag. Write the name of each color of cereal at the bottom of a sheet of grid paper.

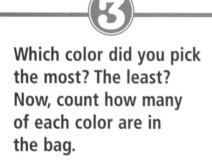

**2**

Pick one piece from the bag. Color a square to show which color you picked. Put the piece back. Repeat step 2 ten times.

**3**

Which color did you pick the most? The least? Now, count how many of each color are in the bag.

How does the total number you counted compare to the result in your graph?

How does a graph give you a picture of data?

**Ready to Go!**

# Collecting and Recording Data

**Getting Started**

**What You'll Need:**
▶ recording sheets

**Vocabulary:**
survey
data
Glossary, p. 516

**Use What You Know**

When you make tally marks, use a slash for every fifth mark.
卌

**W**hen you take a **survey,** you ask questions to collect **data,** or facts. You can use tally marks to record the data as you collect it. Then, you can make a table to show the data you have collected.

# Tally a Table!

**Activity**

- Form groups.
- Each group makes a table like the one below.
- Find out your classmates' favorite school subjects.

**1**

Make a table with your group.

- On your table, write a title and give each column a heading.

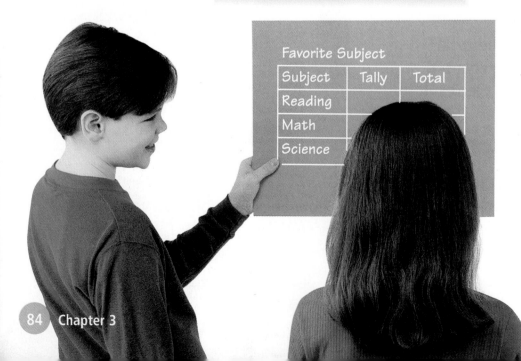

**Favorite Subject**

| Subject | Tally | Total |
|---------|-------|-------|
| Reading |       |       |
| Math    |       |       |
| Science |       |       |

**2**

Take a survey of another group in your class.

- Record the data using tally marks.
- Count the tally marks for each subject. Write the number in the last column.

**3**

Study the data in your table. Compare it to tables other groups have made.

- What two subjects are the favorites?
- How many students chose these subjects?
- Which subject got the least votes?
- How can you tell if the whole class took the survey?

## Show What You Know!

Use the table to help you answer the question.

1. **Critical Thinking** How is this class's table like your group's table? How is it different?

2. How is the data in the table organized?

3. Did Ms. Toro's class take a survey of more students than your group did? How can you tell?

4. What subject got the fewest votes in Ms. Toro's class?

5. **Create Your Own** Think of another survey you could take. Make a table and collect data by taking a survey of your class or another class.

**Ms. Toro's Class**

| Subject | Tally | Total |
|---|---|---|
| Reading | IIII I | 6 |
| Math | IIII III | 8 |
| Science | IIII | 5 |
| Social Studies | IIII II | 7 |

Science MATH

# Organizing Data in a Bar Graph

**S**uppose three classes in your school took a survey to find out about their favorite pets. The table at the right shows the results. Can you think of another way to show the data?

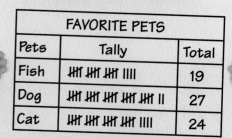

| FAVORITE PETS | | |
|---|---|---|
| Pets | Tally | Total |
| Fish | ℍℍ ℍℍ ℍℍ IIII | 19 |
| Dog | ℍℍ ℍℍ ℍℍ ℍℍ ℍℍ II | 27 |
| Cat | ℍℍ ℍℍ ℍℍ ℍℍ IIII | 24 |

## Here's A Way! Show the data on a bar graph.

**1** Choose the kind of bar graph you will make. Bars can go across or up and down.

**2** Think of a title for the graph. Write it at the top.

**3** Put labels on the graph, for numbers and kind of data.

**4** Decide what numbers to put on the graph. The numbers always start at 0 and are placed the same distance apart on the graph paper.

- The greatest number of votes for one pet is 27. So the numbers on the graph are 0 to 30.
- Count by 5's.

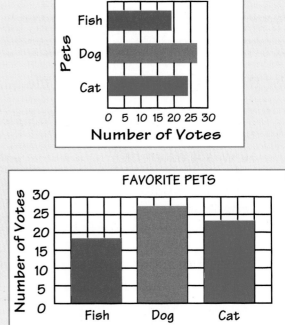

## Talk About It!

- Do the bars in the graphs show the number of pets or the number of votes?
- Why do you think numbers need to be evenly spaced on a bar graph?

## Show What You Know!

**Make a bar graph for the data in the table. Then, answer the question.**

1. Which data from the table did you use in your graph? Which data did you *not* use?

2. By what number did you skip-count to create the number labels? What was the greatest number you used?

3. **Mental Math** How many students voted in the survey? Did more than half of the students choose adventure and sport books? How can you tell?

4. **Critical Thinking** If you wanted to know the results of the survey as quickly as possible, would you use the table or the graph? Why?

### Favorite Types of Books

| Book Type | Tally | Total |
|---|---|---|
| Mystery | ⊥⊥⊥ III | 8 |
| Sport | ⊥⊥⊥ ⊥⊥⊥ IIII | 14 |
| Humor | ⊥⊥⊥ ⊥⊥⊥ I | 11 |
| Adventure | ⊥⊥⊥ ⊥⊥⊥ ⊥⊥⊥ II | 17 |

## Work It Out!

**Use the graph to help you answer the question.**

5. What information can you learn from this graph?

6. Which animal received about twice as many votes as the lion? How can you tell?

7. About how many people voted in this survey?

8. **Create Your Own** Write two questions about the data on the graph. Write the answers on the back of the sheet. Trade questions with a classmate. Check each other's answers.

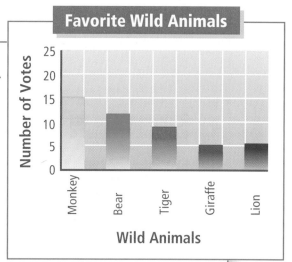

**Favorite Wild Animals**

Number of Votes vs. Wild Animals (Monkey, Bear, Tiger, Giraffe, Lion)

**More Practice Set 3.2, p. 481**

### Math Journal

Look back at the survey you did in Lesson 3.1. How would you show the data in a bar graph?

# LESSON 3

# Problem Solving
## Make a List

Getting Started

**What You'll Need:**
► red, blue, green, and yellow tiles

**Y**ou have 4 tiles—1 red, 1 green, 1 blue, and 1 yellow. How many different ways can you put the tiles in order?

You can count the number of different ways by making a list.

R G B Y

## Here's A Way! Make a List to solve the problem.

### 1 Understand

- How many colors are there?

- Think of one way to put the tiles together. Think of another.

### 2 Plan

- Decide how to organize a list of all the different combinations.

### 3 Try It

- Choose one color. List all the ways that start with that color. Do the same for the other colors.

- Complete the list to solve the problem.

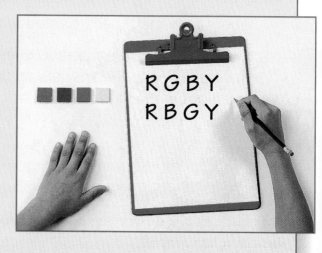

R G B Y
R B G Y

### 4 Look Back

- Can you think of any ways you have not listed?

- There are 24 different ways to put the tiles together.

**Use Make a List to solve the problem.**

1. Suppose you are creating a math test that has 3 different sections. How many ways can you order the sections?

2. **Critical Thinking** What if the test had 6 sections? Would the same strategy help organize it? Why or why not?

| Make a List | | |
|---|---|---|
| 1 | 2 | 3 |
| 1 | 3 | 2 |
| 2 | ☐ | ☐ |
| ☐ | ☐ | ☐ |
| ☐ | ☐ | ☐ |
| ☐ | ☐ | ☐ |

## Work It Out!

**Use Make a List or any other strategy to solve the problem.**

3. You have a kit to make your own T-shirt designs. It has a circle, a square, and a triangle shape. You want to use all 3 shapes in each design. How many ways can you put the shapes in order?

4. You can make different models from an airplane kit. Choose red, blue, or green airplane bodies. Then choose yellow, orange, or purple wings. How many different models can you make?

5. The Treetop Club created a number code for the alphabet. Below is the way they wrote *Treetop Club* in code. Use the code to write the alphabet in numbers.

| 7 | 9 | 22 | 22 | 7 | 12 | 11 | 24 | 15 | 6 | 25 |

6. **Create Your Own** Create a code for the alphabet. Write your name using the code. Have a friend find your code.

7. You have 1 quarter, 1 dime, 1 nickel, and 1 penny. In how many different ways can you put the four coins in order? Which way has the greatest value? Explain.

8. You are taping the 7 songs shown on the graph. Each side of the tape holds up to 30 minutes. In what order can you put the songs on the tape so that no song is split between the two sides?

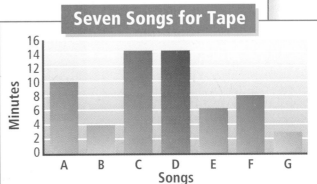

**Seven Songs for Tape**

## Share Your Thinking

9. Which problems did you solve by using Make a List? In which problems did you use a different strategy? Explain.

10. How did you solve problem 8? What other strategy could you use?

# LESSON 4

# Pictographs

**Take a RIDE!**

**Mountain Bike**

## Use What You Know

**Pictographs** use pictures to show data. The pictures stand for numbers.

The **key** in a pictograph tells what each picture or symbol stands for.

**Y**ou are trying to decide what bicycle to buy. To find the kind you want, you look at different types of data.

Suppose you find this chart. How would you make a pictograph to show the number of bicycles sold?

| Bikes sold in August | |
|---|---|
| Racing | 2249 |
| Mountain | 8230 |
| Hybrid | 2528 |
| Youth | 2056 |

## Here's A Way!  Make a pictograph.

**1** Begin by choosing a title and writing the names of each kind of bicycle on your pictograph.

**2** Choose a picture for the key. Use one that can divide in half.

**3** Decide on the number each whole picture will represent. Then, decide how much each half picture will represent.

**Bikes Sold in August**

| Racing | 🚲 🚲 🚲 |
| Mountain | 🚲 🚲 🚲 🚲 🚲 🚲 🚲 🚲 |
| Hybrid | 🚲 🚲 🚲 |
| Youth | 🚲 🚲 |

Key  🚲 = 1000 bikes   🚲 = 500 bikes

## Talk About It!

How does a pictograph help you compare data quickly?

Use the pictograph showing bicycles sold in August to answer the following.

1. Could this graph show 2056 bicycles exactly? Explain your reasoning.

2. Describe how the graph would look if each whole symbol stood for 2000 bicycles instead of 1000.

3. **Critical Thinking** What do you need to know to decide what a whole symbol represents?

## Work It Out!

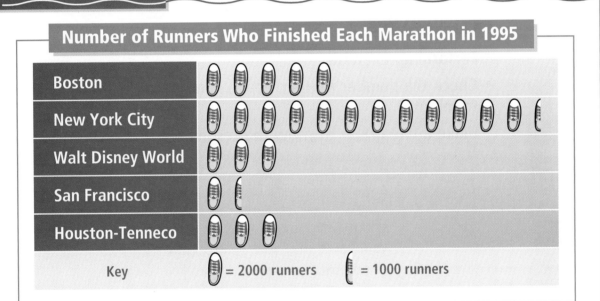

**Number of Runners Who Finished Each Marathon in 1995**

| | |
|---|---|
| Boston | |
| New York City | |
| Walt Disney World | |
| San Francisco | |
| Houston-Tenneco | |

Key  = 2000 runners   = 1000 runners

4. Which marathon had the most finishers?

5. Which marathon had the fewest finishers?

6. About how many runners finished the Boston Marathon?

7. Which marathon had the number of finishers closest to the number in the Walt Disney World Marathon?

8. **Critical Thinking** Suppose the key were changed and the whole symbol stood for 1000 runners instead of 2000. Would there be more or fewer symbols on the pictograph?

9. **Number Sense** Suppose you remake the pictograph without the New York City Marathon. What number would you have the whole symbol stand for? Tell your reasoning.

**More Practice Set 3.4, p. 481**

# Line Graphs

**Getting Started**

**What You'll Need:**
▶ stopwatch, timer, or clock with a second hand
▶ calculator
▶ graph paper

**W**hat happens to your heartbeat when you stop exercising? You can make a line graph to find out. A line graph uses lines and dots to show data that changes over time.

## Shape Up!

**Activity**

- Perform an exercise.
- Check the number of heartbeats, minute to minute.
- Make a line graph to show the results.

**1**

Choose an exercise. You could clap your hands over your head 50 times or do 25 jumping jacks. Before you exercise, take your pulse. Your pulse is the number of times your heart beats a minute.

| Pulse Rate | |
|---|---|
| 15 s | 1 min |
| 31 | 124 |
| 27 | 108 |
| 26 | 104 |
| 25 | 100 |

**2**

To find your pulse, count beats for 15 seconds. Ask someone to look at a stopwatch and tell you when to stop. Use a calculator to add the number 4 times.

**3**

Now that you know how to take your pulse, do the exercise. Then count your pulse once for each minute for the next 5 minutes. Record the data in a table.

| Minutes after Exercising | 1 | 2 | 3 |
|---|---|---|---|
| Heartbeats in a Minute | ? | ? | ? |

**4**

Use the table to make a line graph.

• Choose a title and labels. To label the beats, count by 10's, from 70 through 130. Label the minutes through 6.

• To graph your pulse, draw dots and connect them. First, find the minute at the bottom of the table. Then follow that line up until you arrive at the number of beats. Draw a dot.

• Repeat the steps for each minute. Then connect the dots.

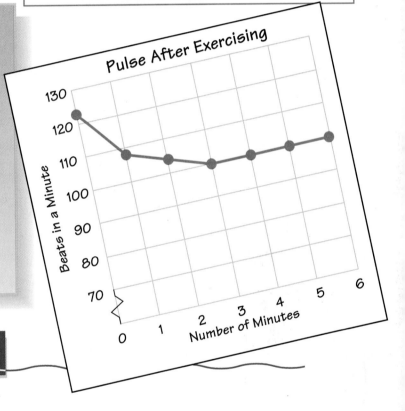

Pulse After Exercising

## Show What You Know!

**Use the graph to answer the question.**

1. What does it mean when the line slopes downward on the graph?

2. Read across the graph to find the number of heartbeats for each minute after exercising. Complete the table.

| Minutes after Exercising | 1 | 2 | 3 | 4 | 5 | 6 |
|---|---|---|---|---|---|---|
| Heartbeats in a Minute | 108 | 104 | ? | ? | ? | ? |

3. **Critical Thinking** Compare the graph above with yours. How are they alike? How are they different?

4. **Write About It** Write your own question about the graph and share it.

**More Practice Set 3.4, p. 481**

# Circle Graphs

**Cooperative Learning**
**Checklist**

☐ Work alone.
☑ Work with a partner.
☐ Work with a group.

**Getting Started**

**What You'll Need:**
▶ clipboard
▶ flat, round object for tracing a circle
▶ scissors
▶ 4 different-colored markers
▶ tape

**Vocabulary:**
**circle graph**
Glossary, p. 516

**A** school newspaper recently reported that students' favorite sports are (1) soccer, (2) swimming, and (3) baseball. Would these results be true for your class?

## Activity

• Ask 16 classmates to pick their favorite sport from the following: soccer, swimming, baseball, and basketball.

• Tally the results. Use the steps to make a circle graph.

**1**

A **circle graph** shows the parts that make up a whole group. Make a circle graph to show the results of your survey.

• Trace a large circle on a piece of paper.
• Cut out the circle.

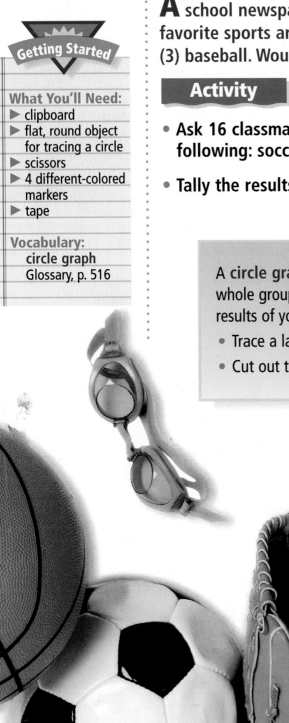

**Favorite Sports**

| Sports | Number of Students |
|------------|--------------------|
| Soccer | 卌 II |
| Swimming | II |
| Baseball | III |
| Basketball | IIII |

**2**

- Fold the circle in half. Then fold it in half again 3 more times.
- Now you have divided the circle into 16 equal parts, one part for each tally mark.

**3**

- Start with the sport that receives the most votes. Color that number of parts in the graph.
- Use different colors for each of the other sports.
- Label the sections.

Basketball
Baseball
Swimming
Soccer

## Show What You Know!

1. In your circle graph, did the results for the most favorite sport match the school newspaper report?

2. **Write About It** Compare the graph above with the one you and your partner made. Write about the different data each shows.

**Use the circle graph above to answer each question.**

3. Is soccer more popular than basketball? How can you tell?

4. Did soccer receive more than or less than half the votes?

5. Put the sports in order from least number of votes to greatest number of votes.

6. **Critical Thinking** With which graph at the right is it easier to compare responses?

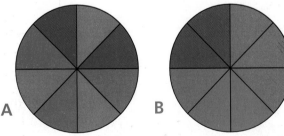

A          B

**Math Journal**

Why would a circle graph be a good choice for showing your day's activities? Would a line graph be a good choice? Why or why not?

More Practice Set 3.7, p. 482

# Using Data

Students are traveling to Dallas to perform in a band contest. The students must decide how to travel. They collected data about the cost and time of travel and put the information in two graphs.

What information do the graphs show?

## Here's A Way! | Read the graphs.

**1** This graph shows roundtrip travel costs from a northeastern city. The longest bar shows that a plane trip to Dallas costs about $275.

**2** The green bar on this graph shows that a train trip to Dallas takes about 8 hours.

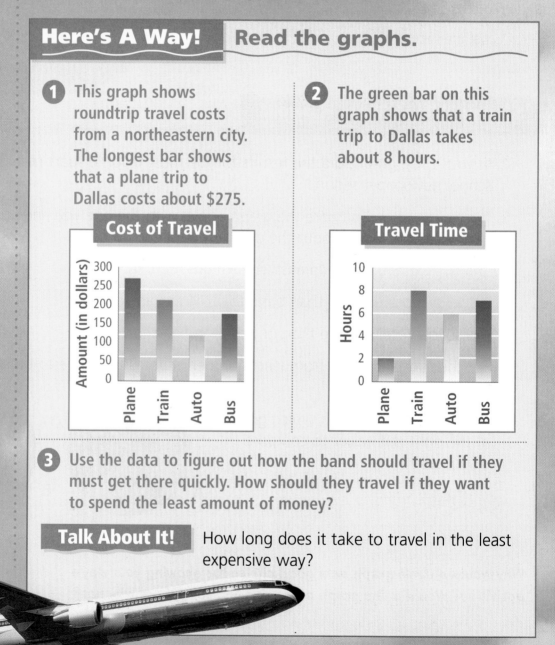

**3** Use the data to figure out how the band should travel if they must get there quickly. How should they travel if they want to spend the least amount of money?

## Talk About It!

How long does it take to travel in the least expensive way?

Compare these line graphs. Answer the questions.

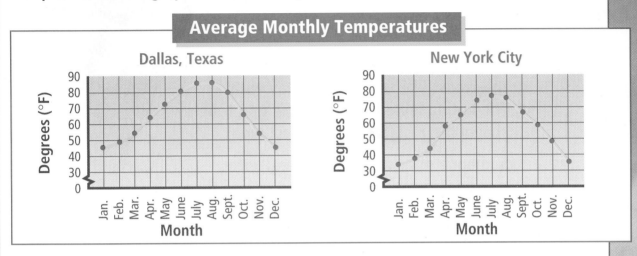

**Average Monthly Temperatures**

1. Are any months colder in New York than the coldest month in Dallas?

2. How are the temperature changes in New York like those in Dallas? How are they different?

3. **Estimation** Can you tell from the graphs what the highest one-day temperature was in these cities? Explain.

4. **Critical Thinking** How would these graphs help someone planning a winter visit to these cities?

## Work It Out!

Compare the circle graphs. Answer the question.

5. Students from different states are coming to the band contest. From which state will the greatest number of students come?

6. Which state will have the fewest students at the contest?

7. Is the fraction of Northeast students from New York greater or less than the fraction of Southwest students from Arizona?

### Problem Solving

8. Suppose there are 100 students from the Southwest. Are there more than 25 students from Texas? How do you decide?

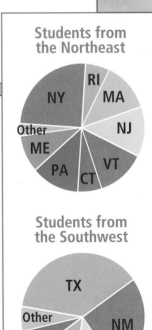

Students from the Northeast

Students from the Southwest

**More Practice Set 3.7, p. 482**

97

# Problem Solving

## Is the Answer Reasonable?

**A**t one museum children voted on what they most like to read and play with. The voting lasted a month. The graph below shows the results from the first week.

Someone asks about how many votes *magazines* received. You answer "less than half." Is this answer reasonable?

### Is the Answer Reasonable?

Ask Yourself:

Did I answer the question?

Did I calculate correctly?

Is the answer labeled with the right units?

Does my answer need to be rounded to a whole number to make sense?

## You Decide

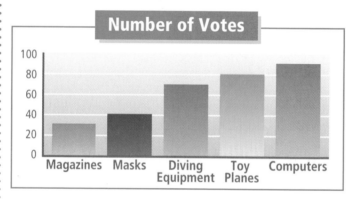

- What information does the graph give you?

- How can the graph help you answer the question?

- Decide whether or not the answer is reasonable. Explain.

## Work It Out!

Is the answer reasonable? Tell why or why not.

1. When the voting is done, more than 500 people will have voted.

2. The total number of votes equals the total number of visitors to the museum.

3. At the end of the voting, computers will still be more popular than masks.

4. Computers are not more popular than all the other toys combined.

## Share Your Thinking

5. Discuss your answers with a friend. What are some differences in the way you made your decisions?

# Midchapter Review

## for Pages 82–98

### Problem Solving

**Solve. Show your work.** (page 88)

1. Your school's bike team wants to choose two colors for its uniforms. The team can choose from turquoise, purple, gold, and black. How many different pairs of colors are possible?

### Concepts

**Use the graph to answer the question.** (page 86)

2. Which animal will have a longer life, a sea lion or a giraffe?

3. About how many more years does an elephant live than a chimpanzee?

4. Which animal lives about double the years a giraffe does?

5. If a kangaroo and a giraffe were both born in the same year, would you expect them to be alive 15 years later? Tell why.

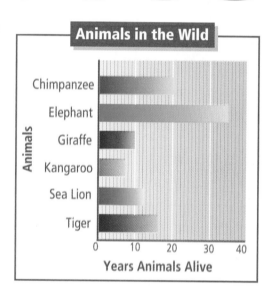

### Skills

**Use the graph to answer each question.** (pages 92, 96)

6. What was the worst year for sales?

7. In what two-year period did sales go up the most?

8. Could a circle graph show this information? Explain.

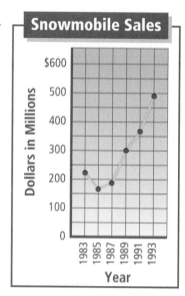

# Math World

## How Many Hugs?

The Malay people of Southeast Asia use the metric system, but they sometimes use their own bodies for units of measure. The Malay word for fingernail is *sebesar kuku* (suh BEH sahr koo koo). So, an object about the size of a fingernail is called *sebesar kuku*. The size of arms forming a hug is known as *sepemeluk* (suh PUH meh luhk). How many hugs of laundry will you have at the end of the week?

## Keeping Track of Data

What does bread have to do with tallies? In France, bakers used tallies to track bread sales. The baker and the customer each had a wooden tally. When a loaf of bread was bought, the baker and the customer each carved a notch in their tallies. When the customer paid his bill, they compared notches. If one of them had made a mistake, the other would know right away. The tallies on the right were used in England.

# Try This!

In some parts of Africa, people use small shells called cowries (COW rees) as money. They also use them to play games. One of these games is called Igba-ita. You and a partner can play a game similar to Igba-ita with pennies instead of cowries.

Materials: 20 pennies per player, paper, pencil

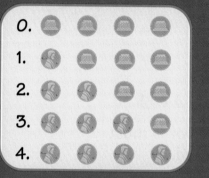

**1** Look at the picture to see all the different ways four pennies tossed at the same time can land.

**2** Make a tally chart. Write the numbers 0 – 4 in a column down the left side of your paper.

**3** Take turns tossing four pennies. After each round, count the number of heads you and your partner tossed. The player with the higher number takes all eight pennies. (Toss again if both players' pennies land the same way.) Mark the tally chart with the combinations you tossed.

**4** Keep playing until one player has all the pennies.

**5** Add the tally marks to show how many times you and your partner tossed each combination.

**Respond**

Work in small groups . . .
to measure objects in your classroom using Malay measurements.

Internet:
**Houghton Mifflin Education Place**
Explore the Math Center at
http://www.eduplace.com

# LESSON 9

# Making Predictions

Cooperative Learning
Checklist
☐ Work alone.
☑ Work with a partner.
☐ Work with a group.

**Y**ou reach into a bag of cubes. Can you predict which color you will pull out? Try this activity to find out.

## Getting Started

**What You'll Need:**
▶ paper bag
▶ 10 cubes (1 yellow, 2 red, 2 green, and 5 blue)
▶ recording sheet

# Take a Guess!

### Activity

• Pull cubes out of a bag.

• Predict which color is most likely to be picked.

## Use What You Know

A **prediction** is what someone thinks may happen. It is sometimes based on what has already happened.

### 1

• Put 1 yellow, 2 red, 2 green, and 5 blue cubes in a bag.
• Without looking, pick a cube.
• Record the color. Put the cube back.

| | Tally | Total |
|---|---|---|
| Blue | | |
| Red | | |
| Green | | |
| Yellow | | |

**2**
- Repeat this process 4 more times.
- Compare your totals. What color did you pick most often?

**3**
- Ask other groups what color they picked the most often. How do their results compare with yours?
- Based on what has already happened, what color is most likely to be picked the next time you try? Discuss your predictions with your partner.

**4**
- Make a prediction about what the results will be for the next 10 picks.
- Pick 10 times and record the results. Compare your predictions to the result.

## Show What You Know!

1. Look at your tallies. What color was picked most often? Why do you think this is so?

2. Before you pick a cube, can you be sure what color you will pick? Why or why not?

3. Suppose you pick cubes 10 more times. Do you think you will get the same results? Why or why not?

4. **Number Sense** Suppose there are 1 yellow, 2 blue, 2 green, and 5 red cubes in a bag.
   a. Which color is most likely to be picked? Why?
   b. Why are blue and green equally likely to be picked?

5. **Critical Thinking** A jar contains 5 blue marbles, 3 red marbles, and 1 yellow marble. If you pick a marble 50 times, is blue most likely to be picked? Is yellow the least likely to be picked? Explain.

# Comparing Probabilities

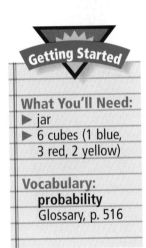
**A**n outcome is any possible result of an experiment. Sometimes you want to know the **probability**, or chance, that an outcome will happen.

In this experiment, which color are you more likely to pick—blue, red, or yellow? Which color are you least likely to pick?

You need to know how many outcomes are possible. Then you can compare the probability of each outcome.

## Here's A Way! — Compare the chances.

Find the probability, or chance, of each outcome.

**1** Of the 6 cubes in the jar, 1 is blue. Therefore, there is 1 chance out of 6 that you will pick blue.

**2** Of the 6 cubes in the jar, 3 are red. There are 3 chances out of 6 that you will pick red.

**3** Of the 6 cubes in the jar, the probability that you will pick yellow is 2 chances out of 6.

Based on the chances, you are most likely to pick red. You are least likely to pick blue.

### Talk About It!

• What could you do to make the probability of picking blue, red, or yellow the same, or equally likely?

• What are your chances of picking a green cube from the same jar? Explain.

## Show What You Know!

**Use spinners A and B to answer each question.**

A

1. What is the chance of spinner A stopping on
   **a.** red?          **b.** green?          **c.** yellow?

2. There are 4 sections in spinner B. Is the chance of spinning green 1 out of 4? Why do you think so?

B

3. On which color is spinner B most likely to stop? On which colors is it least likely to stop? Explain your reasoning.

4. **Mental Math** Which outcome is more likely?
   **a.** spinner A stopping on red     **b.** spinner B stopping on green

5. **Critical Thinking** Is the chance of landing on a certain color different for spinners A and B? Explain your reasoning.

## Work It Out!

**To get each result below, choose spinner C, D, or E. Tell why.**

C

6. You need to spin red to win.   7. If you spin red, you lose.

8. You need to spin blue to win.   9. If you spin green, you lose.

**Use the three spinners at the right and the cubes shown below. Which has a greater chance of happening? Write a, b, or same.**

D

10. **a.** Spinner C stops on red.        **b.** Spinner E stops on red.

11. **a.** A red cube is picked.          **b.** A blue cube is picked.

12. **a.** A green cube is picked.        **b.** A yellow cube is picked.

13. **a.** Spinner C stops on green        **b.** Spinner D stops on green.

E

14. **a.** Spinner D stops on blue.        **b.** Spinner E stops on blue.

15. **a.** Spinner C stops on red.        **b.** A yellow cube is picked.

**More Practice Set 3.10, p. 483**

# Problem Solving
## Using Make a List and Other Strategies

**S**uppose your classroom has a computer. Each of you has your own locked folder. Each folder has a password that only you can use.

**Problem Solving Process**
- ✓ Understand
- ✓ Plan
- ✓ Try It
- ✓ Look Back

**Choose a Strategy You Have Learned**
- ✓ Guess and Check
- ✓ Draw a Picture
- ✓ Make a List
- Make a Table
- Act It Out
- Work a Simpler Problem
- Look for a Pattern
- Work Backward

**Y**ou and your partner are asked to create password codes for the locked folders in the computer. The codes are to be made of 1 letter and 1 number. In each code the letter must be first, then the number. Suppose you can choose from 4 letters and 3 numbers. How many codes can you make?

- What problem needs to be solved?

- How many numbers and letters can you choose from?

- Would you get the same answer with any 4 letters and any 3 digits? Explain.

- Explain a strategy you can use to solve the problem. Then solve it.

**Codes Made**

| Letters RSTU | Numbers 5,6,7 |
|---|---|
|  |  |
|  |  |
|  |  |

## Work It Out!

**Use any strategy to solve the problem. Show your work.**
**For problems 1–4 use the numbers shown.**

1. You buy a combination lock for your bike. You need to create a combination of two numbers. How many combinations can you make that start with 0?

0, 1, 2, 3, 4, 5, 6, 7, 8, 9

2. How many combinations can you make that start with 1?

3. How many combinations can you make that start with 2?

4. How many different combinations can you make in all? Explain how you found your answer.

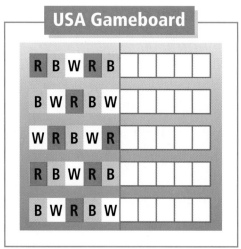

**USA Gameboard**

| R | B | W | R | B |
|---|---|---|---|---|
| B | W | R | B | W |
| W | R | B | W | R |
| R | B | W | R | B |
| B | W | R | B | W |

5. Suppose you play a game about the United States. On the gameboard there are 50 spaces, 1 for each state. The spaces are in a pattern of red, blue, and white. How many spaces are red?

6. The U.S.A. gameboard is 30 inches on each side. If you fold it in half to store it, what size box will you need? Find the length and width.

7. You pick 6 cards from a set numbered 1–9. You use these cards to make a subtraction sentence that has two 3-digit numbers. What is the greatest difference possible?

8. **Create Your Own** Make up a problem about a game with cards that are numbered 0–7. Ask a classmate to solve your problem.

## Share Your Thinking

9. How did you solve problem 7? Discuss your strategy with a friend.

10. Which problems did you use Make a List to solve? How did this strategy keep you from leaving out important information?

# Making Better Predictions

## Getting Started

**What You'll Need:**
- ▶ paper bag
- ▶ 3 cubes (1 red, 1 blue, and 1 green)
- ▶ recording sheet

**T**his activity will show you how you can use what you already know to make better predictions.

# Guess Again!

### Activity

- Find the ways you can put 3 cubes of different colors in order. For example, one order is red-blue-green.

- Make predictions based on the number of possible orders.

**1**

- If a red, a blue, and a green cube were mixed in a bag, in what order could you take them out? List all the possibilities.

- Look at your list. What are the chances that someone picking cubes out of the bag would get a particular order?

- Take turns. Pick 3 cubes, one at a time. Record the order, return the cubes, and pick again.
- Pick the cubes out 30 times. Stop every 5 times.
- After every fifth turn, have someone predict what the next order of colors will be. Would studying the tallies on the sheet help to make a better prediction? Why or why not?
- Compare your tallies with another group's. Are the results similar? Why?

| Making Predictions | | |
|---|---|---|
| Order | Tally | Total |
| Red, Green, Blue | III | |
| Red, Blue, Green | I | |
| Green, Red, Blue | | |
| | | |
| | | |
| | | |
| | | |

## Show What You Know!

1. How often did members of your group get the order they predicted?

2. Look at the results and the predictions your group made. If you were to pick the 3 cubes another 30 times, would you be able to make better predictions? Why or why not?

**Make a chart like this one or use a recording sheet. Record the results of each group. Then answer the questions.**

3. How many times was the order red-green-blue picked?

4. Without looking at the sheet, predict how many times the red cube was picked first.

5. Now combine the results of all the groups. Check your prediction. Write the results for each group on the recording sheet.

| Order | Group | | | | | Total |
|---|---|---|---|---|---|---|
| | A | B | C | D | E | |
| Red-Green-Blue | | | | | | |
| Red-Blue-Green | | | | | | |
| Green-Red-Blue | | | | | | |
| | | | | | | |
| | | | | | | |

## Mixed Review

**Give the value of the underlined digit. Round to the greatest place.**

6. 3̲8          7. 4̲26          8. 5̲95          9. 46̲19          10. 35,6̲82

# Mental Math: Addition and Subtraction

**L**ocal schools are collecting cans to be recycled. How many cans have School C and School D collected so far? How many more cans has School C collected than School D? You can use mental math to find sums and differences.

**Cans Collected**

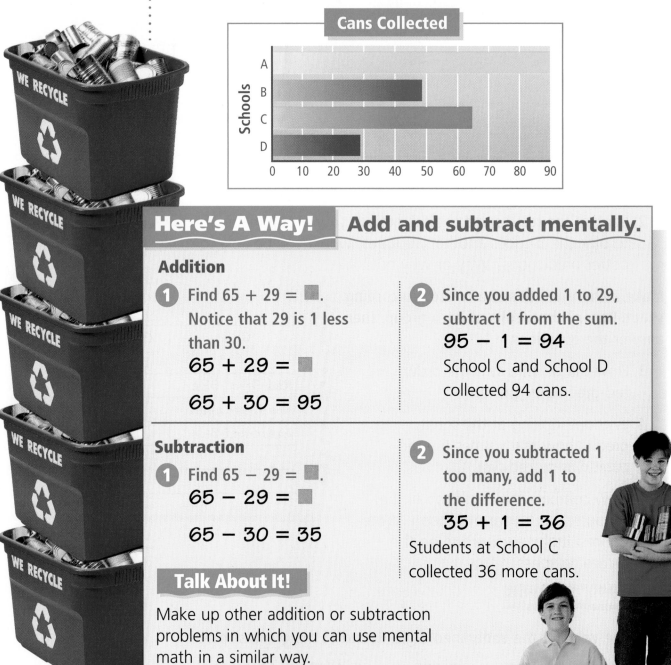

## Here's A Way! Add and subtract mentally.

### Addition

**1** Find $65 + 29 = \blacksquare$.
Notice that 29 is 1 less than 30.
$65 + 29 = \blacksquare$
$65 + 30 = 95$

**2** Since you added 1 to 29, subtract 1 from the sum.
$95 - 1 = 94$
School C and School D collected 94 cans.

### Subtraction

**1** Find $65 - 29 = \blacksquare$.
$65 - 29 = \blacksquare$
$65 - 30 = 35$

**2** Since you subtracted 1 too many, add 1 to the difference.
$35 + 1 = 36$
Students at School C collected 36 more cans.

### Talk About It!

Make up other addition or subtraction problems in which you can use mental math in a similar way.

**Solve. Use mental math.**

| 1. | 2. | 3. | 4. | 5. | 6. |
|---|---|---|---|---|---|
| 44 | 37 | 66 | 62 | 54 | 32 |
| + 29 | − 19 | + 19 | − 19 | − 29 | + 49 |

**Patterns** Find the sum for a. Use it to find the sums for b and c.

7. a. 127 + 500     b. 127 + 499     c. 127 + 498

8. a. 324 + 200     b. 324 + 199     c. 324 + 198

9. a. 248 + 200     b. 248 + 199     c. 248 + 198

10. **Critical Thinking** How did the sum you found in part a help you find the sums in parts b and c? Explain.

## Work It Out!

**Solve. Use mental math when you can.**

11. 75 + 29 = ■     12. 600 + 650 = ■     13. 432 + 199 = ■

14. 37 + 56 = ■     15. 75 − 49 = ■     16. 125 + 372 = ■

17. 55 + 15 = ■     18. 325 + 298 = ■     19. 100 + 90 = ■

20. 390 + 78 = ■     21. 325 + 25 = ■     22. 756 + 444 = ■

23. **Create Your Own** Write your own set of exercises that follow a pattern to help you solve them using mental math.

### Problem Solving    Using Data

24. How many pounds of newspaper did both groups recycle on Tuesday?

25. **Algebraic Thinking** Without adding, how can you tell which group recycled the most newspaper?

**Pounds of Paper Recycled**

| Day | Group A | Group B |
|---|---|---|
| Monday | 30 | 40 |
| Tuesday | 10 | 80 |
| Wednesday | 20 | 40 |

**More Practice Set 3.13, p. 483**

# Chapter 3 Test

## for Pages 82–111

**Test-Taking Tips**
If you are having trouble with an exercise, go on to the next one.

## Problem Solving

**Solve. Show your work.** (pages 88, 106)

1. You and 2 friends go to the movies. You sit together in a row of 3 seats. If you and your best friend sit next to each other, how many ways can your group arrange itself in the 3 seats?

2. You have two 5-pound weights and three 2-pound weights. You must balance weights evenly on each end of a bar. List the different combinations of weights you can use.

## Concepts

**Use the graph to answer the questions.** (pages 94, 96, 98, 102)

3. If 80 students took part in the survey, how many chose bicycling?
   a. 20          b. 40
   c. 50          d. 10

4. Which sport was chosen by half as many students as those who chose bicycling?
   a. soccer      b. bicycling
   c. volleyball  d. softball

5. How many more students chose soccer than softball?
   a. 20          b. 40
   c. 30          d. 10

6. Which pair of sports was chosen by the same number of students?
   a. bicycling and soccer
   b. soccer and softball
   c. volleyball and softball
   d. bicycling and volleyball

**Favorite Sports to Play**

Total Students = 80

7. Write at least two true sentences about the data in the circle graph.

Use the spinners. Tell which is more likely to happen. Write *a*, *b*, or *same.* (pages 102, 104)

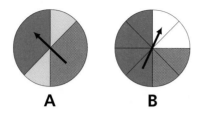

**A**　　　**B**

8. a. Spinner A stops on blue.
   b. Spinner B stops on green.

9. a. Spinner A stops on yellow.
   b. Spinner B stops on white.

10. What are the chances that spinner B will stop on blue?

**Write the answer. Show how you use mental math.** (page 110)

| | |
|---|---|
| 11. 18 + 37 | 12. 24 + 59 |
| 13. 28 + 69 | 14. 33 + 29 |
| 15. 85 − 66 | 16. 75 − 39 |
| 17. 47 − 29 | 18. 92 − 67 |

## Performance Task

(pages 88, 96, 106)

You are making breakfast for the family. You ask if each person would like toast, cereal, or an egg to eat. You then ask who would like apple, orange, cranberry, or grape juice to drink. If the choice is one food item and one drink, how many different breakfast combinations does the family have to choose from?

- How would you organize a list of combinations?

- Explain how you found the total number of possible combinations.

**Keep In Mind . . .**

Your work will be evaluated on the following:
- ☑ An organized list
- ☑ Clearly written details
- ☑ Correct combinations
- ☑ Reasonable explanation

# Cumulative Review

**Mental Math** (Chapter 1)
Find 45 + 55.

Break apart the numbers. Use the fact that 5 + 5 = 10.
45 = 40 + 5
55 = 50 + 5
Add the tens. 40 + 50 = 90
Add the ones. 5 + 5 = 10
Find the total. 90 + 10 = 100
So, 45 + 55 = 100.

Use mental math to find the sum.

1. 25 + 85
2. 450 + 350
3. 1050 + 4050
4. 235 + 745
5. 15 + 45 + 35
6. 2500 + 6500

Find the sum. Think about changing the order of the numbers you are adding. Explain how you got your answer.

7. 15 + 47 + 25
8. 3500 + 500 + 80
9. 550 + 200 + 350

---

**Addition** (Chapter 2)
Find 135 + 256.

Add the ones. Regroup.
Add the tens and then add the hundreds.

$$\begin{array}{r} {\overset{1}{\phantom{0}}135} \\ +\ 256 \\ \hline 391 \end{array}$$

Write the sum.

10. $\begin{array}{r} 15 \\ +\ 29 \\ \hline \end{array}$
11. $\begin{array}{r} 241 \\ +\ 613 \\ \hline \end{array}$
12. $\begin{array}{r} 1865 \\ +\ 2331 \\ \hline \end{array}$

13. 82 + 54 + 36
14. 413 + 350 + 110
15. $1.50 + $3.25 + $4.10
16. Find each pair of numbers with a sum of 1000: 350  550  150  700  195  850  300  450  805  650

---

**Subtraction** (Chapter 2)
Find 81 − 22.

You cannot subtract the ones. Regroup.
Subtract the ones, then the tens.

$$\begin{array}{r} {\overset{7\ 11}{8\ 1}} \\ -\ 2\ 2 \\ \hline 59 \end{array}$$

Find the difference.

17. $\begin{array}{r} 70 \\ -\ 43 \\ \hline \end{array}$
18. $\begin{array}{r} 808 \\ -\ 652 \\ \hline \end{array}$
19. $\begin{array}{r} 7321 \\ -\ 5243 \\ \hline \end{array}$

20. 2000 − 898
21. $20.05 − $15.27
22. 4 quarters − 4 dimes
23. Explain how you regrouped in exercise 20.

## Properties and Rules (Chapter 2)

Complete the number sentence.

1536 + 2983 = 2983 + ■

### Here's A Way!

The order property in addition states that when the order of the addends is changed, the sum stays the same.

1536 + 2983 = 2983 + 1536

Find the missing number to complete the number sentence.

24. 758 + 0 = ■       25. 8458 − 8458 = ■

26. 676 + ■ + 58 = 140 + 58 + 676

27. (64 + 55) + 32 = ■ + (64 + 55)

28. 56 − ■ = 56

29. 450 − 0 = ■

30. $1.76 + $3.20 = $3.20 + ■

31. 14 + (22 + 7) = (14 + ■) + 7

## Estimating Sums (Chapter 2)

About how much is
343 + 462 + 207?

### Here's A Way!

Make a front-end estimate.
Look for groups of about 100 in the other digits.

300 + 400 + 200 = 900

Adjusted estimate:

900 + 100 = 1000

Estimate the sum.

32. 576 + 330       33. 4510 + 3510

34. 2341 + 4512 + 3250

35. How would you find a front-end estimate for 234 + 47?

36. What is a front-end estimate for 1045 + 756 + 24?

## Problem Solving

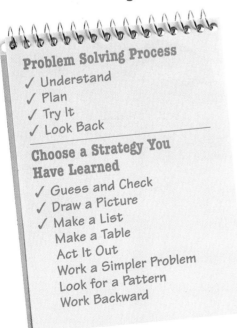

Problem Solving Process

✓ Understand
✓ Plan
✓ Try It
✓ Look Back

Choose a Strategy You Have Learned

✓ Guess and Check
✓ Draw a Picture
✓ Make a List
  Make a Table
  Act It Out
  Work a Simpler Problem
  Look for a Pattern
  Work Backward

Choose any of the strategies you know to solve the problem. Show your work.

37. Suppose your school playground is shaped like a rectangle. It measures 40 yards long and 30 yards wide. Your principal plans to build a fence around the playground. How many yards of fence should she buy?

38. Suppose each lunchroom table is 12 feet long. You plan to place 3 of them end-to-end along a 40-foot wall. How much wall space will be left over?

## CHAPTER · 3 ·

### INVESTIGATION

# Grow Your Vegetables

**Science Connection** | **With Your Group**

### Keep In Mind . . .

Your work will be evaluated on the following:

☑ How well your plan uses the data you were given

☑ Why you decided to choose certain vegetables

☑ Whether your plan makes sense and is neatly done

☑ How well your group works together to complete the plan

**G**rowing your own vegetables can be fun—and you can eat the results! But a vegetable garden needs planning. You can use the planting guides to help you.

Your group will decide which vegetables to plant. Try to get two harvests from the same space. Then, draw your garden on squared paper.

## 1 Plan It

- Find your climate zone on the map.
- Choose vegetables you like. The chart shows sample dates for 3 zones. Select one of these to use, or do research in your library to find the dates for your own zone.

## 2 Put It Together

- Plan for 5 to 7 rows of plants in a space 10 feet wide and 10 feet long.
- Draw your garden design on squared paper.

CLIMATE ZONES

### Planting Dates

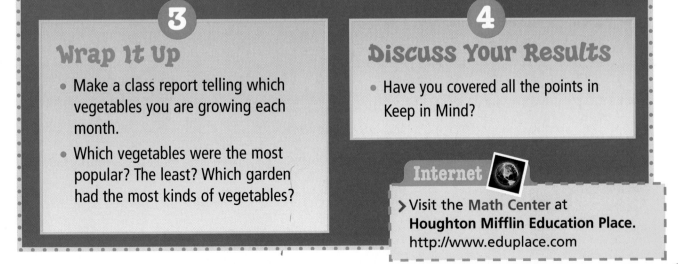

| Vegetable | Zone 4 | Zone 5 | Zone 6 |
|---|---|---|---|
| Beans | March 15 – Aug. 15 | March 1 – May 1<br>July 1 – Sept. 1 | Feb. 1 – April 1<br>Sept. 1 – Nov. 1 |
| Chinese Cabbage | Aug. 1 – Sept. 16 | Sept. 15 – Oct. 15 | Sept. 1 – Dec. 1 |
| Lettuce | Feb. 1 – April 1<br>Aug. 15 – Oct. 1 | Jan. 1 – March 15<br>Sept. 1 – Nov. 1 | Jan. 1 – Feb. 1<br>Sept. 15 – Dec. 31 |
| Pumpkins | June 10 – July 10 | July 1 – Aug. 1 | Aug. 1 – Sept. 1 |
| Sweet Potatoes | April 10 – June 15 | March 20 – July 1 | Feb. 15 – July 1 |
| Tomatoes | April 1 – July 1 | March 1 – Aug. 1 | Feb. 1 – April 1 |

## 3 Wrap It Up

- Make a class report telling which vegetables you are growing each month.
- Which vegetables were the most popular? The least? Which garden had the most kinds of vegetables?

## 4 Discuss Your Results

- Have you covered all the points in Keep in Mind?

### Internet

> Visit the **Math Center** at **Houghton Mifflin Education Place.** http://www.eduplace.com

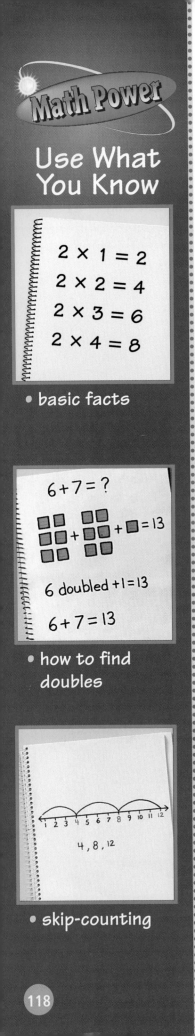

## Math Power

### Use What You Know

$2 \times 1 = 2$
$2 \times 2 = 4$
$2 \times 3 = 6$
$2 \times 4 = 8$

• basic facts

$6 + 7 = ?$

$+$ $+$ $= 13$

6 doubled +1 = 13

$6 + 7 = 13$

• how to find doubles

4, 8, 12

• skip-counting

# CHAPTER 4

# Multiplication and Division Facts

## Try This!

**S**tacking cubes is one way to see multiplication facts. Use what you know about doubles and skip-counting to make and describe stacks of cubes.

### What You'll Need

connecting cubes or any other counters

**1**

Use cubes to build two stacks of three cubes each. Think about which multiplication fact the stacks show. Write this fact down.

$2 \times 3 = 6$

**2**

Build two more stacks of three cubes each. Place them next to the ones you already built. Now, write down the multiplication fact that the four stacks show.

**3**

Build two more stacks of three cubes each. Place them next to the ones already built. Write down the multiplication fact that the six stacks show.

How are the three facts you wrote down related?

$2 \times 3 = 6$

Talk about different ways to multiply. How do skip-counting, doubling, and stacking cubes help you with multiplication facts?

**Ready to Go!**

# Understanding Multiplication

**Getting Started**

**What You'll Need:**
▶ tiles
▶ number cube
▶ grid paper
▶ scissors
▶ markers

**Vocabulary:**
array
Glossary, p. 516

**W**hen you arrange a group of objects in equal rows and equal columns, you make an **array.** Making arrays can help you understand multiplication. In this activity you will build arrays with tiles.

# Square Off!

**Activity**

• Each group makes a chart like the one on page 121.

• Try at least six rounds of Square Off!

**1**
• Roll the number cube. Write the number on your chart under Number of Rows.
• Roll the number cube again. Write that number on your chart under Number in Each Row.

**2**
Use tiles to build an array. Use the numbers you recorded to decide on the number of tiles and the number of rows for each array.

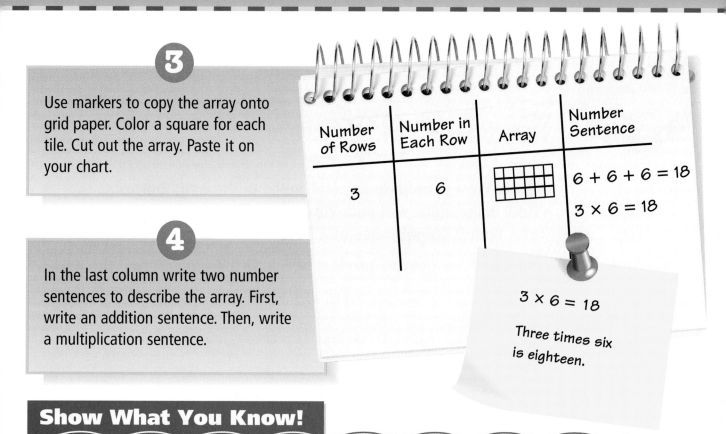

**3**

Use markers to copy the array onto grid paper. Color a square for each tile. Cut out the array. Paste it on your chart.

| Number of Rows | Number in Each Row | Array | Number Sentence |
|---|---|---|---|
| 3 | 6 | | $6 + 6 + 6 = 18$ $3 \times 6 = 18$ |

$3 \times 6 = 18$

Three times six is eighteen.

**4**

In the last column write two number sentences to describe the array. First, write an addition sentence. Then, write a multiplication sentence.

## Show What You Know!

Write an addition sentence and a multiplication sentence for each array.

1. ◆◆◆
   ◆◆◆

2. ●●●●
   ●●●●
   ●●●●

3. ■■■■■■
   ■■■■■■
   ■■■■■■

4. ★★★★★★★★★
   ★★★★★★★★★
   ★★★★★★★★★

5. **Critical Thinking** Explain why you can use repeated addition or multiplication to show 4 groups of 3.

6. **Number Sense** Describe how you can use skip-counting to find a product.

Draw an array. Then, write an addition sentence and a multiplication sentence for each one.

7. four rows of three      8. three rows of four      9. four rows of five

10. two rows of three      11. three rows of two      12. five rows of four

13. **Number Sense** Describe how the arrays and number sentences in exercises 10 and 11 are related.

14. **Critical Thinking** Is it possible to write a multiplication sentence for the group at the right? Why or why not?

●●●
●●●●●●
●●●●

**More Practice Set 4.1, p. 484**

# LESSON 2

# Multiplication Patterns with 5 and 10

**Y**our class is helping to plant bulbs in the neighborhood. How many bulbs will your class plant if it has 5 packages of 4 bulbs? 10 packages of 4 bulbs?

How can you use the product of 5 × 4 to help you find the product of 10 × 4?

---

**Here's A Way!** **Use multiplication patterns.**

**①** This table shows products of 5 and 10.

| X | 1 | 2 | 3 | 4 | 5 |
|---|---|---|---|---|---|
| 5 | 5 | 10 | 15 | 20 | 25 |
| 10 | 10 | 20 | 30 | 40 | 50 |

**Now use the table to help you multiply.**

**②** Multiply 4 by 5.

$$\begin{array}{r} 4 \\ \times\ 5 \\ \hline 20 \end{array}$$

In 5 packages of 4 bulbs, there are 20 bulbs.

**③** Multiply 4 by 10.

$$\begin{array}{r} 4 \\ \times\ 10 \\ \hline 40 \end{array}$$

In 10 packages of 4 bulbs, there are 40 bulbs.

**Talk About It!**

- How can you use the product of 5 × 4 to help you find the product of 10 × 4?

- Look at the products in the table. What patterns do you see when you multiply with 5? with 10?

Bulbs
5 Packages for $4.00
10 Packages for $7.00

1. **Critical Thinking** Will the patterns continue in the 5's row and 10's row? Explain. Copy and extend the table through $5 \times 9$ and $10 \times 9$.

**Write the product.**

2. $10 \times 1$   3. $5 \times 5$   4. $10 \times 8$   5. $5 \times 6$   6. $5 \times 10$

## Work It Out!

**Write the product.**

7. $\begin{array}{r} 7 \\ \times 5 \\ \hline \end{array}$   8. $\begin{array}{r} 10 \\ \times 4 \\ \hline \end{array}$   9. $\begin{array}{r} 5 \\ \times 3 \\ \hline \end{array}$   10. $\begin{array}{r} 10 \\ \times 2 \\ \hline \end{array}$   11. $\begin{array}{r} 10 \\ \times 9 \\ \hline \end{array}$   12. $\begin{array}{r} 8 \\ \times 5 \\ \hline \end{array}$

This multiplication table shows the products of nickels and dimes.

|        | 0      | 1      | 2      | 3      | 4      | 5      |
|--------|--------|--------|--------|--------|--------|--------|
| $ .05  | $ .00  | $ .05  | $ .10  | $ .15  | $ .20  | $ .25  |
| $ .10  | $ .00  | $ .10  | $ .20  | $ .30  | $ .40  | $ .50  |

If the table continued past 10, would the amounts appear in both rows? Write *yes* or *no* for each amount. Explain your answer.

13. $1.25          14. $1.45          15. $1.75          16. $2.70

### Problem Solving  Using Data

17. If Class B plants their bulbs in rows of 8, how many rows can they plant?

18. How many more bulbs did Class C plant than Class A? What is the total number of bulbs the classes planted?

19. **Create Your Own** Use the pictograph to write a word problem. Give it to a friend to solve.

**Bulbs Planted in Class**

Class A
Class B
Class C
Class D
Key   = 10 bulbs    = 5 bulbs

**More Practice Set 4.2, p. 484**

**Math Journal**

Explain about the digit in the ones place of the product when you multiply by 10 and when you multiply by 5.

# LESSON 3

# Understanding Division

Cooperative Learning
**Checklist**
☑ Work alone.
☑ Work with a partner.
☑ Work with a group.

In how many ways can the number 20 be divided equally? Try this activity and find out.

## Getting Started

**What You'll Need:**
▶ 20 tiles
▶ cube labeled 1, 2, 4, 5, 10, and 20
▶ flip card

**Vocabulary:**
dividend
divisor
quotient
Glossary, p. 516

# Divide It!

**Activity**

• Use models to find all the ways to divide 20 evenly.

• Record results on a chart like the one on page 125.

**1**
• Create a flip card.
• Write Number of Groups on one side.
• Write Number in Each Group on the other side.
• Flip the card.

*Number in each group*

**2**
• Roll the number cube.
• Write the number in the column stated on the flip card.
• Use the number you roll as the divisor in step 3.

**3**

Divide your group of 20 tiles by the divisor you rolled in step 2.

**4**

Record your results as shown on the chart. Continue until you have shown all the ways 20 can be divided equally.

| Start with 20 | Number of Groups | Number in Each Group | Picture | Picture in Words and in Numbers |
|---|---|---|---|---|
| 20 | 2 | 10 |  | $20 \div 2 = 10$<br><br>20 divided into 2 groups equals 10 in a group |

## Show What You Know!

1. Look at the picture of the stars. Write a division sentence to describe it.

★★★　★★★　★★★
★★★　★★★　★★★
★★★　★★★　★★★

**Create Your Own** Draw a picture to show the sentence. Then write a division sentence to describe the picture.

2. There are 12 muffins arranged in packages of 4.

3. There are 25 hearts arranged in groups of 5.

4. Copy the chart and add four more rows. Put the numbers 4, 6, 8, and 12 in the Number of Groups column. Complete the chart.

| Start with 24 Objects | Number of Groups | Number in Each Group | Division Number Sentence |
|---|---|---|---|
| 24 | 2 | 12 | $24 \div 2 = 12$ |
| 24 | 3 | 8 | $24 \div 3 = 8$ |

5. **Patterns** What happens to the number in each group as the number of groups increases? Describe other patterns you see.

**Calculator** Count the number of times you can subtract the divisor from the dividend until you reach 0.

6. $12 \div 4$　　7. $15 \div 5$　　8. $18 \div 6$　　9. $21 \div 7$　　10. $24 \div 8$　　11. $27 \div 9$

**More Practice Set 4.3, p. 484**

# Dividing by 5 and 10

**S**uppose you want to buy 40 baseball cards. How many packages would you need to buy if each package has 5 cards? 10 cards?

You can divide to find out.

---

## Here's A Way! Divide 40 by 5 and by 10.

**Divide 40 by 5.**

Use multiplication facts to help you divide.

$$40 \div 5 = n$$

> You can use a letter, like *n*, to stand for a mystery number.

$$5 \times n = 40$$
$$5 \times 8 = 40$$
So, $40 \div 5 = 8$.

> Think: 5 times what number is 40?

If each package has 5 cards, you need to buy 8 packages.

---

**Divide 40 by 10.**

Use the quotient of $40 \div 5$ to help you divide.

$$40 \div 5 = 8$$

$$40 \div 10 = n$$
So, $40 \div 10 = 4$.

> If there are twice as many cards in each, you only need 4 packages.

If each package has 10 cards, you need to buy 4 packages.

### Talk About It!

- Would you buy packages of 5 or packages of 10? Explain your answer.
- How do multiplication facts help you divide?

1. **Critical Thinking** Why is the quotient of 30 ÷ 5 double the quotient of 30 ÷ 10? Use words, models, or pictures to explain.

**Use a pattern or a multiplication fact to find the quotient.**

2. a. 20 ÷ 5   3. a. 40 ÷ 5   4. a. 70 ÷ 5   5. a. 30 ÷ 5   6. a. 80 ÷ 5

   b. $10\overline{)20}$   b. $10\overline{)40}$   b. $10\overline{)70}$   b. $10\overline{)30}$   b. $10\overline{)80}$

## Work It Out!

**Use a pattern or a multiplication fact to find the quotient.**

7. 90 ÷ 5      8. 10 ÷ 10      9. 80 ÷ 5      10. 50 ÷ 10      11. 60 ÷ 5

12. $10\overline{)90}$      13. $5\overline{)10}$      14. $10\overline{)80}$      15. $5\overline{)50}$      16. $10\overline{)60}$

|       | 0 | 10 | 20 | 30 | 40 | 50 | 60 | 70 | 80 | 90 | 100 |
|-------|---|----|----|----|----|----|----|----|----|----|-----|
| ÷5    | 0 | 2  | 4  | 6  | 8  | 10 | 12 | 14 | 16 | 18 | 20  |
| ÷10   | 0 | 1  | 2  | 3  | 4  | 5  | 6  | 7  | 8  | 9  | 10  |

17. **Write About It** Describe patterns you see in the table above.

18. If 90 baseball cards were packaged in 5-packs, how many packs would be filled? Use the table above.

19. **Critical Thinking** The quotient is 8 when you divide the mystery number by 10. What is the quotient when you divide the mystery number by 5? Explain your answer.

### Problem Solving

20. What combination of 5-packs and 10-packs could Sport Shots have sold? List all possibilities.

21. How could you change the key so that the graph would have only whole card symbols? Explain your reasoning.

**Cards Sold at Baseball Expo**

| Green's Sports | |
| Sport Shots | |
| Collectibles | |
| Sports Outlet | |

Key  ▯ = 30 cards  ▯ = 15 cards

**More Practice Set 4.4, p. 485**

# Properties and Rules

Multiplication and division have special properties or rules. You can use these rules to help you find products and quotients.

## Getting Started

**What You'll Need:**
► 3 cubes (with numbers 1–6)
► calculator

## Here's A Way! Use properties and rules.

### Multiplication Properties

**Order Property:** If you change the order of the factors, the product stays the same.

Example: $4 \times 5 = 5 \times 4$

**Property of Zero:** If you multiply any factor and zero, the product is zero.

Example: $3 \times 0 = 0$

**Property of One:** If you multiply any factor and 1, the product is that factor.

Example: $7 \times 1 = 7$

**Grouping Property:** If you change the grouping of the factors, the product remains the same.

Example:

$(1 \times 5) \times 2 = 1 \times (5 \times 2)$
$10 = 10$

### Division Rules

If you divide a number other than zero by itself, the quotient is always 1.

Example: $8 \div 8 = 1$

If you divide zero by any other number, the quotient is always 0.

Example: $0 \div 6 = 0$

If you divide any number by 1, the quotient is always that number.

Example: $2 \div 1 = 2$

A number cannot be divided by zero.

Example: $4 \div 0$ is not possible.

### Talk About It!

How can the grouping property make it easier to multiply?

## Show What You Know!

Two students used number cubes to create examples of multiplication properties. They recorded their examples on charts.

1. List the multiplication properties Student A used.

2. List the multiplication properties Student B used.

3. **Critical Thinking** Use the numbers 2, 4, and 1. Write as many examples as you can to show multiplication properties and division rules. Trade papers with your partner. Identify the properties and rules. Then use your calculator to solve them.

| Numbers Rolled | Example | Property |
|---|---|---|
| 1, 4, 2 | $1 \times 42 = 42$ | |
| 2, 3, 5 | $23 \times 5 = 5 \times 23$ | |

**Student A**

| Numbers Rolled | Example | Property |
|---|---|---|
| 3, 4, 5 | $34 \times 5 = 5 \times 34$ | |
| 2, 6, 4 | $(2 \times 6) \times 4 = 2 \times (6 \times 4)$ | |

**Student B**

Parentheses tell what part of a problem to solve first.

$$(3 \times 2) \times 4 = n$$
$$6 \times 4 = 24$$

## Work It Out!

**Algebraic Reasoning** Copy and solve for *n*.

4. $42 \times 36 = n \times 42$

5. $(4 \times 17) \times 3 = 4 \times (n \times 3)$

6. $110 \times 6 = n \times 110$

7. $n \div 1 = 17$

8. $n \div 500 = 0$

9. $27 \div n = 1$

Copy and complete the number sentence.

10. $4 \times (2 \times 2)$

11. $0 \times 94$

12. $217 \div 217$

13. $1 \times 51$

14. $42 \div 1$

15. $8 \times (0 \times 9)$

16. $35 \div 0$

17. $(7 \times 7) \times 1$

18. $(2 \times 3) \times 2$

19. $5 \times (6 \times 1)$

20. $0 \div 234$

21. $345 \div 1$

22. Show with objects why a number cannot be divided by zero. (For example, $6 \div 0$ is not possible.) Then divide the same number by zero using your calculator. Explain what happens.

23. **Problem Solving** Use any of the numbers in the box to show 3 multiplication properties and 3 division rules. You can use any number more than once. Label each property or rule.

| 5 | 2 | 7 | 0 | 8 | 35 | 10 | 1 |
|---|---|---|---|---|---|---|---|
| | 100 | 50 | | 428 | 80 | | |
| | 48,957 | 3126 | | 654,281 | | | |

**More Practice Set 4.5, p. 484**

# Problem Solving
## Make a Table

**Y**ou want to make 128 price tags for a class sale. You have a long, narrow sheet of paper to fold and cut into tags.

How many times must you fold the paper in half so the fold lines form at least 128 sections?

Some problems can be solved by using Make a Table.

## Here's A Way! Use Make a Table.

### ① Understand

- How many sections do you get by folding the sheet in half one time? Two times?

### ② Plan

- Make a table to keep track of your results.

- Record each fold and the number of sections you have made.

| Folds | Sections |
|-------|----------|
| 1 | 2 |
| 2 | 4 |
| 3 | 8 |
| 4 | 16 |

### ③ Try It

- Look at the number of sections you recorded for each fold. Do you see a pattern?

- Extend the table to solve the problem.

### ④ Look Back

- You will have to fold the paper in half 7 times.

- How did making a table help you solve the problem?

Use Make a Table to solve the problem.

1. You want to buy a computer game. It costs $78. You have $40. Suppose you save $5 a week. How many weeks will it take you to save enough money to buy the game?

2. **Critical Thinking** How is the table you used for problem 1 different from the one you used to solve the problem on page 130? How is it similar?

| Weeks | Now | 1 | 2 | 3 | 4 | 5 |
|-------|-----|-----|-----|-----|-----|-----|
| Money | $40 | $45 | $50 | ? | ? | ? |

## Work It Out!

Use Make a Table or any strategy to solve the problem.

3. You have a baseball card collection. You want to arrange the cards in an album. Each page of the album holds 6 cards. Suppose you have 78 cards. How many pages will you use?

4. You have 3 T-shirts—a white, a green, and a blue T-shirt. You also have a pair of white shorts and a pair of tan shorts. How many different outfits can you make?

5. You buy a bottle of 100 vitamins. You take 1 vitamin a day. How many complete weeks will this bottle last before you have to buy another?

6. You are decorating T-shirts to sell at the arts fair. You want to decorate 12 T-shirts. You can finish 3 T-shirts in an hour. If you begin at 9:00 A.M., at what time will you be finished?

### Share Your Thinking

7. Which problems did you solve by using Make a Table? How are these problems the same?

8. Choose a problem you solved by using Make a Table. How did you complete the table?

# Problem Solving
## Choose a Computation Method

**S**uppose your school holds a book fair. You want to buy 1 history book for yourself and 1 for a friend. How much money will you spend?

Choose a Computation Method

Ask Yourself:

Do I need an exact answer or an estimate?

Should I use a model, paper and pencil, mental math, or a calculator?

What operation should I use?

## You Decide

- Could you use mental math to find out? Explain.
- Could you use paper and pencil to find out? Explain.
- Describe other methods you might use.

| Type of Book | Cost |
|---|---|
| Poetry Books | $1.50 |
| Novels | $2.00 |
| History Books | $1.25 |
| Biographies | $ .50 |

## Work It Out!

Use the prices shown. Decide whether to use mental math or paper and pencil. Solve and explain.

1. You buy 1 poetry book for yourself and 3 other poetry books for friends. How much do you spend?

2. You buy a novel, a poetry book, and a biography. How much do you spend on these three books?

3. You spend $4.25 on books for yourself. Then you buy the same books for two friends. How much change do you receive from $20?

4. **Create Your Own** Use the book prices shown above. Write a problem for a friend to solve. Which method did your friend use to solve the problem?

## Share Your Thinking

5. How do you decide when to use paper and pencil?

# Midchapter Review

## for Pages 118–132

for Pages 118–132

## Problem Solving

**Solve. Show your work.** (page 130)

1. Suppose you want to put photos in a photo album. Each page of the album holds 8 photos. You have 100 photos. How many pages can you fill?

2. You want to buy a cassette player. It costs $44. You have $27. You save $3 a week. How many weeks will it take you to save enough money to buy the cassette player?

## Concepts

**Write an addition sentence and a multiplication sentence for each picture.** (page 120)

3.

4. ◆◆◆◆◆
◆◆◆◆◆
◆◆◆◆◆
◆◆◆◆◆

**Use multiplication and division properties to complete.** (page 128)

5. $(3 \times 4) \times 5 = \blacksquare \times (4 \times 5)$

6. $\blacksquare \div 1 = 25$

7. $9 \div \blacksquare = 1$

8. $(4 \times \blacksquare) \times 2 = 4 \times (2 \times 3)$

## Skills

**Write the product.** (page 122)

9. $6 \times 5$
10. $5 \times 8$
11. $7 \times 10$
12. $10 \times 9$

**Find the quotient.** (page 126)

13. $10\overline{)60}$
14. $5\overline{)15}$
15. $10\overline{)10}$
16. $5\overline{)45}$
17. $10\overline{)900}$

## Multiplication and Division
## Around the World

# Math World

Throughout history, people have used songs, finger games, and tablets to help them multiply.

## Sing about math in Chinese

More than 2000 years ago, the Chinese invented a song for the multiplication table. They used it to help them multiply 1-digit numbers. The song, called the "Nine-nines Rhyme," is still memorized by Chinese schoolchildren today. In English, it begins: "One one makes one, one two makes two, one three makes three . . ."

## What's 4 × 4 in Babylonian?

Scientists know that Babylonians in the Middle East used multiplication at least 4000 years ago. How do they know this? They found ancient clay tablets with multiplication tables written on them. The Babylonians used a kind of writing called cuneiform (KYOO nee uh form). They pressed marks into wet clay tablets. When the clay dried, it formed a permanent, and heavy, record of the writing.

# Try This! EASTERN FINGER MULTIPLICATION

This method of multiplying numbers between 5 and 10 has been used in North Africa, Serbia, Syria, Iran, and Iraq. Follow these steps to solve 6 × 8.

**1** Hold both hands out, face up. Stretch out your fingers.

**2** Because 6 is 1 more than 5, bend one finger down on one hand.

**3** Because 8 is 3 more than 5, bend three fingers down on the other hand.

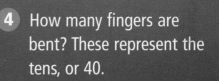

**4** How many fingers are bent? These represent the tens, or 40.

**5** Multiply the raised fingers, 2 on one hand and 4 on the other, to get 8.

**6** Add these two numbers, 40 and 8, to get the product: 48.

**Try:** 6 × 9, 8 × 8, 9 × 9

## Multiply to Count

The Toba people of Paraguay use multiplication in their number words, after the number five. To say the number six, they say 2 × 3. The number 7 is 1 + (2 × 3). Eight is said as 2 × 4, and ten is 2 + (2 × 4). Can you imagine how they might say the number nine?

## Respond

With a partner . . .
to create a song to help you remember some math facts you have trouble with.

Internet:
**Houghton Mifflin Education Place**
Explore the Math Center at
http://www.eduplace.com.

# Multiplying by 2, 4, and 8

**Y**our soccer team is supplying drinks for a game. Each carton has 6 drinks. How many drinks are in 8 cartons?

You can use doubles to help you multiply.

## Here's A Way!  Find 8 × 6.

**1** Think of 2 × 6.

**2 × 6 = 12**

**2** Double the factor 2 to make 4 × 6.

**4 × 6 = 24**
The product is also doubled.

**3** Double the factor 4 to make 8 × 6.

**8 × 6 = 48**
The product is also doubled.

2 × 6

4 × 6

8 × 6

## Talk About It!

• Explain why the product of 4 × 6 is twice as great as 2 × 6.

• Discuss how many times greater the product of 8 × 6 is compared to the product of 2 × 6.

**Algebraic Reasoning** Copy and complete. Write >, <, or =.

1. 4 × 8 ● 8 × 5
2. 3 × 8 ● 2 × 16
3. 12 × 4 ● 6 × 8
4. 3 × 4 ● 4 × 3
5. 3 × 4 ● 8 × 6
6. 6 × 2 ● 5 × 4

7. **Critical Thinking** If you double the product of 2 × 4, will you get the product of 4 × 8? Explain.

**Write a multiplication fact that doubles the product. Draw pictures to show how it is doubled.**

8. 2 × 8    9. 3 × 4    10. 5 × 2    11. 4 × 4    12. 3 × 8    13. 7 × 2

**Find the product.**

14. 5 × 4    15. 10 × 2    16. 7 × 4    17. 3 × 4    18. 7 × 8

19. 3 × 6    20. 8 × 9    21. 6 × 4    22. 6 × 8    23. 5 × 9

24. 3 × 8    25. 5 × 6    26. 9 × 9    27. 3 × 7    28. 4 × 9

29. **Number Sense** One kind of fruit drink comes in packages of 2, 4, and 8. Find out how many fruit drinks the team can buy. In the table $n$ stands for the number of packs. Copy and complete the table.

| $n$ | $2 \times n$ | $4 \times n$ | $8 \times n$ |
|---|---|---|---|
| 3 | 6 | 12 | 24 |
| 6 | ? | ? | 48 |
| 9 | ? | 36 | ? |
| 4 | ? | ? | ? |

30. **Write About It** Compare the products for 3, 6, and 9 in exercise 29. Describe a pattern you see in the completed table.

**Remember, some problems may not have enough information.**

31. The score is 3 to 2 when the second half of the game begins. If you score the only two goals in the second half, which team will win? How do you know?

32. Your team rests during the entire halftime. Each of the 16 players rests for 8 minutes. How long does halftime last?

**More Practice Set 4.8, p. 486**

# Dividing by 2, 4, and 8

**Y**ou are helping the soccer coach set up practice drills. There are 16 players on the team. How many players will be in each group if they form 2 groups? 4 groups? 8 groups?

You can use division to find out.

## Here's A Way! — Divide 16 by 2, 4, and 8.

**1** Find the number in each group, if there are 2 groups.

$16 \div 2 = n$

Think $2 \times 8 = 16$.

So, $16 \div 2 = 8$.

When there are 2 groups, 8 players will be in each group.

**2** Find the number in each group, if there are 4 groups.

$16 \div 4 = n$

Think $4 \times 4 = 16$.

So, $16 \div 4 = 4$.

When there are 4 groups, 4 players will be in each group.

**3** Find the number in each group, if there are 8 groups.

$16 \div 8 = n$

Think $8 \times 2 = 16$.

So, $16 \div 8 = 2$.

When there are 8 groups, 2 players will be in each group.

**Talk About It!** What patterns do you see in the three division problems? Why do you think those patterns occur?

**Find the missing factor.**

1. ■ × 4 = 20    2. ■ × 2 = 10    3. 4 × ■ = 36    4. 8 × ■ = 40

   20 ÷ 4 = ■         10 ÷ 2 = ■          36 ÷ 4 = ■          40 ÷ 8 = ■

**Find the quotient.**

5. 28 ÷ 4    6. 24 ÷ 2    7. 20 ÷ 4    8. 56 ÷ 8    9. 18 ÷ 2    10. 72 ÷ 2

11. **Critical Thinking** If you know that 64 ÷ 8 = 8, explain how you can use this fact to find 64 ÷ 4.

## Work It Out!

**Write the quotient.**

12. a. 16 ÷ 2    13. a. 32 ÷ 4    14. a. 8 ÷ 2    15. a. 24 ÷ 4    16. a. 48 ÷ 4

    b. $4\overline{)16}$         b. $8\overline{)32}$         b. $4\overline{)8}$         b. $8\overline{)24}$         b. $8\overline{)48}$

17. Look at exercises 12–16. How does the quotient in part *a* of each exercise help you find the quotient in part *b*?

**Copy and complete the tables.**

18.

| $n$ | $n \div 2$ | $n \div 4$ |
|---|---|---|
| 8 | 4 | 2 |
| 12 | ? | 3 |
| 16 | 8 | ? |
| 20 | 10 | ? |
| 24 | ? | ? |

19.

| $n$ | $n \div 5$ | $n \div 10$ |
|---|---|---|
| 10 | 2 | ? |
| 20 | 4 | 2 |
| 50 | 10 | 5 |
| 70 | ? | 7 |
| 100 | ? | ? |

20. **Write About It** Look for patterns in the tables above. Use words to describe them.

### Problem Solving

21. Four parents have offered to drive the 16 soccer players to the game. If the players are divided into equal groups, how many players will go with each parent?

22. A number's two digits add up to 3. The number can be divided by 2 or 4 without a remainder, but not 8. What is the number?

**More Practice Set 4.9, p. 486**

# Problem Solving

## Using Make a Table and Other Strategies

Plastic bottles are packed into bales before being recycled.

**R**ecycled plastic helps keep people warm! Some factories use recycled plastic, combined with other fabrics, to make winter jackets.

**Y**ou are in charge of making sure the factory has enough recycled plastic to make clothes. The warehouse has 46 truckloads of recycled plastic. When fewer than 10 truckloads are left, you need to order more. Suppose you use 8 truckloads a day. When will you need to order more?

- What problem are you trying to solve?

- How many truckloads will you have left after 2 days? 3 days?

- Explain a strategy you can use to solve the problem. Then solve it.

**Problem Solving Process**
- ✓ Understand
- ✓ Plan
- ✓ Try It
- ✓ Look Back

**Choose a Strategy You Have Learned**
- ✓ Guess and Check
- ✓ Draw a Picture
- ✓ Make a List
- ✓ Make a Table
-    Act It Out
-    Work a Simpler Problem
-    Look for a Pattern
-    Work Backward

## Work It Out!

**Use any strategy to solve the problem. Show your work.**

1. You have plastic recycled from a total of 175 two-liter bottles. You make a jacket an hour. You start at 11:00 A.M. and finish at 5:00 P.M. Will you use plastic from all 175 bottles? How many jackets do you make?

2. How many jackets can you make with the plastic from 150 two-liter bottles?

3. How many two-liter bottles does it take to make 8 jackets?

*Twenty-five two-liter bottles make 1 pullover jacket.*

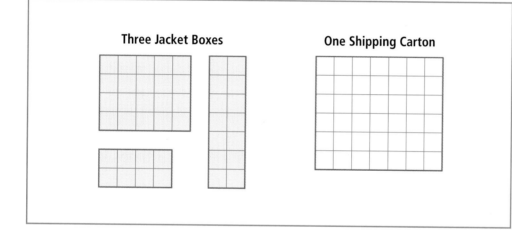

Three Jacket Boxes

One Shipping Carton

4. Look at the diagrams shown above. Describe how you can pack the 3 jacket boxes in the shipping carton. Suppose that the carton and the boxes are the same height.

5. The shipping cartons are placed in large trucking crates. A total of 9 cartons fit in each crate. How many of the jacket boxes will you need for each trucking crate?

## Share Your Thinking

6. Describe how you solved problem 1. Explain how patterns helped you.

7. **Create Your Own** Write a problem for a friend to solve. Use any of the information on this page. Did your friend use the strategy you expected? Explain.

# Multiplying and Dividing with 3 and 6

**Y**ou know that multiplication and division are related. You can use this understanding to learn the facts for multiplying and dividing with 3 and 6.

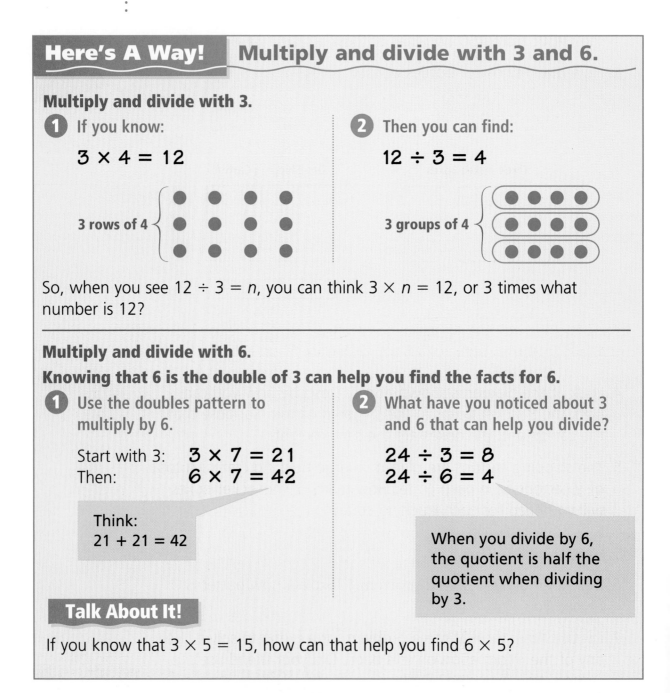

## Here's A Way! Multiply and divide with 3 and 6.

**Multiply and divide with 3.**

**1** If you know:

$$3 \times 4 = 12$$

3 rows of 4

**2** Then you can find:

$$12 \div 3 = 4$$

3 groups of 4

So, when you see $12 \div 3 = n$, you can think $3 \times n = 12$, or 3 times what number is 12?

**Multiply and divide with 6.**

**Knowing that 6 is the double of 3 can help you find the facts for 6.**

**1** Use the doubles pattern to multiply by 6.

Start with 3:  $3 \times 7 = 21$
Then:  $6 \times 7 = 42$

Think:
$21 + 21 = 42$

**2** What have you noticed about 3 and 6 that can help you divide?

$$24 \div 3 = 8$$
$$24 \div 6 = 4$$

When you divide by 6, the quotient is half the quotient when dividing by 3.

### Talk About It!

If you know that $3 \times 5 = 15$, how can that help you find $6 \times 5$?

Write the answer.

1. 3 × 3
2. 3 × 9
3. 3)‾18
4. 3)‾24
5. 3 × 4

6. 6 × 3
7. 6 × 9
8. 6)‾18
9. 6)‾24
10. 6 × 4

11. **Critical Thinking** What other strategies can you use to help you find multiplication facts for 3 or 6?

## Work It Out!

12. **Patterns** Copy the table. Use patterns to complete.

| Factors | Factors | | | | | | | | | |
|---------|---|---|---|---|---|---|---|---|---|---|
| | 0 | 1 | 2 | 3 | 4 | 5 | 6 | 7 | 8 | 9 |
| x 3 | ? | ? | ? | ? | ? | ? | ? | ? | ? | ? |
| x 6 | ? | ? | ? | ? | ? | ? | ? | ? | ? | ? |

| Divisors | Dividends | | | | | | | | | |
|----------|---|---|---|---|---|---|---|---|---|---|
| | 0 | 3 | 6 | 9 | 12 | 15 | 18 | 21 | 24 | 27 |
| ÷ 3 | ? | ? | ? | ? | ? | ? | ? | ? | ? | ? |
| ÷ 6 | ? | | ? | | ? | | ? | | ? | |

13. What patterns do you see in the multiplication table for 3 and 6? What patterns are in the division table for 3 and 6?

Write the answer.

14. 3 × 7
15. 5 × 6
16. 6)‾30
17. 6)‾48
18. 3 × 5

### Problem Solving

19. You buy 3 packages of 3 custard buns and 6 packages of 4 custard buns. How many custard buns have you bought?

20. You want to buy 24 custard buns to share with your class. There are 6 in a package. How many packages will you buy?

### Mixed Review   Add or subtract.

| 21. | 603 | 22. | 1555 | 23. | 984 | 24. | 43,456 | 25. | 6479 |
|-----|-----|-----|------|-----|-----|-----|--------|-----|------|
| | − 58 | | + 394 | | − 390 | | − 3,948 | | + 42 |

**More Practice Set 4.11, p. 487**

143

# Multiplying and Dividing with 7 and 9

**W**hen you divide with 7 or 9, think of multiplication facts.

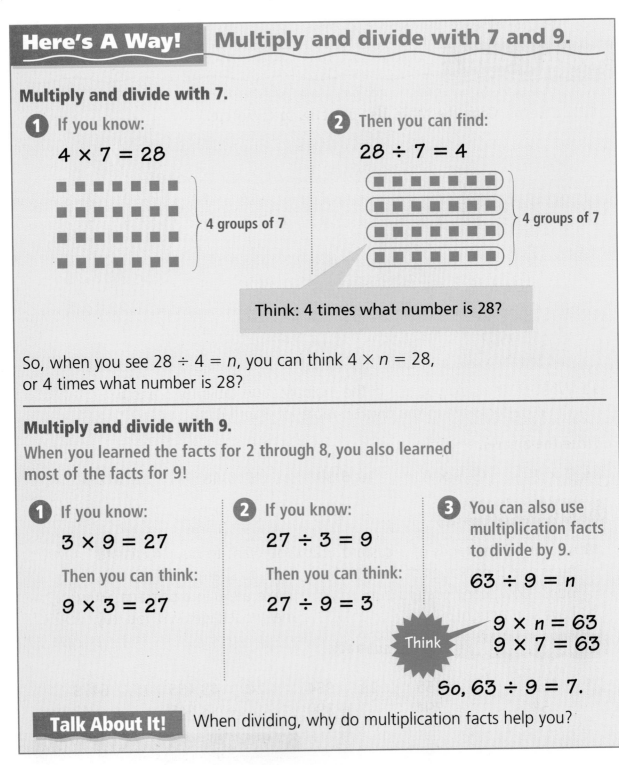

**Here's A Way!** | **Multiply and divide with 7 and 9.**

**Multiply and divide with 7.**

**1** If you know:

$4 \times 7 = 28$

} 4 groups of 7

**2** Then you can find:

$28 \div 7 = 4$

} 4 groups of 7

Think: 4 times what number is 28?

So, when you see $28 \div 4 = n$, you can think $4 \times n = 28$, or 4 times what number is 28?

**Multiply and divide with 9.**

When you learned the facts for 2 through 8, you also learned most of the facts for 9!

**1** If you know:

$3 \times 9 = 27$

Then you can think:

$9 \times 3 = 27$

**2** If you know:

$27 \div 3 = 9$

Then you can think:

$27 \div 9 = 3$

**3** You can also use multiplication facts to divide by 9.

$63 \div 9 = n$

Think

$9 \times n = 63$
$9 \times 7 = 63$

So, $63 \div 9 = 7$.

**Talk About It!** | When dividing, why do multiplication facts help you?

**Write the answer.**

1. $7 \times 3$    2. $7 \times 6$    3. $9 \times 5$    4. $9\overline{)45}$    5. $3 \times 9$    6. $7\overline{)21}$

7. **Critical Thinking** How can the answer to exercise 1 help you answer exercise 2?

**Copy and complete the fact families.**

8. ■ $\times 4 = 36$      9. $7 \times$ ■ $= 42$    10. ■ $\times 7 = 49$    11. $9 \times$ ■ $= 54$

■ $\times 9 = 36$        $6 \times 7 =$ ■        $7 \times 7 =$ ■          $6 \times 9 =$ ■

$36 \div$ ■ $= 9$        ■ $\div 6 = 7$        $49 \div$ ■ $= 7$        $54 \div$ ■ $= 9$

■ $\div 9 = 4$        $42 \div$ ■ $= 6$        $49 \div 7 =$ ■        $54 \div 9 =$ ■

## Work It Out!

**Write the product.**

12. $7 \times 5$      13. $9 \times 6$      14. $4 \times 9$      15. $9 \times 8$      16. $0 \times 9$

17. $9 \times 9$      18. $0 \times 7$      19. $1 \times 9$      20. $7 \times 8$      21. $7 \times 7$

**Write the quotient.**

22. $7\overline{)21}$      23. $9\overline{)81}$      24. $9\overline{)63}$      25. $7\overline{)28}$      26. $7\overline{)35}$

**Mental Math Is each quotient greater than or less than $36 \div 9$?**

27. $18 \div 6$      28. $45 \div 5$      29. $28 \div 4$      30. $36 \div 12$      31. $72 \div 9$

### Problem Solving

32. Suppose your class plans to visit a sugar mill. The sign-up list shows that there are 7 groups with 5 students in each group. How many students are going?

33. A company received 3 equal shipments of sugar cane from Brazil. The total amount was 27 tons. How many tons was each shipment?

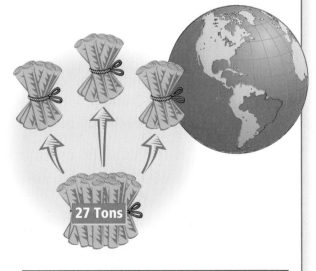

27 Tons

**More Practice Set 4.12, p. 487**

145

# Patterns and Multiples

**A** **multiple** of a number is the product of that number and any other whole number. A **common multiple** is a number that is a multiple of two or more numbers.

One way to find multiples is by counting.

| 1 | 2 | 3 | 4 | 5 | 6 | 7 | 8 | 9 | 10 |
|---|---|---|---|---|---|---|---|---|---|
| 11 | 12 | 13 | 14 | 15 | 16 | 17 | 18 | 19 | 20 |
| 21 | 22 | 23 | 24 | 25 | 26 | 27 | 28 | 29 | 30 |
| 31 | 32 | 33 | 34 | 35 | 36 | 37 | 38 | 39 | 40 |
| 41 | 42 | 43 | 44 | 45 | 46 | 47 | 48 | 49 | 50 |
| 51 | 52 | 53 | 54 | 55 | 56 | 57 | 58 | 59 | 60 |
| 61 | 62 | 63 | 64 | 65 | 66 | 67 | 68 | 69 | 70 |
| 71 | 72 | 73 | 74 | 75 | 76 | 77 | 78 | 79 | 80 |
| 81 | 82 | 83 | 84 | 85 | 86 | 87 | 88 | 89 | 90 |
| 91 | 92 | 93 | 94 | 95 | 96 | 97 | 98 | 99 | 100 |

## Here's A Way! Count to find multiples.

You can use a hundreds chart to count.

**1** To find multiples of 2, start at 2 and count by 2's from 2 to 100.

- Shade the numbers as you say them.
- Do you notice a pattern in the shaded numbers?

| 1 | 2 | 3 | 4 | 5 | 6 | 7 | 8 | 9 | 10 |
|---|---|---|---|---|---|---|---|---|---|
| 11 | 12 | 13 | 14 | 15 | 16 | 17 | 18 | 19 | 20 |
| 21 | 22 | 23 | 24 | 25 | 26 | 27 | 28 | 29 | 30 |
| 31 | 32 | 33 | 34 | 35 | 36 | 37 | 38 | 39 | 40 |
| 41 | 42 | 43 | 44 | 45 | 46 | 47 | 48 | 49 | 50 |
| 51 | 52 | 53 | 54 | 55 | 56 | 57 | 58 | 59 | 60 |
| 61 | 62 | 63 | 64 | 65 | 66 | 67 | 68 | 69 | 70 |
| 71 | 72 | 73 | 74 | 75 | 76 | 77 | 78 | 79 | 80 |
| 81 | 82 | 83 | 84 | 85 | 86 | 87 | 88 | 89 | 90 |
| 91 | 92 | 93 | 94 | 95 | 96 | 97 | 98 | 99 | 100 |

**2** To find multiples of 3, start at 3 and count by 3's from 3 to 100.

- Use a different color to circle the numbers.

**3** To find some common multiples of 2 and 3, look at the multiples of each number up to 50.

| 1 | 2 | ③ | 4 | 5 | ⑥ | 7 | 8 | ⑨ | 10 |
|---|---|---|---|---|---|---|---|---|---|
| 11 | ⑫ | 13 | 14 | ⑮ | 16 | 17 | ⑱ | 19 | 20 |
| ㉑ | 22 | 23 | ㉔ | 25 | 26 | ㉗ | 28 | 29 | ㉚ |
| 31 | 32 | ㉝ | 34 | 35 | ㊱ | 37 | 38 | ㊴ | 40 |
| 41 | ㊷ | 43 | 44 | ㊺ | 46 | 47 | ㊽ | 49 | 50 |
| ㊿ | 52 | 53 | 54 | 55 | 56 | 57 | 58 | 59 | 60 |
| 61 | 62 | 63 | 64 | 65 | 66 | 67 | 68 | 69 | 70 |
| 71 | 72 | 73 | 74 | 75 | 76 | 77 | 78 | 79 | 80 |
| 81 | 82 | 83 | 84 | 85 | 86 | 87 | 88 | 89 | 90 |
| 91 | 92 | 93 | 94 | 95 | 96 | 97 | 98 | 99 | 100 |

- Write the common multiples up to 50: 6, 12, 18, 24, 30, 36, 42, 48.

**Talk About It!** Why are the numbers on your list called common multiples?

1. Use a hundreds chart to count and shade multiples of 5 up to 100.

2. List common multiples of 2 and 5 up to 100.

3. List common multiples of 3 and 5 up to 100.

4. **Critical Thinking** Is it possible to list all the multiples of 2, 3, or 5? Explain.

## Work It Out!

5. Use a hundreds chart to count and shade multiples of 6 up to 100.

6. **Critical Thinking** Compare the multiples of 6 with multiples of 2 and 3. What do you notice? Why do you think this occurs?

7. **Algebraic Reasoning** What number has no multiple other than itself?

8. **Number Sense** Do you think a hundreds chart that starts at 201 has the same pattern for 2, 3, and 5 as a 0–100 chart? Try it. Share your results.

9. **Critical Thinking** Think about the pattern on a hundreds chart made by multiples of 4. Will it be similar to the pattern made by multiples of 8? Why or why not?

### Problem Solving

**Use a hundreds chart for the following.**

10. Hamburger patties come in packages of 6. Buns come in packages of 8. How can you buy the same number of each?

11. Pizza appears on the school lunch menu every third day. Hamburger appears every fifth day. When will they both appear? Explain.

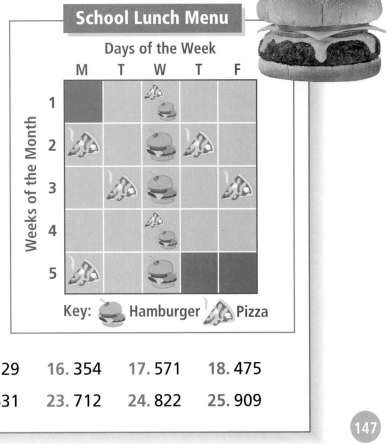

School Lunch Menu

### Mixed Review

**Round to the nearest ten. Then, round to the nearest hundred.**

| | | | | | | |
|---|---|---|---|---|---|---|
| 12. 56 | 13. 92 | 14. 87 | 15. 129 | 16. 354 | 17. 571 | 18. 475 |
| 19. 64 | 20. 99 | 21. 77 | 22. 631 | 23. 712 | 24. 822 | 25. 909 |

# Factors

**Getting Started**

**What You'll Need:**
▶ grid paper
▶ recording sheet
▶ a red, a blue, and a yellow crayon

**Vocabulary:**
**common factor**
Glossary, p. 516

**S**uppose you have 24 square tiles. If you put them in 4 equal rows, you will have 6 squares in each row. This is a rectangular array. The numbers 4 and 6 are factors of 24.

You can use arrays to find factors.

**Activity**

**1** How many squares are in each array?

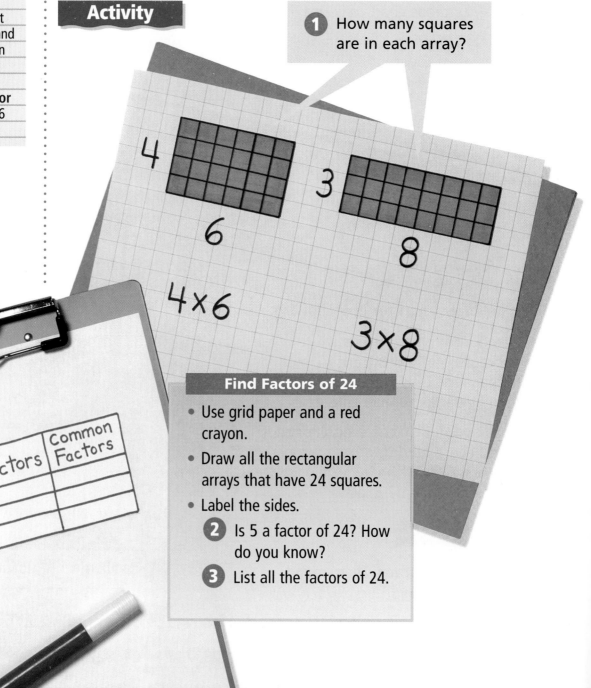

4

6

4 × 6

3

8

3 × 8

**Find Factors of 24**

• Use grid paper and a red crayon.
• Draw all the rectangular arrays that have 24 squares.
• Label the sides.
  **2** Is 5 a factor of 24? How do you know?
  **3** List all the factors of 24.

| Number | Factors | Common Factors |
|--------|---------|----------------|
| 24 | | |
| 18 | | |
| 18 and 24 | | |

## Find Factors of 18

- Use grid paper and a blue crayon.
- Draw all the rectangular arrays that have 18 squares.
- Label the sides.
- **4** List all the factors of 18.

## Find Common Factors

- Compare the arrays with 18 squares to the arrays with 24 squares.
- Find the arrays that have a side of the same length.
- **5** List matching sides common to the array with 18 squares and the array with 24 squares. The lengths of the matching sides are **common factors**.

*Common factors are numbers that are factors of two or more products.*

## Find Factors of 16

- Use grid paper and a yellow crayon.
- Draw all the rectangular arrays that have 16 squares.
- Label the sides.
- **6** List all the factors of 16.

## Find Common Factors

- Compare the arrays with 16 squares to the arrays with 24 squares.
- Find the arrays with matching sides.
- **7** List the common factors of 16 and 24.
- **8** List the common factors of 16, 18, and 24.

# Show What You Know!

**Use the recording sheet.**

1. Why is every number a factor of itself?

2. What two numbers are common factors of all even numbers?

3. Do you think a number that has 8 as a factor will have 4 as a factor? Explain.

4. How would you use multiplication to find the factors of a number?

## Mixed Review

**Write the number in word form and expanded form.**

5. 4300    6. 2345    7. 787    8. 185    9. 8901    10. 55,786

# Multiplication Patterns

LESSON 15 LESSON

**H**ow would you find the product of 3 × 2000? You can use basic facts and patterns to help you multiply by tens, hundreds, and thousands.

**Getting Started**

**What You'll Need:**
► calculator
► recording sheet

## Here's A Way! Find 3 × 2000.

**Multiply by tens, hundreds, and thousands.**

**1** Write a multiplication sentence with the digits that are not 0. ➤ $3 \times 2 = 6$

**2** Build a pattern with multiples of 10, 100, and 1000.

$3 \times 20 = 60$ ➤

$3 \times 200 = 600$ ➤

$3 \times 2000 = 6000$ ➤

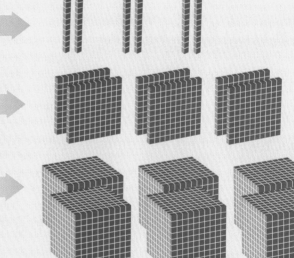

## Talk About It!

- What pattern do you see in the multiplication sentences?
- How will the multiplication sentences and place-value blocks change if you multiplied by 6 instead of 3?

## Show What You Know!

**Copy and complete the patterns.**

1. 3 × 10 = ■    2. 9 × ■ = 90    3. 4 × ■ = 240    4. 6 × ■ = 420

  3 × ■ = 300      9 × 100 = ■      4 × 600 = ■      6 × 700 = ■

  3 × 1000 = ■     9 × ■ = 9000     4 × ■ = 24,000   6 × ■ = 42,000

5. **Create Your Own** Write a rule for multiplying by tens, hundreds, and thousands.

## Work It Out!

**Copy and complete the patterns.**

6. 8 × ■ = 32     7. ■ × 7 = 35     8. 5 × 1 = 5      9. ■ × 8 = 56

  8 × 40 = ■       5 × 70 = ■        ■ × 10 = 50       7 × ■ = 560

  8 × ■ = 3200     5 × ■ = 3500      5 × ■ = 500       7 × 800 = ■

  8 × 4000 = ■     5 × 7000 = ■      5 × 1000 = ■      7 × ■ = 56,000

### Problem Solving   Using Data

10. **Calculator** Work with a partner. The chart shows how many blocks you need to build different kinds of buildings. Suppose you have 100,000 blocks. Use as many of them as you can. Use a recording sheet to show your plan. You may use a calculator.

| Dog house | Garage | House | Store | School | Apartment | Office building |
|-----------|--------|-------|-------|--------|-----------|-----------------|
| 15 blocks | 90 blocks | 700 blocks | 2000 blocks | 3000 blocks | 4000 blocks | 5000 blocks |

# Problem Solving
## Using Strategies

LESSON 16

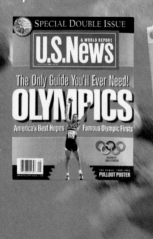

**S**wimming is a popular Olympic event. Swimmers compete using different kinds of strokes. These include the backstroke, breaststroke, butterfly, and freestyle.

**One Lap**

To one end

and back

You can read more about the Olympics in the pages of *U.S. News and World Report.*

SPECIAL DOUBLE ISSUE

**U.S.News** & WORLD REPORT

The Only Guide You'll Ever Need!

**OLYMPICS**

America's Best Hopes    Famous Olympic Firsts

PULLOUT POSTER

**Problem Solving Process**
✓ Understand
✓ Plan
✓ Try It
✓ Look Back

**Choose a Strategy You Have Learned**
✓ Guess and Check
✓ Draw a Picture
✓ Make a List
✓ Make a Table
  Act It Out
  Work a Simpler Problem
  Look for a Pattern
  Work Backward

**A** freestyle swimmer and a breaststroke swimmer are practicing laps. The freestyle swimmer takes 1 minute. The breaststroke swimmer takes 2 minutes. They swim for 12 minutes. How many laps will each complete?

• How many laps will the freestyle swimmer complete after 2 minutes? After 4 minutes?

• How many laps will the other swimmer complete after 2 minutes? After 4 minutes?

• Explain a strategy that can help you solve the problem. Then solve it.

# Work It Out!

**Use any strategy to solve the problem. Show your work.**

1. An Olympic diver plans to use 3 out of 6 of the dives shown. She will do each dive only once. In how many different orders can she do these 3 dives?

2. A diver adds one more dive to her routine. If she also does this dive only once, how many more orders are possible?

3. Suppose a swimmer swims 2 meters a second and a runner runs 10 meters a second. The swimmer gets a 8-second head start. How long will it take the runner to catch up?

4. One half of a lap is 50 meters. A freestyle swimmer goes 50 meters in 20 seconds. If he keeps the same speed, how many meters will he swim in a minute?

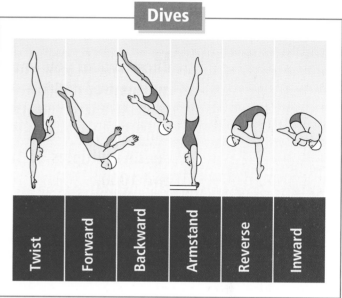

**Dives**

Twist | Forward | Backward | Armstand | Reverse | Inward

5. An Olympic pool is 50 meters long. One swimmer swims to one end and back. Another swimmer swims all the way around the edge of the pool. Who has swum farther? Explain.

6. Two swimmers challenge each other to a race. They plan to use a different stroke for each of 3 laps. How many possible choices of strokes can each swimmer use?

7. A freestyle swimmer swims 50 meters in 30 seconds. A backstroke swimmer takes 40 seconds to swim this distance. Both start at the same time. The freestyle swimmer finishes 150 meters. How many seconds behind him is the other swimmer?

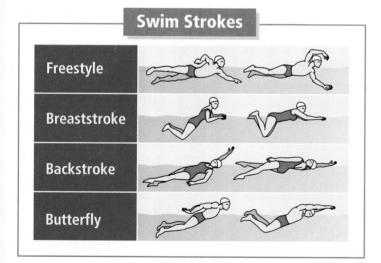

**Swim Strokes**

Freestyle

Breaststroke

Backstroke

Butterfly

## Share Your Thinking

8. Discuss problem 7 with a partner. Describe why you used the strategy you did. Would another strategy have worked? Explain.

# Division Patterns

**H**ow would you find the quotient of $4000 \div 2$? Division facts and patterns can help you mentally divide multiples of 10, 100, and 1000.

Two trucks delivered 4000 lb of hay to the Wildlife Habitat. Each truck delivered the same amount of hay. How many pounds of hay did each truck deliver?

$$4000 \div 2 = n$$

---

**Here's A Way!**    **Divide 4000 by 2.**

**Divide tens, hundreds, and thousands.**

1️⃣ Use a related basic fact to write a division sentence. ➡️ $4 \div 2 = 2$

2️⃣ Build a pattern with multiples of 10, 100, and 1000.

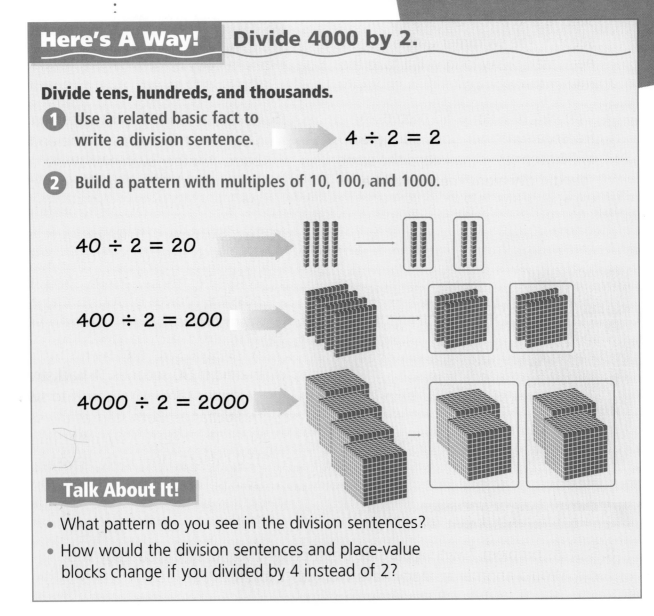

$40 \div 2 = 20$

$400 \div 2 = 200$

$4000 \div 2 = 2000$

**Talk About It!**

- What pattern do you see in the division sentences?
- How would the division sentences and place-value blocks change if you divided by 4 instead of 2?

Use a division fact. Build a pattern with multiples of 10, 100, and 1000.

1. $3 \div 3 = 1$    2. $63 \div 7 = 9$    3. $45 \div 5 = 9$    4. $36 \div 6 = 6$    5. $56 \div 8 = 7$

6. **Number Sense** Extend each pattern in exercises 1–5 using the multiples of 10,000.

7. **Create Your Own** Write a rule for dividing multiples of 10, 100, and 1000.

## Work It Out!

**Find the quotient.**

8. $250 \div 5$      9. $30 \div 5$      10. $240 \div 4$      11. $720 \div 8$

12. $2800 \div 7$      13. $4900 \div 7$      14. $3200 \div 4$      15. $6000 \div 6$

16. $5600 \div 8$      17. $81,000 \div 9$      18. $3000 \div 6$      19. $20,000 \div 4$

20. **Critical Thinking** In exercises 18 and 19, does the quotient have the same number of zeros as the dividend? Why or why not?

### Problem Solving Using Data

Use the pictograph to solve each problem.

21. How many pounds does each animal weigh?

22. Which animal weighs twice as much as another animal?

23. Write a division sentence to show your answer to exercise 22.

24. Suppose you added another row to the pictograph for a 5000-pound rhinoceros. How many symbols would you add?

**Comparing Weights**

| Animals | Pounds |
|---------|--------|
| American Black Bear | 🐻🐻🐻 |
| Atlantic Leatherback Turtle | 🐢🐢🐢🐢🐢 |
| Bison | 🐂🐂🐂🐂🐂🐂🐂🐂🐂🐂🐂🐂 |

Key 🔵 = 200 Pounds    🔹 = 100 Pounds

**More Practice Set 4.17, p. 488**

# Line Plots

**Getting Started**

Vocabulary:
line plot
Glossary, p. 516

**S**uppose you ask your friends how many hours a week they spend doing homework. How can you show the results?

You can use a line plot to show results that can be read and compared easily. A **line plot** is a diagram that shows data on a number line.

Make a line plot to show the results of the homework survey.

## Homework Survey

| | |
|---|---|
| Marci | 10 hours |
| Anna | 9 hours |
| Chris | 6 hours |
| Elaine | 7 hours |
| Juan | 8 hours |
| Maria | 8 hours |
| Dawn | 5 hours |
| Paul | 8 hours |
| Ray | 10 hours |
| David | 7 hours |
| Tawana | 5 hours |
| Alex | 6 hours |

## Here's A Way! Make a line plot.

**To make a line plot, begin by drawing a number line.**

**1** Use the information to decide how long to make the number line.

**2** Mark an X over the number for each student's answer.

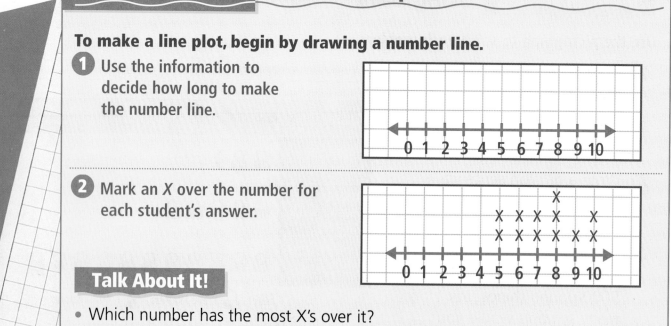

### Talk About It!

• Which number has the most X's over it?

• What does that tell you?

## Show What You Know!

This line plot shows the hours students spend reading each week. Use the line plot to answer each question.

```
                    X
          X  X  X        X
          X  X  X        X
       X  X  X  X  X  X  X
    <------|--|--|--|--|--|------>
       0  1  2  3  4  5
```

1. How many students read for 2 hours each week?

2. How many students answered the survey? Explain your answer.

3. Did more students read for 3 hours or for 5 hours? Explain.

4. **Critical Thinking** Can you tell which person read for 5 hours by looking at the line plot? Explain.

## Work It Out!

Make a line plot. Then, use the line plot to answer exercises 6–8.

5. Students were surveyed about how many brothers and sisters they had. Make a line plot to show the data.
   Data: 0, 3, 1, 2, 0, 4, 2, 1, 5, 0, 1, 0

6. How many students voted in the survey?

7. What is the most number of brothers and sisters anyone has?

8. What answer was given most often? Explain.

9. **Problem Solving** A group of 15 students took a math quiz. Here are their scores: 8, 5, 5, 9, 10, 2, 3, 3, 5, 5, 8, 7, 4, 5, 4. Make a line plot to show the data.

10. **Write About It** Look at your completed line plot in exercise 9. Write three facts from the data. Share your findings.

### Mixed Review

Use the bar graph to answer each question.

11. About how many students voted?

12. Which subject received twice as many votes as art?

13. Did more than or fewer than half the students vote for spelling?

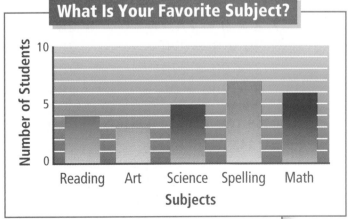

**What Is Your Favorite Subject?**

More Practice Set 4.18, p. 488

# Chapter 4 Test

## for Pages 118–157

**Test-Taking Tips**
Use related multiplication and division facts to help you find and check answers.

## Problem Solving

**Solve. Show your work.** (pages 130, 132, 140)

1. You and your friends have $5 in all. How many lemonades can you buy?

2. Can you buy spaghetti, fruit salad, and a lemonade for less than $5? How do you know?

3. Suppose you buy one of each item, and you pay with a $10 bill. Should you get more than $5 in change? Explain your answers.

| School Lunch Menu | |
| --- | --- |
| Lemonade | $1.25 |
| Spaghetti | $1.70 |
| Roll | $0.40 |
| Fruit Salad | $0.85 |

## Concepts

**Find the multiples of a number.** (page 146)

4. List the multiples of 2 up to 20.

5. List the multiples of 3 up to 30.

6. List the common multiples of 4 and 6 up to 30.

**Use patterns to find the missing number.** (pages 150, 154)

7. $3 \times 9 = 27$
   $30 \times 9 = 270$
   $3 \times 90 = 270$
   $3 \times 900 = \blacksquare$

8. $28 \div 7 = 4$
   $280 \div 7 = 40$
   $280 \div 70 = 4$
   $2800 \div 70 = \blacksquare$

9. $5 \times 6 = 30$
   $5 \times 60 = 300$
   $50 \times 60 = 3000$
   $\blacksquare \times 60 = 30,000$

**Choose two related division sentences for each exercise.**
(pages 142, 144)

10. $4 \times 9 = 36$  a. $9 \div 1 = 9$  b. $36 \div 4 = 9$  c. $4 \div 4 = 1$  d. $36 \div 9 = 4$

11. $8 \times 7 = 56$  a. $56 \div 8 = 7$  b. $56 \div 1 = 56$ c. $8 \div 1 = 8$  d. $56 \div 7 = 8$

12. $6 \times 9 = 54$  a. $9 \div 9 = 1$  b. $54 \div 6 = 9$  c. $54 \div 9 = 6$  d. $6 \div 1 = 6$

**Write the product or the quotient.** (pages 122, 136, 138, 142, 144)

13. $\begin{array}{r} 6 \\ \times\, 6 \\ \hline \end{array}$   14. $\begin{array}{r} 4 \\ \times\, 5 \\ \hline \end{array}$   15. $\begin{array}{r} 5 \\ \times\, 8 \\ \hline \end{array}$   16. $\begin{array}{r} 9 \\ \times\, 3 \\ \hline \end{array}$

17. $4\overline{)32}$   18. $9\overline{)36}$   19. $7\overline{)42}$   20. $5\overline{)40}$

21. $\begin{array}{r} 8 \\ \times\, 8 \\ \hline \end{array}$   22. $\begin{array}{r} 8 \\ \times\, 4 \\ \hline \end{array}$   23. $\begin{array}{r} 7 \\ \times\, 2 \\ \hline \end{array}$   24. $\begin{array}{r} 3 \\ \times\, 7 \\ \hline \end{array}$

25. $8\overline{)56}$   26. $3\overline{)24}$   27. $6\overline{)30}$   28. $7\overline{)42}$

29. $\begin{array}{r} 7 \\ \times\, 5 \\ \hline \end{array}$   30. $\begin{array}{r} 9 \\ \times\, 7 \\ \hline \end{array}$   31. $\begin{array}{r} 9 \\ \times\, 5 \\ \hline \end{array}$

## Performance Task

Keep In Mind . . .

Your work will be evaluated on the following:

☑ A line plot with suitable numbers

☑ Clearly recorded survey data

☑ Accurate interpretation

☑ Reasonable questions

(page 156)

A group of friends took a survey of how many videos they watched each week. Which number was the most common?

| | | | |
|---|---|---|---|
| Roberto | 2 | Leon | 2 |
| Amber | 1 | Gail | 3 |
| Thomas | 3 | Maria | 3 |
| Vinnie | 0 | Peter | 3 |

- How would you record the survey data in a line plot?

- Write two questions that can be answered by the line plot.

# Cumulative Review

## Number Sense (Chapter 1)

Put these numbers in order from greatest to least: 353, 443, 676.

To compare numbers, start with the greatest place value. Then if you need to, compare the digits from left to right.

least      greatest

353, 443, 676

So, greatest to least order is
676, 443, 353.

---

Compare the numbers. Write >, <, or =.

1. 1464 ● 1446

2. 3005 ● 3050

3. $2.10 ● $2.15

4. 731 ● 7310

5. 531 ● 531

6. 2963 ● 2961

Write the numbers in order from greatest to least.

7. 382  302  322

8. 436  485, 442

---

## Addition and Subtraction (Chapter 2)

Find 100 − 34 and 25 + 38 + 86.

Subtract. Regroup when you need to.

$$
\begin{array}{r}
{}^{9}\phantom{0}{}^{10}\phantom{0} \\
10\,0 \\
-\phantom{0}3\,4 \\
\hline
6\,6
\end{array}
$$

Line up the digits.
Add. Regroup when you need to.

$$
\begin{array}{r}
{}^{1}\phantom{0} \\
25 \\
36 \\
+\,86 \\
\hline
147
\end{array}
$$

---

Write the answer. Use mental math when you can.

9. 100 − 66

10. 15 + 2 + 5

11. 545 − 545

12. 1758 + 0

13. 600 − 145

14. 1000 − 116

15. $2.06 − $1.99

16. $1.24 + $6.54 + $.87

## Estimating Sums (Chapter 2)

Estimate $38 + $24.

**Here's A Way!**

Round up or down.
Add the rounded amounts.

$$\begin{array}{c} \$38 \\ +\ 24 \end{array} \quad \Rightarrow \quad \begin{array}{c} \$40 \\ +\ 20 \\ \hline \$60 \end{array}$$

**Estimate by rounding.**

17. $59 + $18

18. 45 + 7

19. 203 + 659

20. $.15 + $.46

## Graphing (Chapter 3)

**What does the bar graph show?**

**Here's A Way!**

Find the highest and lowest bars.

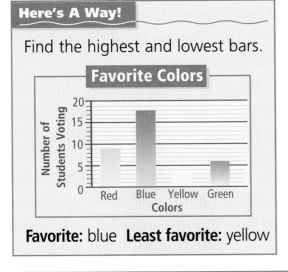

**Favorite Colors**

Number of Students Voting / Colors

**Favorite:** blue  **Least favorite:** yellow

**Use the graph to answer the question.**

21. How many students voted for blue? For yellow?

22. How many students voted for red? For green?

23. How many students in all voted?

24. Draw the graph as a pictograph.

## Problem Solving

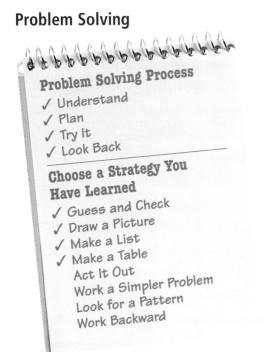

**Problem Solving Process**
- ✓ Understand
- ✓ Plan
- ✓ Try It
- ✓ Look Back

**Choose a Strategy You Have Learned**
- ✓ Guess and Check
- ✓ Draw a Picture
- ✓ Make a List
- ✓ Make a Table
-   Act It Out
-   Work a Simpler Problem
-   Look for a Pattern
-   Work Backward

**Choose one of the strategies you know to solve the problem. Show your work.**

25. Your school has a weekly soup and salad special. You can choose chicken, vegetable, or mushroom soup and mixed greens, spinach, or fruit salad. If you wish, you may have a roll also. How many different combinations can you make?

# Can You Dig It?

**Science Connection**    **With Your Group**

**Keep In Mind . . .**

Your work will be evaluated on the following:

· · · · · · · · · ·

☑ The accuracy of your math in describing your squares

· · · · · · · · · ·

☑ How well the grid you create shows the site

· · · · · · · · · ·

☑ How accurately you record your findings

· · · · · · · · · ·

☑ Whether your group divides the work among all the members

**H**ow do we know that the Maya peoples had calendars and the Sumerians "signed" their letters? Archaeologists help us learn such things. They dig in the earth to find buried objects that give them clues to the past.

Archaeologists begin their work by taking a sample. They take samples by digging and studying a small part of an area. You can create your own site and take a sample. What objects will you find?

| Item | Count |
|---|---|
| Utensils | 8 |
| Coins | 15 |
| Keys | 10 |
| Toys | 12 |

## 1 Plan It

- Gather lots of small objects. Think what kind of object each one is. Write down how many objects you have for each kind.
- Place the objects in a large, shallow box and cover them with sand.
- Put string over the sand to make a grid. Draw a grid with the same number of squares on grid paper. Number each square.
- Make a table to record how many objects of each kind you find.

## 2 Put It Together

- Choose a grid square as your first sample space.
- Carefully dig up its contents. If an object is partly in your square, dig it up!
- As you uncover each item, draw it on the paper grid.
- Count the number of objects that you found in your square. Record your findings by kind.
- Repeat by digging up another square.

## 3 Wrap It Up

- Multiply the number of each kind of object you found by the total number of grid squares in the box. Do this for both samples.
- Do the products from either sample come close to the actual contents?

## 4 Discuss Your Results

- Have you covered all the points in Keep In Mind?
- Report your results to the class. Which group's samples predict their box contents most closely?

# Geometry

## Math Power

### Use What You Know

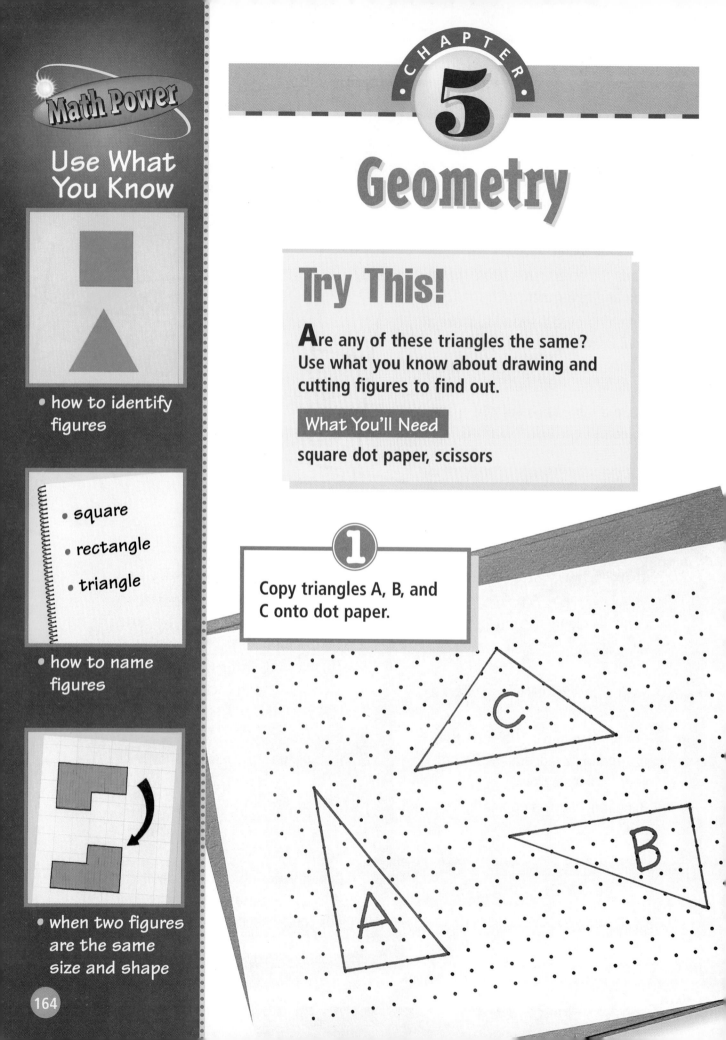

- how to identify figures

- square
- rectangle
- triangle

- how to name figures

- when two figures are the same size and shape

## Try This!

**A**re any of these triangles the same? Use what you know about drawing and cutting figures to find out.

**What You'll Need**

square dot paper, scissors

**1**

Copy triangles A, B, and C onto dot paper.

**2**

Cut out the triangles you drew.

**3**

Move or flip the triangles. Which two match?

How did turning and flipping the triangles help you find the matching pair?

What kinds of things make two figures match? What makes them not match?

**Ready to Go!**

# Flips

Cooperative Learning
**Checklist**

☑ Work alone.
☑ Work with a partner.
☑ Work with a group.

**H**ave you ever noticed how a reflection in a mirror makes things look backward? A **flip** is a move that makes a figure face in the opposite direction.

You can use dot paper to show flips.

**Getting Started**

**What You'll Need:**
▶ dot paper
▶ ruler
▶ markers

**Vocabulary:**
flip
congruent
Glossary, p. 516

## Up, Down, or Over!

**Activity**

• **Fold dot paper in half.**

• **Draw a simple figure on one side of the fold line.**

• **Copy your figure on the other side to show a flip.**

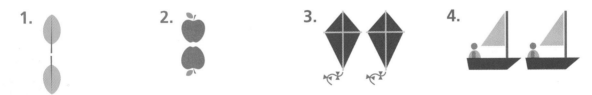

### 1
- Fold a sheet of dot paper in half.
- On one side of the fold line, draw a simple figure. Use straight lines to connect dots.

### 2
- Turn your paper over. Hold it up to the light.
- Mark the corners of the figure that you see through the paper.
- Use a ruler to connect the marks.

### 3
- Open your paper. Look at the two figures.
- Your second figure is a flip of the first figure.
- The two figures are congruent. Congruent figures are the same size and shape.

## Show What You Know!

**Does the picture show a flip? Write *yes* or *no*.**

1.

2.

3.

4.

5. What are some examples of flips that you see in your classroom?

6. **Create Your Own** If you flip a figure several times, you can make a pattern. Create a flip pattern and share it with your classmates.

7. **Critical Thinking** Does the direction a figure faces make a difference in whether it is congruent to another figure?

8. Is a square that measures 4 inches on one side congruent to another square that measures 4 inches on one side?

# Turns

**What You'll Need:**
▶ heavy paper
▶ scissors
▶ pattern blocks

**M**any things work by turning. Door knobs, bicycle wheels, and Ferris wheels are only a few.

By rotating a figure, you can show a whole turn.

## Here's A Way! Show a whole turn.

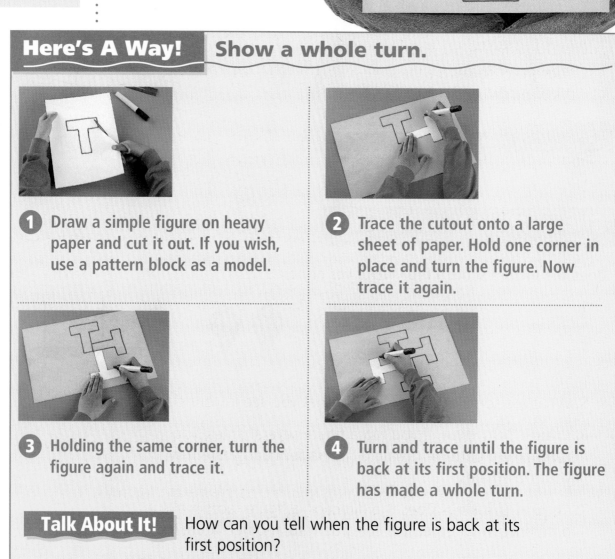

**1** Draw a simple figure on heavy paper and cut it out. If you wish, use a pattern block as a model.

**2** Trace the cutout onto a large sheet of paper. Hold one corner in place and turn the figure. Now trace it again.

**3** Holding the same corner, turn the figure again and trace it.

**4** Turn and trace until the figure is back at its first position. The figure has made a whole turn.

**Talk About It!** How can you tell when the figure is back at its first position?

## Show What You Know!

Which of these drawings show a turn? Explain how you know.

1. V
   •<

2. B
   •B

3. ⌇ • ⌇

4. A
   •
   A

How many turns were used to make each design?

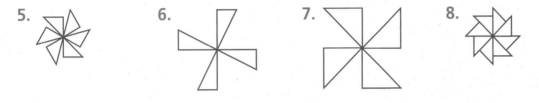

5.

6.

7.

8.

9. **Critical Thinking** Use the pattern block that is a yellow hexagon. As you turn it, why is it difficult to tell when it is back at its first position?

## Work It Out!

Is the figure a turn of the shaded figure? Write *yes* or *no*.

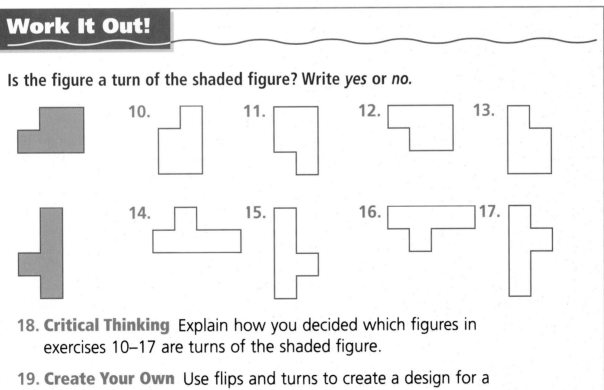

10.

11.

12.

13.

14.

15.

16.

17.

18. **Critical Thinking** Explain how you decided which figures in exercises 10–17 are turns of the shaded figure.

19. **Create Your Own** Use flips and turns to create a design for a book cover. Share with classmates how you created your design.

# Angles

**Vocabulary:**
angle
perpendicular
right angle
vertex (vertices)
Glossary, p. 516

**A**n **angle** is a figure that is formed when two rays meet. The hands of a clock form angles. You can learn more about turns and angles using the hands of a clock.

## Activity

### Right angle

A quarter turn is the same as turning a quarter of the way around a circle.

Put the hands of a clock together. Then move one hand a quarter turn. This makes a **right angle**.

### Vertex

An angle is formed by two rays that meet at a common point. The point is called a **vertex**.

Find the vertex on your clock face.

## Perpendicular lines

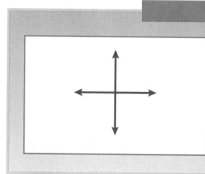

Two lines that meet to form right angles are called **perpendicular** lines.

Look at clock hands that form a right angle. Suppose you could extend the hands past the vertex. You would create perpendicular lines.

# Show What You Know!

**Is the angle a right angle? Write *yes* or *no*.**

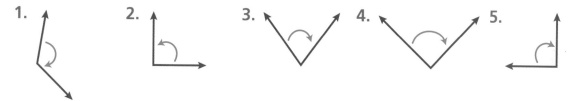

1.    2.    3.    4.    5.

6. **Critical Thinking** If you extend the rays in exercise 5, will they be perpendicular? Explain how you know.

7. How many right angles does a square have? Draw a square and check your answer.

8. Look at the path from *A* to *B* in the photograph. How many right angles appear along the path?

9. On dot paper mark a square with 5 dots on each side. Mark points *A* and *B* like those in the photograph. Draw a path from *A* to *B* with 3 right angles. Draw a path with 4, and then 5 right angles. Compare the lengths of the paths.

10. Can you draw a path from *A* to *B* that has 6 right angles? Show how you got your answer.

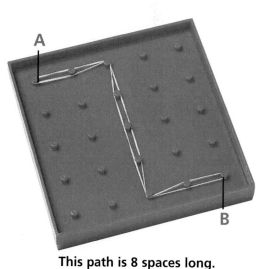

**This path is 8 spaces long.**

## Math Journal

List examples of right angles you see around you at school and at home. Choose an object on your list and draw it without right angles. What happens?

More Practice Set 5.3, p. 489

# Symmetry

**What You'll Need:**
► recording sheet
► scissors
► grid paper

**Vocabulary:**
line of symmetry
Glossary, p. 516

**T**his design shows symmetry. If you draw a line from top to bottom through the center, the design on each side will match. This line is called a **line of symmetry.**

How can you find out if a figure has one or more lines of symmetry?

## Here's A Way! Find lines of symmetry.

**1** Cut a simple figure out of grid paper. Fold it through the center so that both parts match. The fold line is a line of symmetry.

**2** Unfold the figure. Does it have other lines of symmetry? Fold the figure again to check.

### Talk About It!

To create a line of symmetry, does it matter where you fold a figure? Why or why not?

## Show What You Know!

Use the recording sheet.

1. Which letters of the alphabet have a line of symmetry?

2. If a letter has one or more lines of symmetry, draw the lines on your recording sheet.

ABCDEF
GHIJKL
MNOPQ
RSTUV
WXYZ

## Work It Out!

**Is the dotted line a line of symmetry for the figure? Write *yes* or *no*.**

3.

4.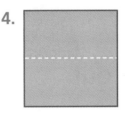

5.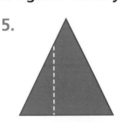

6.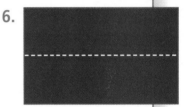

7. Does the figure in exercise 6 have more than one line of symmetry? Explain.

8. Predict how many lines of symmetry this figure has. Trace the shape, cut it out, and fold it. Were you correct?

9. **Critical Thinking** If a square is larger or smaller, does that change the number of lines of symmetry it has? Explain.

### Problem Solving

**A builder dropped and broke the tiles below. Match the missing piece to the tile. Hint: The tiles had lines of symmetry.**

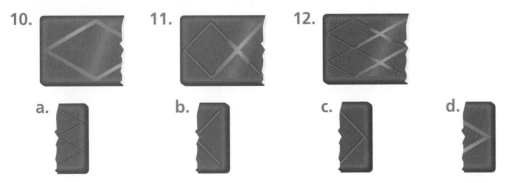

10.  11.  12.

a. b. c. d.

13. **Create Your Own** Design your own symmetrical tile. How many lines of symmetry does it have?

# Problem Solving

## Act It Out

**Getting Started**

**What You'll Need:**
▶ scrap paper
▶ tape
▶ ruler

**Y**ou are making a crown to fit a puppet. The bottom edge of the crown will be the same length as the distance around the puppet's head. Its head is 2 inches across. How long will the bottom edge be? You can solve this problem by acting it out.

## Here's A Way! Use Act It Out

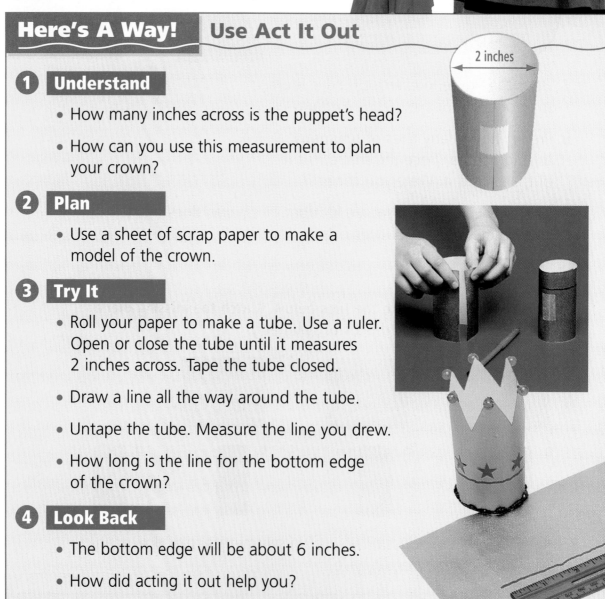

2 inches

**1 Understand**

- How many inches across is the puppet's head?

- How can you use this measurement to plan your crown?

**2 Plan**

- Use a sheet of scrap paper to make a model of the crown.

**3 Try It**

- Roll your paper to make a tube. Use a ruler. Open or close the tube until it measures 2 inches across. Tape the tube closed.

- Draw a line all the way around the tube.

- Untape the tube. Measure the line you drew.

- How long is the line for the bottom edge of the crown?

**4 Look Back**

- The bottom edge will be about 6 inches.

- How did acting it out help you?

# Show What You Know!

**Use Act It Out to solve the problem.**

1. You are designing a blanket. You want to use one circle surrounded by other circles as a design pattern. All the circles will be the same size. How many circles will fit around one circle?

2. **Critical Thinking** Will the answer to problem 1 change if you use smaller or larger circles? Explain.

# Work It Out!

**Use Act It Out or any other strategy to solve the problem. Show your work.**

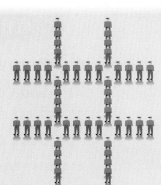

3. Twelve groups of marchers line up in a ticktacktoe formation. How can they make 3 identical squares if only 4 groups move? Hint: The squares touch only at the corners.

4. How can you arrange 9 toothpicks to form 4 equal-sized triangles?

5. First draw a square. Then draw a line from the top left corner to the bottom right corner. Is this line the same length as a side of the square? Explain.

6. You have two pitchers. One holds 5 cups. The other holds 3 cups. You need 2 cups for a recipe. How can you use the two pitchers to measure 4 cups?

7. The artist Leonardo da Vinci kept notes. He wrote some notes so you can read them only by holding them up to a mirror. How might you write your name in mirror writing?

8. **Create Your Own** Write a problem that you think can best be solved by acting it out. Challenge a friend to solve your problem.

## Share Your Thinking

9. Discuss one problem you solved by acting it out. What is different about solving problems like this?

10. **Write About It** Describe how you decided what type of model to use to act out two of the problems.

**Getting Started**

**What You'll Need:**
▶ pattern blocks
▶ heavy paper
▶ scissors
▶ colored markers

**T**he Ndebele (en duh BEL ay) peoples of southern Africa produce a beautiful form of art. The women cover the walls of their houses with bright colors in bold patterns. You can use slides to create similar patterns.

# Design a Bookmark!

### Activity

- Draw a figure. Cut it out. Trace around it.
- Slide the figure, without turning or flipping it. Trace it again.
- Slide the figure again to make a pattern.

**1**

- Copy a figure used in an Ndebele design onto heavy paper. (Or trace a pattern block.)
- Cut it out.
- Trace around it on dot paper.

- Slide the figure in one direction on your dot paper. Be careful not to turn the figure when sliding it.
- Trace the figure again.

- Continue to slide and trace until you have created a row that shows many slides.
- Color your design. Cut off extra paper around the pattern to form a strip. This is your bookmark.

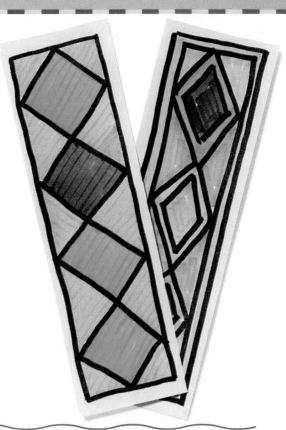

## Show What You Know!

1. **Critical Thinking** When you traced your figure, did you make congruent figures? Remember that figures are congruent when they have the same size and shape. Make another design with the figures you traced.

**The arrow shows the direction to slide the figure. Copy each figure and cut it out. Then trace it, slide it, and trace it again.**

2.     3.     4.     5.

6. Will the figure in exercise 2 be congruent no matter what distance you slide it? Will that be true for exercises 3–5?

7. **Patterns** The pattern shows a slide. Draw the figure used for the slide.

**Mixed Review**   Write the answer.

8. 7 × 6      9. 10 × 5      10. 56 ÷ 7      11. 63 ÷ 9

12. 9 × 4     13. 8 × 9      14. 64 ÷ 8      15. 70 ÷ 10

**More Practice Set 5.6, p. 489**

# Ordered Pairs

## Hidden Treasure

This map shows hidden treasures. How could clues be given to find them? One way is to use **ordered pairs.** An ordered pair represents a point on the grid.

You can use ordered pairs to locate the treasures. Where is the crown?

### Here's A Way!  Use ordered pairs.

**1** In ordered pairs, the first number represents how many spaces to move across. The second number represents how many spaces to move up. Use your fingers to help you find the point where the lines cross.

Start at point 0. Count spaces across to find 2. Count spaces up to find 4.

**2** Write the ordered pair.

Your clue for the treasure hidden there would be (2,4).

The crown is located at point (2,4).

### Talk About It!

Would the treasure hunters find the same treasure if you changed the order of the pair of numbers? Explain.

Write the ordered pairs for the other hidden treasures. Use the map on page 178.

1. vase

2. coin

3. ring

4. **Critical Thinking** Why is it important to make sure the numbers in an ordered pair are in the correct order? Explain.

## Work It Out!

Where do the students sit? Use the map of desks in a classroom to write an ordered pair to locate each student.

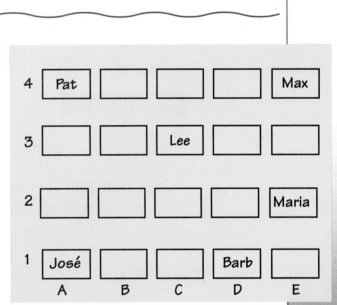

5. José

6. Pat

7. Lee

8. Barb

9. Maria

10. Max

11. **Patterns** What are the two ordered pairs that come next in the pattern?
   a. (1,3)  (1,5)  (1,7)  (1,9)
   b. (0,1)  (2,3)  (4,5)  (6,7)

### Problem Solving

12. An old oak tree is located at (3,3) on a map. A valuable ring is located at (2,1). A jeweled sword is located at (4,6). Is the ring or the sword closer to the oak tree? How do you know?

13. **Create Your Own** Draw a treasure map on grid paper. Use ordered pairs to locate 6 treasures at different points. Give your map to a classmate. Have your classmate find the ordered pair for each treasure.

**More Practice Set 5.7, p. 490**

# Quadrilaterals and Other Polygons

Cooperative Learning
**Checklist**

☐ Work alone.
☑ Work with a partner.
☐ Work with a group.

**H**ave you ever noticed the different figures in flag designs from around the world? You can make figures like these by using a geoboard and dot paper.

Czech Republic

## Making Flags!

### Activity

• **Find polygons in flag designs.**

• **Copy polygons and other figures on a geoboard.**

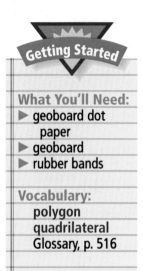

**Getting Started**

**What You'll Need:**
▶ geoboard dot paper
▶ geoboard
▶ rubber bands

**Vocabulary:**
polygon
quadrilateral
Glossary, p. 516

**1**

Look at *a, b,* and *c.* Figure *a* is an open figure. Figures *b* and c are closed figures. They have an inside and an outside.

Figures *b* and c are also polygons. A **polygon** is a closed figure made of line segments. It has three or more sides.

Make a few open and closed figures.

a

b

c

A polygon with four sides is called a **quadrilateral**.
- Use geoboards to copy the figures that you find in the two flags on these pages. Record them on dot paper.
- Use several polygons and quadrilaterals together to draw a flag design.

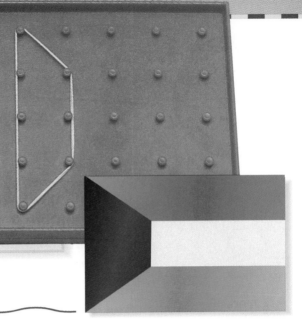

Kuwait

## Show What You Know!

1. Copy and complete the chart.

| Shape | | | | | | | |
|---|---|---|---|---|---|---|---|
| **Name** | square | rectangle | triangle | parallelogram | hexagon | pentagon | octagon |
| **Sides** | 4 | ? | 3 | ? | ? | ? | ? |
| **Vertices** | ? | ? | ? | 4 | ? | ? | 8 |

2. Draw different polygons and label them with the number of sides and the number of vertices.

3. **Critical Thinking** If you draw a figure that has 3 vertices and 4 sides, will it be open or closed?

4. Try to draw a figure that has 4 vertices and 3 sides. Describe what you discover.

**Is the figure a polygon? Write *yes* or *no*. Explain your answer.**

5.

6.

7.

8.

**Create the figure on a geoboard. Then record it on dot paper.**

9. a triangle with one pair of perpendicular sides

10. a quadrilateral with only two right angles

11. a polygon with at least one right angle

12. **Logical Reasoning** Suppose you hike on your favorite trail. The trail forms a closed figure. How far from your starting point will you be when you finish your hike?

# Problem Solving
## Is There Enough Information?

**A** friend gives you directions from sculpture A to sculpture B. "Start at sculpture A. Walk 4 squares east. Make a quarter turn to the left. Walk to the big tree. Then walk 3 squares."

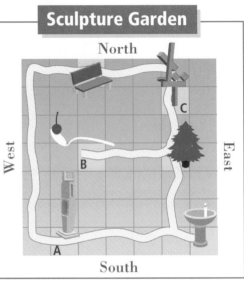

**Sculpture Garden**

North

West

East

South

C

B

A

### Is There Enough Information?

Ask Yourself:

Do I have all the facts I need?

If not, what information do I need?

## You Decide

- Do your friend's directions give you enough information to get from sculpture A to sculpture B? Why or why not?
- What extra information might help you to get from sculpture A to sculpture B more easily? Explain.

## Work It Out!

Use the map for each problem. If there is not enough information to get to a landmark or sculpture, provide better directions.

1. Walk 3 squares south from the tree. Make a turn. Walk 1 square. Where are you?

2. Begin at sculpture A. Walk 1 square west. Walk north 6 squares. Where are you?

3. Begin at the water fountain. Walk 3 squares north on the path. Turn and walk 3 squares. Where are you?

4. **Create Your Own** Write directions to a place near your school. Make sure your directions are complete.

## Share Your Thinking

5. What is easy about giving directions? What is difficult?

This sculpture, *Spoonbridge and Cherry*, is in the Minneapolis Sculpture Garden.

# Midchapter Review

## for Pages 164–182

## Problem Solving

**Solve. Show your work.** (pages 174, 182, 198)

1. Read across and then up to find the ordered pair for each boat.

   **a.** Which boat is the ordered pair (2,2) closest to?

2. How can you flip this triangle to form a quadrilateral on your paper?

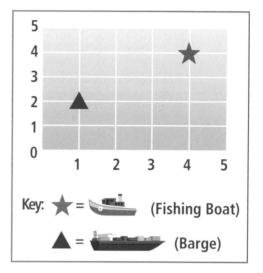

Key: ★ = (Fishing Boat)
▲ = (Barge)

## Concepts

**Choose between a flip, a turn, and a slide. Write a, b, or c.** (pages 166, 168, 172)

3. Which shows a slide?

4. Which shows a flip?

5. Which shows a turn?

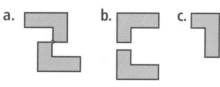

a.   b.   c.

## Skills

**Is the dotted line a line of symmetry? Write yes or no.** (page 172)

6. 7. 8. 9. 10.

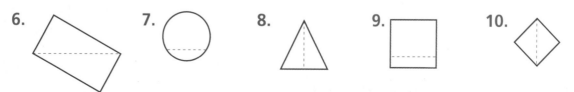

# Math World

Geometry has helped people make patterns, build monuments, and measure land throughout history.

## A Pattern Fit for a King

For hundreds of years, the Kuba kings of Zaire created beautiful new patterns named after themselves. Kings put these patterns on drums and other objects. Sometimes kings borrowed new patterns from designs found on plants and animals. One king in the 1920s got his idea from the tire tracks a motorcycle had made in the sand!

## Giant Geometry

Native Americans living near the Mississippi River hundreds of years ago built huge mounds. As you can see in this picture taken above Ohio, these mounds often formed geometric figures. A similar group of mounds has sides measuring 928 feet, 926 feet, 939 feet, and 951 feet. Its corners form almost perfect right angles.

# Try This!

## KUBA GEOMETRIC PATTERNS

The Kuba people used symmetry and geometric figures to make cloth and carved objects. People who created new patterns were rewarded by having the patterns named after them. What kind of pattern would you want to have named after you?

**1** Create a design by tracing pattern blocks or other small objects.

**2** Cut out the figures you drew or traced.

**3** Slide, flip, or turn the figures you cut out to help you create a pattern.

**4** Decorate personal items, such as a notebook cover, with your own pattern.

## The Sky's the Limit

People have been using geometry to measure and divide land for thousands of years. Today, as cities have become more crowded, the air above them has become as valuable as the land below. Now people are measuring and dividing the air above cities too!

**Respond**

Work with a partner . . .
to find and describe examples of geometric patterns in your classroom.

**Internet:**
**Houghton Mifflin Education Place**
Explore the Math Center at
http://www.eduplace.com

# Counting Squares

**Getting Started**

**What You'll Need:**
► dot or grid paper
► tiles
► markers

**W**hen you have a figure made out of squares, you can count the squares to find out how many square units are in the figure.

# Figure It Out!

### Activity

- **Use tiles to build figures.**
- **Copy the figures.**
- **Count the square units.**
- **Continue the pattern.**

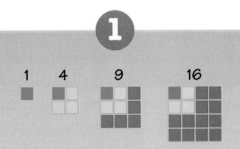

**1**

1  4  9  16

- Use tiles to build the figures shown above.
- Each tile equals one square unit.
- Copy the figures onto grid paper.
- Count the square units. Record the numbers.

**3**

Continue the pattern. Build the sixth figure. Record the number of square units in the figure. What shape is in every figure in the pattern?

**2**

What would the next figure in the pattern look like? Use tiles and grid paper to build the figure. Record the number of square units in the figure.

## Show What You Know!

1. Use grid paper or tiles. Draw the figures shown. Continue the pattern. Draw the figure that will come next. Record the number of square units in each figure.

2. **Write About It** Describe in words the pattern in c.

3. Make 5 different figures using 4 tiles. Be sure the tiles are connected along one whole side when you make each figure. Draw the figures on grid paper.

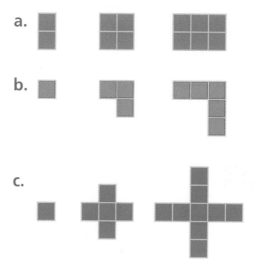

a.

b.

c.

4. **Logical Reasoning** Can one rectangle be longer than another but have fewer square units? Use words and pictures to explain your thinking.

**Copy the figure onto grid paper. Tell how many square units are in the figure.**

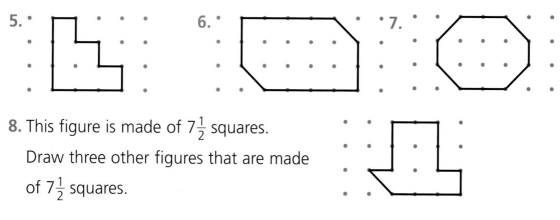

5.

6.

7.

8. This figure is made of $7\frac{1}{2}$ squares.

Draw three other figures that are made of $7\frac{1}{2}$ squares.

# Area

Getting Started

**What You'll Need:**
▶ tiles
▶ squared paper
▶ centimeter-squared paper

**Vocabulary:**
area
Glossary, p. 516

**T**he **area** of a figure is the number of square units it covers. One way to measure area is to count the number of square units. You can also use addition and multiplication.

## Here's A Way!  Find the area.

**Count**

There are 6 tiles in each figure, so the area for each figure is 6 square units.

---

**Add and Multiply**

Arrange the tiles of one figure into an array. You can add to find the area.

**2 + 2 + 2 = 6**

Or you can multiply the number of rows in the array by the number of tiles in each row.

**3 × 2 square units = 6 square units**

### Talk About It!

If you rearrange the tiles to make different figures, will the area be the same? Explain your answer.

**What is the area of the figure? Explain how you found your answer.**

1.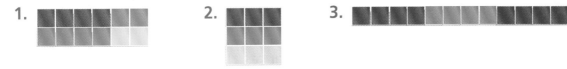

2.

3.

4. **Mental Math** What numbers could you multiply to find the area of the figure in exercise 3?

5. **Estimation** Estimate the area of the triangle at right.

6. Use squared paper to draw three rectangles with different shapes, but the same area. Each rectangle should have an area of 18 square units.

## Work It Out!

Suppose these squares are drawn on centimeter-squared paper. Give the area of each in square centimeters.

7.

8.

9.

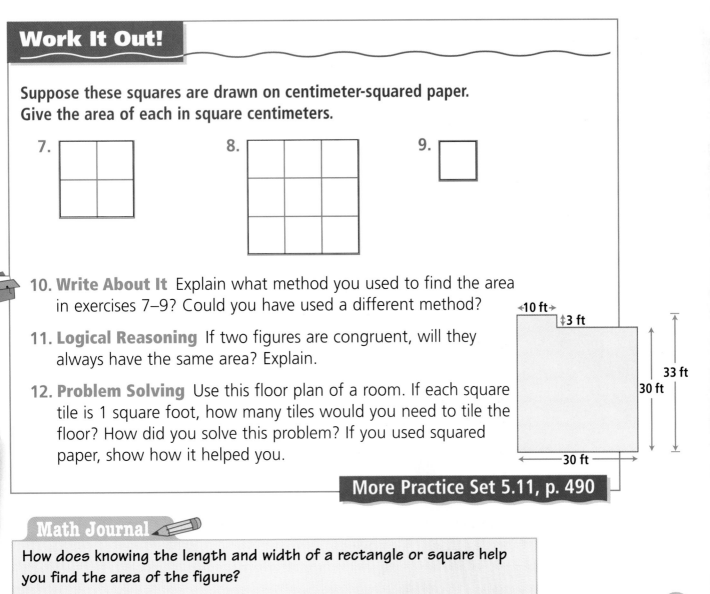

10. **Write About It** Explain what method you used to find the area in exercises 7–9? Could you have used a different method?

11. **Logical Reasoning** If two figures are congruent, will they always have the same area? Explain.

12. **Problem Solving** Use this floor plan of a room. If each square tile is 1 square foot, how many tiles would you need to tile the floor? How did you solve this problem? If you used squared paper, show how it helped you.

**10 ft** **3 ft**

**33 ft**

**30 ft**

**30 ft**

**More Practice Set 5.11, p. 490**

### Math Journal

How does knowing the length and width of a rectangle or square help you find the area of the figure?

# LESSON 12

# Congruence and Similarity

Cooperative Learning
Checklist

☑ Work alone.
☐ Work with a partner.
☐ Work with a group.

**Getting Started**

**What You'll Need:**
▶ dot paper or
tracing paper
▶ markers
▶ rulers
▶ scissors

**Vocabulary:**
similar figures
Glossary, p. 516

**S**ometimes you can have figures that are the same shape but are not the same size. These are called **similar figures**.

# Triangle Mystery!

**Activity**

• Copy these 5 triangles.

• Cut them out.

• Solve the mystery. Fit the four smaller triangles together to match the large one.

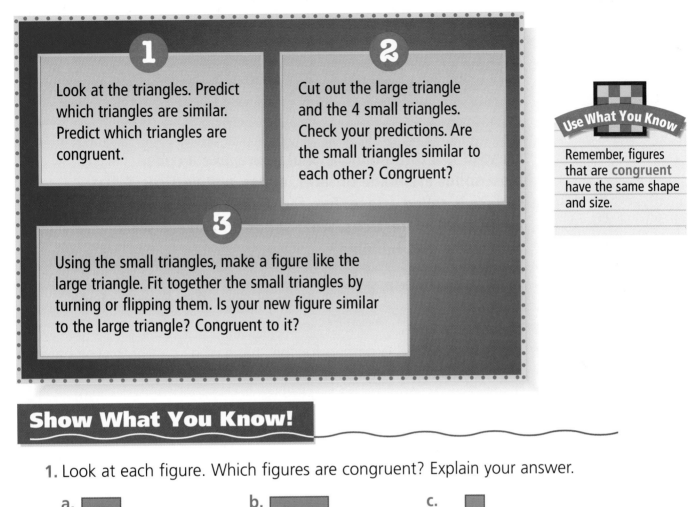

**1** Look at the triangles. Predict which triangles are similar. Predict which triangles are congruent.

**2** Cut out the large triangle and the 4 small triangles. Check your predictions. Are the small triangles similar to each other? Congruent?

**3** Using the small triangles, make a figure like the large triangle. Fit together the small triangles by turning or flipping them. Is your new figure similar to the large triangle? Congruent to it?

## Show What You Know!

1. Look at each figure. Which figures are congruent? Explain your answer.

a.

b.

c.

d.

e.

f.

**Are the figures similar? Write *yes* or *no*.**

2.

3.

4.

5. **Critical Thinking** Are all congruent figures similar? Are all similar figures congruent? Explain.

6. Copy the figure. Draw as many triangles as you can inside the box that are congruent to this triangle.

**Mixed Review**  Find the answer.

7. 5 × 400    8. 5 × 40    9. 1397 + 67    10. 5006 − 1597

# Solids

A solid is a three-dimensional figure, like a cube. Most solids are made of faces, edges, and vertices. A flat surface is called a **face**. Two faces meet at an **edge**. Edges meet at **vertices**. What solids do you see when you look at this building?

## Here's A Way! Name geometric solids.

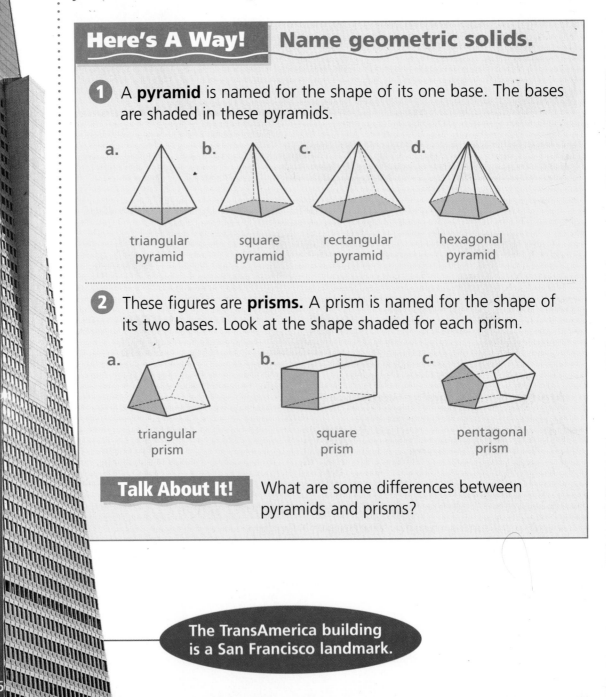

**1** A **pyramid** is named for the shape of its one base. The bases are shaded in these pyramids.

a. triangular pyramid

b. square pyramid

c. rectangular pyramid

d. hexagonal pyramid

**2** These figures are **prisms.** A prism is named for the shape of its two bases. Look at the shape shaded for each prism.

a. triangular prism

b. square prism

c. pentagonal prism

**Talk About It!** What are some differences between pyramids and prisms?

The TransAmerica building is a San Francisco landmark.

How many faces are on each of the solids below? How many edges? How many vertices?

1.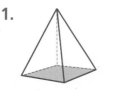

2.

3.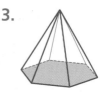

4. How many faces and vertices do you think a hexagonal prism has?

5. **Critical Thinking** Cylinders, spheres, and cones are solids, but they are neither prisms nor pyramids. How are they different from prisms and pyramids?

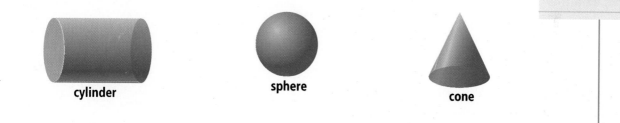

cylinder

sphere

cone

**Use What You Know**

Architects and other designers use nets. A net is a flat pattern that makes a solid when it is folded.

## Work It Out!

6. The cube is a special prism. What is special about it?

7. **Write About It** Look at the nets on your recording sheet. Each net builds a solid. Name each solid.

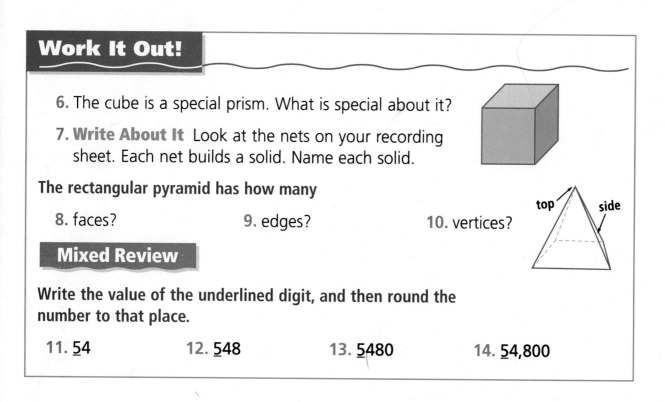

**The rectangular pyramid has how many**

8. faces?

9. edges?

10. vertices?

top   side

## Mixed Review

Write the value of the underlined digit, and then round the number to that place.

11. 5̲4

12. 5̲48

13. 5̲480

14. 5̲4,800

# LESSON 14

# Problem Solving
## Using Act It Out and Other Strategies

**A**rtists make birdhouses and so do some kids. Their birdhouses may look like castles, log cabins, or famous buildings. The birds do not seem to care! A simple box can satisfy them.

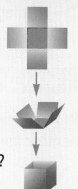

## Getting Started

**What You'll Need:**
▶ grid paper
▶ scissors

**Vocabulary:**
net
Glossary, p. 516

In 1918, students in New York posed with birdhouses they made for a school contest.

### Problem Solving Process
✓ Understand
✓ Plan
✓ Try It
✓ Look Back

### Choose a Strategy You Have Learned
✓ Guess and Check
✓ Draw a Picture
✓ Make a List
✓ Make a Table
✓ Act It Out
  Work a Simpler Problem
  Look for a Pattern
  Work Backward

**S**uppose you are using nets to design a birdhouse. A **net** is a flat pattern that folds into a solid. The net shown folds to form a cube with one face missing. You decide to make the main part of your birdhouse a cube. What 4 other nets could you use?

- How many faces should be on the cube you make?

- What do you need to remember about the size of the faces?

- How will you test each net to see if it forms a cube?

- Explain a strategy you can use to solve the problem. Then solve it.

**Use any strategy to solve the problem. Show your work.**

1. Which nets will work as a model for an open cube? Which will not? Explain.

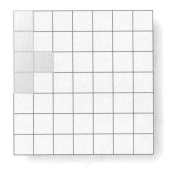

2. You have a single sheet of cardboard. You must cut out as many birdhouse patterns from the sheet as possible. Use this grid as a model. How many of the nets shown will fit on the grid?

3. Use grid paper and scissors to make a net for a pyramid-shaped birdhouse.

4. Each student on a team can put together 3 birdhouses in an hour. Each team has 3 students. How many birdhouses can a team put together in 2 hours?

5. How many students would you need to make 36 birdhouses in 1 hour?

6. You and other students make 36 birdhouses. You plan to place them on a fence 3 feet apart. If the fence is 50 feet long, will there be enough room? Why or why not?

7. A factory in your town makes cardboard birdhouse patterns. Workers can make 50 patterns every 30 minutes. How many patterns do the workers produce in an 8-hour day?

8. Look at the patterns shown. How many boxes made from net A can fit inside boxes made from net B?

A    B

## Share Your Thinking

9. Explain how you solved problem 8.

10. Sometimes you can use two strategies together to solve a problem. What two strategies could you use to solve problem 6? Explain.

# Volume

**S**uppose you want to know how much a box can hold. You need to know the volume of the box. **Volume** is the number of cubic units that a solid contains.

You can use cubes to find the volume of the box.

## Here's A Way! Find the volume.

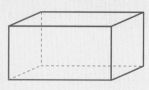

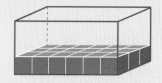

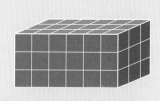

**1** The total number of cubes you use to fill the box is the volume.

**2** Start filling the box. How many cubes wide is it? How many cubes long?

**Cubes wide = 3**

**Cubes long = 6**

Finish filling the box with cubes.

**3** How many cubes high is the box?

**Cubes high = 3**

Count the total number of cubes you used.

It took 54 cubes to fill this box. The volume is 54 cubic units.

## Talk About It!

- How many cubes do you think you used to cover the base of the box? How are these cubes like an array?

- Instead of counting cubes one by one, can you find the volume of a box another way?

**Find the volume in cubic units.**

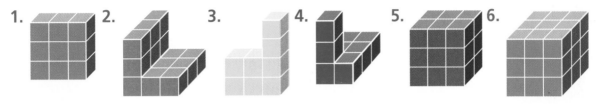

1.   2.   3.   4.   5.   6.

7. In 1–6 which pairs of solids have the same volume?

8. **Logical Reasoning** Suppose you do not have enough blocks to fill a box. How could you find the volume of that box?

## Work It Out!

9. **Critical Thinking** If two solids have the same volume, are they the same shape? Explain.

10. Use cubes to make three different rectangular prisms, each with a volume of 8 cubic units.

11. Copy and complete Chart A for the shapes you made in exercise 10.

12. Copy Chart B. Use cubes to make two different rectangular prisms based on the numbers in this chart. Complete the chart.

### Chart A

| Length | Width | Height | Volume |
|--------|-------|--------|--------|
| 2 | 2 | 2 | 8 |
| ? | ? | ? | ? |
| ? | ? | ? | ? |

### Chart B

| Length | Width | Height | Volume |
|--------|-------|--------|--------|
| 3 | ? | ? | 9 |
| 2 | ? | 3 | 12 |

13. **Create Your Own** Choose a volume for a figure. Draw it. Tell a classmate only the length, width, and height in cubic units. Ask your classmate to build the box with cubes. Did the cubes match your drawing?

**More Practice Set 5.15, p. 491**

### Math Journal

Write about a situation in which you would need to know the volume of a container. Explain how you would measure the volume.

# LESSON 16

# Problem Solving
## Using Strategies

You can read more about tornadoes in the pages of *Kids Discover*.

**Tornadoes**

**A** tornado is a very powerful storm. Its funnel of winds can swirl at speeds greater than 300 miles each hour. "Storm chasers" are scientists who predict the path that a tornado will probably follow. They use their predictions to warn people to seek shelter before a dangerous tornado hits.

## Problem Solving Process
- ✓ Understand
- ✓ Plan
- ✓ Try It
- ✓ Look Back

## Choose a Strategy You Have Learned
- ✓ Guess and Check
- ✓ Draw a Picture
- ✓ Make a List
- ✓ Make a Table
- ✓ Act It Out
  - Work a Simpler Problem
  - Look for a Pattern
  - Work Backward

**S**uppose you are part of a team that predicts the paths of tornadoes. Study the map and the compass shown. If the tornado on the map is traveling north at 60 miles each hour, where might it strike in one hour?

- How can you name some points on the map?

- Between what two points do you need to draw a line?

- Explain a strategy that can help you solve the problem. Then solve it.

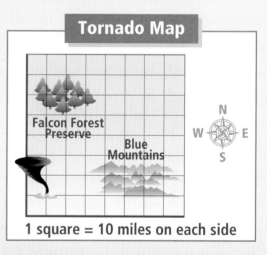

**Tornado Map**

Falcon Forest Preserve

Blue Mountains

1 square = 10 miles on each side

**Use any strategy to solve the problem.
Show your work.**

1. Carson Eads is a storm chaser. He has studied about 22 tornadoes in 8 years. About how many tornadoes has he seen each year? Hint: Suppose he saw about the same number each year.

2. Estimate how many tornados Eads will have seen after 9 years.

3. Suppose Eads began chasing a tornado in Dallas, Texas. Driving a van with special equipment, he followed the tornado for 412 miles. Then he turned around and he drove the same route back to Dallas. How far did he drive all together?

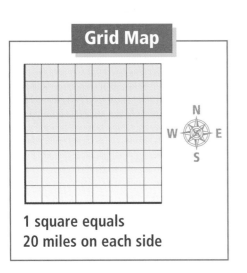

**Grid Map**

1 square equals
20 miles on each side

4. A tornado travels from south to north. It moves 35 miles each hour. How might you use a grid to show the path the tornado takes in 4 hours?

5. A powerful tornado struck the Midwest. It traveled on the ground for 160 miles, headed west. How might you show the track of this tornado?

6. Three towns are 32 miles apart. A tornado passes near one town at 2:10 P.M. and the next town at 3:10 P.M. When might people in the third town expect to see it? Explain.

7. How long might it take a tornado traveling at 30 miles each hour to move 15 miles?

## Share Your Thinking

8. Explain how you solved problem 6.

9. Choose another problem that you solved. What strategy did you use? Explain how your strategy helped you to solve the problem.

# Chapter 5 Test

## for Pages 164–199

**Test-Taking Tips**
Be sure to answer every question.

## Problem Solving

**Solve. Show your work.** (pages 174, 188)

1. In your garden you want to raise one row each of lettuce, tomatoes, carrots, beans, and corn. Plan your garden so that the corn shades the beans from the afternoon sun in the west and the lettuce is closest to the gate. What is one way you could order all of the rows?

2. If you leave a 2-ft path all around the inside edge of the garden, how long can each row be?

3. Draw the plan of this garden. Put in 5 rows. Each row is 1 ft wide. The distance between rows is 2 ft, and the path around the garden is 2 ft wide. Is there room to plant one more row of vegetables? Show your drawing.

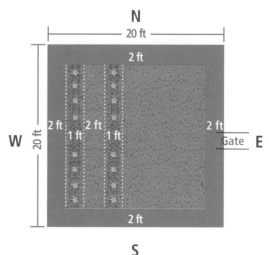

## Concepts

**Match the figure to the name. Write the letter of your answer.** (pages 171, 180, 192)

4. pyramid

5. prism

6. circle

7. cylinder

8. perpendicular lines

9. quadrilateral

a.  b.  c.

d.  e.  f.

**Find the answer.** (page 170)

10. When the hands of a clock are at 1 and 5, is the angle greater than or less than a right angle?

**Choose the correct pair of figures. Write the letter of your answer.**
(page 190)

11. Which figures are similar?

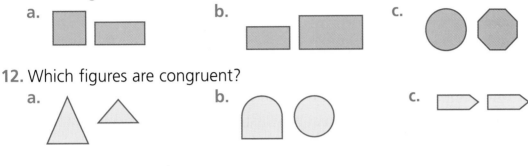

a.    b.    c.

12. Which figures are congruent?

a.    b.    c.

**Find the volume of each solid.** (pages 192, 196)

13.
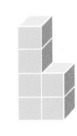

14.
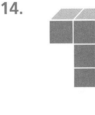

15.

16.

**Performance Task**

(pages 178, 180)

How would you use this grid to show the location of the figures below?

A triangle at (5, 4)

A square at (2, 3)

A circle at (6, 2)

A diamond at (3, 2)

```
7
6
5
4
3
2
1
0  1  2  3  4  5  6  7
```

• Explain how you used the ordered pairs to find locations on the grid.

**Keep In Mind . . .**

Your work will be evaluated on the following:

☑ Clearly numbered grid

☑ Correct figures

☑ Correct placement on ordered pairs

☑ Reasonable explanation

# Cumulative Review

**Place Value** (Chapter 1)
**What number is 10 more than 1135?**

> ### Here's A Way!
>
> Look at the tens place. There are 3 tens.  **1135**
>
> One more ten makes 4 tens. So, 10 more than 1135 is 1145.

Write the correct number.

**1.** 10 more than 130  **2.** 1 more than 1452

**3.** 100 more than 3826  **4.** 10 less than 234

**5.** 1000 more than 452  **6.** 1 less than 999

---

**Estimating Sums** (Chapter 2)
**Estimate 224 + 182.**

> ### Here's A Way!
>
> To make a front-end estimate, add the digits in the greatest place: 200 + 100 = 300
>
> For a closer estimate, look for groups of hundreds.
>
> Adjusted estimate:
> 20 + 80 = 100
> 300 + 100 = 400

Make a front-end estimate Then, adjust your estimate.

**7.** 137 + 273 + 99

**8.** 562 + 140 + 310

**9.** 786 + 504

**10.** 3250 + 2898

**11.** 2969 + 4973

**12.** 1847 + 999

---

**Probability** (Chapter 3)
**If you roll one number cube, what is the probability of rolling a 3?**

> ### Here's A Way!
>
> The faces of a number cube are numbered 1–6. The 3 appears on just one face. So, your chance of rolling a 3 is 1 out of 6.

Use a list to find the probability of rolling the following numbers:

**13.** the number 6 with one cube

**14.** the number 1 with a pair of cubes

**15.** two number 3's with a pair of cubes

## Multiplication and Division Patterns
(Chapter 4)
**Find 400 ÷ 4.**

**Here's A Way!**

Use a division pattern. You know that 4 ÷ 4 = 1 and 40 ÷ 4 = 10. So, 400 ÷ 4 = 10 × 10 = 100.

**Use a pattern to answer the question.**

**16.** If 25 ÷ 5 = 5, what is 250 ÷ 5?

**17.** If 3 × 4 = 12, what is 30 × 4?

**18.** If 16 ÷ 4 = 4, what is 1600 ÷ 4?

**19.** If 7 × 2 = 14, what is 700 × 2?

## Factors (Chapter 4)
**List the factors of 6.**

**Here's A Way!**

Think of the different ways you can arrange six tiles in an array.

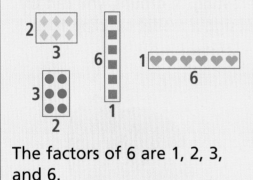

The factors of 6 are 1, 2, 3, and 6.

**List the factors of the following numbers:**

**20.** 12

**21.** 15

**22.** 5

**List the common factors of the following numbers:**

**23.** 20 and 10

**24.** 9 and 18

**25.** 16 and 24

## Problem Solving

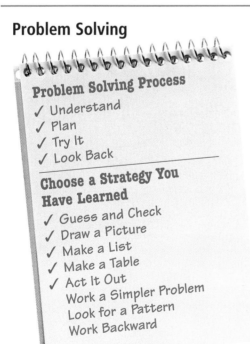

Problem Solving Process
✓ Understand
✓ Plan
✓ Try It
✓ Look Back

Choose a Strategy You Have Learned
✓ Guess and Check
✓ Draw a Picture
✓ Make a List
✓ Make a Table
✓ Act It Out
Work a Simpler Problem
Look for a Pattern
Work Backward

**Choose any strategy you know to solve the problem. Show your work.**

**26.** You have a recipe that makes enough food to feed 10 people. The recipe takes 4 pounds of mashed potatoes. Suppose you need to feed 45 people one day and 55 people the next day. If you use the recipe, how many pounds of mashed potatoes will you need for both days?

**27.** How many quarters does it take to make $5.25?

# Be an Architect!

**Social Studies Connection**   **With Your Group**

Keep In Mind . . .

Your work will be evaluated on the following:

☑ How you use geometry to help design your model

☑ How you find and combine geometric shapes

☑ Whether you make use of many different shapes

☑ How well your group works together

**H**ow can you use geometry to build a house or a school? Architects know that certain shapes are easier to build with. They also use different shapes to make their buildings more interesting. In groups, you can try out different shapes to design a model building for a new community.

## Town Hall

### 1 Plan It

- Look at the list of shapes. Discuss how you can use them in your design.
- Decide what kind of building you want to make. A house? A school? Each group should make a different building.
- Design your model building. Draw a picture of it.

### 2 Put It Together

- Find as many of the shapes from the list as you can. Use everyday objects and materials.
- Make shapes if you need to, using heavy paper.
- Put together your model.

| | |
|---|---|
| Cone | Cube |
| Sphere | Cylinder |
| Triangular pyramid | Triangular prism |
| Rectangular pyramid | Rectangular prism |
| Square pyramid | Square prism |
| Pentagonal pyramid | Pentagonal prism |

### 4 Discuss Your Results

- Have you covered all the points in Keep In Mind?
- Share your model with other groups. Explain why you designed it the way you did.
- Find out which group used the most shapes. What kind of building did that group make?

### 3 Wrap It Up

- Review your model. How many different shapes did you use in your building?
- How did using geometric shapes help you build it?

**Internet**

> Visit the **Math Center** at **Houghton Mifflin Education Place.** http://www.eduplace.com

## Math Power

### Use What You Know

- how to make an array

---

$4 \times 1 = 4$
$4 \times 2 = 8$
$4 \times 3 = 12$
$4 \times 4 = 16$
$4 \times 5 = 20$
$4 \times 6 = 24$

- basic facts

---

- product
- factor
- multiple

- the vocabulary

# Multiplying by 1-Digit Numbers

## Try This!

**Y**ou know how to make an array to find $4 \times 3$ and $4 \times 10$. You can put the arrays together to find $4 \times 13$.

### What You'll Need

grid paper, construction paper, blue marker, tape, scissors

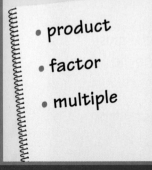

**①**

Draw an array to show $4 \times 3$. Color it blue. Cut out the array.

## ②

Draw an array to show 4 × 10. Color it blue. Cut out the array.

## ③

Tape the arrays together. What is the product?

How does putting the arrays together help you show 4 × 13?

Create your own multiplication problem like 4 × 13. Make arrays to find the product.

**Ready to Go!**

# 1

# Estimating Products

Cooperative Learning
Checklist
☐ Work alone.
☐ Work with a partner.
☑ Work with a group.

**Y**ou've learned how to estimate sums and differences using front-end estimation and rounding. Use what you know to estimate products.

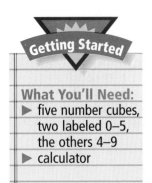

**Getting Started**

**What You'll Need:**
▶ five number cubes, two labeled 0–5, the others 4–9
▶ calculator

# Roll the Cube!

**Activity**

- Form two teams.
- Each team makes one of the charts shown below.
- Try at least six rounds of Roll the Cube!

| Team A: Front-End Estimation | | | | |
|---|---|---|---|---|
| Problem | Estimate | Product | High or low estimate? | Which is closer? |
| | | | | |

| Team B: Rounding | | | | |
|---|---|---|---|---|
| Problem | Estimate | Product | High or low estimate? | Which is closer? |
| | | | | |

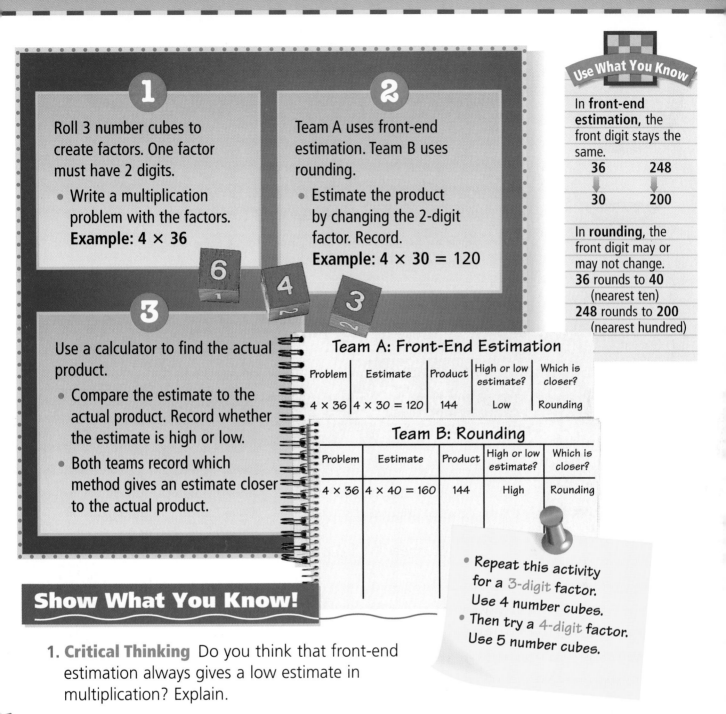

**1**

Roll 3 number cubes to create factors. One factor must have 2 digits.

- Write a multiplication problem with the factors.
  **Example: 4 × 36**

**2**

Team A uses front-end estimation. Team B uses rounding.

- Estimate the product by changing the 2-digit factor. Record.
  **Example: 4 × 30 = 120**

In **front-end estimation**, the front digit stays the same.

| 36 | 248 |
|----|-----|
| ↓ | ↓ |
| 30 | 200 |

In **rounding**, the front digit may or may not change.
**36** rounds to **40** (nearest ten)
**248** rounds to **200** (nearest hundred)

**3**

Use a calculator to find the actual product.

- Compare the estimate to the actual product. Record whether the estimate is high or low.
- Both teams record which method gives an estimate closer to the actual product.

**Team A: Front-End Estimation**

| Problem | Estimate | Product | High or low estimate? | Which is closer? |
|---------|----------|---------|----------------------|------------------|
| 4 × 36 | 4 × 30 = 120 | 144 | Low | Rounding |

**Team B: Rounding**

| Problem | Estimate | Product | High or low estimate? | Which is closer? |
|---------|----------|---------|----------------------|------------------|
| 4 × 36 | 4 × 40 = 160 | 144 | High | Rounding |

- Repeat this activity for a 3-digit factor. Use 4 number cubes.
- Then try a 4-digit factor. Use 5 number cubes.

## Show What You Know!

1. **Critical Thinking** Do you think that front-end estimation always gives a low estimate in multiplication? Explain.

2. **Write About It** Do you think rounding always gives a closer estimate than front-end estimation does? Explain. Give examples.

**Patterns** Write the numbers of the exercises in which rounding and front-end estimation give the same estimate.

3. 6 × 33    4. 6 × 34    5. 6 × 35    6. 6 × 36    7. 3 × 252

8. 3 × 257    9. 3 × 230    10. 3 × 249    11. 5 × 4498    12. 5 × 4499

13. **Number Sense** When is it better to use rounding instead of front-end estimation? Explain.

More Practice Set 6.1, p. 492

# Multiplying with Arrays

**What You'll Need:**
► tens and ones blocks
► grid paper
► markers
► scissors

**A** school van can carry 24 students. How many students can ride in 3 vans? Multiply 24 by 3 to find out.

You can use an array of tens and ones blocks, or a diagram, to find 3 × 24.

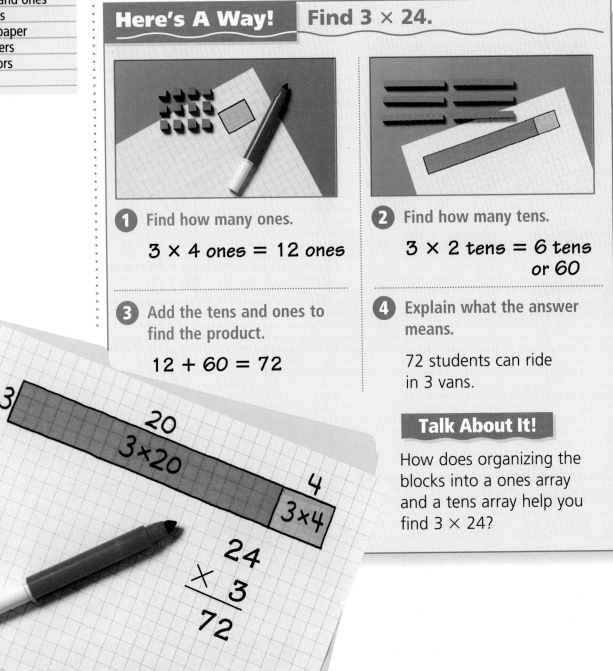

**Here's A Way!**   Find 3 × 24.

**1** Find how many ones.

3 × 4 ones = 12 ones

**2** Find how many tens.

3 × 2 tens = 6 tens or 60

**3** Add the tens and ones to find the product.

12 + 60 = 72

**4** Explain what the answer means.

72 students can ride in 3 vans.

**Talk About It!**

How does organizing the blocks into a ones array and a tens array help you find 3 × 24?

3
20
3×20
4
3×4

$$\begin{array}{r} 24 \\ \times\ 3 \\ \hline 72 \end{array}$$

## Show What You Know!

**Solve and explain.**

1. What multiplication problem does the array of blocks at right show?

2. **Estimation** Is the product greater than 100? How can you tell?

3. Draw a diagram of the array of blocks. Find the product.

**Find the product.**

4.

5.

| 7 tens | 4 ones |

6

**Find the product. Use blocks or a diagram.**

6. 3 × 23      7. 5 × 37      8. 8 × 46      9. 7 × 62      10. 9 × 42

## Work It Out!

**Find the product. Use blocks, a diagram, or mental math.**

11. 4 × 20      12. 37 × 10      13. 8 × 27      14. 1 × 97      15. 6 × 52

16.  26          17.  57          18.  79          19.  12          20.  44
    × 2              × 4              × 3              × 7              × 7

21.  12          22.  27          23.  21          24.  37          25.  64
    × 5              × 8              × 6              × 9              × 7

26. **Mental Math** In exercises 11–25, which products did you find by using mental math? Explain how.

### Problem Solving

27. A bus has 12 rows of 4 seats. If only 3 seats are empty, how many riders are seated on the bus? How did you find the answer?

28. You go to school 20 days this month. You ride 3 miles there and 3 miles back each day. In total, how many miles do you ride this month?

### Mixed Review    Write the answer.

29.    258          30.    601          31.    3695          32.   6          33.   9
     + 229               − 519               + 489              × 7              × 5

**More Practice Set 6.2, p. 492**

# Multiplying 2-Digit Numbers

In the last lesson, you used arrays to find 3 × 24. Now try a different way.

## Here's A Way!  Find 3 × 24.

**1** Multiply the ones. Regroup if you need to.

$$\begin{array}{r} \overset{1}{2}4 \\ \times\ 3 \\ \hline 2 \end{array}$$

4 ones
× 3
12 ones

**2** Multiply the tens.

$$\begin{array}{r} \overset{1}{2}4 \\ \times\ 3 \\ \hline 2 \end{array}$$

2 tens
× 3
6 tens

**3** Add the regrouped tens.

$$\begin{array}{r} \overset{1}{2}4 \\ \times\ 3 \\ \hline 72 \end{array}$$

6 tens
+ 1 ten
7 tens

**Talk About It!**  Why do you need to regroup in step 1?

**Other Examples**  How are these examples like the one above? How are they different?

a.
$$\begin{array}{r} 34 \\ \times\ 2 \\ \hline 68 \end{array}$$

b.
$$\begin{array}{r} 70 \\ \times\ 8 \\ \hline 560 \end{array}$$

c.
$$\begin{array}{r} \overset{2}{4}4 \\ \times\ 7 \\ \hline 308 \end{array}$$

d. 3 × 43 = 129

## Show What You Know!

Find the product. Use diagrams or blocks to help you.

1. 3 × 12   2. 6 × 80   3. 9 × 72   4. 5 × 34   5. 6 × 53

## Work It Out!

**Multiply. Circle the product if you used mental math.**

| 6. | 36 | 7. | 19 | 8. | 45 | 9. | 32 | 10. | 12 |
|---|---|---|---|---|---|---|---|---|---|
| | × 3 | | × 5 | | × 6 | | × 2 | | × 8 |

| 11. | 32 | 12. | 33 | 13. | 34 | 14. | 30 | 15. | 60 |
|---|---|---|---|---|---|---|---|---|---|
| | × 4 | | × 4 | | × 4 | | × 9 | | × 9 |

16. **Patterns** Look at exercises 11–13. What patterns do you see in the factors and products?

17. **Number Sense** How can you use the answer to exercise 14 to find the answer to exercise 15?

**Copy and complete.**

18. 4 × 78 = ■

19. 5 × 39 = ■

20. 9 × 17 = ■

21. 2 × 55 = ■

22. 7 × 60 = ■

23. 8 × 34 = ■

24. 1 × 63 = ■

25. 2 × 46 = ■

26. 3 × 37 = ■

27. 6 × 82 = ■

28. 5 × 79 = ■

29. 9 × 26 = ■

## Problem Solving  Using Data

**Use the chart to answer the question.**

30. Two groups of students sold cups of lemonade for $.50 each. Without multiplying, tell which group earned more money. Then find exactly how much money each group earned.

31. Suppose Group B sells 11 cups on Friday and 6 cups on Saturday. How much will the group earn during those two days?

**Cups of Lemonade Sold**

| Day | Group A | Group B |
|---|---|---|
| Monday | 7 | 10 |
| Tuesday | 9 | 10 |
| Wednesday | 8 | 10 |
| Thursday | 9 | 10 |

More Practice Set 6.3, p. 493

**Math Journal**

You can multiply in more than one way. What method do you prefer? Explain why.

# Multiplying 3-Digit Numbers

**G**ray whales migrate from the Arctic to waters near the coast of Mexico. They can travel 125 miles in 1 day. If they go that far each day, how far will they have traveled after 3 days?

Humpback whales also migrate from Arctic waters.

## Here's A Way! Find 3 × 125.

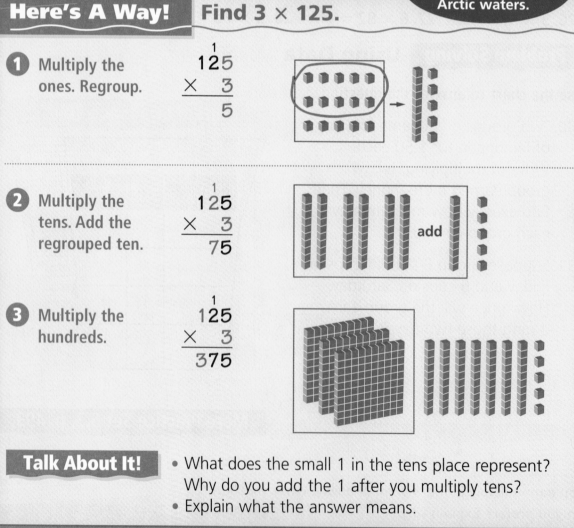

**1** Multiply the ones. Regroup.

$$\begin{array}{r} \overset{1}{1}25 \\ \times\ \ \ 3 \\ \hline 5 \end{array}$$

**2** Multiply the tens. Add the regrouped ten.

$$\begin{array}{r} \overset{1}{1}25 \\ \times\ \ \ 3 \\ \hline 75 \end{array}$$

add

**3** Multiply the hundreds.

$$\begin{array}{r} \overset{1}{1}25 \\ \times\ \ \ 3 \\ \hline 375 \end{array}$$

## Talk About It!

• What does the small 1 in the tens place represent? Why do you add the 1 after you multiply tens?
• Explain what the answer means.

## Show What You Know!

**Estimate. If the actual product will be greater than 1000, find the product.**

| 1. | 2. | 3. | 4. | 5. |
|---|---|---|---|---|
| 403 | 312 | 372 | 321 | 124 |
| × 3 | × 2 | × 5 | × 8 | × 4 |

6. **Calculator** Gray whales can migrate 805 miles in 1 week. How many weeks will it take to migrate 6000 miles from the Arctic to Mexico? Explain how multiplication helps you find the answer.

## Work It Out!

**Solve. Show your work.**

| 7. | 8. | 9. | 10. | 11. |
|---|---|---|---|---|
| 403 | 327 | 671 | 802 | 974 |
| × 4 | × 3 | × 8 | × 9 | × 6 |

| 12. | 13. | 14. | 15. | 16. |
|---|---|---|---|---|
| 397 | 545 | 545 | 121 | 121 |
| × 7 | × 3 | × 6 | × 4 | × 8 |

17. **Critical Thinking** Explain how you solved two of the exercises above.

18. **Patterns** Copy this diagram. Then draw diagrams for exercises 15 and 16. What pattern do you see in these diagrams?

|  | 100 | 20 | 1 |
|---|---|---|---|
| 2 | 2 × 100 = 200 | 2 × 20 = 40 | 2 × 1 = 2 |

**Copy and complete.**

19. $9 \times 729 =$ ■    20. $8 \times 777 =$ ■    21. $5 \times 829 =$ ■    22. $7 \times 222 =$ ■

### Problem Solving  Using Data

**Write the number to complete the chart.**

### Whale Migration

| Distance | Blue whale | Gray whale | Beluga whale |
|---|---|---|---|
| Daily distance traveled | 210 miles | 125 miles | 105 miles |
| Weekly distance traveled | 23. ? | 875 miles | 24. ? |
| Distance traveled in 4 weeks | 25. ? | 26. ? | 27. ? |
| Migration distance | 2500 miles | 6000 miles | 3000 miles |

28. Can any of these whales finish migrating in 4 weeks? Explain.

**More Practice Set 6.4, p. 493**

**LESSON 5**

# Problem Solving
## Guess and Check

There are 5 cards whose numbers total 93. Four of the cards have the same mystery number. The fifth card is 25. What is the mystery number?

Try using Guess and Check to solve this kind of problem.

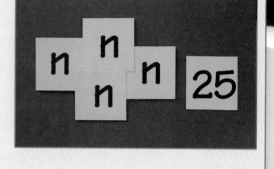

## Here's A Way!   Use Guess and Check.

### 1 Understand

- Four of 5 numbers are equal. The fifth number is 25.

### 2 Plan

- If you guessed at the answer, could you tell if the guess was right? How?
- Start with a guess that's easy to check.

### 3 Try It

- Try 10. What happens?
- Will your next guess be higher or lower?
- Guess and check until you solve the problem.

### 4 Look Back

- The mystery number is 17.
- How did checking each guess help you to solve the problem?

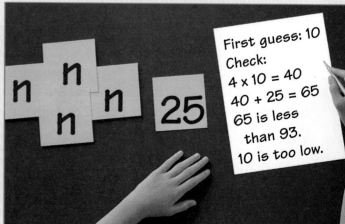

First guess: 10
Check:
4 x 10 = 40
40 + 25 = 65
65 is less
   than 93.
10 is too low.

**Use Guess and Check to solve the problem.**

1. Suppose you had only nickels and dimes in your pocket. You lost 10 coins that totaled 85¢. How many of each coin did you lose?

2. **Critical Thinking** Why did starting with 5 nickels and 5 dimes make sense? Can you think of another way to start?

First guess:
5 nickels and 5 dimes

$5 \times \$.05 = \$.25$
$5 \times \$.10 = \$.50$

$$\begin{array}{r} \$.25 \\ + \phantom{0}.50 \\ \hline \$.75 \end{array}$$

So, 5 nickels and 5 dimes is too low.

## Work It Out!

**Use Guess and Check or any strategy to solve the problem.**

3. What three numbers in a row make the second number sentence true?

$1 + 2 + 3 = 6$
$\blacksquare + \blacksquare + \blacksquare = 6 \times 6$

4. If you subtract 24 from a mystery number, the result is $2 \times 24$. Find the mystery number.

5. A store is ordering T-shirts. Each shirt costs $5. How many can the store order for $208? Why?

6. What two numbers in a row have a product of 110?

7. Suppose you have 5 coins that are dimes and quarters. Their total value is $.95. How many of each coin do you have?

**Use the chart to solve the problem.**

8. Suppose each car of a fun ride can hold up to 400 pounds. The weights of 6 family members are shown at right. How can they fit into 2 cars?

9. The sum of the weights of 4 of the people is 10 more than 600 pounds. Who are the 4 people?

| Brother | 98 pounds |
|---------|-----------|
| Sister | 79 pounds |
| Uncle | 176 pounds |
| Aunt | 137 pounds |
| Father | 151 pounds |
| Mother | 146 pounds |

### Share Your Thinking

10. Which problems did you solve by using Guess and Check? How are these problems alike?

11. When you used Guess and Check, how did your first guesses help you find the answer?

# Problem Solving
## Choose a Computation Method

**S**uppose you were in the parade shown. You want to tell a friend how many people saw you march by. The newspaper estimates that there were 500 people in each city block. The parade traveled 8 city blocks. What do you tell your friend?

*Chinese New Year parade, Chicago, Illinois*

### Choose a Computation Method

**Ask Yourself:**

Do I need an exact answer or an estimate?

Should I use a model, paper and pencil, mental math, or a calculator?

What operation should I use?

## You Decide

- Do you need to know the exact number of people who were at the parade? Why or why not?
- Could you estimate? Describe an estimate that would be close enough to tell your friend.
- Decide whether you would find an estimate or an exact answer. Explain your decision.

## Work It Out!

**Decide to estimate or find an exact answer. Solve and explain.**

1. You see 8 people holding up some dragons and 10 people holding up others. There are 15 dragons in the parade. How many people are holding them all up?

2. Your class raises $567.83 for a trip to the parade. The class spends $124.95. Is there enough left to pay $435.88 for the senior citizens group, too?

3. You have $10. Will that be enough to buy a dragon puppet for $7.95 and a fan for $2.95?

4. **Create Your Own** Write a problem for a friend to solve either by estimating or finding an exact answer.

## Share Your Thinking

5. How do you know when to estimate? Give examples from problems 1–3.

# Midchapter Review

## for Pages 206–218

### Problem Solving

**Solve. Show your work. (page 216)**

1. John tried to find the mystery weight by using Guess and Check. His first guess was 10. Should his next guess be higher or lower? Why?

2. How you can toss 10 beanbags onto the mat and score exactly 100 points? Show your work.

### Concepts

**Find the answers. (pages 208, 210, 212)**

3. Use front-end estimation and rounding to solve. Which gives a closer estimate? Why?
   a. 9 × 88
   b. 7 × 175

4. Why was a 2 written above the 3? What does it represent?

5. Draw an array diagram that would help you find the product of 6 × 738.

$$\overset{2}{37} \\ \underline{\times\ 4} \\ 148$$

### Skills

**Multiply. Show your work. (pages 212, 214)**

| 6. | 7. | 8. | 9. | 10. |
|---|---|---|---|---|
| 55 | 83 | 347 | 602 | 199 |
| × 6 | × 3 | × 4 | × 3 | × 4 |

11. 5 × 288    12. 8 × 406    13. 6 × 53    14. 7 × 690    15. 3 × 95

**Estimate. Choose the answer that describes the actual product. (pages 208, 212, 214)**

16. 4 × 80       a. less than 320    b. greater than 320    c. equal to 320

17. 4 × 352      a. less than 352    b. greater than 1200   c. equal to 1600

# Math World

Throughout history, multiplication has been written and carried out in many ways.

## A different kind of multiplication table

Today, electronic calculators are so small that they can even fit into pockets. People can carry their calculators around with them and use them wherever they want. Calculators weren't always that small, however. In 17th century Europe, people had to do their calculating in one place. The device they used to make their calculations was about the size of a pingpong table!

A teacher shows students how to add with chips on a reckoning table. This woodcut was made in 1543.

# Try This!

Ancient Egyptians understood that multiplication is just a shorter way to add. They multiplied two numbers together by halving and doubling them. People still multiply this way in Russia and other countries. Find 26 × 52 with this method.

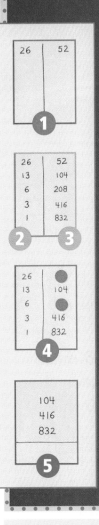

**1** Make two columns on a sheet of paper. Write 26 at the top of the left column and write 52 at the top of the right column.

**2** Divide 26 by 2. Write the result below. Continue halving each number in the left column. Ignore remainders. Stop when you get to 1.

**3** Multiply 52 by 2. Write the result below. Continue doubling each number in the right column and recording the result. Stop when the left and right columns are equal in length.

**4** Find all even numbers in the left column. Use counters to cover the numbers across from them in the right column.

**5** Add the remaining numbers in the right column to find the product. Check your answer by multiplying 26 and 52 using a calculator.

**Try:** 246 × 7

## X marks the spot

People have been using the symbol *x* to multiply for at least 300 years. Throughout history, other symbols have been used, like the ones shown here. Look at a computer keyboard. Does it use an x to multiply, or some other symbol?

### Respond

**Think about it!**

Why do you think some people did not want to use the letter x to multiply?

**Internet:**
**Houghton Mifflin Education Place**
Explore the Math Center at
http://www.eduplace.com

# Multiplying 4-Digit Numbers

**D**id you know that if you fly enough miles on an airline, you can earn a free ticket? Suppose Wingtip Airlines offered a free ticket every 16,000 miles. Would a passenger on this airline get a free ticket if she flew 6 flights between New York and Los Angeles?

You can multiply to find out.

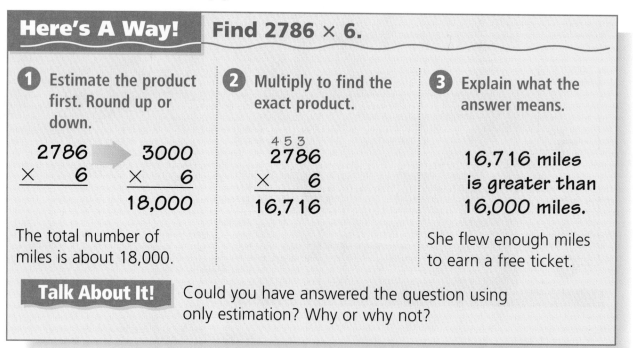

## Here's A Way!   Find 2786 × 6.

**1** Estimate the product first. Round up or down.

$$2786 \Rightarrow \begin{array}{r} 3000 \\ \times \quad 6 \\ \hline 18,000 \end{array}$$
$$\begin{array}{r} 2786 \\ \times \quad 6 \end{array}$$

The total number of miles is about 18,000.

**2** Multiply to find the exact product.

$$\begin{array}{r} {\scriptstyle 4\,5\,3} \\ 2786 \\ \times \quad 6 \\ \hline 16,716 \end{array}$$

**3** Explain what the answer means.

16,716 miles is greater than 16,000 miles.

She flew enough miles to earn a free ticket.

**Talk About It!** Could you have answered the question using only estimation? Why or why not?

## Show What You Know!

Estimate the product. Record your estimate.

1. 7 × 6492    2. 9 × 2345    3. 5 × 1995    4. 6 × 3594

5. **Critical Thinking** Without multiplying, predict which estimate in exercises 1–4 will be closest to the actual product. Explain your prediction. Then find the actual products.

## Work It Out!

**Estimate first. Record your estimate. Then choose the actual product.**

6. 4 × 4792
   a. 1658
   b. 19,168
   c. 1916

7. 6 × 7231
   a. 43,386
   b. 433,386
   c. 4338

8. 8 × 2095
   a. 1676
   b. 1776
   c. 16,760

9. 5 × 5672
   a. 28,360
   b. 2800
   c. 30,000

**Multiply. Circle the product if you used mental math.**

10.  3412
   ×    2

11.  3007
   ×    6

12.  2999
   ×    8

13.  2999
   ×    7

14.  6345
   ×    5

15. 3 × 3021   16. 2 × 2419   17. 4 × 1372   18. 2 × 4953   19. 8 × 7650

20. **Critical Thinking** Is 4 × 4792 closer to 16,000 or 20,000? Explain.

21. **Mental Math** If 4 × 1325 is 5300, then what is 8 × 1325?

## Problem Solving  Using Data

**Use the chart to solve the problem.**

22. Which is the longer distance: 4 roundtrips between Chicago and Los Angeles, or one 13,000-mile trip?

23. A passenger jet can fly 600 miles in 1 hour. Is the flight from Seattle to New York longer than 3 hours? Explain.

24. Suppose planes are checked for safety after every 10,000 miles. A plane flies 3 roundtrips from New York to San Antonio. If it is checked in New York, where would it be checked next?

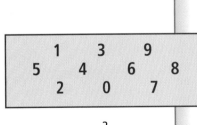

### Flight Distances

| Cities | Distance |
| --- | --- |
| New York to San Antonio | 1587 miles |
| Seattle to New York | 2421 miles |
| Chicago to Los Angeles | 1747 miles |

**Logical Reasoning** Copy and complete each exercise choosing from the digits shown. Use each digit only once. You may use a calculator.

```
  1   3   9
5    4    6    8
  2    0    7
```

25.  ¹ ¹ ¹
    2■45
   ×    3
   ‾‾‾‾‾‾
    79■5

26.      ⁴
    20■8
   ×    5
   ‾‾‾‾‾‾
    1■,090

27.   ³
    9■
   ×  6
   ‾‾‾‾
    5■0

28.    1343
    ×    ■
   ‾‾‾‾‾‾‾
    26■6

29.     ²
    ■17
   ×    ■
   ‾‾‾‾‾‾
    3668

**More Practice Set 6.7, p. 494**

223

# Problem Solving
## Using Guess and Check and Other Strategies

**Getting Started**

**What You'll Need:**
► grid paper

**S**uppose designers plan to make a sign for a dinosaur show. They want to use red and gold tiles. The sign will read:

## GIANTS OF THE EARTH

A worker welds a frame for a dinosaur skeleton.

**Problem Solving Process**
✓ Understand
✓ Plan
✓ Try It
✓ Look Back

**Choose a Strategy You Have Learned**
✓ Guess and Check
✓ Draw a Picture
✓ Make a List
✓ Make a Table
✓ Act It Out
   Work a Simpler Problem
   Look for a Pattern
   Work Backward

**T**he sign will be made up of columns of tiles. Each tile is a square that measures 5 inches on each side. The sign will be 10 feet high. The designers need to know how many red and gold tiles will be in each of the columns.

- What problem needs to be solved?
- How many feet high will the sign be?
- What is the size of each tile?
- Should you use inches or feet to decide how many tiles will be in each column?
- Explain a strategy you can use to solve the problem. Then solve it.

## Work It Out!

**Use any strategy to solve the problem. Show your work.**

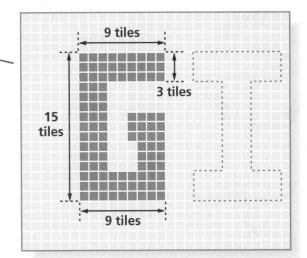

9 tiles

3 tiles

15 tiles

9 tiles

1. About how many red tiles will be in the letter *I*? Use the partly drawn plan at the right.

2. Which letter in the sign do you think will use the least number of tiles? Explain.

3. Workers put up a sign like the one shown below. Suppose they didn't pay attention and hung the letters upside down. Which tiles would still look right?

| T | Y | R | A | N | N | O | S | A | U | R | U | S | | R | E | X |

4. Suppose you have 4 red tiles and 2 gold tiles and want to put them together like the figure shown below. Draw the possible color arrangements.

5. A box of tiles costs $50. There are 24 tiles in each box.
   a. Does each tile cost more than or less than $2? How do you know?
   b. A sign will be around 200 tiles long. Will the total cost of the tiles be more than or less than $10,000? How do you know?

6. **Create Your Own** On grid paper design your own sign for a museum exhibit. How will you arrange the tiles?

### Share Your Thinking

7. What strategy did you use to solve problem 5? Explain why you chose that strategy.

8. Discuss the strategy you used for problem 5 with a classmate. Think of another way to solve the problem. Explain how to solve the problem using that strategy.

# LESSON 9

# Multiplying Money

**Getting Started**

**What You'll Need:**
▶ calculator

**Y**our class has earned $49.00 to buy games for the library. Do you have enough money to buy 3 mancala games?

Try an estimate first. Round the price to the nearest 10 dollars.

$$3 \times \$10 = \$30$$

Is this estimate enough to help you decide? Why not? Now try the calculator.

---

## Here's A Way!  Find $13.95 × 3.

**1** Press these keys. **3** **×** **1** **3** **.** **9** **5** **=**
Remember that a calculator does not have a $ key.

**2** Write what is in the display as dollars and cents.

`41.85`  **$41.85**

**3** Explain what the answer means.

Since $41.85 is less than $49.00, your class does have enough money to buy 3 mancala games.

**Talk About It!**
• In what situations is an estimate enough?
• How do you know when to use a calculator to find an answer?

**Other Examples** Compare the calculator display with the written amount. How are they alike? How are they different?

a. `0.75`

$$\begin{array}{r} \overset{1}{\$.25} \\ \times \quad 3 \\ \hline \$.75 \end{array}$$

b. `137.5`

$$\begin{array}{r} \overset{3\,2}{\$27.50} \\ \times \quad 5 \\ \hline \$137.50 \end{array}$$

## Show What You Know!

Estimate the product. Record. Predict whether the product will be greater than or less than the estimate. Use a calculator to find out.

1. 7 × $48.23
2. 5 × $3.65
3. 9 × $35.96
4. 5 × $4.10

5. 8 × $1.28
6. 6 × $.95
7. 4 × $15.35
8. 3 × $6.75

9. **Critical Thinking** Why is it helpful to estimate before using a calculator?

## Work It Out!

Estimate. If your estimate is greater than $10.00, use a calculator to find the product.

| 10. | $3.26<br>× 2 | 11. | $2.50<br>× 5 | 12. | $3.65<br>× 6 | 13. | $9.57<br>× 4 | 14. | $4.97<br>× 2 |
|---|---|---|---|---|---|---|---|---|---|

15. 8 × $1.05
16. 3 × $34.67
17. 3 × $19.95
18. 5 × $.07

19. **Algebraic Reasoning** Use a calculator to find 3 × 4.75. Record the product. Now find 4.75 × 3. Is the product the same? Does it matter which factor you enter first when multiplying? Explain.

| Games | Price |
|---|---|
| Mancala | $13.95 |
| Go | $11.35 |
| Backgammon | $ 7.69 |
| Checkers | $ 8.25 |

### Problem Solving Using Data

Use the chart to solve the problem.

20. If your class has $47, do you have enough money to buy one of each game? Is an estimate enough to answer the question? Why or why not?

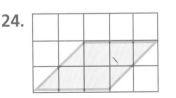

21. **Write About It** Another class also raised money for games for the library. Together you have $120 to spend. You want to purchase at least one of each game. Which games would you buy. Why?

### Mixed Review  Tell how many squares are in each figure.

22.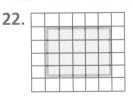

23.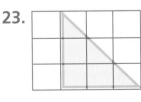

24.

**More Practice Set 6.9, p. 494**

# Problem Solving
## Using Strategies

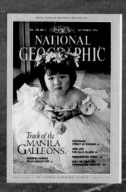

**D**uring 1987 and 1988, divers aboard a recovery vessel salvaged treasure from the *Concepción* (kon sep see ON), a Spanish merchant ship that sank in the 1600s.

You can read more about sunken treasure in the pages of *National Geographic* magazine.

This map shows an area of the Pacific Ocean, where treasures were found near one of the Mariana (mar ee AN uh) Islands.

**Problem Solving Process**

✓ Understand
✓ Plan
✓ Try It
✓ Look Back

**Choose a Strategy You Have Learned**

✓ Guess and Check
✓ Draw a Picture
✓ Make a List
✓ Make a Table
✓ Act It Out
   Work a Simpler Problem
   Look for a Pattern
   Work Backward

**I**magine that divers found these two ends of a jeweled belt, along with 95 other jewels that came from the belt. How long was the original belt?

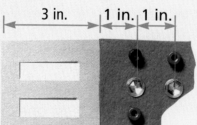

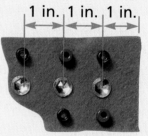

3 in.   1 in. 1 in.     1 in. 1 in. 1 in.

- What is the question you must answer?
- What is the total number of jewels?
- How many jewels are in each column?
- Look at the diagram. What other information do you know about the belt?
- Explain a strategy that can help you solve the problem. Then solve it.

# Work It Out!

**Use any strategy to solve the problem. Show your work.**

1. Suppose that a jeweled bracelet was found in 5 pieces as shown. In what order do you think the pieces should be put together? How did you decide?

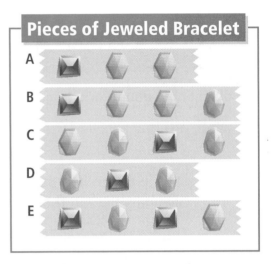

**Pieces of Jeweled Bracelet**

A

B

C

D

E

2. Long air hoses connected divers to the anchored ship. Imagine the greatest possible area divers could explore while connected to their hoses. What would be the shape of the area of the ocean floor? Hint: Try drawing a picture of the boat with the hose attached to it, or act out the problem using a string.

3. Divers found 32 gold chains, each 5 feet long. If they link the 32 chains to make 1 chain, the total length would be less than 160 feet. How can that be? Hint: Think about the links.

4. Divers found 156 storage jars from the *Concepción*. Each jar was full of sand and water and weighed more than 100 pounds. Was the total weight more than half a ton? More than a ton? How do you know? Hint: 1 ton = 2000 pounds.

5. Divers need to search a rectangular area on the ocean floor that is 90 yards long and 60 yards wide. In each dive, they search an area 15 yards long and 10 yards wide. What is the fewest number of dives they will need to make?

## Share Your Thinking

6. What strategy did you use to solve problem 5? How did you decide to use this strategy?

7. What methods can you use to organize the information in a problem? How does organizing information help you to find a solution?

# Chapter 6 Test

## for Pages 206–229

**Test-Taking Tips**
Sometimes it helps to estimate an answer before looking at the multiple-choice options.

## Problem Solving

**Solve. Show your work.** (page 216)

1. If you buy exactly $6.25 worth of Dugout and Bleacher packs, how many packs of each will you get?

2. As of 1996, the Red Sox, the Reds, the Giants, and the Pirates had all won the same number of World Series.

   • The New York Yankees held the record for 22 wins.

   • Five teams had a total of 42 wins. How many World Series has each team won?

| Team | World Series Won |
|------|------|
| Yankees | 22 |
| Red Sox | n |
| Reds | n |
| Giants | n |
| Pirates | n |
| Total | 42 |

| | |
|------|------|
| Dugout Pack | $ .89 a pack |
| Bleacher Pack | $2.69 a pack |

## Concepts

**Find the answer.** (pages 206, 208, 210)

3. Is the actual product greater than or less than the estimate?
   a. 8 × 76; Estimate 560  b. 4 × 4715; Estimate 20,000

4. You need to buy 9 baseball caps for your baseball team. Each cap costs $4.85. You have $44. Do you have enough money? Should you estimate or find the exact cost?

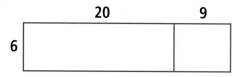

5. Write a multiplication word problem for this array diagram. Then, solve the problem.

Use front-end estimation to choose a reasonable estimate for each problem. Write a, b, c, or d, (pages 208, 214, 226)

6. 7 × 32
   a. 345
   b. 23
   c. 210
   d. none of the above

7. 4 × 288
   a. 12,442
   b. 1000
   c. 622
   d. none of the above

8. 6 × $46.00
   a. $150.00
   b. $170.00
   c. $240.00
   d. none of the above

Choose the correct product. Write a, b, c, or d. (pages 208, 222, 226)

9. 7 × 9520
   a. 6664          b. 66,640          c. 76,640          d. 91,240

10. 5 × $3.50
   a. $1.75          b. $30.00          c. $12.00          d. $17.50

Multiply. Show your work. (pages 212, 214, 222)

| 11. | 18 | 12. | 408 | 13. | 334 | 14. | 2216 | 15. | 39 |
|---|---|---|---|---|---|---|---|---|---|
| | × 5 | | × 3 | | × 6 | | × 7 | | × 4 |

Multiply. Circle the product if you used mental math. (pages 212, 214, 226)

16. 7 × 200          17. 4 × 175          18. 8 × 175

19. 10 × 47          20. 1 × $82.15

## Performance Task

(pages 216, 224, 228)

Suppose you are putting 15 lb of apples into crates. You have 2-lb crates and 3-lb crates, and you must use both sizes. How many of each crate will you fill?

- How can you use Guess and Check and any other strategy to help you solve the problem?

- Explain how you made your guesses and adjusted them.

**Keep In Mind . . .**
Your work will be evaluated on the following:
..........
☑ Checks guesses
..........
☑ Adjusts guesses
..........
☑ Uses accurate math
..........
☑ Gives a reasonable explanation

# Cumulative Review

**Rounding** (Chapter 1)

Round 6610 to the nearest thousand.

**Here's A Way!**

Find the thousands place. **6**610
Find the digit to the right. 6**6**10
If it is less than 5, round down.
If 5 or greater, round up.
6610 ➡ 7000

**Round the number to the nearest thousand.**

1. 5431  2. 8649  3. 4021

4. 1501  5. 6980  6. 7750

7. Do you think the number below is an exact number or an estimate? Why?
**34,000 people at a parade**

---

**Subtraction** (Chapter 2)

Find 82 − 34.

**Here's A Way!**

Regroup.
Subtract.
$$\begin{array}{r} \overset{7\,12}{8\,2} \\ -\ 3\,4 \\ \hline 4\,8 \end{array}$$

Check: 48 + 34 = 82

**Find the difference.**

8. 85 − 25   9. 435 − 36   10. 525 − 66

11. 10 − 0   12. 350 − 250   13. 804 − 76

14. In the Here's A Way! box, why is 7 written over the 8 in the tens place?

---

**Reading Graphs** (Chapter 3)

Find the month with the greatest sales.

**Here's A Way!**

Locate the point that shows the greatest sales. Go down to the labels to find the month. (August)

**Vegetable Stand Sales**

**Use the graph to answer each question.**

15. What data does the graph show?

16. About how much was sold in August?

17. Which month had the least sales?

18. About how much did sales increase between July and August?

19. About how much did sales decrease between August and September?

20. How much more was sold in August than in September?

## Multiplication Patterns (Chapter 4)
Write the product for 3 × 6000.

**Here's A Way!**

Use a pattern.
3 × 6 = 18
3 × 60 = 180
3 × 600 = 1800
3 × 6000 = 18,000

**Find the product.**

21. 5 × 400   22. 3 × 2000   23. 2 × 60

24. 4 × 8       25. 2 × 10       26. 8 × 50

27. In 3 × 5000, how are the number of zeros in the factor and the number of zeros in the product related?

## Ordered Pairs (Chapter 5)
Write the ordered pair for point G.

**Here's A Way!**

Find G on the graph.
Go down to the 5. (5,  )
Go across left to the 4. (5, 4).

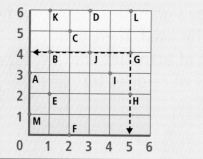

**Use the grid to write the ordered pair for each point.**

28. A           29. B           30. C

31. D           32. E           33. F

**Use the grid to write the letter for the ordered pair.**

34. (3,4)       35. (5,2)       36. (1,4)

37. (4,3)       38. (5,6)       39. (0,1)

40. Is point (5,1) the same as point (1,5)? Explain.

## Problem Solving

**Problem Solving Process**
- ✓ Understand
- ✓ Plan
- ✓ Try It
- ✓ Look Back

**Choose a Strategy You Have Learned**
- ✓ Guess and Check
- ✓ Draw a Picture
- ✓ Make a List
- ✓ Make a Table
- ✓ Act It Out
- Work a Simpler Problem
- Look for a Pattern
- Work Backward

**Choose one of the strategies you know to solve the problem. Show your work.**

41. Your friend wants to buy a game that costs $34. She saves $2 each week. How many weeks will it take her to save enough money to buy the game?

42. Your sister gets $3 each time she walks her neighbor's dog. She does this two times a week. How long will it take her to make $36?

# ·CHAPTER·
# 6
### INVESTIGATION

# Calorie Kids

**Health Connection**   **With Your Group**

**D**id you eat breakfast this morning? Right now, as you read this, your body is using up energy from the food you ate. The energy is measured in calories. All foods contain calories, and everything you do each day uses up calories. Even sleeping uses calories!

First, you will record a day's activities. Figure out how many calories each activity used. Then, your group will make a chart of activities and find the total number of calories for each.

Eating

30 min. = 60 calories

activity | time | calories
--- | --- | ---
eating | 90 | 180
bike riding | 120 | 720

# 1

## Plan It

- What did you do last Saturday? Write down your activities.
- Don't forget sleeping and eating. Look at the chart below to remind you of activities.
- Estimate the time you spent doing each activity. For example, if you ate 3 meals, you probably spent about 90 minutes eating.

# 2

## Put It Together

- Look at the chart to see how many calories each activity uses in a minute. Multiply that number by how many minutes you spent on each activity.
- Make a list of your activities and the total number of calories used.

# 3

## Wrap It Up

- Add your group's calories together. For each activity, you should now have the total number of calories used for the whole group.
- Make a chart that shows your group's activities and the calories used. Which activities used the most? The least?

# 4

## Discuss Your Results

- Have you covered all the points in Keep In Mind?
- What does your chart show? If you are tired, which activities might help you save energy?

### Calories Used in a Minute

| Activity | Calories |
| --- | --- |
| Sleeping | 1 |
| Watching TV | 2 |
| Reading, studying | 2 |
| Eating | 2 |
| Bathing or showering | 3 |
| Walking slowly | 3 |
| Bike riding | 6 |
| Climbing stairs | 6 |
| Playing sports | 7 |
| Rollerskating fast | 11 |

### Internet

> Visit the **Math Center** at **Houghton Mifflin Education Place.** http://www.eduplace.com

# Dividing by 1-Digit Numbers

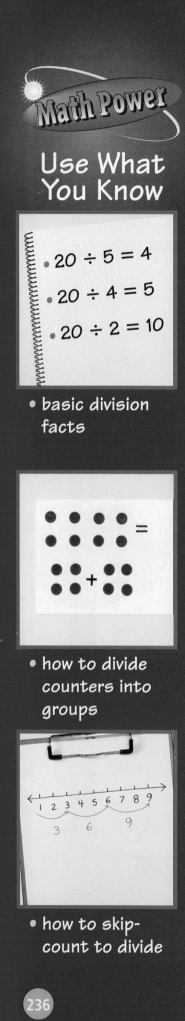
## Try This!

**W**hich number has a remainder of 3 when divided by 5 and a remainder of 2 when divided by 7? Use division to help you find the mystery number.

### What You'll Need

30 counters

**1**

Make a list of the numbers 1 through 30.

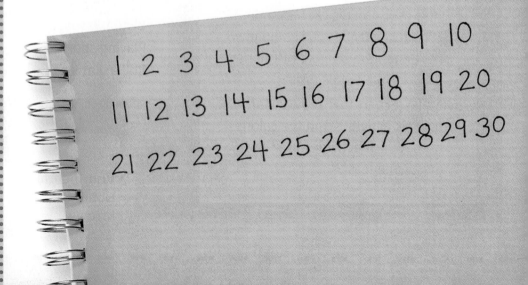

1 2 3 4 5 6 7 8 9 10
11 12 13 14 15 16 17 18 19 20
21 22 23 24 25 26 27 28 29 30

## 2

Using the counters, find all the numbers having a remainder of 3 when divided by 5. Circle all these numbers on your list.

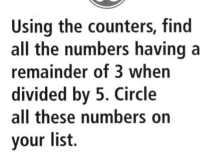

X 2 B 4B 6 7 8 9 10
11 12 13 14 15 16 17 18 19 20
21 22 23 24 25 26 27 28 29 30

## 3

Now, look at the numbers you circled. Which of these numbers has a remainder of 2 when divided by 7? Use the counters to find out. Circle that number. What is the mystery number?

How do basic facts help you find remainders?

Use counters and basic multiplication facts to create your own problem. Have a friend solve it.

**Ready to Go!**

# Division with Remainders

**Getting Started**

**What You'll Need:**
▶ number cards, 0–9
▶ spinner, numbered 3–9
▶ place-value blocks

**Vocabulary:**
remainder
Glossary, p. 516

**S**ometimes when you divide, numbers do not divide evenly. In this activity, you will explore division with remainders. The **remainder** is the number left over when you divide a number into equal parts.

# Spin and Divide!

### Activity

• Make a chart like the one shown.

• Take turns playing Spin and Divide!

• Record results in your chart.

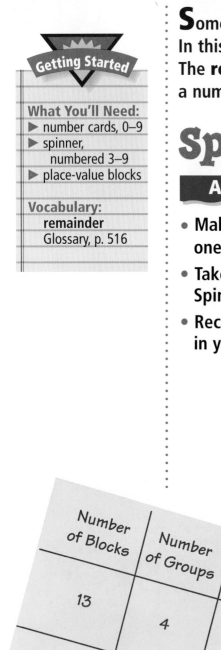

| Number of Blocks | Number of Groups | Number in Each Group | Number Left Over | Division |
|---|---|---|---|---|
| 13 | 4 | 3 | 1 | 3R1<br>4)13 |
| 34 | 7 | 4 | 6 | 4R6<br>7)34 |

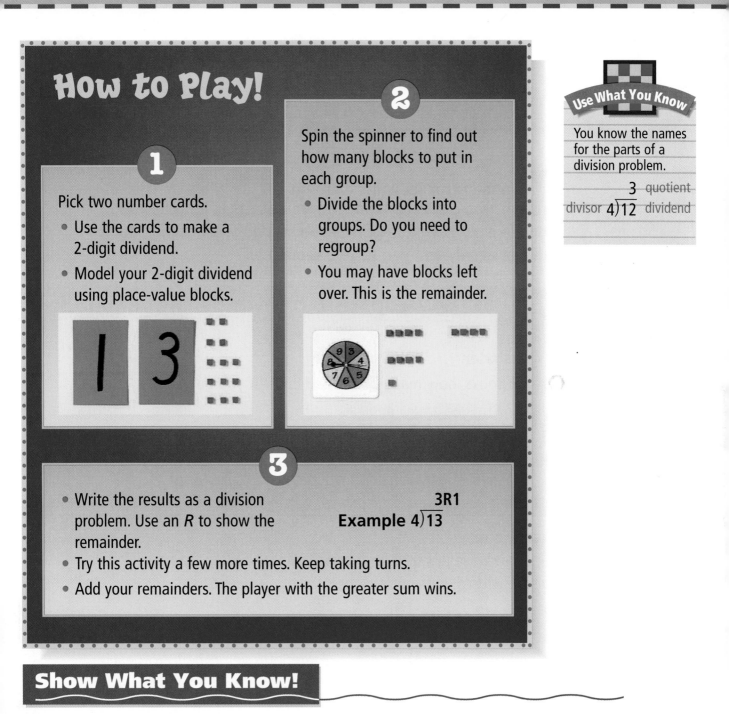

# How to Play!

## 1

Pick two number cards.

- Use the cards to make a 2-digit dividend.
- Model your 2-digit dividend using place-value blocks.

## 2

Spin the spinner to find out how many blocks to put in each group.

- Divide the blocks into groups. Do you need to regroup?
- You may have blocks left over. This is the remainder.

## 3

- Write the results as a division problem. Use an *R* to show the remainder.

$$\text{Example } 4\overline{)13}\ \ ^{3R1}$$

- Try this activity a few more times. Keep taking turns.
- Add your remainders. The player with the greater sum wins.

**Use What You Know**

You know the names for the parts of a division problem.

divisor $4\overline{)12}$ dividend, quotient 3

## Show What You Know!

Divide. You may use place-value blocks.

1. $8\overline{)34}$  2. $4\overline{)27}$  3. $6\overline{)51}$  4. $5\overline{)39}$  5. $7\overline{)49}$  6. $8\overline{)46}$

7. $21 \div 3$  8. $42 \div 6$  9. $72 \div 9$  10. $56 \div 8$  11. $66 \div 8$  12. $89 \div 9$

13. $33 \div 8$  14. $56 \div 7$  15. $46 \div 9$  16. $76 \div 8$  17. $25 \div 4$  18. $55 \div 8$

19. **Number Sense** What multiplication fact can help you divide 27 by 5? Explain how you would use it.

20. **Algebraic Reasoning** Can the remainder ever be greater than the divisor? Why or why not?

**More Practice Set 7.1, p. 495**

# Understanding Remainders

**Y**ou and 5 friends help clean out your neighbor's attic. In return, you can keep whatever you want, as long as you divide everything fairly. What do you do when things don't divide evenly and you have a remainder?

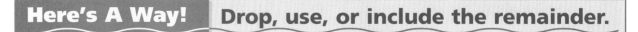

## Here's A Way! Drop, use, or include the remainder.

### Drop the remainder.

If you share 26 books, how many books will each of you get?

$$\begin{array}{r} 4 \text{ R2} \\ 6\overline{)26} \\ -24 \\ \hline 2 \end{array}$$

You can't split up 2 books among 4 people. So, you and your friends will each get an even share of 4 books.

### Use the remainder.

Your neighbor makes 15 sandwiches for you and your friends. How many sandwiches will you each get?

$$\begin{array}{r} 2 \text{ R3} \\ 6\overline{)15} \\ -12 \\ \hline 3 \end{array}$$

Divide the 3 sandwiches that are left over in half. You each get 2 and a half sandwiches.

### Include the remainder.

You find 61 marbles and some plastic cups to hold them. If each cup holds 7 marbles, how many cups will you need?

$$\begin{array}{r} 8 \text{ R5} \\ 7\overline{)61} \\ -56 \\ \hline 5 \end{array}$$

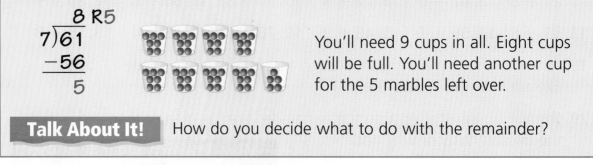

You'll need 9 cups in all. Eight cups will be full. You'll need another cup for the 5 marbles left over.

**Talk About It!** How do you decide what to do with the remainder?

Solve each problem. Decide what to do with the remainder.

1. You and 5 friends fill 21 bags with trash. Each of you make the same number of trips, carrying only one bag at a time. How can you get all the bags downstairs without being unfair to anyone?

2. You find an old train set in the attic. There are 39 cars in all. If you can fit 7 cars in a box, how many boxes will you need?

## Work It Out!

Solve each exercise.

3. You and your 5 friends find 21 tennis balls. How many balls will each of you get?

4. Your neighbor buys 2 packages of yogurt bars and divides them evenly among you and 5 friends. The bars come in packages of 8. How many left-over bars will he put in his freezer?

5. You find a toy Ferris wheel and 45 tin soldiers. There are 12 seats on the Ferris wheel, and each seat has room for 3 soldiers. If you fill all the seats, how many tin soldiers will not fit on the Ferris wheel?

6. There are 4 windows in the attic and each window has 8 panes of glass. One friend cleans every third pane. Two of you clean the rest. Who cleans the least number of panes?

7. You find a wind-up mouse. It travels 6 feet and then goes back 2 feet. If the attic is 37 feet long, how many times will you have to wind up the mouse to make it run all the way across the floor?

8. You use 19 boxes to pack what you want. You borrow your sister's red wagon to take the boxes home. Only 3 boxes can fit on the wagon at a time. How many trips will you have to make?

9. **Create Your Own** Write a division word problem in which the answer has a remainder. Trade it with a classmate to solve. Make sure your classmate decides what to do with the remainder.

**Mixed Review**  Write the answer.

10. $7 \times 4$   11. $7 \times 5$   12. $7 \times 6$   13. $7 \times 7$   14. $7 \times 8$   15. $7 \times 9$

16. $36 \div 9$   17. $45 \div 9$   18. $54 \div 9$   19. $63 \div 9$   20. $72 \div 9$   21. $81 \div 9$

More Practice Set 7.2, p. 495

# Estimating Quotients

**Use What You Know**

You know how to multiply multiples of 10.

$6 \times 3 = 18$
$60 \times 3 = 180$
$600 \times 3 = 1800$

**Y**ou can use division patterns to help you estimate quotients.

$18 \div 3 = 6$
$180 \div 3 = 60$
$1800 \div 3 = 600$

You can use compatible numbers to find division patterns. **Compatible numbers** are numbers that are easy to work with. They also divide evenly.

Try estimating $147 \div 3$.

What are compatible numbers?

4 and 2     10 and 5
9 and 3     12 and 4

You can divide these numbers easily and there is no remainder.

---

## Here's A Way! Estimate $147 \div 3$.

**1** Think of compatible numbers and a division pattern that can help you estimate the quotient.

compatible numbers

$12 \div 3 = 4$         $15 \div 3 = 5$

$120 \div 3 = 40$     $150 \div 3 = 50$

**2** Choose the numbers that will give you the best estimate.

$150 \div 3$ is close to $147 \div 3$.

So, the estimate, 50, is close to the actual quotient.

**Talk About It!** Why is it helpful to choose the compatible numbers that are closest to the numbers you are dividing?

**Other Examples:** Estimate $2579 \div 8$.

Find a division pattern.

$24 \div 8 = 3$
$240 \div 8 = 30$
$2400 \div 8 = 300$

Think of compatible numbers.

$2400 \div 8$ is close to $2579 \div 8$.
So, the estimate is 300.

Write the letter of the compatible numbers that help you estimate the quotient.

1. 492 ÷ 6
   a. 42 ÷ 6 = 7
   b. 48 ÷ 6 = 8
   c. 54 ÷ 6 = 9

2. 377 ÷ 7
   a. 28 ÷ 7 = 4
   b. 35 ÷ 7 = 5
   c. 42 ÷ 7 = 6

3. 2317 ÷ 8
   a. 16 ÷ 8 = 2
   b. 24 ÷ 8 = 3
   c. 32 ÷ 8 = 4

4. **Critical Thinking** Look at exercise 3. How many zeros will the quotient have? How do you know?

**Estimate the quotient.**

5. 372 ÷ 6     6. 592 ÷ 8     7. 539 ÷ 7     8. 1908 ÷ 6     9. 1696 ÷ 4

## Work It Out!

Write the letter of the better estimate.

10. 629 ÷ 5     a. less than 200
                b. less than 300

11. 523 ÷ 8     a. less than 60
                b. less than 70

12. 1953 ÷ 3    a. less than 700
                b. less than 800

13. 4913 ÷ 7    a. less than 700
                b. less than 800

**Estimate the quotient.**

14. 268 ÷ 5     15. 856 ÷ 5     16. 773 ÷ 6     17. 349 ÷ 7     18. 834 ÷ 2

19. 1725 ÷ 4     20. 3338 ÷ 8     21. 7247 ÷ 8     22. 2703 ÷ 9     23. 2457 ÷ 6

### Problem Solving   Using Data

24. Suppose you and 5 friends go camping. You have to carry your supplies, and you want to divide the weight fairly. About how many ounces will you each carry?

25. Suppose you pick up 1 tent to carry. Your hiking partner picks up 2 sleeping bags. How many more ounces does your partner need to carry to equal the weight of your tent?

**Camping Gear**

| Supplies | Total Weight |
|---|---|
| Food | 456 oz |
| Water | 332 oz |
| 6 Sleeping Bags | 240 oz |
| 3 Tents | 504 oz |

**More Practice Set 7.3, p. 496**

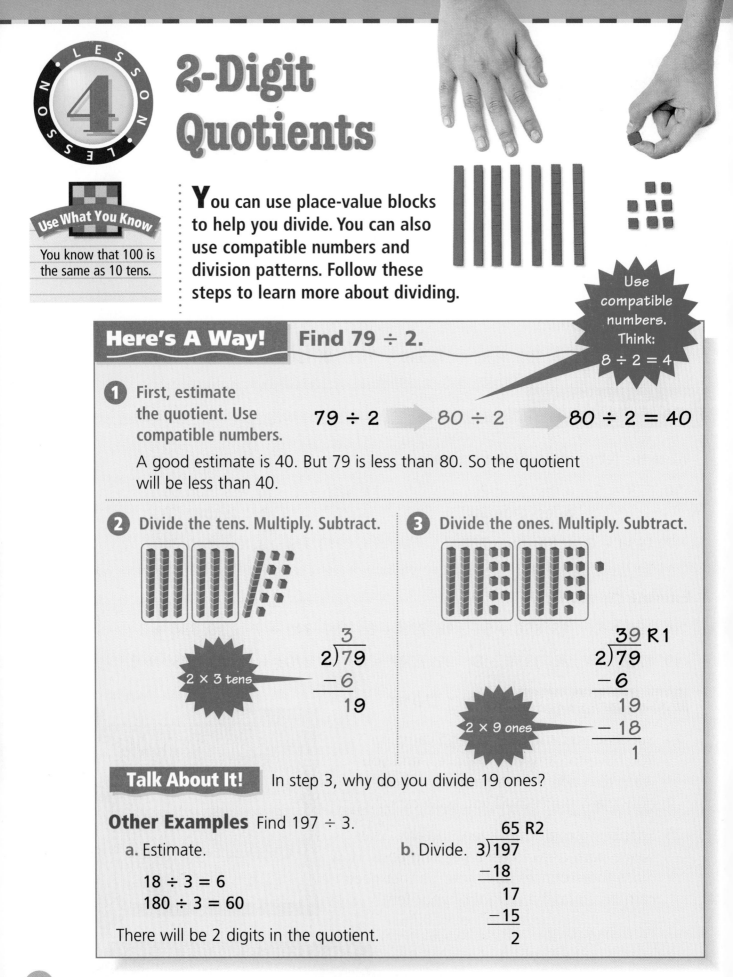

# LESSON 4

# 2-Digit Quotients

**Use What You Know**

You know that 100 is the same as 10 tens.

**Y**ou can use place-value blocks to help you divide. You can also use compatible numbers and division patterns. Follow these steps to learn more about dividing.

**Here's A Way!**  Find 79 ÷ 2.

*Use compatible numbers. Think: 8 ÷ 2 = 4*

**1** First, estimate the quotient. Use compatible numbers.

$$79 ÷ 2 \Rightarrow 80 ÷ 2 \Rightarrow 80 ÷ 2 = 40$$

A good estimate is 40. But 79 is less than 80. So the quotient will be less than 40.

**2** Divide the tens. Multiply. Subtract.

*2 × 3 tens*

$$\begin{array}{r} 3 \\ 2\overline{)79} \\ -6 \\ \hline 19 \end{array}$$

**3** Divide the ones. Multiply. Subtract.

*2 × 9 ones*

$$\begin{array}{r} 39 \text{ R1} \\ 2\overline{)79} \\ -6 \\ \hline 19 \\ -18 \\ \hline 1 \end{array}$$

**Talk About It!**  In step 3, why do you divide 19 ones?

**Other Examples**  Find 197 ÷ 3.

**a.** Estimate.

$$18 ÷ 3 = 6$$
$$180 ÷ 3 = 60$$

There will be 2 digits in the quotient.

**b.** Divide.

$$\begin{array}{r} 65 \text{ R2} \\ 3\overline{)197} \\ -18 \\ \hline 17 \\ -15 \\ \hline 2 \end{array}$$

**Write an estimate. Then divide.**

1. $6\overline{)566}$    2. $5\overline{)89}$    3. $3\overline{)48}$    4. $4\overline{)248}$    5. $9\overline{)552}$    6. $7\overline{)674}$

7. $8\overline{)193}$    8. $9\overline{)340}$    9. $2\overline{)74}$    10. $7\overline{)364}$    11. $6\overline{)437}$    12. $9\overline{)724}$

13. **Critical Thinking** If 7 is the divisor in a division problem, what is the greatest possible number for the remainder? Explain.

## Work It Out!

**Estimation** If the estimate is greater than 30, find the quotient.

14. $4\overline{)396}$    15. $5\overline{)75}$    16. $8\overline{)236}$    17. $6\overline{)93}$    18. $7\overline{)98}$

19. $2\overline{)151}$    20. $9\overline{)532}$    21. $4\overline{)125}$    22. $3\overline{)93}$    23. $5\overline{)435}$

24. $5\overline{)193}$    25. $7\overline{)201}$    26. $8\overline{)256}$    27. $6\overline{)583}$    28. $9\overline{)865}$

29. **Number Sense** If $158 \div 9 = 17$ R5, what is $159 \div 9$?

**Divide and check. Solve as many as you can by using mental math.**

30. $7\overline{)574}$    31. $7\overline{)581}$    32. $7\overline{)588}$    33. $7\overline{)595}$    34. $7\overline{)602}$

35. **Patterns** Look at exercises 30–34. What happens to the quotient as the dividend increases? Why?

36. **Create Your Own** Write a division word problem that can be solved using the compatible numbers $42 \div 6$. Be sure to include the answer to your problem.

## Problem Solving  Using Data

**Use the map to answer the question.**

37. The map shows a hiking trail at Brazos Bend State Park in Texas. You leave Point A at 11 A.M. and walk at a steady speed. You get to Point B at 1 P.M. How many yards did you walk each hour?

38. Suppose you eat lunch at Point B for 1 hour and then continue walking at the same speed. Will you get to Point D before 4 P.M.? Explain.

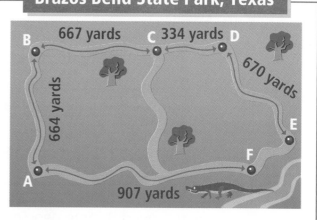

**Brazos Bend State Park, Texas**

B — 667 yards — C — 334 yards — D
664 yards
670 yards
E
F
A
907 yards

**More Practice Set 7.4, p. 496**

# LESSON 5

# Problem Solving
## Work a Simpler Problem

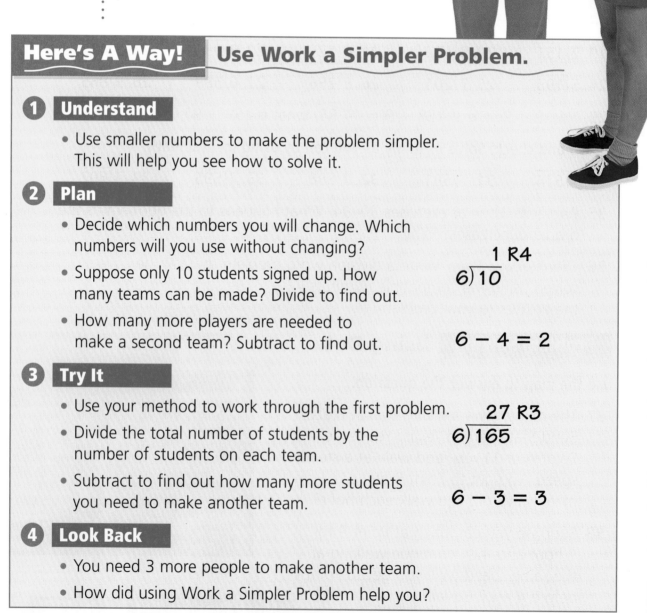

**Y**ou are organizing a volleyball tournament. So far, 165 students have signed up. You want each team to have 6 players. How many more students must sign up before this is possible?

You can start by working a simpler problem.

## Here's A Way! Use Work a Simpler Problem.

### 1 Understand

- Use smaller numbers to make the problem simpler. This will help you see how to solve it.

### 2 Plan

- Decide which numbers you will change. Which numbers will you use without changing?
- Suppose only 10 students signed up. How many teams can be made? Divide to find out.

$$6\overline{)10} \quad 1\text{ R}4$$

- How many more players are needed to make a second team? Subtract to find out.

$$6 - 4 = 2$$

### 3 Try It

- Use your method to work through the first problem.
- Divide the total number of students by the number of students on each team.

$$6\overline{)165} \quad 27\text{ R}3$$

- Subtract to find out how many more students you need to make another team.

$$6 - 3 = 3$$

### 4 Look Back

- You need 3 more people to make another team.
- How did using Work a Simpler Problem help you?

**Use Work a Simpler Problem to solve the problem.**

1. Eight teams practice for the volleyball tournament. Each team plays every other team one game. How many games are played?

2. **Critical Thinking** How did working a simpler problem help you find a pattern in problem 1? Explain.

## Work It Out!

**Use Work a Simpler Problem or any strategy to solve the problem. Show your work.**

3. There are 16 teams in your volleyball tournament. On the first day, 8 games are played. The teams that lose drop out. The teams that win play each other. How many games will be played in all before one team has won the tournament?

4. How many ways can you make $1.00 with nickels, dimes, and quarters? Suppose you always use at least 1 quarter.

5. A store is having a sale on volleyballs: Buy 2 get 1 free. One volleyball costs $9.50. How many can you get for $100?

6. The sum of two numbers is 18. If you divide one of these numbers by the other, the quotient is 5. What are the two numbers?

7. You use 6 lines to divide a rectangle. What is the greatest number of sections you can make?

8. **Create Your Own** Write a problem you can solve by working a simpler problem. Then trade with a classmate and solve each other's problem.

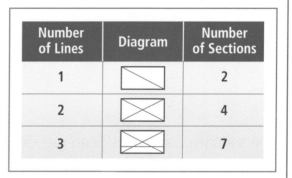

| Number of Lines | Diagram | Number of Sections |
|---|---|---|
| 1 | | 2 |
| 2 | | 4 |
| 3 | | 7 |

9. You set your computer at 3:30 P.M. on Friday so it will chime every hour on the hour. How many times will it chime before 8:15 P.M. on Sunday?

## Share Your Thinking

10. Describe the strategy you used to solve problem 9. Explain a different strategy you could use to solve this problem.

# 3-Digit Quotients

**A** saguaro (suh GWAR oh) cactus can grow about 4 inches each year. Suppose a saguaro cactus has grown 498 inches tall. About how many years has it been growing?

You can divide to find out.

## Here's A Way!   Find 498 ÷ 4.

**1** Estimate.   $4 \div 4 = 1$   ➡   $400 \div 4 = 100$

The number 498 is greater than 400. So, the quotient will be greater than 100.

**2** Divide the hundreds. Multiply. Subtract.

$$\begin{array}{r} 1\phantom{00} \\ 4\overline{)498} \\ -4\phantom{00} \end{array}$$

**3** Divide the tens. Multiply. Subtract.

$$\begin{array}{r} 12\phantom{0} \\ 4\overline{)498} \\ -4\phantom{00} \\ \hline 9\phantom{0} \\ -8\phantom{0} \\ \hline 1\phantom{0} \end{array}$$

**4** Divide the ones. Multiply. Subtract. Write the remainder if there is one.

$$\begin{array}{r} 124 \text{ R2} \\ 4\overline{)498} \\ -4\phantom{00} \\ \hline 9\phantom{0} \\ -8\phantom{0} \\ \hline 18 \\ -16 \\ \hline 2 \end{array}$$

The saguaro cactus has been growing for about 124 years.

## Talk About It!

• If the saguaro cactus grows about 4 inches a year, why can't you be sure that this cactus has grown for exactly 124 years?

• When checking the answer to a division problem, why do you add the remainder after multiplying and not before?

**Check your answer:**

$$\begin{array}{r} 124 \leftarrow \text{quotient} \\ \times \phantom{00} 4 \leftarrow \text{divisor} \\ \hline 496 \\ + \phantom{00} 2 \leftarrow \text{remainder} \\ \hline 498 \leftarrow \text{dividend} \end{array}$$

## Show What You Know!

**Estimate** Decide whether the quotient will be greater than or less than the estimate. Then divide.

1. 5)17    2. 9)270    3. 5)555    4. 4)488    5. 9)8289    6. 6)728

7. 3)298    8. 8)729    9. 7)892    10. 5)476    11. 8)648    12. 9)8118

13. **Calculator** Suppose the division key is broken. How can you still use your calculator to find 475 ÷ 4?

## Work It Out!

Estimate. Then divide and check. Use mental math when you can.

14. 7)187    15. 5)285    16. 8)247    17. 2)1578    18. 4)526    19. 3)494

20. 8)839    21. 6)366    22. 5)3972    23. 9)564    24. 9)4630    25. 8)6859

**Patterns** Divide. Use the answer from a to solve b and c.

26. a. 9)815    27. a. 3)745    28. a. 7)173    29. a. 6)4215
    b. 9)816        b. 3)746        b. 7)175        b. 6)4216
    c. 9)817        c. 3)747        c. 7)177        c. 6)4217

30. **Write About It** Explain how you found the answers to b and c in exercise 29.

### Problem Solving   Using Data

Use the chart to solve the problem.

31. An old-man cactus grows about 3 inches each year. Which of the cactuses on the chart is older, the old-man cactus or the saguaro? How do you know?

32. The saguaro grows about 4 inches each year. Which is older, the saguaro in this chart or the one described on page 248? How much older? Explain.

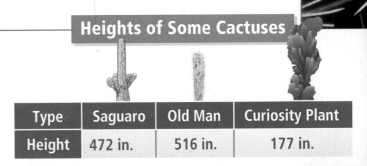

**Heights of Some Cactuses**

| Type | Saguaro | Old Man | Curiosity Plant |
|---|---|---|---|
| Height | 472 in. | 516 in. | 177 in. |

**More Practice Set 7.6, p. 497**

## Problem Solving
### Is the Answer Reasonable?

**Y**ou are studying India in school. All the fourth graders are going to see a movie that was made in India. There are 74 students. Some parents have agreed to drive. Each car holds 5 students.

Your friend divides 74 by 5. "We need 14 cars," he says. Did he use the remainder correctly?

More movies are made in India than any other place, including Hollywood.

### You Decide

- What does the quotient show? What does the remainder show?

$$5\overline{)74} = 14 \text{ R}4$$

- What if you only used 14 cars? Would all the students be able to go?

- Decide how many cars you need. Explain your answer.

### Work It Out!

**Solve. Then decide how to use the remainder. Explain.**

1. If you could go to 6 movies each week, how many weeks would it take for you to see 50 movies?

2. A theater has 126 seats. Each row except the first row has 8 seats. How many seats are in the first row?

3. A student film club earned $97 to buy movie tickets. A cinema sells student tickets for $4 each. How many tickets can the club buy?

4. **Create Your Own** Write a problem about movies that uses the remainder to answer the problem. Share your problem with a friend.

### Share Your Thinking

5. How do you decide what to do with a remainder?

# Midchapter Review

## for Pages 236–250

for Pages 236–250

## Problem Solving

**Solve. Show your work.** (pages 246, 250)

1. Your class and another class are going on a white-water rafting trip. In the group are 38 students and 2 teachers. Each raft can carry 7 passengers. How many rafts do you need?

2. The raft trip is 18 miles. You start at 11:00 A.M. If you travel 4 miles each hour, will you finish by 3:00 P.M.?

## Concepts

**Estimate. Write the letter of the better estimate.** (page 242)

3. $252 \div 3$  a. between 70 and 80
  b. between 80 and 90

4. $504 \div 7$  a. between 70 and 80
  b. between 80 and 90

5. $1235 \div 4$  a. less than 300
  b. between 300 and 400

6. $2476 \div 5$  a. less than 400
  b. between 400 and 500

**Estimate the quotient to compare. Write >, <, or =.** (page 244)

7. $359 \div 5 \bullet 376 \div 6$

8. $212 \div 3 \bullet 424 \div 6$

9. $459 \div 9 \bullet 459 \div 5$

10. $658 \div 8 \bullet 641 \div 9$

## Skills

**Divide.** (pages 238, 240, 244, 248)

11. $2\overline{)246}$

12. $3\overline{)639}$

13. $4\overline{)924}$

14. $5\overline{)798}$

15. $8\overline{)184}$

16. $6\overline{)883}$

17. $7\overline{)296}$

18. $9\overline{)466}$

# Math World

Use math to find leap years. Find out what division has to do with a well-known cheer.

Divide two numbers the Egyptian way.

## Why Do We Leap?

What would it be like to have winter in July? This could happen if our calendars were based on actual time. The earth takes between 365 and 366 days to orbit the sun. But our calendars have only 365 days. After a few hundred years, the extra time would build up, and our seasons would be turned around. Long ago, people came up with a solution—leap year. A leap year has an extra day at the end of February.

You can find out which years are leap years. Pick a year from 1900 to 1997. If you can divide the year evenly by 4, it is a leap year.

# Try This! EGYPTIAN DIVISION

To make division problems easier, the Egyptians turned them into addition problems. Follow these steps to learn how you can use addition to solve a division problem like 147 ÷ 7.

**1** Draw two columns. Write 7 (the divisor) at the top of the left column. Write 1 at the top of the right column.

**2** Double both numbers and write the results below.

**3** Repeat step 2 until you get a number in the left column that is greater than 147 (the dividend).

**4** Circle the numbers in the left column with a sum of 147.

**5** Add the numbers in the right column that are across from the circled numbers. This is the quotient.
Since 1 + 4 + 16 = 21, 147 ÷ 7 = 21.

**Try:** 126 ÷ 9   148 ÷ 4

## Three Cheers for Division

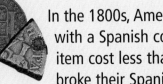

In the 1800s, Americans could buy things with a Spanish coin worth a dollar. If an item cost less than a dollar, people broke their Spanish coin into eight small pieces, or bits. These are the "bits" in the cheer, "Two bits, four bits, six bits, a dollar . . ."

## Respond

Work with a Partner . . .
to find the years since you were born that were leap years.

Internet:
**Houghton Mifflin Education Place**
Explore the Math Center at
http://www.eduplace.com

# LESSON 8

# Zeros in the Quotient

**Y**ou have 634 beads. You want to make 6 masks. Each mask will have the same number of beads. How many beads will be on each mask?

You can divide to solve this problem.

---

## Here's A Way! Find 634 ÷ 6.

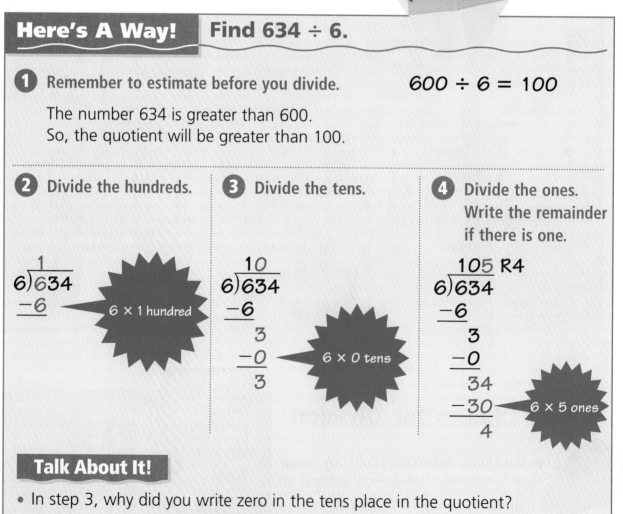

**1** Remember to estimate before you divide.

$$600 \div 6 = 100$$

The number 634 is greater than 600.
So, the quotient will be greater than 100.

---

**2** Divide the hundreds.

$$
\begin{array}{r}
1\phantom{00} \\
6\overline{)634} \\
-6\phantom{00} \\
\end{array}
$$

6 × 1 hundred

**3** Divide the tens.

$$
\begin{array}{r}
10\phantom{0} \\
6\overline{)634} \\
-6\phantom{00} \\
\hline
3\phantom{0} \\
-0\phantom{0} \\
\hline
3\phantom{0} \\
\end{array}
$$

6 × 0 tens

**4** Divide the ones. Write the remainder if there is one.

$$
\begin{array}{r}
105 \text{ R4} \\
6\overline{)634} \\
-6\phantom{00} \\
\hline
3\phantom{0} \\
-0\phantom{0} \\
\hline
34 \\
-30 \\
\hline
4 \\
\end{array}
$$

6 × 5 ones

---

## Talk About It!

- In step 3, why did you write zero in the tens place in the quotient?
- In step 4, why was 5 written in the ones place and not the tens place?
- What would you do with the leftover beads?

## Show What You Know!

**Estimate the quotient. Then divide and check.**

1. $7\overline{)705}$    2. $3\overline{)322}$    3. $2\overline{)808}$    4. $8\overline{)861}$    5. $9\overline{)641}$    6. $9\overline{)918}$

7. $7\overline{)728}$    8. $4\overline{)2480}$    9. $9\overline{)918}$    10. $3\overline{)2762}$    11. $9\overline{)9083}$    12. $7\overline{)7050}$

**Algebraic Reasoning** Write >, < or =.

13. $345 \div 8$ ● 60        14. $5793 \div 7$ ● 80        15. $563 \div 4$ ● 40

16. **Critical Thinking** Does a zero in the ones place of a quotient mean that there is no remainder? Explain.

## Work It Out!

**Estimate. Then divide and check. Use mental math when you can.**

17. $6\overline{)609}$    18. $8\overline{)5616}$    19. $7\overline{)490}$    20. $3\overline{)1891}$    21. $3\overline{)309}$    22. $4\overline{)414}$

23. $6\overline{)642}$    24. $4\overline{)4426}$    25. $3\overline{)2314}$    26. $7\overline{)760}$    27. $8\overline{)8051}$    28. $7\overline{)5483}$

**Mental Math** Describe how you can use mental math to solve these exercises. Then write the answers.

29. a. $6\overline{)600}$    30. a. $4\overline{)436}$    31. a. $7\overline{)756}$    32. a. $9\overline{)936}$    33. a. $8\overline{)840}$

 b. $6\overline{)606}$     b. $4\overline{)440}$     b. $7\overline{)763}$     b. $9\overline{)945}$     b. $8\overline{)848}$

 c. $6\overline{)612}$     c. $4\overline{)444}$     c. $7\overline{)770}$     c. $9\overline{)954}$     c. $8\overline{)856}$

34. **Create Your Own** Write a division problem that has two zeros in the dividend but no zeros in the quotient.

### Problem Solving   Using Data

**Use the chart to solve the problem.**

35. You have 1 package of string. How many pieces would you have if you cut the string into pieces 3 inches long?

36. You and 2 friends want to make imitation African masks. You buy 4 packages of paper and share the paper equally. How many sheets of paper will each of you have?

| Supplies for Making Masks | |
| --- | --- |
| Supplies | Amount per Package |
| Beads | 100 |
| String | 325 in. |
| Paper | 36 sheets |
| Paint | 6 bottles |

**More Practice Set 7.8, p. 497**

Cooperative Learning
**Checklist**

☐ Work alone.
☑ Work with a partner.
☐ Work with a group.

# LESSON 9

# Divisibility

**Getting Started**

**What You'll Need:**
▶ calculator
▶ poster paper
▶ recording sheet

**Vocabulary:**
divisible
Glossary, p. 516

**H**ow do you tell when one number is divisible by another? We say a number is **divisible** when it can be divided by another number and there is no remainder. For example, 18 is divisible by 3 but not by 4.

You can find surprising patterns as you work with numbers that are divisible. Try this activity and see what you find!

## Divide and Discover!

**Activity**

- Make a chart like the one shown.
- Use the list on the left. Find numbers that are divisible by 2, 3, 4, 5, and 10.
- Look for patterns in the numbers you find.

| 8 | 9 | 10 | 12 | 15 |
| 16 | 22 | 24 | 25 | 27 |
| 30 | 38 | 39 | 45 | 46 |
| 48 | 50 | 54 | 66 | 70 |
| 78 | 88 | 95 | 98 | 99 |
| 105 | 106 | 108 | 125 | 129 |
| 130 | 155 | 166 | 168 | 172 |
| 175 | 190 | 195 | 202 | 210 |
| 224 | 207 | 270 | 320 | |

**Divisible Numbers**

| Divisible by 2 | Divisible by 3 | Divisible by 4 | Divisible by 5 | Divisible by 10 |
|---|---|---|---|---|
| 8 | 9 | 8 | | |
| 10 | 12 | 12 | | |
| 12 | 15 | | | |
| 16 | 24 | | | |
| 22 | | | | |

**1**

Look at the numbers on the list above.

- Use a calculator to find numbers that are divisible by 2.
- List these numbers on the poster paper.

**Look at the numbers you found that were divisible by 2.**

- What do you notice about them?
- Can you find any patterns?

Hint: Numbers divisible by 2 are even numbers. They also end in 0, 2, 4, 6, or 8.

**Now find the numbers that are divisible by 3.**

- Use a calculator.
- Look for patterns in the numbers.
- Add the digits in each number. Is the sum of the digits divisible by 3?

REPEAT
- Find numbers that are divisible by 4, 5, and 10.
- Look for patterns in the numbers you find.

## Show What You Know!

**Use the recording sheet to complete the following.**

1. Write a rule about divisibility by 4.    2. Write a rule about divisibility by 3.

3. Use your rules about divisibility by 3 to complete the first column of the chart on the recording sheet. Write *yes* or *no* in each box.

4. Write a rule about divisibility by 5.    5. Write a rule about divisibility by 10.

6. Use your rules about divisibility by 2 to complete the second column of the chart on the recording sheet. Which numbers divisible by 2 are also divisible by 4?

7. **Number Sense** Are numbers that are multiples of 4 also multiples of 2? Why or why not?

8. **Patterns** Look at the chart on the recording sheet. What do you notice about the numbers that are divisible by both 2 and 3? Could these numbers be divisible by a third number? If so, what is it?

9. Use your rules about divisibility by 5 to complete the third column of the chart on the recording sheet. Which numbers divisible by 5 are also divisible by 10?

10. **Critical Thinking** Is this statement true or false? All numbers that are divisible by 5 are also divisible by 10. Explain.

**Math Journal**

*What does divisibility mean? Give examples.*

# Problem Solving
## Using Work a Simpler Problem and Other Strategies

**The** Little League World Series is held in Williamsport, Pennsylvania, every year. Teams from around the United States, Canada, Latin America, and many other countries compete for the championship.

**Problem Solving Process**
- ✓ Understand
- ✓ Plan
- ✓ Try It
- ✓ Look Back

**Choose a Strategy You Have Learned**
- ✓ Guess and Check
- ✓ Draw a Picture
- ✓ Make a List
- ✓ Make a Table
- ✓ Act It Out
- ✓ Work a Simpler Problem
  Look for a Pattern
  Work Backward

**You** are the coach of a team at the Little League World Series. There are 18 players on your team. Only 9 players can play in each inning. Your team is playing a six-inning game. How can every player play the same number of innings?

- What information do you know? What do you need to find out?
- Suppose you only played a three-inning game. Suppose also that there were 3 players on your team and only 2 could play at a time.
- How many places does your team have for players in each inning?
- What are the total number of places in a game?
- Explain a strategy you can use to solve the problem. Then solve it.

## Work It Out!

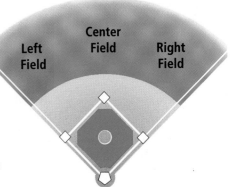

**Choose any strategy to solve the problem. Show your work.**

1. You have three outfielders on your team. They each can play right field, left field, and center field. In how many different ways can they trade these positions?

2. Your team plans to put a 120-foot fence along one side of a baseball field. The fence posts will be 6 feet apart, with a post at each end. How many posts will you need?

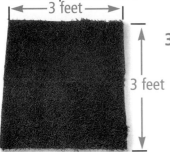

3. A rectangular area on your baseball field needs new grass. The area is 24 feet long and 30 feet wide. Your team plans to order square pieces of sod. Each piece of sod is 3 feet long and 3 feet wide. How many pieces should you order?

4. At the end of a game, each player on your team shakes hands with every player from the other team. Suppose each team has 12 players. How many handshakes will there be?

5. The product of your uniform number and your teammate's uniform number is 128. The quotient of the two numbers is 2. What are the numbers?

6. Your team is playing at home. The scoreboard shows the runs scored in six innings. A friend says the visitors will score 4 runs in the next inning. Do you agree? Explain.

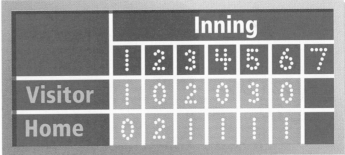

7. **Create Your Own** Make up a problem about baseball. Solve it. Then see if a friend can solve it.

8. There are 12 players on your team. Each player brings 2 or 3 bats to practice. If there are 32 bats in all, how many players brought 2 bats and how many players brought 3 bats?

## Share Your Thinking

9. Discuss problem 8 with a classmate. What strategy did you each use to solve it? How were your strategies different? Were they helpful in different ways? How?

259

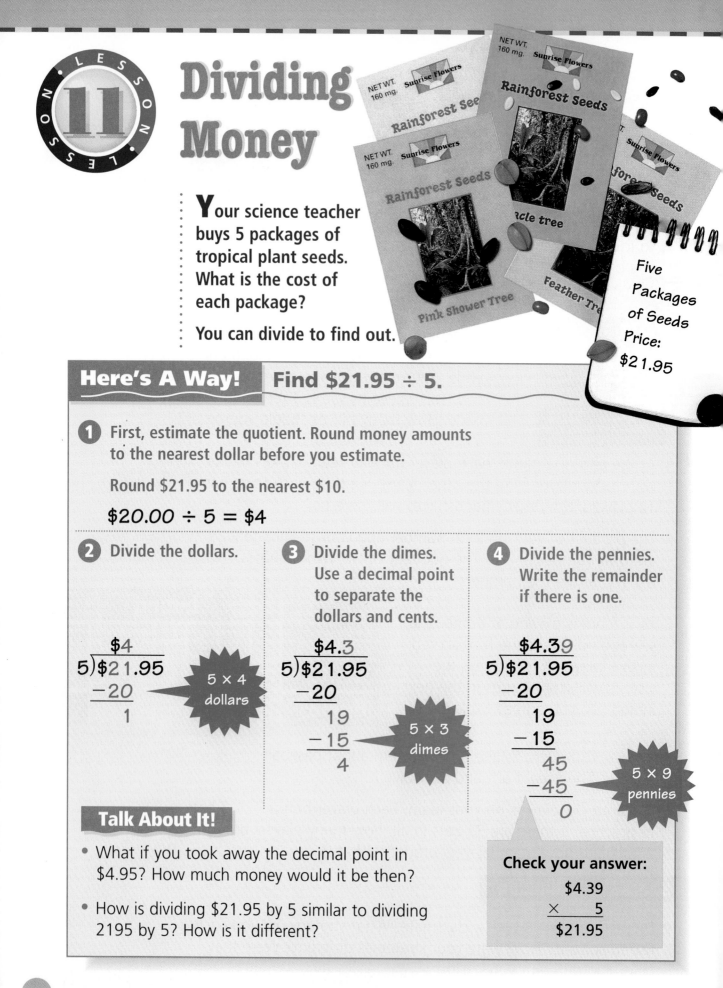

# Dividing Money

**Y**our science teacher buys 5 packages of tropical plant seeds. What is the cost of each package?

You can divide to find out.

Five Packages of Seeds Price: $21.95

## Here's A Way! Find $21.95 ÷ 5.

**1** First, estimate the quotient. Round money amounts to the nearest dollar before you estimate.

Round $21.95 to the nearest $10.

$$\$20.00 \div 5 = \$4$$

**2** Divide the dollars.

$$\begin{array}{r} \$4 \\ 5)\overline{\$21.95} \\ -20 \\ \hline 1 \end{array}$$

5 × 4 dollars

**3** Divide the dimes. Use a decimal point to separate the dollars and cents.

$$\begin{array}{r} \$4.3 \\ 5)\overline{\$21.95} \\ -20 \\ \hline 19 \\ -15 \\ \hline 4 \end{array}$$

5 × 3 dimes

**4** Divide the pennies. Write the remainder if there is one.

$$\begin{array}{r} \$4.39 \\ 5)\overline{\$21.95} \\ -20 \\ \hline 19 \\ -15 \\ \hline 45 \\ -45 \\ \hline 0 \end{array}$$

5 × 9 pennies

### Talk About It!

• What if you took away the decimal point in $4.95? How much money would it be then?

• How is dividing $21.95 by 5 similar to dividing 2195 by 5? How is it different?

**Check your answer:**

$$\begin{array}{r} \$4.39 \\ \times \quad 5 \\ \hline \$21.95 \end{array}$$

Find the quotient. Circle the answers you found by using mental math.

1. 2)$11.24  2. 4)$.28  3. 5)$.90  4. 8)$16.08  5. 9)$9.27

6. 7)$7.14  7. 3)$.60  8. 4)$22.00  9. 9)$70.20  10. 6)$6.66

11. 6$)24.06  12. 9)$9.63  13. 8)$6.64  14. 5)$16.50  15. 4)$4.36

16. **Critical Thinking** In exercise 15, why is there a zero in the quotient?

## Work It Out!

Find the quotient. Circle the answers you found by using mental math.

17. 3)$3.72  18. 4)$1.64  19. 9)$.81  20. 2)$.50  21. 3)$18.33

22. 2)$8.00  23. 4)$1.00  24. 5)$6.55  25. 6)$5.58  26. 8)$12.36

27. 5)$10.00  28. 6)$36.60  29. 2)$8.80  30. 7)$15.47  31. 7)$28.14

### Problem Solving  Using Data

32. The librarian buys plants for the school library. The plants are on sale. Three climbing vines cost $7.50. How much does the librarian save?

33. Red and yellow ferns are on sale. You can buy 2 plants for $19.95. What is the price for each plant?

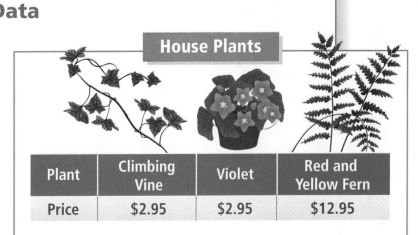

**House Plants**

| Plant | Climbing Vine | Violet | Red and Yellow Fern |
|-------|---------------|--------|---------------------|
| Price | $2.95 | $2.95 | $12.95 |

### Mixed Review

Write the answer.

| 34. | 35. | 36. | 37. | 38. |
|-----|-----|-----|-----|-----|
| 7034 + 8669 | 7999 × 4 | 4589 × 6 | 3006 × 5 | 5543 + 629 |

Use the order property. Rewrite the number sentence.

39. 9 + 8 = 17  40. 7 + 17 = 24  41. 32 + 19 = 51  42. 63 + 25 = 88

More Practice Set 7.11, p. 498

# Using Division Sense

**Plant Stores**

**ROLLING MEADOWS**
**Flowering Shrubs!**
**8 for $229**

**Green Hills**
**Flowering Shrubs**
**6 for $189**

**T**wo plant stores are having a sale. Which store has the better buy in flowering shrubs?

Estimation and division can help you decide.

## Here's A Way! Compare costs.

**1** Estimate the cost of a shrub at Rolling Meadows Plant Store.

8 shrubs for $229

$229 ÷ 8 ⟶ $240 ÷ 8 = $30

Your estimate is $30. But $229 is less than $240. So the cost for a shrub is less than $30.

**2** Estimate the cost of one shrub at Green Hills Plant Store.

6 shrubs for $189

$189 ÷ 6 ⟶ $180 ÷ 6 = $30

Again, your estimate is $30. But $189 is greater than $180. So, the cost for a shrub is more than $30.

**3** Compare your estimates.

The shrubs at Rolling Meadows Plant Store cost less.

**Talk About It!** How could you have solved the problem by finding exact answers?

**Estimate. Then write the letter of the correct answer.**

| 1. $7\overline{)924}$ | 2. $9\overline{)387}$ | 3. $8\overline{)376}$ | 4. $6\overline{)576}$ | 5. $7\overline{)378}$ | 6. $4\overline{)256}$ |
|---|---|---|---|---|---|
| a. 82 | a. 23 | a. 47 | a. 96 | a. 44 | a. 64 |
| b. 102 | b. 43 | b. 87 | b. 106 | b. 54 | b. 56 |
| c. 132 | c. 93 | c. 107 | c. 46 | c. 78 | c. 78 |

7. **Number Sense** You estimate that Rolling Meadows sells pine trees for less than $40 each. You also estimate that Green Hills sells them for more than $30. How would you decide where to buy pine trees? Explain.

## Work It Out!

**Compare. Which quotient is greater? Explain how you decided.**

8. $98 \div 7$ or $98 \div 8$     9. $739 \div 4$ or $739 \div 3$     10. $409 \div 7$ or $609 \div 7$

11. $525 \div 5$ or $620 \div 4$   12. $735 \div 7$ or $880 \div 8$   13. $472 \div 9$ or $668 \div 8$

**Estimate. Write the letter of the correct answer.**

| 14. $6\overline{)498}$ | 15. $5\overline{)455}$ | 16. $8\overline{)688}$ | 17. $7\overline{)777}$ | 18. $8\overline{)896}$ | 19. $9\overline{)1224}$ |
|---|---|---|---|---|---|
| a. 23 | a. 71 | a. 69 | a. 111 | a. 92 | a. 136 |
| b. 83 | b. 61 | b. 86 | b. 96 | b. 72 | b. 86 |
| c. 53 | c. 91 | c. 102 | c. 77 | c. 112 | c. 106 |

**Write the answer.**

20. $9\overline{)845}$   21. $8\overline{)987}$   22. $5\overline{)1525}$   23. $4\overline{)3244}$   24. $9\overline{)5427}$   25. $7\overline{)4949}$

### Problem Solving   Using Data

**Use the chart to solve the problem.**

26. A school buys 25 rakes from Rolling Meadows. Would the school have saved money by buying from Green Hills? Explain.

27. Students have $36.75 to spend on tools and supplies. At which store could they spend exactly this amount of money?

**Prices of Tools and Supplies**

| | Rolling Meadows Plant Store | Green Hills Plant Store |
|---|---|---|
| Rake | 2 for $17 | 4 for $33.40 |
| Shovel | 4 for $53 | 3 for $37.50 |
| Plant Food | 6 lb for $15 | 4 lb for $8 |

**More Practice Set 7.12, p. 498**

# 13 Finding Averages

**Getting Started**

**Vocabulary:**
average
Glossary, p. 516

**S**uppose a friend asks how much fruit you eat in a week. You make a chart each week for a month. But at the end of the month, every week has a different number. How do you answer your friend's question?

You can answer the question by finding the average. An **average** is a way of describing a group of numbers.

## Here's A Way! Find the average of 12, 14, 8, 10.

**1** Make 4 stacks of counters showing the number of fruit you ate each week.

Record the number of counters in each stack.

12, 14, 8, 10

**2** Put all the counters together in a group.

Record the total.

$12 + 14 + 8 + 10 = 44$

**3** Divide the group into 4 equal stacks—one stack for each week.

Record the number in each stack.

$44 \div 4 = 11$

The average number of fruit you ate in a week was 11 pieces.

### Talk About It!

• How can an average be different from all the original numbers?
• In what other situations might you use averages?

**Write the number you divide by to find the average. Then find the average.**

1. 2, 5, 7, 4, 7
2. 242, 187, 300
3. 93, 73, 65
4. 62, 71, 83, 96
5. 56, 54, 49
6. 112, 116, 117
7. 243, 233, 235
8. 76, 86, 96, 86
9. 127, 154, 148
10. 99, 96, 87
11. 987, 993, 975
12. 83, 83, 83

13. **Number Sense** Did you need to add and divide to find the average for exercise 12? Why or why not?

14. **Critical Thinking** Suppose this list shows the number of pieces of paper you use at school each day for a week. Explain how you would find the average. Then find it.

| | |
|---|---|
| Mon. | 3 |
| Tues. | 3 |
| Wed. | 2 |
| Thurs. | 7 |
| Fri. | 0 |

## Work It Out!

**Find the average for the set of numbers.**

15. 17, 28, 36
16. 55, 59, 96
17. 43, 55, 64
18. 87, 92, 85, 72
19. 7, 8, 9
20. 12, 13, 14
21. 19, 20, 21
22. 65, 68, 69, 74
23. 32, 33, 34
24. 123, 145, 155
25. 765, 647, 712
26. 832, 822, 899

27. **Estimation** Estimate the average for the set of numbers shown. Then find the average.

| 35 | 40 | 45 | 50 | 55 |
|---|---|---|---|---|

28. **Create Your Own** List three numbers that have an average of 121. Explain how you chose the three numbers.

### Problem Solving   Using Data

29. The cash register at a sandwich shop records the drinks sold at lunch every day. On which days did the store sell more juice than average?

30. Compare the average amounts of the drinks that the sandwich shop sells. Which kind of drink does the store sell the most?

**Drinks Sold at Lunch**

| | Strawberry Milk | Whole Milk | Fruit Juice |
|---|---|---|---|
| Monday | 204 | 155 | 103 |
| Tuesday | 93 | 85 | 163 |
| Wednesday | 79 | 77 | 100 |
| Thursday | 111 | 119 | 76 |
| Friday | 128 | 99 | 108 |

**More Practice Set 7.13, p. 499**

# Problem Solving
## Using Strategies

LESSON 14

You can read more about the Florida National Scenic Trail in the pages of *Outside*.

**T**he Florida National Scenic Trail winds through Florida for about 1300 miles. One of the most beautiful sections of this trail is the part that runs through the Ocala National Forest. Here, hikers pass tiny lakes, cypress swamps, and the birds and animals that live in them.

Ocala National Park

FLORIDA

### Problem Solving Process
✓ Understand
✓ Plan
✓ Try It
✓ Look Back

### Choose a Strategy You Have Learned
✓ Guess and Check
✓ Draw a Picture
✓ Make a List
✓ Make a Table
✓ Act It Out
✓ Work a Simpler Problem
   Look for a Pattern
   Work Backward

**S**uppose you hike 21 miles along the Ocala Trail. You hike the first 8 miles at 4 miles each hour. It takes you 4 hours to hike the next 11 miles. You spend an hour eating lunch and then finish the hike in an hour. If you started at 7 A.M., at what time do you finish?

• What is the problem you have to solve?

• How long will it take to hike the first 8 miles?

• How long will the entire hike take?

• Explain a strategy that can help you solve the problem. Then solve it.

**Use any strategy to solve the problem. Show your work.**

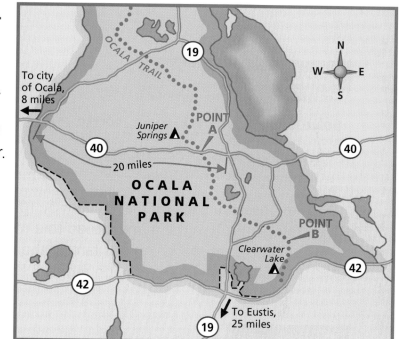

1. Suppose Point A and Point B are 24 miles apart. You leave Point A at 9:00 A.M. You hike 3 miles each hour. Will you reach Point B by 3:00 P.M.? Explain your answer.

2. Your hike ends near Route 42. Suppose it is 30 miles from where your car is parked to the intersection of Route 40 and Route 19. If your family drives at 30 miles each hour, about how long will it take to reach the city of Ocala?

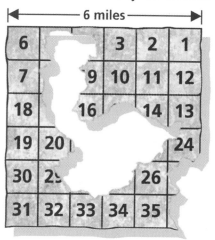

3. Maps use a grid like the one shown. The larger square is called a township. It is 6 miles long and 6 miles wide. The smaller sections are numbered in a particular way. Copy the grid and complete the numbering.

4. Suppose you hike 4 miles an hour. Can you hike from the beginning of section 6 to the end of section 30 in an hour? Explain.

5. Your hiking group takes a 72-mile hike. You will start on June 5 and end on June 8. Each day you will hike from 7 A.M. to 5 P.M., with a 1-hour break. How many miles each hour should you hike?

6. The sun moves across the sky from east to west. How can you use the shadows of the trees to tell which way is north?

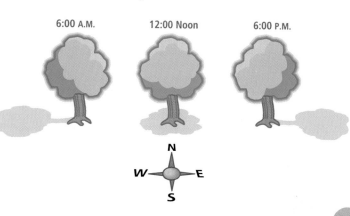

7. How can problem solving strategies help you when you are hiking?

# Chapter 7 Test

## for Pages 236–267

**Test-Taking Tips**
Picture in your mind what is going on in the problems.

## Problem Solving

**Solve. Show your work.** (pages 246, 250, 258)

1. An astronaut spends 100 days in space. About how many weeks is 100 days? How many months?

2. Suppose you and five friends earn $210 cleaning out an attic. You plan to use the money to go to a rodeo. Each ticket costs $17.00. Each round-trip bus fare to the rodeo costs $12.50. Do you have enough money? Explain.

## Concepts

**Find the value. Look for ways to use a pattern.** (pages 254, 262)

3. a. 700 ÷ 7    b. 707 ÷ 7    c. 714 ÷ 7    d. 721 ÷ 7

4. a. 387 ÷ 3    b. 390 ÷ 3    c. 393 ÷ 3    d. 396 ÷ 3

5. a. 630 ÷ 6    b. 636 ÷ 6    c. 642 ÷ 6    d. 648 ÷ 6

6. a. 120 ÷ 3    b. 120 ÷ 4    c. 120 ÷ 6    d. 120 ÷ 8

7. a. 480 ÷ 3    b. 480 ÷ 4    c. 480 ÷ 6    d. 480 ÷ 8

**Use mental math to find the quotient.** (page 260)

8. $27.63 ÷ 9    9. $15.95 ÷ 5    10. $2.04 ÷ 6

11. $7.14 ÷ 7    12. $11.24 ÷ 2

**Which division does not come out even? Write the letter.** (pages 238, 240)

13. a. 35 ÷ 6    b. 27 ÷ 3    c. 63 ÷ 9    d. 40 ÷ 8

14. a. 56 ÷ 7    b. 32 ÷ 8    c. 32 ÷ 5    d. 45 ÷ 9

Write the letter of the correct answer. (pages 244, 248, 254, 260)

15. $7\overline{)2282}$    a. 343       b. 320 R6     c. 326       d. 290

16. $4\overline{)978}$     a. 246       b. 219        c. 232       d. 244 R2

17. $4\overline{)\$3957}$  a. $989.25   b. $994.25    c. $892.75   d. $955.95

Divide. Show your work. (pages 244, 248, 254, 260)

18. $7\overline{)58}$      19. $9\overline{)452}$      20. $8\overline{)1956}$      21. $7\overline{)2103}$

22. $9\overline{)\$12.96}$  23. $6\overline{)495}$     24. $7\overline{)69}$       25. $3\overline{)1296}$

Find the average. (page 264)

26. $12.50, $7.50, $4.00        27. 88, 37, 65, 102

28. 386, 260                    29. $96.00, $84.75, $12.44, $3.25

## Performance Task

(page 264)

Suppose you kept a chart showing the number of minutes you exercised each day last week. How can you use the chart to help you find the average number of minutes you exercised each day?

- Explain how you will find this average. What number will you divide by? Why?

- What is the average number of minutes you exercised last week?

**Minutes of Exercise**

| Sunday | 15 |
|---|---|
| Monday | 25 |
| Tuesday | 15 |
| Wednesday | 30 |
| Thursday | 10 |
| Friday | 0 |
| Saturday | 24 |

# Cumulative Review

**Rounding** (Chapter 1)
Round 24 to the nearest 10.

> **Here's A Way!**
>
> Use a number line.
> You see that 24 is closer to 20 than to 30. So, 24 rounded to the nearest 10 is 20.
>
>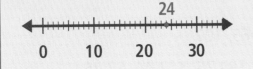
>
> 0   10   20   30

**Round the number to the nearest 100.**

1. 256

2. 447

3. 1269

4. When you round to the nearest 100, does 951 or 1141 round to 1000?

5. When you round to the nearest 10, does 96 or 108 round to 100?

---

**Addition** (Chapter 2)
Find 278 + 137.

> **Here's A Way!**
>
> Add the ones. Regroup.    $\overset{1\ 1}{278}$
> Add the tens. Regroup.    $+\ 137$
> Add the hundreds.         $415$

**Find the sum.**

| 6. | 532 | 7. | 1001 | 8. | 731 |
|---|---|---|---|---|---|
| | 452 | | 327 | | 66 |
| | + 376 | | + 764 | | + 9 |

9. Which three numbers have the sum of 1000? 744, 159, 123, 674, 133

**Copy and complete. Use >, <, or =.**

10. 0 + 5512 ⬤ 5500 + 12

11. 17 + 17 + 17 ⬤ 16 + 16 + 16

---

**Division** (Chapter 4)
Find 400 ÷ 8.

> **Here's A Way!**
>
> Use multiplication facts to help you divide.
>
> 8 × 5 = 40        40 ÷ 8 = 5
> 8 × 50 = 400      400 ÷ 8 = 50

**Find the quotient. Think of a multiplication fact to help you.**

12. $9\overline{)36}$     13. $9\overline{)360}$     14. $9\overline{)3600}$

15. $7\overline{)63}$     16. $7\overline{)630}$     17. $7\overline{)6300}$

18. 72 ÷ 9     19. 54 ÷ 6     20. 81 ÷ 9

## Area (Chapter 5)

Find the area of each rectangle you can make with four square tiles.

**Here's A Way!**

You can make a 2 × 2 square, a 4 × 1 rectangle, or a 1 × 4 rectangle. To find the area, count the tiles.

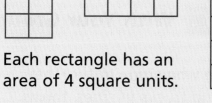

Each rectangle has an area of 4 square units.

Find the area.

21.
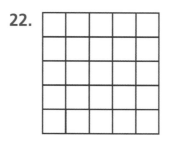

22.

23.
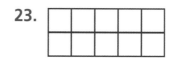

## Multiplication (Chapter 6)

Find 24 × 3.

**Here's A Way!**

Multiply the ones.
Regroup.
Multiply the tens.
Add the tens.

$$\begin{array}{r} 1 \\ 24 \\ \times\ 3 \\ \hline 72 \end{array}$$

Find the product.

24.
$$\begin{array}{r} 46 \\ \times\ 6 \\ \hline \end{array}$$

25.
$$\begin{array}{r} \$29 \\ \times\ 7 \\ \hline \end{array}$$

26.
$$\begin{array}{r} 415 \\ \times\ 8 \\ \hline \end{array}$$

27.
$$\begin{array}{r} \$76 \\ \times\ 5 \\ \hline \end{array}$$

28.
$$\begin{array}{r} 1001 \\ \times\ 5 \\ \hline \end{array}$$

29.
$$\begin{array}{r} 9999 \\ \times\ 9 \\ \hline \end{array}$$

## Problem Solving

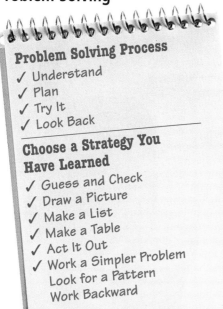

Problem Solving Process
✓ Understand
✓ Plan
✓ Try It
✓ Look Back

Choose a Strategy You Have Learned
✓ Guess and Check
✓ Draw a Picture
✓ Make a List
✓ Make a Table
✓ Act It Out
✓ Work a Simpler Problem
Look for a Pattern
Work Backward

Choose any strategy you have learned to solve each problem. Show your work.

30. Suppose 8 ounces of milk costs $.64. If the milk goes on sale for $.56, how much less is the cost per ounce?

31. Suppose your library book is due on January 24. You return it on February 7. The fee for a late book is $.10 a day. How much do you owe?

YIELD

# Go with the Flow!

ONE WAY

**Social Studies Connection**  **With Your Group**

**T**raffic engineers are people who study traffic. They watch the patterns of cars and trucks in cities, towns, and on highways. The data they collect helps them decide where to put signs and traffic lights to make traffic flow smoothly.

Your group will gather information about the traffic in your school. You can use averages to help you. Then, you can make decisions about how to improve the flow of your school's traffic.

Day: Monday
Outside of Library

Number
of People
||||| |||

Notes:
dropped books

## 1 Plan It

- Divide into groups. Select a site in the school to watch. Choose places such as hallways, doorways, and cafeteria entrances.
- Make a chart for the place you have chosen. Observe the site from Monday through Friday, at the same time each day.

Location: Outside of Library

| Day | Number of People | Notes |
|---|---|---|
| Monday | 30 | Traffic Jam! |
| Tuesday | | |

## 2 Put It Together

- Watch your site for 10 minutes. Count each person who walks by, using numbers or tally marks. Make notes about what you see.
- On Friday, find the average number of people who passed your site each day. Note this on your chart.

## STOP

## 3 Wrap It Up

- Compare your site with those of other groups. Which locations were busiest? Which were the least busy?
- Talk about how you could improve traffic in your school. Where would you put up traffic signs? Would you make some areas one-way?

## 4 Discuss Your Results

- Have you covered all the points in Keep In Mind?
- How do averages give you a clearer picture of your school's traffic than just watching people?

### Internet

> Visit the **Math Center** at **Houghton Mifflin Education Place.** http://www.eduplace.com

## Math Power

### Use What You Know

- halves
- thirds
- fourths

• words for some fractions

$$\frac{1}{4} + \frac{1}{4} = \frac{1}{2}$$

• how to write fractions

- 10 ÷ 5 = 2
- 10 ÷ 2 = 5

• basic division facts

# CHAPTER 8

# Fractions

## Try This!

**H**ow can two fractions look different but represent the same amount? Fold and color strips of paper to help you explore fractions.

### What You'll Need

scissors, paper, crayons or markers, a sheet of paper

**1**

Cut the piece of paper into three equal strips. Fold each strip of paper in half. Unfold each strip and color half of it. Use a different color for each strip.

## 2

Fold one strip to make four sections. Fold another to make eight sections. Fold the third strip into more equal parts. Draw a line along each fold.

$\frac{2}{4}$

## 3

Count the total number of sections for each strip. Count the sections in color. Write a fraction for each paper strip.

What fraction are all the fractions you wrote equal to? How do you know?

How can you show the same fraction in other ways?

**Ready to Go!**

# Fractions

**S**ailors use flags to send messages. Each flag stands for a letter. The flag for *D* is divided into three equal parts. Each part is one third of the whole. The fraction one third can be written as $\frac{1}{3}$. You can learn about fractions by drawing flags.

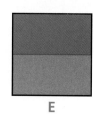
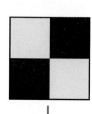

D   G

E   L

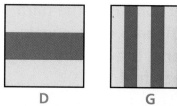

Z

### Activity

- **Choose four flags to color. Each partner can make two flags.**

- **Use markers to color the flags.**

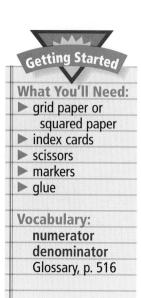

**1**

Use grid paper to draw square shapes that will fit on index cards. Use each square to make a flag.

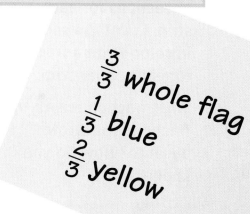

$\frac{3}{3}$ whole flag
$\frac{1}{3}$ blue
$\frac{2}{3}$ yellow

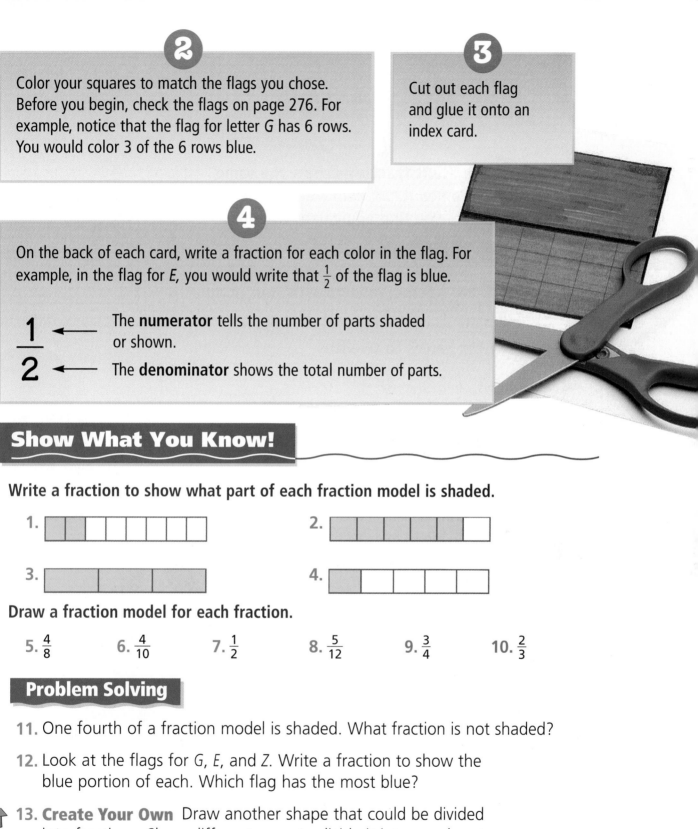

**2**

Color your squares to match the flags you chose. Before you begin, check the flags on page 276. For example, notice that the flag for letter *G* has 6 rows. You would color 3 of the 6 rows blue.

**3**

Cut out each flag and glue it onto an index card.

**4**

On the back of each card, write a fraction for each color in the flag. For example, in the flag for *E*, you would write that $\frac{1}{2}$ of the flag is blue.

$$\frac{1}{2}$$

The **numerator** tells the number of parts shaded or shown.

The **denominator** shows the total number of parts.

## Show What You Know!

Write a fraction to show what part of each fraction model is shaded.

1.

2.

3.

4.

**Draw a fraction model for each fraction.**

5. $\frac{4}{8}$  6. $\frac{4}{10}$  7. $\frac{1}{2}$  8. $\frac{5}{12}$  9. $\frac{3}{4}$  10. $\frac{2}{3}$

### Problem Solving

11. One fourth of a fraction model is shaded. What fraction is not shaded?

12. Look at the flags for *G*, *E*, and *Z*. Write a fraction to show the blue portion of each. Which flag has the most blue?

13. **Create Your Own** Draw another shape that could be divided into fractions. Show different ways to divide it into equal parts.

### Mixed Review  Multiply or divide.

14.  2500
      × 4

15. 3)798

16.  356
      × 9

17. 4)1000

18.  1017
      × 6

# LESSON 2

# Fractions and Equivalence

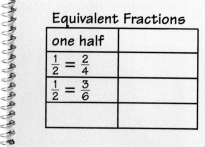

**E**quivalent fractions show the same, equal, amount. Shading fraction models can help you find equivalent fractions.

## Activity

- Share fraction models with your group.

- Have several models for fractions, from halves to twelfths.

**Equivalent Fractions**

| one half | |
|---|---|
| $\frac{1}{2} = \frac{2}{4}$ | |
| $\frac{1}{2} = \frac{3}{6}$ | |

**1**

Copy the chart. Get a fraction model with two parts. Shade $\frac{1}{2}$ of the model.

This model will be your guide for shading other fraction models. Hold a fourths model under it. Shade the fourths model to equal the half model. On your chart, write $\frac{1}{2} = \frac{2}{4}$ under *one half*.

**Equivalent Fractions**

| one half | two thirds |
|---|---|
| $\frac{1}{2} = \frac{2}{4}$ | |

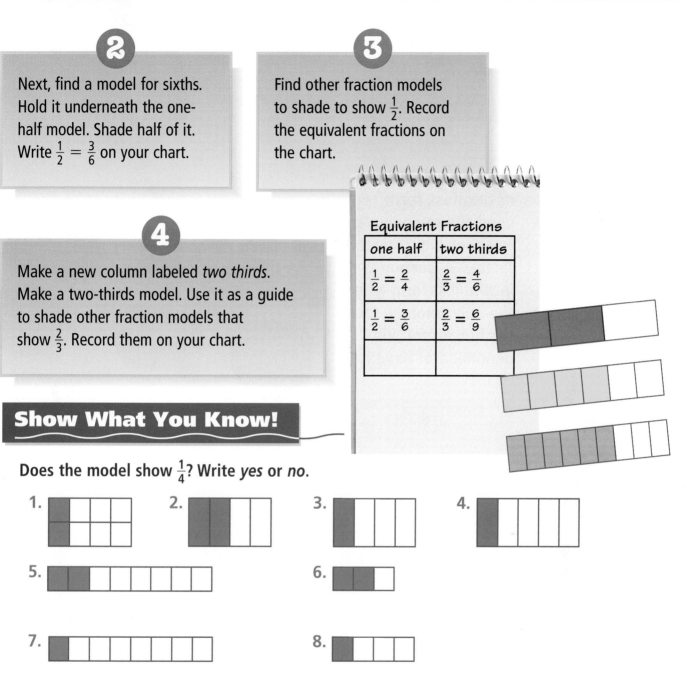

**2**

Next, find a model for sixths. Hold it underneath the one-half model. Shade half of it. Write $\frac{1}{2} = \frac{3}{6}$ on your chart.

**3**

Find other fraction models to shade to show $\frac{1}{2}$. Record the equivalent fractions on the chart.

**4**

Make a new column labeled *two thirds*. Make a two-thirds model. Use it as a guide to shade other fraction models that show $\frac{2}{3}$. Record them on your chart.

**Equivalent Fractions**

| one half | two thirds |
|---|---|
| $\frac{1}{2} = \frac{2}{4}$ | $\frac{2}{3} = \frac{4}{6}$ |
| $\frac{1}{2} = \frac{3}{6}$ | $\frac{2}{3} = \frac{6}{9}$ |
| | |

## Show What You Know!

Does the model show $\frac{1}{4}$? Write *yes* or *no*.

1. 
2. 
3. 
4. 

5. 
6. 

7. 
8. 

9. Cut out a strip of paper. Then:
   a. Fold the strip in half. Then fold it in half again to make fourths. Color two fourths. Fold the strip in half a third time. Write the equivalent fractions that the shaded parts show.
   b. Fold the strip in half again. Write another fraction that is equivalent to one half.

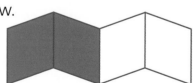

10. **Critical Thinking** What number does a fraction model name when all of its parts are shaded?

**Math Journal**

Write about some of the times you have used fractions outside of math class.

# Equivalence and Simplest Form

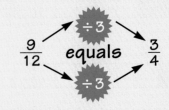

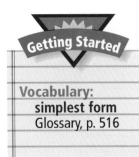
**Getting Started**

**Vocabulary:**
simplest form
Glossary, p. 516

**T**o write a fraction in **simplest form** you need to use equivalent fractions and common factors. A fraction is in simplest form when the only common factor the numerator and denominator have is 1.

**Use What You Know**

A **common factor** is a number that is a factor of two or more numbers.

3 is a common factor of 3 and 6.

---

## Here's A Way!   Find the simplest form.

### Equivalent Fractions

You can find some equivalent fractions by multiplying the numerator and denominator by the same number.

You can find other equivalent fractions by dividing the numerator and denominator by a common factor.

$$\frac{2}{3} \text{ equals } \frac{4}{6}$$

$$\frac{9}{12} \text{ equals } \frac{3}{4}$$

---

### Simplest Form

These fractions are in simplest form.

$$\frac{1}{3} \quad \frac{5}{6} \quad \frac{7}{9} \quad \frac{2}{5} \quad \frac{3}{4}$$

The only common factor of 3 and 4 is 1.

These fractions are not.

$$\frac{6}{10} \quad \frac{2}{8} \quad \frac{3}{9} \quad \frac{4}{6} \quad \frac{2}{4}$$

6 and 10 have two common factors: 1 and 2

### Talk About It!

How do you know when a fraction is in simplest form?

What number has the denominator been multiplied by? Complete
the equivalent fraction.

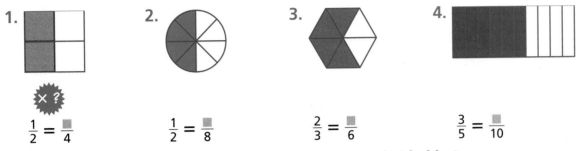

1.

$\frac{1}{2} = \frac{\blacksquare}{4}$

2.

$\frac{1}{2} = \frac{\blacksquare}{8}$

3.

$\frac{2}{3} = \frac{\blacksquare}{6}$

4.

$\frac{3}{5} = \frac{\blacksquare}{10}$

What number has the numerator or denominator been divided by?
Complete the equivalent fraction.

5. $\frac{4}{10} = \frac{\blacksquare}{5}$
6. $\frac{15}{20} = \frac{3}{\blacksquare}$
7. $\frac{10}{16} = \frac{\blacksquare}{8}$
8. $\frac{6}{9} = \frac{\blacksquare}{3}$
9. $\frac{18}{20} = \frac{9}{\blacksquare}$

10. **Critical Thinking** In Exercises 1–9, what happened to the numerator and
denominator when you wrote the equivalent fraction?

Decide whether the fraction is in simplest form. If not, write the
simplest form.

11. $\frac{2}{4}$
12. $\frac{5}{8}$
13. $\frac{9}{10}$
14. $\frac{3}{12}$
15. $\frac{4}{8}$

16. $\frac{10}{11}$
17. $\frac{3}{7}$
18. $\frac{1}{3}$
19. $\frac{8}{10}$
20. $\frac{10}{12}$

21. Write three fractions equivalent to $\frac{1}{5}$.

22. **Number Sense** Use the models to explain
why $\frac{3}{5}$ is not equivalent to $\frac{4}{10}$.

**Patterns** Find and extend the pattern.
Write the next three equivalent fractions.

23. $\frac{2}{3}$ $\frac{4}{6}$ $\frac{6}{9}$ $\frac{\blacksquare}{\blacksquare}$ $\frac{\blacksquare}{\blacksquare}$ $\frac{\blacksquare}{\blacksquare}$

24. $\frac{2}{4}$ $\frac{4}{8}$ $\frac{6}{12}$ $\frac{\blacksquare}{\blacksquare}$ $\frac{\blacksquare}{\blacksquare}$ $\frac{\blacksquare}{\blacksquare}$

25. $\frac{1}{5}$ $\frac{2}{10}$ $\frac{3}{15}$ $\frac{\blacksquare}{\blacksquare}$ $\frac{\blacksquare}{\blacksquare}$ $\frac{\blacksquare}{\blacksquare}$

**Problem Solving**

26. In a kit of clay there are 8 bars. If 6 of the bars are red, what
fraction of the kit is that?

27. If 4 of the bars are red, what fraction of the kit is that?

More Practice Set 8.3, p. 499

# Exploring Order of Fractions

**A**t a glance, you know that 2 is greater than 1. It is not so easy to compare fractions and put them in order. This activity shows you how fraction models can help.

**Getting Started**

**What You'll Need:**
▶ fraction models
▶ markers

# Compare Fractions!

**Activity**

- Use fraction models.

- Compare and order them.

**1**

Copy the chart shown below.

Label three columns:

$$> \frac{1}{2} \qquad < \frac{1}{2} \qquad = \frac{1}{2}$$

Then, shade fraction models to show $\frac{1}{2}$ $\frac{2}{4}$ $\frac{2}{3}$ and $\frac{1}{5}$.

| $> \frac{1}{2}$ | $< \frac{1}{2}$ | $= \frac{1}{2}$ |
|---|---|---|
| $\frac{2}{3}$ | $\frac{1}{5}$ | $\frac{2}{4}$ |
| $\frac{4}{5}$ | | |
| | | |

**2**

Compare each model to the $\frac{1}{2}$ fraction model. Is it greater than, less than, or equal to $\frac{1}{2}$? Write the fraction in the correct column on your chart.

**3**

Then, arrange the models in order from least to greatest. On another sheet, write the fractions in order.

**4**

Create a model for the fraction $\frac{4}{5}$. Compare it to the $\frac{1}{2}$ strip. Put it in order with the other strips. Then, list the fractions in order.

**Comparing Fractions**

| | |
|---|---|
| $\frac{1}{5}, \frac{2}{4}, \frac{2}{3}$ | |
| $\frac{1}{5}, \frac{2}{4}, \frac{2}{3}, \frac{4}{5}$ | |
| | |

## Show What You Know!

1. **Critical Thinking** What is an easy way to order fractions that have the same denominator? How would you order fractions that have the same numerator?

**Algebraic Reasoning** Write a number for *m* and *n* to make each statement true. Check your work with fraction models.

2. $\frac{n}{2} = \frac{m}{4}$

3. $\frac{n}{3} > \frac{m}{6}$

4. $\frac{n}{8} < \frac{m}{12}$

5. $\frac{n}{2} > \frac{m}{4}$

6. $\frac{n}{3} < \frac{m}{6}$

7. $\frac{n}{8} = \frac{m}{12}$

Put the fractions in order from least to greatest. Use fraction models to check your work.

8. $\frac{1}{3}$ $\frac{1}{4}$ $\frac{1}{6}$

9. $\frac{2}{3}$ $\frac{1}{2}$ $\frac{2}{6}$

10. $\frac{3}{3}$ $\frac{4}{6}$ $\frac{0}{2}$ $\frac{9}{12}$

11. $\frac{1}{2}$ $\frac{2}{10}$ $\frac{5}{5}$ $\frac{7}{10}$

### Mixed Review

Divide or multiply.

12. $7\overline{)333}$

13. $\begin{array}{r} 427 \\ \times\ \ 8 \end{array}$

14. $5\overline{)2000}$

15. $\begin{array}{r} 1500 \\ \times\ \ 4 \end{array}$

16. $4\overline{)876}$

# Comparing and Ordering Fractions

**Y**ou can compare fractions by using fraction models. You can also compare two or more fractions by finding equivalent fractions.

Once you have fractions with the same denominator, you can compare them and put them in order.

## Here's A Way! Compare and order.

**Compare fractions.**

Compare $\frac{5}{6}$ and $\frac{7}{12}$.

**1** Write both fractions with the same denominator. Find a fraction equivalent to $\frac{5}{6}$ with a denominator the same as $\frac{7}{12}$.

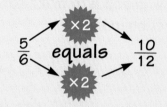

$$\frac{5}{6} \xrightarrow{\times 2} \text{equals} \xrightarrow{\times 2} \frac{10}{12}$$

**2** Compare the numerators.

Think: **10 > 7**

$$\frac{10}{12} > \frac{7}{12}$$

So, $\frac{5}{6}$ is greater than $\frac{7}{12}$.

**Order fractions.**

Write $\frac{5}{6}$, $\frac{7}{12}$, and $\frac{1}{2}$ in order from least to greatest.

**1** Write the fractions with the same denominator.

$$\frac{5}{6} = \frac{10}{12}, \quad \frac{7}{12} = \frac{7}{12}, \quad \frac{1}{2} = \frac{6}{12}$$

**2** Compare the fractions.

$$\frac{6}{12} < \frac{7}{12} \text{ and } \frac{7}{12} < \frac{10}{12}$$

**3** Write the fractions in order from least to greatest.

The order is $\frac{1}{2}$, $\frac{7}{12}$, $\frac{5}{6}$.

**Talk About It!** Why find equivalent fractions to compare fractions with different denominators?

Leaf Cutter Ants from Monteverde, Costa Rica

**Algebraic Reasoning** Write >, <, or =.

1. $\frac{2}{4}$ ● $\frac{4}{12}$    2. $\frac{1}{2}$ ● $\frac{5}{10}$    3. $\frac{2}{6}$ ● $\frac{5}{12}$    4. $\frac{3}{4}$ ● $\frac{7}{8}$    5. $\frac{2}{3}$ ● $\frac{4}{9}$    6. $\frac{4}{5}$ ● $\frac{9}{10}$

Write the fractions in order from least to greatest.

7. $\frac{6}{6}$ $\frac{1}{6}$ $\frac{3}{6}$    8. $\frac{2}{10}$ $\frac{2}{5}$ $\frac{7}{10}$ $\frac{3}{5}$    9. $\frac{2}{4}$ $\frac{1}{8}$ $\frac{6}{8}$    10. $\frac{1}{9}$ $\frac{1}{3}$ $\frac{4}{9}$    11. $\frac{2}{6}$ $\frac{1}{12}$ $\frac{3}{12}$ $\frac{5}{6}$

12. **Critical Thinking** Describe how you decided the order of the fractions in exercise 11.

---

**Work It Out!**

**Algebraic Reasoning** Write >, <, or =.

13. $\frac{1}{2}$ ● $\frac{9}{12}$    14. $\frac{7}{8}$ ● $\frac{1}{4}$    15. $\frac{6}{6}$ ● $\frac{3}{3}$    16. $\frac{3}{6}$ ● $\frac{8}{12}$    17. $\frac{1}{10}$ ● $\frac{2}{5}$

Write the fractions in order from greatest to least.

18. $\frac{3}{4}$ $\frac{1}{2}$ $\frac{7}{8}$    19. $\frac{4}{5}$ $\frac{1}{10}$ $\frac{10}{10}$    20. $\frac{10}{12}$ $\frac{3}{4}$ $\frac{1}{12}$    21. $\frac{2}{3}$ $\frac{3}{6}$ $\frac{3}{3}$    22. $\frac{1}{4}$ $\frac{5}{8}$ $\frac{2}{4}$

Draw a number line from 0 to 1 for each set of fractions. Place the fractions on the number line. Which fraction in each set is closest to 1?

23. $\frac{3}{4}$ $\frac{1}{2}$ $\frac{1}{4}$    24. $\frac{4}{5}$ $\frac{5}{10}$ $\frac{1}{5}$    25. $\frac{1}{3}$ $\frac{1}{6}$ $\frac{2}{3}$    26. $\frac{7}{8}$ $\frac{6}{8}$ $\frac{1}{4}$    27. $\frac{4}{6}$ $\frac{5}{12}$ $\frac{10}{12}$

**Problem Solving**

28. One leaf cutter ant cuts a leaf and carries away $\frac{4}{5}$ of it. Another ant cuts a leaf of the same size and carries away $\frac{7}{10}$ of it. Which is the larger piece of leaf, $\frac{4}{5}$ or $\frac{7}{10}$?

29. Suppose leaf cutter ants have cut $\frac{2}{3}$ of the leaves on a vine. Were most of the leaves cut by the ants?

**More Practice Set 8.5, p. 500**

# Problem Solving
## Is the Answer Reasonable?

**Y**our family is driving to a World Cup soccer game. The trip takes one hour. After going $\frac{2}{3}$ of the way, your father says, "Only half an hour to go and we're there!"

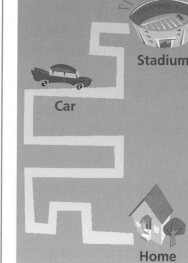

**The Trip**

Stadium

Car

Home

## You Decide

- What fraction of the trip is left?

- How long will it take to drive this distance?

- Is the last sentence reasonable? Explain.

## Work It Out!

**Decide if the sentence in color is reasonable. Tell why or why not.**

1. Italy won the 1994 World Cup. In that game Baggio made $\frac{1}{2}$ of the team's goals, Costacurta made $\frac{1}{2}$ of them, and Albertini made $\frac{1}{2}$ of them.

2. In one soccer game, Baggio played in $\frac{1}{2}$ of the game, and so did Costacurta and Albertini.

3. On the U.S. team, $\frac{1}{2}$ of the players were born in the United States. Nine players were born in other countries. So, there are 18 players on the U.S. team.

4. **Create Your Own** Write a problem about a soccer game. Give the answer. Challenge a classmate to decide if your answer is reasonable.

### Share Your Thinking

5. How did you decide if each sentence in color was reasonable? Explain.

# Midchapter Review
## for Pages 274–286

## Problem Solving

**Solve. Show your work. (page 286)**

1. A movie ticket costs $6.75 for an adult and $4.25 for a child. You have $35.75. How much money will you have left after buying tickets for 2 adults and 2 children?

2. Suppose you and three friends buy a large pizza. You each pay with a $5 bill. The pizza costs $12.75. You will also pay an $.83 tax on the pizza. How much change will you and your friends get?

## Concepts

**Draw a model for each fraction. (page 276)**

3. $\frac{2}{3}$    4. $\frac{1}{4}$    5. $\frac{3}{8}$    6. $\frac{2}{5}$

**Write the fraction. (pages 278, 280)**

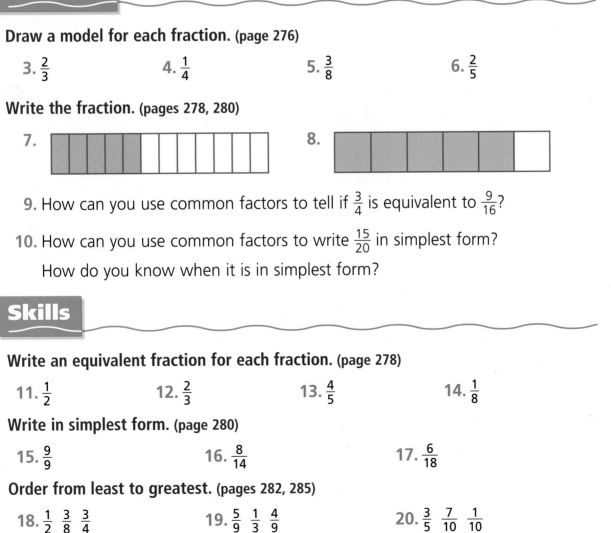

7.

8.

9. How can you use common factors to tell if $\frac{3}{4}$ is equivalent to $\frac{9}{16}$?

10. How can you use common factors to write $\frac{15}{20}$ in simplest form? How do you know when it is in simplest form?

## Skills

**Write an equivalent fraction for each fraction. (page 278)**

11. $\frac{1}{2}$    12. $\frac{2}{3}$    13. $\frac{4}{5}$    14. $\frac{1}{8}$

**Write in simplest form. (page 280)**

15. $\frac{9}{9}$    16. $\frac{8}{14}$    17. $\frac{6}{18}$

**Order from least to greatest. (pages 282, 285)**

18. $\frac{1}{2}$  $\frac{3}{8}$  $\frac{3}{4}$    19. $\frac{5}{9}$  $\frac{1}{3}$  $\frac{4}{9}$    20. $\frac{3}{5}$  $\frac{7}{10}$  $\frac{1}{10}$

## Fractions Around the World

# Math World

Use fractions to study the population of Kenya. Make a diagram that compares areas of countries and continents.

## Young and Old Fractions

People use fractions every day to describe things. For example, people use fractions to talk about populations. Did you know that about $\frac{1}{3}$ of the world's population is under the age of 15? In Kenya, closer to $\frac{1}{2}$ of the population is under the age of 15. Is the population of Kenya older or younger than the total population of the world?

## Look at Egyptian fractions!

Egyptians measured grain with a unit called the hekat. It equals a little more than a gallon. They measured smaller amounts of grain in fractions of a hekat. Each fraction had a special sign. When the fractions were put together to show a whole hekat, they formed a symbol that looked like an eye!

# Try This!

## CONTINENTAL DIAGRAM

South America is the fourth largest continent in the world. The land area of South America makes up about $\frac{1}{8}$ of Earth's total land. Follow these steps to make a fraction model that shows the same thing.

**1** Make a model that shows all of Earth's land. Begin by drawing a rectangle 24 cm long and 2 cm wide.

**2** Cut out the rectangle. Divide it into 8 equal parts.

**3** Shade one part of the bar. This represents the part of Earth's total land taken up by South America.

**4** Now find North America's land mass. Cut out another rectangle of the same size. Divide the rectangle into 6 parts. Shade one part. What is the fraction?

**5** Compare the strips. Which is larger?

## Respond

**Work with a Partner . . .**
to use your library to find out all the countries in South America.

 Internet:
Houghton Mifflin Education Place
Explore the Math Center at
http://www.eduplace.com

## First Things First

In the Middle Ages, some writers wrote the fraction part of a mixed number before the whole number.

# Exploring Fractional Parts of a Number

**What You'll Need:**
▶ 36 counters
▶ recording sheet

**H**ow can you show part of a group of things? One way is to separate the whole group into a number of equal parts. Then, you can write a fraction to show a part of the group.

**Activity**

## Begin with 36 Counters

Separate the counters into three equal parts. Use the recording sheet or a piece of paper to record the answers.

**1** How many parts are there?

**2** What fraction names each part?

**3** How many counters are in the whole?

**4** How many counters are in each part?

**5** What part of the whole is 12 counters?

**6** What is $\frac{1}{3}$ of 36?

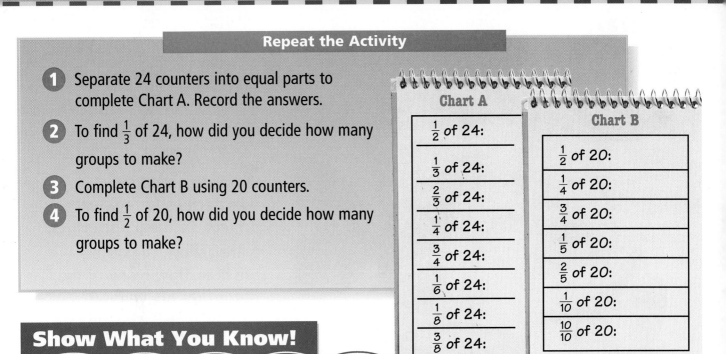

**Repeat the Activity**

1  Separate 24 counters into equal parts to complete Chart A. Record the answers.

2  To find $\frac{1}{3}$ of 24, how did you decide how many groups to make?

3  Complete Chart B using 20 counters.

4  To find $\frac{1}{2}$ of 20, how did you decide how many groups to make?

**Chart A**

| |
|---|
| $\frac{1}{2}$ of 24: |
| $\frac{1}{3}$ of 24: |
| $\frac{2}{3}$ of 24: |
| $\frac{1}{4}$ of 24: |
| $\frac{3}{4}$ of 24: |
| $\frac{1}{6}$ of 24: |
| $\frac{1}{8}$ of 24: |
| $\frac{3}{8}$ of 24: |

**Chart B**

| |
|---|
| $\frac{1}{2}$ of 20: |
| $\frac{1}{4}$ of 20: |
| $\frac{3}{4}$ of 20: |
| $\frac{1}{5}$ of 20: |
| $\frac{2}{5}$ of 20: |
| $\frac{1}{10}$ of 20: |
| $\frac{10}{10}$ of 20: |

## Show What You Know!

1. Which is greater, $\frac{1}{3}$ of 15 or $\frac{1}{4}$ of 12? Use pictures, symbols, or words to explain your answer.

2. **Number Sense** Is $\frac{1}{2}$ of 12 equal to $\frac{3}{6}$ of 12? Use pictures, symbols, or words to explain your answer.

**Write the fractional part.**

3. $\frac{1}{3}$ of 12

4. $\frac{5}{6}$ of 12

5. $\frac{1}{6}$ of 12

6. $\frac{1}{4}$ of 12

7. $\frac{3}{4}$ of 12

8. $\frac{12}{12}$ of 12

9. $\frac{1}{2}$ of 12

10. $\frac{2}{3}$ of 12

11. In exercises 3 through 10, which answers did you figure out without using counters? Explain how you found your answer.

12. **Mental Math** How is finding $\frac{1}{3}$ of 15 like dividing 15 by 3?

13. **Critical Thinking** If $\frac{1}{3}$ is greater than $\frac{1}{4}$, why is $\frac{1}{3}$ of 15 less than $\frac{1}{4}$ of 24?

## Problem Solving

**You have 8 library books. You return 6 and renew the rest.**

14. What fraction of your library books did you return? Explain how you found the answer.

15. What fractional part of your library books did you renew? Write a number sentence to show the number of renewed books.

# Fractional Parts of a Number

Blue Morpho butterfly

Swallowtail butterfly

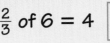

You are observing 6 butterflies for a science project. Of the 6 butterflies, $\frac{2}{3}$ are yellow. The others are blue. How many of the butterflies are yellow?

You need to find $\frac{2}{3}$ of 6 to answer the question.

## Here's A Way!  Find $\frac{2}{3}$ of 6.

**Use counters.**

Use 6 counters.

**1** Divide the counters into three equal parts. Find how many are in one part.

$\frac{1}{3}$ of 6 = 2

**2** Add the counters in two parts to get two thirds of the whole.

$\frac{2}{3}$ of 6 = 4

**Multiply.**

You can also find $\frac{2}{3}$ of 6 by multiplying.

**1** Multiply the numerators.

$$\frac{2}{3} \times \frac{6}{1} = \frac{12}{3}$$

$$6 = \frac{6}{1}$$

**2** Then simplify.

$$\frac{12}{3} = 4$$

So $\frac{2}{3}$ of 6 is 4. Four of the butterflies are yellow.

**Talk About It!**  Why is the product less than the whole number that was multiplied?

## Show What You Know!

Write the answer. Use counters or draw pictures if you need to.

1. $\frac{1}{3}$ of 18
2. $\frac{2}{3}$ of 18
3. $\frac{1}{2}$ of 30
4. $\frac{3}{6}$ of 30
5. $\frac{1}{5}$ of 30

6. **Write About It** How does exercise 1 help you answer exercise 2?

**Mental Math** Do you need to multiply, divide, or do both to find the answer? Tell why.

7. $\frac{1}{5}$ of 20
8. $\frac{2}{3}$ of 15
9. $\frac{5}{5}$ of 40
10. $\frac{1}{2}$ of 14

11. **Critical Thinking** When you multiply a fraction and a whole number, will the product always be less than the whole number? Explain your answer.

## Work It Out!

Write the answer. Use counters or draw pictures if you need to.

12. $\frac{1}{3}$ of 18
13. $\frac{3}{4}$ of 24
14. $\frac{3}{5}$ of 20
15. $\frac{5}{6}$ of 30
16. $\frac{5}{8}$ of 32

17. **Create Your Own** Write a problem about butterflies that uses $\frac{1}{3}$ of 18.

### Problem Solving Using Data

18. You and a friend decide to split equally the cost of flower seeds to plant in a garden. You give your friend 2 quarters. How much should you get back?

19. You have two-thirds of the money you need to buy a packet of herb seeds. What one coin would give you just enough money?

**Seed Prices**

| Seed | Price |
| --- | --- |
| Flower Seeds | $ .80 |
| Herb Seeds | $ .75 |

More Practice Set 8.8, p. 500

**Math Journal**

Explain how to find a fractional part of a number. Use the example $\frac{5}{6}$ of 30.

# Problem Solving
## Look for a Pattern

**Y**ou are adding red squares and then white squares to the center of the design shown. The largest square is 32 cm wide. You continue adding squares until the smallest red square is 1 cm wide. How many red squares will be in your design altogether?

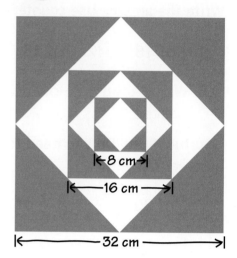

|←8 cm→|
|←—16 cm—→|
|←————— 32 cm —————→|

## Here's A Way! Use Look for a Pattern.

**1 Understand**

• What are you supposed to find out?

• What do you know about the measurements of each red square?

**2 Plan**

• How does the size of each red square change?

• Can you find a pattern in the way the size of each red square changes? Explain.

| Red Square | Width |
|---|---|
| 1 | 32 cm |
| 2 | 16 cm |
| 3 | 8 cm |
| 4 | 4 cm |

**3 Try It**

• How can you show this pattern in numbers?

• Can you continue the number pattern without drawing more squares? Explain.

**4 Look Back**

• There will be 6 red squares in all.

• How did using Look for a Pattern help you to solve the problem?

**Use Look for a Pattern to solve the problem.**

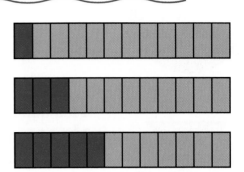

1. Draw and label the next two fraction models in the pattern shown.

2. **Critical Thinking** Write the number pattern in problem 1. How did fraction models help you see the number pattern?

## Work It Out!

**Use Look for a Pattern or any other strategy to solve the problem. Show your work.**

3. Copy and complete this number pattern:
   2, 8, 6, 12, 10, 16, 14, 20, 18, ■, ■, ■.

4. Copy and complete this number pattern: $\frac{1}{2}$ $\frac{2}{3}$ $\frac{3}{4}$ $\frac{4}{5}$ ■ ■ ■.

5. A plant is 1 in. tall. Suppose that for 5 days, its height doubles each day. How tall will it be at the end of the fifth day?

6. Fifty-two tulips are planted in this repeating pattern: red, white, red, yellow. What color is the thirty-sixth tulip?

7. **Create Your Own** Make up your own design or number pattern. See if a classmate can continue the pattern.

8. The price of a jacket is $256. This price will be cut by $\frac{1}{2}$ until the jacket sells or the price drops below $10. If the price is changed every day, how many days will it take to get below $10?

9. Suppose that in September all the students in your class walk to school. In October, $\frac{2}{3}$ walk to school. In November, $\frac{1}{2}$ walk to school. A friend says that in December $\frac{1}{3}$ will walk to school. Do you agree? Explain.

### Share Your Thinking

10. Describe how you solved problem 8. What strategy did you use?

11. Find and describe two patterns in your classroom.

# Mixed Numbers

Getting Started

**What You'll Need:**
▶ ruler

**Vocabulary:**
  mixed number
  Glossary, p. 516

**T**his quilt square measures $2\frac{1}{2}$ inches on each side. A number that has a whole number part and a fraction is a **mixed number**. A mixed number can also be written as a fraction.

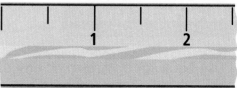

## Here's A Way!   Write mixed numbers and fractions.

**Write $2\frac{1}{2}$ as a fraction.**

**1** Use the ruler to count by halves to $2\frac{1}{2}$. Remember one whole equals two halves.

**2** Count the number of halves there are. Then, write the fraction.

2 halves   2 halves   1 half

$2\frac{1}{2}$ is equivalent to $\frac{5}{2}$

### Talk About It!

What two whole numbers is $2\frac{1}{2}$ between?

**Write $\frac{5}{2}$ as a mixed number.**

**1** Use a ruler or divide. On a ruler, $2\frac{1}{2}$ is equal to 2 wholes and 1 half. Count out $\frac{5}{2}$ on the ruler. The ruler shows $\frac{5}{2}$ is the same as $2\frac{1}{2}$.

$1 = \frac{2}{2}$   $1 = \frac{2}{2}$   $\frac{1}{2}$

$\frac{5}{2} = 2\frac{1}{2}$

**2** Another way is to divide the numerator by the denominator. Then, write the remainder as a fraction of the divisor.

$\frac{5}{2}$ ➡ $2\overline{)5}$ as $2\frac{1}{2}$
$\phantom{2\overline{)}}\underline{-4}$
$\phantom{2\overline{)}}1$

$\frac{5}{2} = 2\frac{1}{2}$

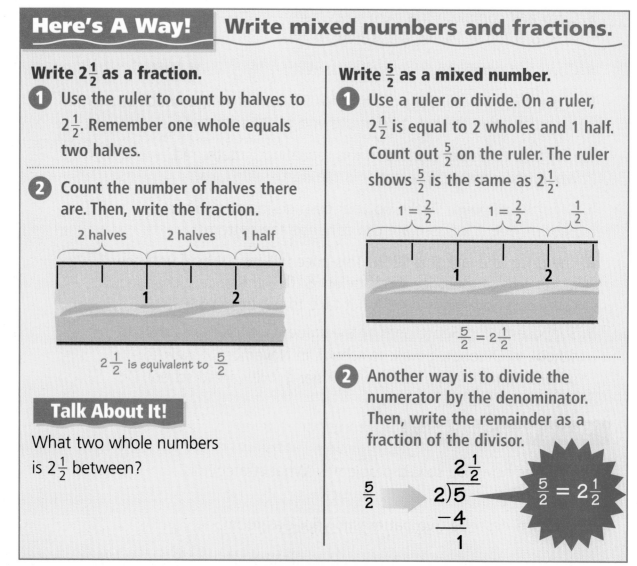

## Show What You Know!

**Write a mixed number and a fraction for each diagram.**

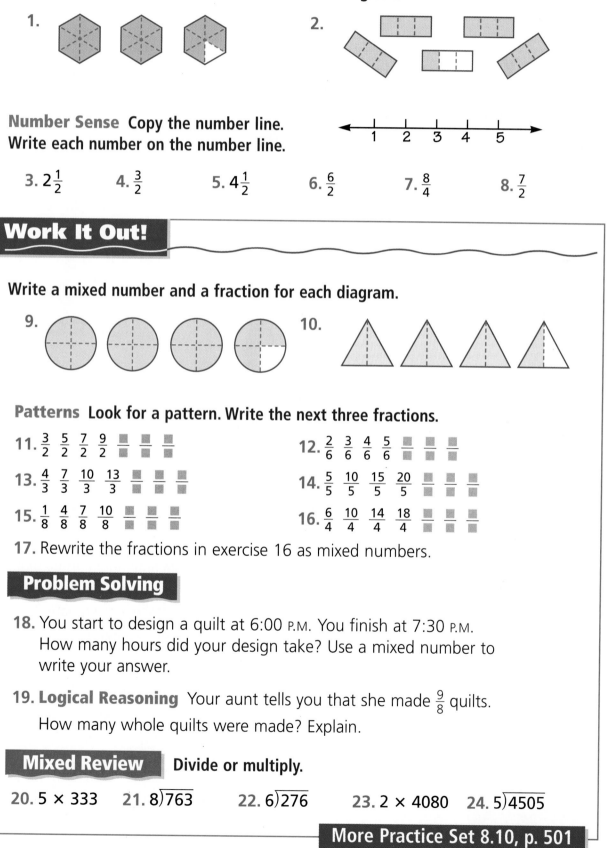

1.

2.

**Number Sense** Copy the number line.
Write each number on the number line.

3. $2\frac{1}{2}$    4. $\frac{3}{2}$    5. $4\frac{1}{2}$    6. $\frac{6}{2}$    7. $\frac{8}{4}$    8. $\frac{7}{2}$

## Work It Out!

**Write a mixed number and a fraction for each diagram.**

9.

10.

**Patterns** Look for a pattern. Write the next three fractions.

11. $\frac{3}{2}$ $\frac{5}{2}$ $\frac{7}{2}$ $\frac{9}{2}$ ▓ ▓ ▓

12. $\frac{2}{6}$ $\frac{3}{6}$ $\frac{4}{6}$ $\frac{5}{6}$ ▓ ▓ ▓

13. $\frac{4}{3}$ $\frac{7}{3}$ $\frac{10}{3}$ $\frac{13}{3}$ ▓ ▓ ▓

14. $\frac{5}{5}$ $\frac{10}{5}$ $\frac{15}{5}$ $\frac{20}{5}$ ▓ ▓ ▓

15. $\frac{1}{8}$ $\frac{4}{8}$ $\frac{7}{8}$ $\frac{10}{8}$ ▓ ▓ ▓

16. $\frac{6}{4}$ $\frac{10}{4}$ $\frac{14}{4}$ $\frac{18}{4}$ ▓ ▓ ▓

17. Rewrite the fractions in exercise 16 as mixed numbers.

### Problem Solving

18. You start to design a quilt at 6:00 P.M. You finish at 7:30 P.M.
How many hours did your design take? Use a mixed number to
write your answer.

19. **Logical Reasoning** Your aunt tells you that she made $\frac{9}{8}$ quilts.
How many whole quilts were made? Explain.

### Mixed Review    Divide or multiply.

20. $5 \times 333$    21. $8\overline{)763}$    22. $6\overline{)276}$    23. $2 \times 4080$    24. $5\overline{)4505}$

More Practice Set 8.10, p. 501

# LESSON 11

# Problem Solving
## Using Look for a Pattern and Other Strategies

You can make a bubble organ by filling bottles with different amounts of water. The bottle with the least amount of water will make the lowest note. The bottle with the most water will make the highest note.

**Problem Solving Process**

✓ Understand
✓ Plan
✓ Try It
✓ Look Back

**Choose a Strategy You Have Learned**

✓ Guess and Check
✓ Draw a Picture
✓ Make a List
✓ Make a Table
✓ Act It Out
✓ Work a Simpler Problem
✓ Look for a Pattern
  Work Backward

You and your partner have 3 bottles. One bottle plays a high note, one plays a low note, and one plays a middle note. Your partner writes a song. He uses dots in 3 different rows to show the 3 different notes. But he erases some of the notes. Can you find the missing notes?

| | | | | | | | | | | | | | | | | |
|---|---|---|---|---|---|---|---|---|---|---|---|---|---|---|---|---|
| **High** | | ·· | | ··· | ·· | | | | | | | | ··· | ·· | |
| **Medium** | ·· | | · | · | ·· | · | | | | · | | · | | ·· | · |
| **Low** | | | ··· | | | | | | | | ··· | | | | ··· |

- What is the question you have to answer?
- Do you need to play the song on the 3 bottles?
- Can you find a pattern in the song that your partner wrote?
- Find the missing part of the pattern.

## Work It Out!

**Use any strategy to solve the problem. Show your work.**

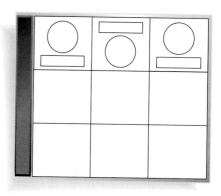

1. You and your friends are in a band. Your band records a CD. Design a cover for your CD by copying and completing the pattern shown.

2. The CD cover will be printed in 2 colors on a white background. You can choose from black, yellow, green, or purple. If all the circles will be one color and all the rectangles another, how many different combinations can you make?

3. Each member of your band either plays one instrument or sings. Of the 6 members, $\frac{1}{3}$ play guitar and $\frac{1}{3}$ are singers. You are the only drummer. How many people play keyboard?

4. You make a wind instrument out of a cardboard tube. You cut holes in the pattern shown. How long should the tube be to fit 12 holes in this pattern?

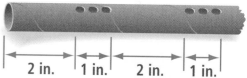

2 in.   1 in.   2 in.   1 in.

5. You plan a poster with a photo of each band member. The poster will be 24 in. wide. The 6 photos will be the same size, placed in 2 rows of 3 across. How many inches wide can each photo be?

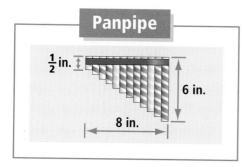
**Panpipe**
$\frac{1}{2}$ in.
6 in.
8 in.

6. Write the next fraction in the pattern: $\frac{1}{2}$ $\frac{1}{4}$ $\frac{1}{8}$ $\frac{1}{16}$ ■.

7. Copy the diagram of this panpipe. The length of each pipe increases by the same amount each time. Write measurements for the length of the other pipes in the panpipe.

8. **Create Your Own** Fill a cup with beans or pebbles. Shake it. Then empty some out. Shake it again. Repeat. How do different amounts change the sound?

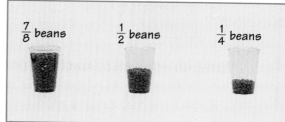

$\frac{7}{8}$ beans   $\frac{1}{2}$ beans   $\frac{1}{4}$ beans

## Share Your Thinking

9. Discuss problem 7 with a partner. What strategy did you each use to solve it?

299

# Chapter 8 Test

## for Pages 274-299

**Test-Taking Tips**

If you have trouble understanding a problem, try drawing a picture to see what's going on.

## Problem Solving

**Solve. Show your work.** (pages 286, 294, 298)

1. The figures are part of a design pattern you are creating for an art contest. Draw what the next figure will look like. Write a fraction to show how much of the square is shaded.

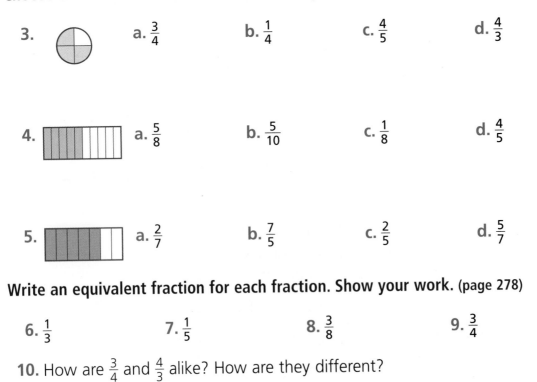

2. If you were to continue this pattern, what would the sixth fraction be?

## Concepts

**Choose the fraction that names the shaded part.** (page 276)

3.    a. $\frac{3}{4}$      b. $\frac{1}{4}$      c. $\frac{4}{5}$      d. $\frac{4}{3}$

4.    a. $\frac{5}{8}$      b. $\frac{5}{10}$      c. $\frac{1}{8}$      d. $\frac{4}{5}$

5.    a. $\frac{2}{7}$      b. $\frac{7}{5}$      c. $\frac{2}{5}$      d. $\frac{5}{7}$

**Write an equivalent fraction for each fraction. Show your work.** (page 278)

6. $\frac{1}{3}$        7. $\frac{1}{5}$        8. $\frac{3}{8}$        9. $\frac{3}{4}$

10. How are $\frac{3}{4}$ and $\frac{4}{3}$ alike? How are they different?

Write each fraction in simplest form. (page 280)

11. $\frac{3}{15}$

12. $\frac{12}{16}$

13. $\frac{5}{10}$

Write the numbers in order from least to greatest. (page 282)

14. $3\frac{1}{2}$  $\frac{3}{4}$  $1\frac{1}{2}$

15. $1\frac{2}{3}$  $1\frac{1}{3}$  $\frac{2}{3}$

16. $\frac{2}{9}$  $\frac{5}{9}$  $\frac{1}{3}$

Complete each number sentence. (page 290)

17. $\frac{1}{3}$ of 9 = ■

18. $\frac{3}{5}$ of 15 = ■

19. $\frac{3}{4}$ of 20 = ■

Write the mixed number as a fraction. (page 296)

20. $3\frac{1}{2}$

21. $1\frac{3}{4}$

22. $5\frac{3}{5}$

Write the fraction as a mixed number. (page 296)

23. $\frac{12}{7}$

24. $\frac{11}{9}$

25. $\frac{4}{3}$

## Performance Task

How can you use the fraction model to show an equivalent fraction? Include drawings to make your answer clear. (pages 276, 278)

Keep In Mind . . .

Your work will be evaluated on the following:

☑ Clear and correct models

☑ Accurate shading

☑ Correctly written equivalent fractions

☑ Clear explanation

- Explain how you decided the amount to shade on each fraction model.

# Cumulative Review

## Subtraction (Chapter 2)

What is the difference between $4.00 and $2.59?

**Here's A Way!**

Regroup.
Then subtract.

$$\begin{array}{r} 3 \; \overset{9}{\cancel{1}}\overset{}{0}10 \\ \$4.\cancel{0}\cancel{0} \\ - \$2.59 \\ \hline \$1.41 \end{array}$$

Find the difference between the pair of numbers.

**1.** 365 and 420       **2.** 909 and 111

**3.** $5.72 and $3.90   **4.** $6.01 and $1.19

Which pair has the greater difference? Write a or b.

**5. a.** $13.76 − $9.22  **b.** $4.00 − $3.50

**6. a.** $23.23 − $10.21 **b.** $53.15 − $40.06

---

## Multiples (Chapter 4)

What is the least common multiple of 3 and 6?

**Here's A Way!**

Count by 3's.
Then count by 6's.
The multiples common to 3 and 6 include 6, 12, 18 . . .
The least common multiple is 6.

List the first five multiples of the number.

**7.** 2              **8.** 5              **9.** 9

Find the least common multiple of the pair.

**10.** 2 and 5    **11.** 9 and 12   **12.** 3 and 7

**13.** What is special about the multiples of the number 1?

---

## Geometric Solids (Chapter 5)

What is this solid?

**Here's A Way!**

This solid is a cube. It has 6 faces, 12 edges, and 8 vertices.

edge→ face
vertex↗

Match.

**14.** flat surface          **a.** where faces meet

**15.** vertex                **b.** pyramid

**16.** edge                  **c.** cone

**17.** 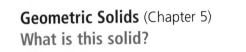   **d.** face

**18.**                       **e.** corner point

**19.**                       **f.** sphere

## Estimate Products (Chapter 6)
About how much is 6 × 48?

### Here's A Way!

You can make a rough estimate with front-end estimation.
6 × 40 = 240
You can make a closer estimate with rounding.
6 × 50 = 300
The exact answer is between 240 and 300.

**Make a front-end estimate. Then, use rounding to estimate.**

20. 7 × 52    21. 5 × 129    22. 10 × 1213

23. 451 × 3    24. 2 × 8672    25. 4 × 1147

26. When will front-end estimation and rounding produce the same estimate?

27. Look at the numbers. Which two have a product of about 1500?

   48  20  38  30  68  40  28

## Averages (Chapter 7)
Find the average of 20, 40, and 75.

### Here's A Way!

Add.    20
        40
      + 75
       135

To find the average,        45
divide by 3.            3)135

**Find the average.**

28. 15, 20, 40

29. 62, 17, 38, 42, 51

30. 0, 3, 7, 10, 5, 5

31. $1.00, $1.50, $2.00

32. 124, 176, 188, 113, 104

33. $23.75, $1.99, $13.66, $12.60

## Problem Solving

Problem Solving Process
✓ Understand
✓ Plan
✓ Try It
✓ Look Back

Choose a Strategy You Have Learned
✓ Guess and Check
✓ Draw a Picture
✓ Make a List
✓ Make a Table
✓ Act It Out
✓ Work a Simpler Problem
✓ Look for a Pattern
  Work Backward

**Choose any strategy you have learned to solve the problem. Show your work.**

34. Suppose you count aloud the multiples of 3, starting with 3. What is the twenty-fifth number you will say?

35. Suppose you are planning a bus trip. The bus goes 60 miles in an hour. You plan to travel 6 hours each day. If your trip starts on Monday, on what day will you have traveled 1080 miles?

36. You have 5 coins. Some are dimes and the rest are quarters. Their total value is $.95. What coins do you have?

INVESTIGATION

# Plan a Park

**Geography Connection**   **With Your Group**

**H**ow do city planners plan cities and parks? They think about what fractions of the land should be used for different purposes. They also use the geography and natural features of the land to guide them.

Your group can plan your own park. You will decide how much land to use for each part of your park.

## 1

### Plan It

- Use this map to plan your park. Look carefully at its features, such as rivers and lakes.

- Look at the chart below. Discuss the categories you want to have in your park. Compare them. What needs to be built? Where should each category go on the map?

- Talk about each category and how much land it will take up.

## 2

### Put It Together

- Copy the map onto a grid. How many grid squares are there?

- Draw the categories you chose. Label them with different colors.

- About how many squares of land does each category use? Make a fraction for each category showing what part of the park land it uses.

| Categories of Land Use | Fraction of Total Land |
|---|---|
| Nature preserves | |
| Sports areas | |
| Playgrounds | |
| Gardens | |
| Walking trails | |
| Eating places | |

## 3

### Wrap It Up

- Work together to report on how you planned your park. Tell what worked well and what you might have done differently.

## 4

### Discuss Your Results

- Have you covered the points in Keep In Mind?

- Share your park map, chart, and report with other groups.

- Which park would you most like to visit? Why?

**Internet**

> Visit the **Math Center** at **Houghton Mifflin Education Place.** http://www.eduplace.com

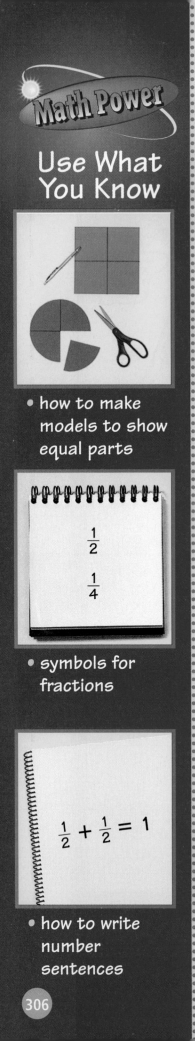

- how to make
models to show
equal parts

$\frac{1}{2}$

$\frac{1}{4}$

- symbols for
fractions

$\frac{1}{2} + \frac{1}{2} = 1$

- how to write
number
sentences

# CHAPTER 9

# Addition and Subtraction of Fractions

## Try This!

**H**ave you ever seen someone sew a quilt? You can design your own fraction quilt using what you know about fractions.

### What You'll Need

scissors, 4 sheets of paper in different colors

**1**

Fold and cut one sheet of paper into halves, one sheet into fourths, and another into eighths. Label each piece $\frac{1}{2}$, $\frac{1}{4}$, or $\frac{1}{8}$.

$\frac{1}{2}$   $\frac{1}{4}$   $\frac{1}{8}$

**2**

Combine pieces to cover a whole sheet of paper. This is your fraction quilt.

$\frac{1}{2}$

$\frac{1}{4}$

$\frac{1}{8}$

$\frac{1}{8}$

**3**

Write a number sentence for your fraction quilt.
$\frac{1}{2} + \frac{1}{4} + \frac{1}{8} + \frac{1}{8} = 1$.

How did you combine parts to make a whole?

What other ways can you combine parts to make a whole?

**Ready to Go!**

# Adding and Subtracting Like Fractions

**F**ractions that have the same denominator are called **like fractions**. To add or subtract fractions, think about adding or subtracting parts of a whole.

**Use What You Know**

$\dfrac{3}{8}$ ← numerator
      ← denominator

The **numerator** is the number of parts you are talking about. The **denominator** is the number of equal parts in the whole.

## Activity

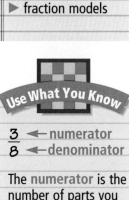

### Add $\dfrac{5}{8}$ and $\dfrac{2}{8}$.

$\dfrac{5}{8}$

$\dfrac{2}{8}$

$\dfrac{5}{8} + \dfrac{2}{8}$

- Use a fraction model to show the first fraction.

- Use another fraction model to show the second fraction.

- Line up the $\dfrac{5}{8}$ model and the $\dfrac{2}{8}$ model as shown.

- Count the number of equal shaded parts. You are adding 5 parts and 2 parts. The total is 7 parts.

- Write the number sentence.

$$\dfrac{5}{8} + \dfrac{2}{8} = \dfrac{7}{8}$$

Think about adding whole numbers:

$$5 + 2 = 7$$

  5 eighths
+ 2 eighths
  7 eighths

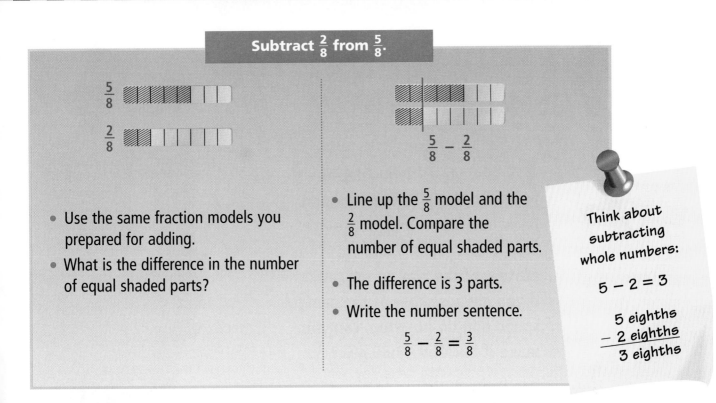

**Subtract $\frac{2}{8}$ from $\frac{5}{8}$.**

$\frac{5}{8}$

$\frac{2}{8}$

$\frac{5}{8} - \frac{2}{8}$

- Use the same fraction models you prepared for adding.
- What is the difference in the number of equal shaded parts?

- Line up the $\frac{5}{8}$ model and the $\frac{2}{8}$ model. Compare the number of equal shaded parts.
- The difference is 3 parts.
- Write the number sentence.

$$\frac{5}{8} - \frac{2}{8} = \frac{3}{8}$$

Think about subtracting whole numbers:

$5 - 2 = 3$

5 eighths
− 2 eighths
3 eighths

## Show What You Know!

**Discuss each question and explain your answer.**

1. **Critical Thinking** How does thinking about whole numbers help you add or subtract fractions?

2. **Critical Thinking** Suppose you have two like fractions. Write a rule for adding them. Write a rule for subtracting them.

**Write the answer. Use fraction models or think about whole numbers.**

3. $\frac{1}{6} + \frac{2}{6}$
4. $\frac{2}{10} + \frac{6}{10}$
5. $\frac{2}{5} + \frac{2}{5}$
6. $\frac{5}{8} - \frac{2}{8}$
7. $\frac{1}{3} + \frac{1}{3}$

8. $\frac{7}{10} - \frac{3}{10}$
9. $\frac{6}{8} - \frac{2}{8}$
10. $\frac{3}{5} + \frac{1}{5}$
11. $\frac{1}{4} + \frac{1}{4}$
12. $\frac{7}{12} - \frac{2}{12}$

**Mental Math** Use mental math to solve the exercises.

13. $\frac{1}{4} + \frac{2}{4}$
14. $\frac{2}{3} - \frac{1}{3}$
15. $\frac{4}{5} - \frac{2}{5}$
16. $\frac{3}{6} + \frac{2}{6}$
17. $\frac{7}{10} - \frac{5}{10}$

18. $\frac{6}{8} + \frac{1}{8}$
19. $\frac{5}{6} - \frac{2}{6}$
20. $\frac{7}{8} - \frac{5}{8}$
21. $\frac{2}{5} + \frac{2}{5}$
22. $\frac{1}{6} + \frac{2}{6}$

**Mixed Review** Copy and complete. Write >, <, or =.

23. $\frac{5}{6} \bullet \frac{2}{3}$
24. $\frac{3}{8} \bullet \frac{3}{4}$
25. $\frac{2}{3} \bullet \frac{5}{9}$
26. $\frac{5}{6}$ of 12 $\bullet$ $\frac{2}{3}$ of 9

**More Practice Set 7.1, p. 501**

# Problem Solving
## Draw a Picture

**Getting Started**

**What You'll Need:**
▶ grid paper

You and your friends decide to in-line skate to the park and back. You leave your house at 9:00 A.M. It takes $\frac{1}{2}$ hour to skate $\frac{3}{4}$ of the way to the park. If you always skate at the same speed and do not stop, can you make it back by 10:30 A.M.?

Use Draw a Picture to solve the problem.

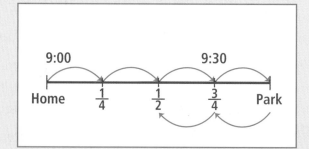

## Here's A Way!   Use Draw a Picture.

**1  Understand**

- What are you supposed to find out?
- How far can you go in $\frac{1}{2}$ hour?

**2  Plan**

- How might a picture help you?
- What would you show in the picture?

**3  Try It**

- Why does it help to divide the distance to the park into fourths?
- Use the picture to solve the problem.

**4  Look Back**

- You will make it back before 10:30 A.M.
- How did using Draw a Picture help you to solve the problem?

**Use Draw a Picture to solve the problem.**

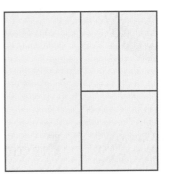

1. You bring along a large box of raisins. You give $\frac{1}{2}$ to a friend. Then you give $\frac{1}{2}$ of what is left to another friend. Then you meet one more friend. The same thing happens. What fraction of the original box do you have left for yourself?

2. **Critical Thinking** Did you need to know the number of raisins to solve problem 1? Why or why not?

## Work It Out!

**Use Draw a Picture or any other strategy to solve the problem.**

3. Two friends meet you $\frac{1}{2}$ of the way to the park. They skate the rest of the way there. But they only skate $\frac{1}{2}$ of the way home with you. If the entire trip is 4 mi long, how many miles did they skate with you?

4. Your family drives to an in-line skating event. Driving $\frac{3}{4}$ of the way there uses $\frac{1}{2}$ tank of gasoline. Can you make it back home without getting more gasoline? Explain.

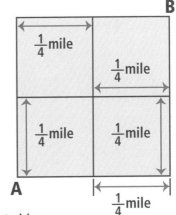

5. Look at the map. How many different 1-mile skating paths are there from Point A to Point B?

6. You pour the powder of a drink mix into a pitcher. Now you need to add $2\frac{1}{4}$ cups of water. You have only measuring cups for $\frac{3}{4}$ and $\frac{1}{2}$ cups. How can you use these to measure $2\frac{1}{4}$ cups?

7. Suppose you and nine friends are skating in a parking lot. You skate behind each other in a line. At the first lamppost, every third skater reaches out and gently taps it. Every fourth skater taps the second lamppost. Every fifth skater taps the third lamppost. Which skaters do not touch any of these lampposts?

## Share Your Thinking

8. How did you solve problem 7? Discuss the problem with a classmate. Compare the strategies you used.

# Adding and Subtracting Unlike Fractions

**Use What You Know**

Equivalent fractions name the same number.

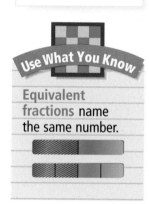

**F**ractions that don't have the same denominator are called **unlike fractions.**

Before you add or subtract unlike fractions, you have to find equivalent fractions.

**Activity**

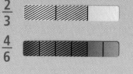

Add $\frac{2}{3}$ and $\frac{1}{6}$.

$\frac{2}{3} + \frac{1}{6}$

$\frac{2}{3}$

$\frac{4}{6}$

$\frac{4}{6} + \frac{1}{6}$

- Use fraction models for $\frac{2}{3}$ and $\frac{1}{6}$.

- Line up the models.

- The models represent fractions with different denominators.

- Find a sixths model that has the same amount shaded as the $\frac{2}{3}$ model.

- How many sixths equal $\frac{2}{3}$?

- Because $\frac{2}{3}$ is equivalent to $\frac{4}{6}$, you can replace $\frac{2}{3}$ with $\frac{4}{6}$ to find the sum.

- Find the sum.

$$\frac{4}{6} + \frac{1}{6} = \frac{5}{6}$$

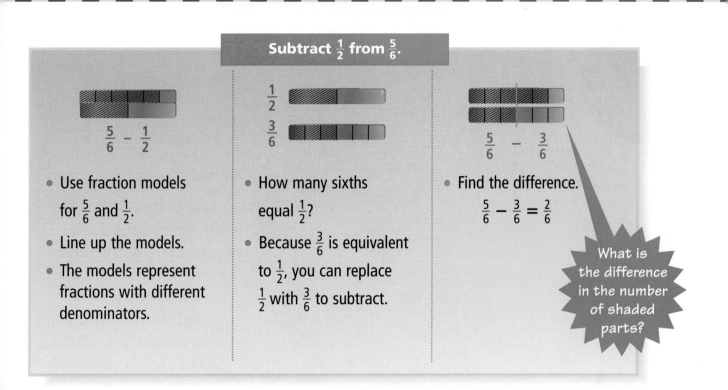

$$\frac{5}{6} - \frac{1}{2}$$

$\frac{1}{2}$

$\frac{3}{6}$

$$\frac{5}{6} - \frac{3}{6}$$

- Use fraction models for $\frac{5}{6}$ and $\frac{1}{2}$.

- Line up the models.

- The models represent fractions with different denominators.

- How many sixths equal $\frac{1}{2}$?

- Because $\frac{3}{6}$ is equivalent to $\frac{1}{2}$, you can replace $\frac{1}{2}$ with $\frac{3}{6}$ to subtract.

- Find the difference.

$$\frac{5}{6} - \frac{3}{6} = \frac{2}{6}$$

What is the difference in the number of shaded parts?

## Show What You Know!

1. **Critical Thinking** Describe how to add and subtract fractions with different denominators. How did fraction models help you?

2. **Write About It** Compare adding and subtracting like fractions to adding and subtracting unlike fractions. How are they the same? How are they different?

**Add or subtract. Use fraction models if you wish.**

3. $\frac{4}{12} + \frac{1}{4}$    4. $\frac{3}{6} + \frac{1}{3}$    5. $\frac{3}{4} - \frac{1}{2}$    6. $\frac{2}{3} - \frac{6}{12}$    7. $\frac{3}{8} + \frac{2}{4}$

8. $\frac{1}{2} - \frac{1}{4}$    9. $\frac{2}{3} + \frac{2}{12}$    10. $\frac{5}{6} - \frac{1}{3}$    11. $\frac{3}{6} + \frac{1}{12}$    12. $\frac{9}{10} - \frac{1}{2}$

**Patterns** Find the sum. Describe a pattern in each addition set.

13. a. $\frac{1}{4} + \frac{1}{12}$    14. a. $\frac{2}{5} + \frac{1}{10}$    15. a. $\frac{1}{4} + \frac{1}{8}$    16. a. $\frac{3}{6} + \frac{1}{12}$

  b. $\frac{2}{4} + \frac{1}{12}$      b. $\frac{3}{5} + \frac{1}{10}$      b. $\frac{2}{4} + \frac{1}{8}$      b. $\frac{4}{6} + \frac{1}{12}$

  c. $\frac{3}{4} + \frac{1}{12}$      c. $\frac{4}{5} + \frac{1}{10}$      c. $\frac{3}{4} + \frac{1}{8}$      c. $\frac{5}{6} + \frac{1}{12}$

17. **Problem Solving** You and your friend are building a tower.

  You build $\frac{2}{3}$ of it. Your friend builds $\frac{1}{6}$ of it. Then your dog

  knocks over $\frac{1}{2}$. How much of the tower is left?

# Problem Solving
## Choose a Computation Method

| Alaska Time Zone | Pacific Time Zone | Mountain Time Zone | Central Time Zone | Eastern Time Zone |
|---|---|---|---|---|

**T**he United States has six time zones. Each time zone is one hour different from the next. Suppose you are the producer of a television news show in California. When should you show your program so people across the country can watch it live?

Hawaii Time Zone

## You Decide

- When do you add hours? When do you subtract hours?
- What might people be doing at different times?

## Work It Out!

**Choose a Computation Method**

**Ask Yourself:**

Do I need an exact answer or an estimate?

Should I use a model, paper and pencil, mental math, or a calculator?

What operation should I use?

**Decide what computation method to use. Solve and explain.**

1. A television network offers to show your program at 10:00 P.M. Pacific Time. Your program lasts an hour. Will most people in Texas still be awake to watch it?

2. You are in California, and you want to telephone your aunt at her office in Illinois. She leaves work by 6:00 P.M. What's the latest time you can call, Pacific Time?

3. You have tickets to a concert in Colorado that starts at 5:00 P.M. You board a plane in Florida at 1:00 P.M. The flight lasts 4 hours. Will you make it on time?

## Share Your Thinking

4. Explain the strategy you used to solve problem 3.

# Midchapter Review

## for Pages 306–314

## Problem Solving

**Solve. Show your work.** (page 314)

1. You have 3 equal stacks of baseball cards. You give a friend one of the stacks. You have 40 cards left. How many cards did you start with?

2. Suppose you live in New York. At 9:00 A.M. you phone a relative in Denver, Colorado. What time is it there? An hour later, you call your mom, who is in Texas. What time is it there?

## Concepts

**Use the fraction model to complete the addition or subtraction sentence.** (page 308)

3.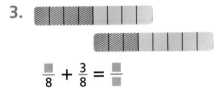

$$\frac{\blacksquare}{8} + \frac{3}{8} = \frac{\blacksquare}{\blacksquare}$$

4.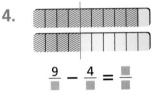

$$\frac{9}{\blacksquare} - \frac{4}{\blacksquare} = \frac{\blacksquare}{\blacksquare}$$

**Find the answer.** (pages 308, 312)

5. When you add or subtract fractions, why do you add or subtract the numerators but not the denominators?

## Skills

**Add or subtract. Use fraction models when helpful.** (pages 308, 312)

6. $\frac{2}{5} + \frac{1}{5}$     7. $\frac{4}{12} - \frac{1}{12}$    8. $\frac{5}{6} - \frac{4}{6}$    9. $\frac{1}{4} + \frac{2}{4}$    10. $\frac{5}{8} - \frac{1}{8}$

11. $\frac{7}{8} - \frac{2}{8}$    12. $\frac{4}{6} + \frac{1}{6}$    13. $\frac{1}{4} + \frac{3}{4}$    14. $\frac{7}{10} - \frac{5}{10}$    15. $\frac{5}{8} + \frac{2}{8}$

# Math *World*

Read about fractions and shoe sizes. Learn how ancient people used addition to write fractions. Set fractions to a Caribbean beat.

## If the shoe fits

An Englishman's shoe from the 1300s

How are English shoe sizes different from American? Both countries base their shoe sizes on an old English system for sizing shoes. In this system, each shoe size increases $\frac{1}{3}$ inch from the one before it. The English system begins at 4 inches, with size 0. The American system, however, begins at $3\frac{11}{12}$ inches with size 0. So, if you wear a size 4 in England, the shoe measures $5\frac{1}{3}$ inches. In the United States, the same size shoe measures $5\frac{1}{4}$ inches.

# Try This!

Counting fractions is an important part of keeping the beat in music. Look at the Puerto Rican folk song below. The notes are like fractions. In one measure, the notes will add up to one.

Follow these steps to keep the song's beat.

**1** Copy the notes of the first measure. Use the chart and write the fraction for each note. Add the fractions.

**2** Repeat step 1 for the second measure. Do you find the same sum?

**3** The first symbol in the third measure is called a *rest*. The sound stops for the length of an eighth note. Write $\frac{1}{8}$. Add it to the other beats in the measure.

**4** Find the fractions for measure 4. Then, start at measure 1 and tap the rhythm for the song.

| | | |
|---|---|---|
| ○ | 1 | whole note |
| ♩ | $\frac{1}{2}$ | half note |
| ● | $\frac{1}{4}$ | quarter note |
| ♪ | $\frac{1}{8}$ | eighth note |

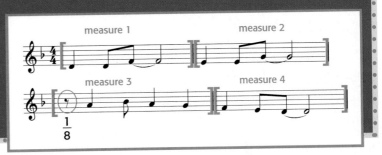

measure 1    measure 2

measure 3    measure 4

$\frac{1}{8}$

## Sum fractions

How did ancient Egyptians write $\frac{3}{4}$? They thought of this fraction as $\frac{1}{2} + \frac{1}{4}$ and wrote it that way, but without the addition sign. Which fraction is shown on the right? Do you think this is easier or harder than how you write fractions?

$\frac{1}{3}$    $\frac{1}{15}$

## Respond

Work in small groups . . .
to write math sentences for a piece of music you find in your library.

**Internet:**
Houghton Mifflin Education Place
Explore the Math Center at
http://www.eduplace.com

317

# Adding Unlike Fractions

| DAY | RAINFALL |
|---|---|
| Monday | 0 |
| Tuesday | $\frac{3}{8}$ inch |
| Wednesday | 0 |
| Thursday | $\frac{1}{4}$ inch |
| Friday | 0 |
| Saturday | 0 |
| Sunday | 0 |

**MY NOTES:**

- I set up the rain gauge in the schoolyard.
- I checked it twice a day.

**Use What You Know**

You can find equivalent fractions by multiplying the numerator and the denominator by the same number.

**Y**ou measured the rainfall for one week as a weather project. On Monday it rained $\frac{3}{8}$ inch. On Thursday it rained $\frac{1}{4}$ inch. How much rain fell that week?

You can add $\frac{3}{8}$ and $\frac{1}{4}$ even though they have different denominators.

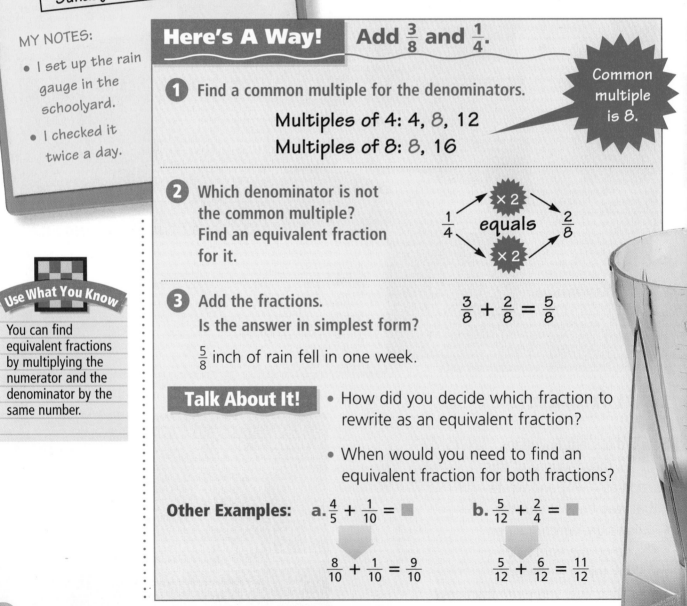

## Here's A Way! Add $\frac{3}{8}$ and $\frac{1}{4}$.

❶ Find a common multiple for the denominators.

Multiples of 4: 4, **8**, 12

Multiples of 8: **8**, 16

Common multiple is 8.

❷ Which denominator is not the common multiple? Find an equivalent fraction for it.

$\frac{1}{4}$ equals $\frac{2}{8}$ (×2)

❸ Add the fractions. Is the answer in simplest form?

$$\frac{3}{8} + \frac{2}{8} = \frac{5}{8}$$

$\frac{5}{8}$ inch of rain fell in one week.

**Talk About It!**
- How did you decide which fraction to rewrite as an equivalent fraction?
- When would you need to find an equivalent fraction for both fractions?

**Other Examples:**

a. $\frac{4}{5} + \frac{1}{10} = \blacksquare$

$$\frac{8}{10} + \frac{1}{10} = \frac{9}{10}$$

b. $\frac{5}{12} + \frac{2}{4} = \blacksquare$

$$\frac{5}{12} + \frac{6}{12} = \frac{11}{12}$$

Write the sum. Use fraction models if you need them.

1. $\frac{7}{10} + \frac{1}{5}$   2. $\frac{1}{4} + \frac{4}{12}$   3. $\frac{3}{8} + \frac{1}{2}$   4. $\frac{2}{5} + \frac{3}{10}$   5. $\frac{3}{6} + \frac{2}{6}$   6. $\frac{5}{12} + \frac{1}{3}$

7. **Critical Thinking** Why don't you add the denominators when you add fractions?

## Work It Out!

Write the sum. Use fraction models if you need them.

8. $\frac{5}{12} + \frac{4}{12}$   9. $\frac{1}{5} + \frac{3}{10}$   10. $\frac{2}{3} + \frac{1}{6}$   11. $\frac{2}{10} + \frac{7}{10}$   12. $\frac{1}{6} + \frac{5}{12}$

13. $\frac{3}{8} + \frac{1}{4}$   14. $\frac{2}{3} + \frac{1}{12}$   15. $\frac{3}{8} + \frac{1}{2}$   16. $\frac{1}{6} + \frac{1}{2}$   17. $\frac{7}{12} + \frac{1}{4}$

**Mental Math** Use mental math to solve the exercises.

18. $\frac{3}{5} + \frac{1}{5}$   19. $\frac{1}{2} + \frac{1}{4}$   20. $\frac{7}{8} - \frac{1}{8}$   21. $\frac{2}{6} + \frac{1}{3}$   22. $\frac{3}{10} + \frac{4}{10}$

### Problem Solving   Using Data

23. In El Paso, $\frac{3}{10}$ inch of rain fell on February 10. On February 15, $\frac{1}{2}$ inch of rain fell. What was the total amount of rain on these two days?

24. What was the total amount of rain that fell on San Antonio on February 24 and 25?

25. Which city had more rain on the days shown, San Antonio or El Paso?

### Rainfall in Two Texas Cities

| Date | San Antonio | El Paso |
|------|-------------|---------|
| February 10 | 0 inch | $\frac{3}{10}$ inch |
| February 15 | 0 inch | $\frac{1}{2}$ inch |
| February 24 | $\frac{1}{12}$ inch | 0 inch |
| February 25 | $\frac{5}{6}$ inch | 0 inch |

### Mixed Review   Put the fractions in order from least to greatest.

26. $\frac{4}{10}$  $\frac{9}{10}$  $\frac{6}{10}$   27. $\frac{6}{8}$  $\frac{5}{8}$  $\frac{2}{8}$   28. $\frac{1}{6}$  $\frac{1}{4}$  $\frac{1}{12}$   29. $\frac{5}{6}$  $\frac{2}{3}$  $\frac{5}{12}$   30. $\frac{1}{4}$  $\frac{1}{3}$  $\frac{1}{6}$

Write the answer.

31. $575 \div 9$   32. $465 \div 8$   33. $524 \div 8$   34. $888 \div 8$   35. $764 \div 9$

More Practice Set 9.5, p. 502

# LESSON 6

# Subtracting Unlike Fractions

## Use What You Know

How do you convert fractions to simplest form? Divide both the numerator and the denominator by the same number

$$\frac{3}{12} = \frac{1}{4}$$

**Y**ou are studying how young rain forest frogs grow into adults. Suppose a young frog measures $\frac{1}{4}$ inch. The expected length of an adult is $\frac{7}{12}$ inch. How much will the young frog grow before it becomes an adult? You can subtract to find out.

Rain forest frogs can be less than one inch long.

## Here's A Way! Subtract $\frac{1}{4}$ from $\frac{7}{12}$.

1 Find a common multiple for the denominators.

> Common multiple is 12.

Multiples of 4: 4, 8, 12, 16
Multiples of 12: 12, 24

2 Which denominator is not the common multiple? Find an equivalent fraction for it.

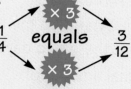

$$\frac{1}{4} \quad \text{equals} \quad \frac{3}{12}$$

3 Subtract the fractions. Write the answer in simplest form.

$$\frac{7}{12} - \frac{3}{12} = \frac{4}{12}$$

$$\frac{4}{12} = \frac{1}{3}$$

The young rain forest frog will probably grow $\frac{1}{3}$ inch.

## Talk About It!

How is subtracting fractions with unlike denominators similar to adding fractions with unlike denominators?

Find the difference. Use fractions models if you need to.

1. $\frac{1}{2} - \frac{1}{8}$    2. $\frac{6}{12} - \frac{1}{3}$    3. $\frac{3}{5} - \frac{1}{10}$    4. $\frac{5}{8} - \frac{1}{2}$    5. $\frac{2}{3} - \frac{1}{6}$    6. $\frac{5}{6} - \frac{3}{6}$

7. $\frac{5}{6} - \frac{2}{3}$    8. $\frac{3}{6} - \frac{1}{3}$    9. $\frac{2}{6} - \frac{1}{12}$    10. $\frac{4}{6} - \frac{1}{3}$    11. $\frac{3}{8} - \frac{1}{4}$    12. $\frac{7}{8} - \frac{6}{8}$

13. **Critical Thinking** Why don't you subtract the denominators when you subtract fractions?

## Work It Out!

Find the difference. Use fraction models if you need to.

14. $\frac{7}{8} - \frac{2}{4}$    15. $\frac{7}{8} - \frac{1}{2}$    16. $\frac{9}{10} - \frac{2}{5}$    17. $\frac{7}{10} - \frac{6}{10}$    18. $\frac{9}{12} - \frac{3}{4}$    19. $\frac{7}{12} - \frac{1}{3}$

20. $\frac{3}{4} - \frac{2}{8}$    21. $\frac{1}{2} - \frac{1}{6}$    22. $\frac{2}{3} - \frac{1}{6}$    23. $\frac{3}{4} - \frac{1}{2}$    24. $\frac{3}{5} - \frac{2}{5}$    25. $\frac{2}{3} - \frac{1}{12}$

**Estimation** Solve the exercises that have a difference of less than $\frac{1}{2}$.

26. $\frac{5}{8} - \frac{1}{4}$    27. $\frac{9}{10} - \frac{4}{5}$    28. $\frac{5}{6} - \frac{2}{3}$    29. $\frac{9}{10} - \frac{1}{5}$    30. $\frac{9}{12} - \frac{1}{2}$

31. **Write About It** In exercises 26–30, how did you decide which subtraction sentences had a difference of less than $\frac{1}{2}$? Explain.

### Problem Solving

Solve the problem.

32. You discover a frog that has red, green, and yellow markings. Red markings cover $\frac{1}{3}$ of his body. Green markings cover $\frac{5}{12}$ of his body. What fraction of his body do the yellow markings cover?

33. Suppose you measure many frogs from one species. You discover that $\frac{1}{4}$ are less than 4 inches long and $\frac{5}{8}$ are between 4 and 5 inches long. What fraction of these frogs is greater than 5 inches long?

More Practice Set 9.6, p. 503

### Math Journal

How can you use what you know about adding fractions to check your answers when you subtract fractions?

# Adding and Subtracting Mixed Numbers

**N**ow try adding and subtracting mixed numbers. Remember that a **mixed number** has a whole number part and a fraction part, like $1\frac{1}{2}$.

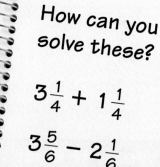

How can you solve these?

$$3\frac{1}{4} + 1\frac{1}{4}$$

$$3\frac{5}{6} - 2\frac{1}{6}$$

## Here's A Way!  Add and subtract mixed numbers.

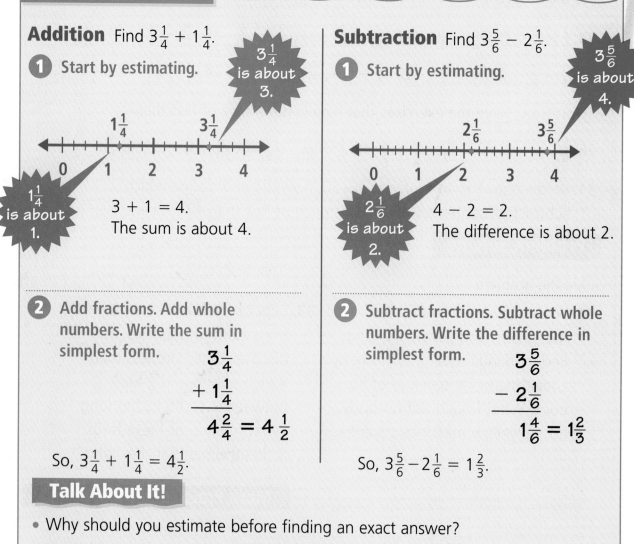

**Addition** Find $3\frac{1}{4} + 1\frac{1}{4}$.

❶ Start by estimating.

$3\frac{1}{4}$ is about 3.

$1\frac{1}{4}$ is about 1.

$3 + 1 = 4.$
The sum is about 4.

❷ Add fractions. Add whole numbers. Write the sum in simplest form.

$$3\frac{1}{4}$$
$$+ 1\frac{1}{4}$$
$$\overline{\phantom{+}4\frac{2}{4}} = 4\frac{1}{2}$$

So, $3\frac{1}{4} + 1\frac{1}{4} = 4\frac{1}{2}$.

**Subtraction** Find $3\frac{5}{6} - 2\frac{1}{6}$.

❶ Start by estimating.

$3\frac{5}{6}$ is about 4.

$2\frac{1}{6}$ is about 2.

$4 - 2 = 2.$
The difference is about 2.

❷ Subtract fractions. Subtract whole numbers. Write the difference in simplest form.

$$3\frac{5}{6}$$
$$- 2\frac{1}{6}$$
$$\overline{\phantom{-}1\frac{4}{6}} = 1\frac{2}{3}$$

So, $3\frac{5}{6} - 2\frac{1}{6} = 1\frac{2}{3}$.

## Talk About It!

- Why should you estimate before finding an exact answer?
- How do you know when a fraction is in simplest form?

## Show What You Know!

**Estimate first. Then record the exact answer.**

1. $7\frac{1}{3} + 2\frac{1}{3}$    2. $5\frac{5}{6} + 4\frac{1}{6}$    3. $3\frac{3}{8} + 2\frac{1}{8}$    4. $2\frac{1}{2} + 1\frac{1}{2}$    5. $6\frac{2}{3} + 1\frac{1}{3}$

6. **Critical Thinking** In exercises 1–5, which numbers did you round up? Which did you round down? Tell your reasoning.

**Find the sum.**

7. $7 + 1\frac{9}{10}$    8. $11 + 2\frac{9}{10}$    9. $8 + 1\frac{1}{12}$    10. $9 + 2\frac{1}{2}$    11. $13 + 2\frac{2}{8}$

12. **Number Sense** Explain how you solved the number sentences in exercises 7–11.

## Work It Out!

**Estimate first. Then record the exact answer.**

13. $5\frac{3}{10} + 2\frac{4}{10}$    14. $4\frac{1}{3} + 2\frac{1}{3}$    15. $3\frac{1}{8} + 2\frac{3}{8}$    16. $6\frac{1}{4} + 1\frac{2}{4}$

17. $2\frac{3}{6} + 1\frac{1}{6}$    18. $3\frac{6}{8} + \frac{2}{8}$    19. $5\frac{4}{12} + 3\frac{5}{12}$    20. $9\frac{3}{10} + 4\frac{4}{10}$

### Problem Solving    Using Data

**Use the chart to solve the problem.**

21. How many bananas will you need to make both of these recipes?

22. **Estimation** Which container would you use to carry the Apple-Coconut Shake to a party?

    a. a container that holds 5 cups
    b. a container that holds 10 cups
    c. a container that holds 15 cups

23. **Logical Reasoning** Could you use the same size container to carry the Orange-Pineapple Shake to the party? Explain.

**More Practice Set 9.7, p. 503**

### Orange-Pineapple Fruit Shake

$4\frac{1}{2}$ cups orange juice

$2\frac{1}{4}$ cups pineapple juice

$5\frac{1}{4}$ bananas

1 tablespoon ginger root

$5\frac{1}{2}$ cups crushed ice

### Apple-Coconut Fruit Shake

$3\frac{1}{2}$ cups apple juice

3 tablespoons coconut milk

$4\frac{1}{3}$ bananas

3 teaspoons ginger root

$3\frac{3}{4}$ cups crushed ice

# Problem Solving
## Using Draw a Picture and Other Strategies

### Getting Started

**What You'll Need:**
▶ grid paper
▶ ruler
▶ colored pencils, markers, or crayons

**N**ative Americans have been weaving on looms for over a thousand years. They make clothes, rugs, and blankets.

Suppose you want to design a blanket that uses a pattern similar to those that Native Americans use. Drawing a picture can help you plan your project.

### Problem Solving Process
✓ Understand
✓ Plan
✓ Try It
✓ Look Back

### Choose a Strategy You Have Learned
✓ Guess and Check
✓ Draw a Picture
✓ Make a List
✓ Make a Table
✓ Act It Out
✓ Work a Simpler Problem
✓ Look for a Pattern
　Work Backward

**Y**our blanket pattern is made up of small red squares inside larger yellow squares. The yellow squares measure 6 in. on each side. The red squares measure 3 in. on each side. What fraction of each larger square is red?

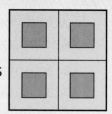

- Use grid paper and a ruler.

- Draw a square that measures 6 in. on each side. Then draw a square inside it that measures 3 in. on each side.

- How many 3 in. squares can you fit inside one 6 in. square?

- Explain why $\frac{1}{2}$ is not the correct answer.

- How did using Draw a Picture help you to solve this problem?

Use Draw a Picture or any other strategy to solve the problem.
Show your work.

1. What fraction of the design shown is blue? Explain.

2. A square blanket is divided into fourths. The top half is
   blue and red, and the bottom half is green and yellow.
   The left half is blue and green, and the right half is red
   and yellow. Explain how this blanket is designed. Hint:
   There is more than one way of dividing a square in half.

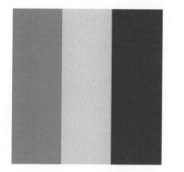

3. Look at the design to the left. Is it greater than
   or less than $\frac{1}{4}$ green? Explain.

4. Suppose this design is 10 in. on each
   side. Someone uses this design to make a
   square blanket. The blanket repeats the
   design 25 times. What size is the blanket?

5. A blanket is made up of red, blue, and yellow squares. Of
   these squares, $\frac{1}{2}$ are red, $\frac{1}{4}$ are blue, and $\frac{1}{4}$ are yellow. If
   there are 30 red squares, how many squares are blue?

6. A blanket has 14 stripes. Some are yellow, some orange, and
   some green. There are twice as many yellow stripes as there are
   orange stripes. There are twice as many orange stripes as green
   stripes. How many orange stripes are there?

7. **Create Your Own** You have 3 different
   colors of yarn. Design a blanket that uses
   equal amounts of all 3 colors. Explain how
   your design does this.

8. If the pattern shown on this blanket continues,
   what fraction of the blanket will be red?

## Share Your Thinking

9. How did you solve problem 8? Explain how patterns helped you.

10. **Critical Thinking** What if the colors shown in problem 8
    were inside circles? Would it be easier or harder to tell what
    fraction of the blanket is red? Discuss this with a classmate.

# LESSON 9

# Problem Solving
## Using Strategies

You can read more about the solar system in the pages of *Kids Discover*.

**A** year is the time it takes a planet to go around the sun. Different planets take different amounts of time to do this. Venus travels faster around the sun than Earth does. In the time it takes Venus to make the trip, Earth has only gone $\frac{3}{5}$ of the way.

### Problem Solving Process
✓ Understand
✓ Plan
✓ Try It
✓ Look Back

### Choose a Strategy You Have Learned
✓ Guess and Check
✓ Draw a Picture
✓ Make a List
✓ Make a Table
✓ Act It Out
✓ Work a Simpler Problem
✓ Look for a Pattern
  Work Backward

**E**arth and Venus are lined up on the same side of the sun. When will these two planets be lined up in the same spot again? How many times will Earth circle the sun before this happens?

- How far has Earth traveled around the sun in B?
- Where will Earth be when Venus completes a second trip?
- Explain a strategy that can help you solve the problem. Then solve it.

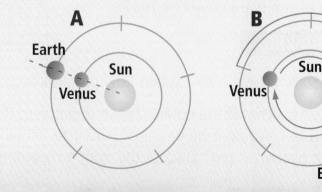

**Use any strategy to solve the problem. Show your work.**

1. Draw the missing picture.

2. You buy a set of planet cards at the planetarium. You get cards for Mercury, Venus, Earth, and Mars. In how many different ways can you put these cards in order?

3. In the time it takes Mercury to travel once around the sun, Earth has only gone $\frac{1}{4}$ of the way. Suppose Mercury has made 8 complete trips around the sun. How many trips has Earth made during this same time?

4. As Mercury travels around the sun, its distance from the sun changes. The closest it comes to the sun is about 28 million miles. The farthest is about 43 million miles. Draw the the shape of the path Mercury follows around the sun.

 **Use a calculator and the chart to solve the problem.**

5. Your weight changes on different planets. Suppose you weigh 104 pounds when you climb into a spaceship on Earth. You weigh 39 pounds when you climb out of the spaceship. What 2 planets might you be on?

6. You continue to travel around the solar system in your spaceship. Your weight changes in the following way: You weigh about 117 pounds, then about 265 pounds, and then about 4 pounds. List the planets in the order you visited them.

7. **Create Your Own** Write a problem about the solar system. Use data shown here or data you find somewhere else. Give your problem to a classmate to solve.

| Planets and Weights ||
| Planet | Fraction of Your Weight on Earth |
| --- | --- |
| Mercury | $\frac{3}{8}$ |
| Venus | $\frac{8}{9}$ |
| Earth | 1 |
| Mars | $\frac{3}{8}$ |
| Jupiter | $2\frac{5}{8}$ |
| Saturn | $1\frac{1}{16}$ |
| Uranus | $1\frac{1}{16}$ |
| Neptune | $1\frac{1}{8}$ |
| Pluto | $\frac{1}{25}$ |

## Share Your Thinking

8. Describe the strategies you used to solve problems 5 and 6.

9. What problem solving strategies could scientists use? Discuss this with a classmate. Think of some examples.

# Problem Solving
## Choose a Computation Method

**M**eteor is another name for a falling star. Most meteors never fall to Earth. They burn up miles above the ground, making streaks of light across the night sky.

Suppose you are an astronomer. Predict how many meteors you will see in 4 hours on August 20.

---

**Choose a Computation Method**

Ask Yourself:

Do I need an exact answer or an estimate?

Should I use a model, paper and pencil, mental math, or a calculator?

What operation should I use?

---

Meteor Showers On the same dates every year, large numbers of meteors appear in the sky. These events are called **meteor showers.** Each meteor shower has a peak day. Scientists keep track of the most meteors you might see during an hour.

## Meteor Showers

| Dates of Meteor Showers | Peak Day | Most Meteors in an Hour |
|---|---|---|
| January 1 – 5 | January 4 | 100 |
| April 19 – 24 | April 22 | 14 |
| June 10 – 21 | June 16 | 10 |
| July 25 – Aug 18 | August 12 | 70 |
| August 18 – 22 | August 20 | 10 |
| December 7 – 15 | December 13 | 55 |

This meteor shower was photographed in December

- Would you use mental math, paper and pencil, or a calculator to solve the problem?

- Solve the problem. Explain why you chose the method you used.

## Work It Out!

**Decide what computation method to use. Solve and explain.**

1. Suppose you watch every meteor shower listed in the chart on page 328. But you can watch each shower for only 4 hours. Might you see more than 800 meteors?

2. You are watching a meteor shower on January 4. The sky is covered with clouds until 8:15 P.M. Then the sky clears. You watch meteors until 10:45 P.M, when clouds cover the sky again. What is the greatest number of meteors you might expect to see?

3. The atmosphere is the air that surrounds Earth. Scientists estimate that as many as 20 million meteors, both large and small, enter Earth's atmosphere every day. How many meteors enter the atmosphere in a week?

4. Meteors can travel at 45 miles each second. Suppose a meteor is 400 miles above Earth. How long would it take the meteor to reach the lower atmosphere?

5. A meteor is traveling at 45 miles each second. It is first visible 55 miles above Earth. The meteor is visible for $\frac{2}{3}$ of a second, and then it disappears. How far did it travel while it was still visible?

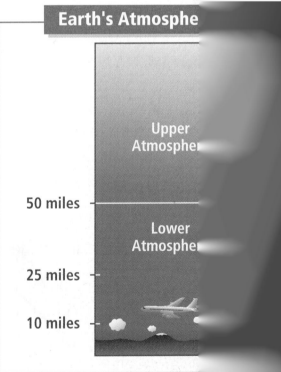

**Earth's Atmosphe**

Upper
Atmosphe

50 miles

Lower
Atmosphe

25 miles

10 miles

### Share Your Thinking

6. Choose one of the problems that you solved. Discuss it with a classmate. Explain why you chose the strategy you used.

7. How do you decide when to use a calculator instead of a paper and pencil?

# Chapter 9 Test

## for Pages 306–329

**Test-Taking Tips**
With multiple-choice questions, cross out all choices you are sure are incorrect.

## Problem Solving

**Solve. Show your work.** (pages 310, 324)

1. A square room has sides that are 12 feet long. Suppose you want to place a square rug that is 3 feet long in the middle of the room. How much space will be between each side of the rug and the wall?

2. You plan an array with 3 rows of 8 tiles each. You want $\frac{1}{4}$ of the array to be red and the rest blue. How many blue tiles will you need?

## Concepts

**Choose the correct answer. Write *a*, *b*, or *c*.**
(pages 318, 320, 322)

3. How can you change $\frac{1}{4}$ to an equivalent fraction with 12 as a denominator?
   a. Multiply the numerator and the denominator by 12.
   b. Multiply the denominator by 3.
   c. Multiply the numerator and the denominator by 3.

4. What must you do first to subtract $\frac{3}{5}$ from $\frac{7}{10}$?

   a. Change $\frac{7}{10}$ to an equivalent fraction with 5 as the denominator.

   b. Change $\frac{3}{5}$ to an equivalent fraction with 10 as the denominator.

   c. Subtract the numerators.

5. Which is true about adding mixed numbers?
   a. The sum is always greater than 1.
   b. The sum is always a mixed number.
   c. Both a and b are always true.

**Choose the correct answer. Write *a, b, c,* or *d.*** (pages, 308 312)

6. $\frac{1}{8} + \frac{3}{8}$    a. $\frac{4}{16}$    b. $\frac{2}{8}$    c. $\frac{4}{8}$    d. $\frac{12}{8}$

7. $\frac{10}{12} - \frac{4}{12}$    a. $\frac{6}{24}$    b. $\frac{5}{12}$    c. $\frac{14}{12}$    d. $\frac{6}{12}$

8. $\frac{7}{8} + \frac{1}{8}$    a. $\frac{8}{16}$    b. $\frac{1}{2}$    c. $\frac{6}{8}$    d. $\frac{8}{8}$

9. $\frac{3}{4} + \frac{1}{2}$    a. $\frac{4}{6}$    b. $\frac{1}{2}$    c. $1\frac{1}{4}$    d. $\frac{3}{8}$

**Record the exact answer in simplest form.** (pages 318, 320, 322)

10. $\frac{1}{4} + \frac{3}{8}$     11. $\frac{7}{9} - \frac{1}{3}$     12. $1\frac{1}{4} + 2\frac{1}{2}$     13. $4\frac{7}{8} - \frac{3}{8}$

14. $6\frac{2}{8} - 4$     15. $7\frac{5}{6} - 2\frac{1}{6}$     16. $12\frac{3}{8} + 1\frac{3}{8}$     17. $\frac{7}{9} - \frac{4}{9}$

**Write the correct time to answer the question.** (page 314)

18. At 3:00 P.M. Eastern Standard Time, what is the Pacific Standard Time?

19. At 1:30 A.M. Mountain Standard Time, what is the Central Standard Time?

20. If it is noon in Hawaii, what time is it in Alaska?

## Performance Task

(pages 312, 328)

What computation method will you use to solve this problem? You are writing a book. You have finished the first half, and you have 36 pages left to write. The publisher will add 16 pages of pictures. By the time you finish, how many pages will you have written?

- Tell how many pages are in the complete book.

- Describe the method you used to solve this problem. Explain why you used it.

**Keep In Mind . . .**

Your work will be evaluated on the following:

☑ Method selected

☑ Reasonable solution found

☑ Method identified

☑ Clear explanation given

# Cumulative Review

**Reading a Bar Graph** (Chapter 3)
How many CDs were sold in May?

**Here's A Way!**

Use the labels to find the answer.

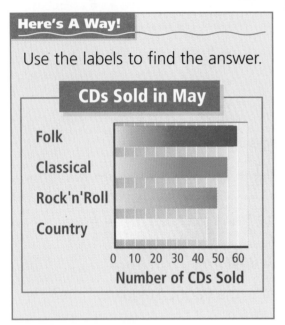

**CDs Sold in May**

Folk
Classical
Rock'n'Roll
Country

0 10 20 30 40 50 60
**Number of CDs Sold**

Use the graph to answer each question.

1. What type of music sold the most CDs?

2. How many more folk CDs were sold than country?

3. What was the total number of folk and classical CDs sold?

4. How many rock'n'roll CDs sold?

5. Was the total number of classical and country CDs sold greater or less than the total number of folk CDs? By how much?

---

**Polygons** (Chapter 5)
How many sides and vertices does this polygon have?

**Here's A Way!**

Name the figure.
An octagon has eight
sides and eight vertices.

Write how many sides and vertices each figure has.

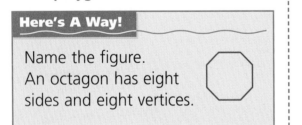

6. 7. 8.

---

**Multiplying Money** (Chapter 6)
Find 5 × \$2.90.

**Here's A Way!**

Estimate first. 5 × \$3 = \$15
Use a calculator to find the exact
answer. 5 × \$2.90 = \$14.50
Is your answer reasonable?

Estimate the product. Then, use a calculator to find the exact answer.

9. 6 × \$3.22          10. 8 × \$4.55

11. 7 × \$18.76          12. 2 × \$33.45

13. What happens when you multiply \$7.15 by 10? Will that happen each time you multiply a price by 10?

## Division (Chapter 7)
Find 345 ÷ 5.

**Here's A Way!**

| | |
|---|---|
| | 69 |
| Divide tens. | 5)345 |
| Multiply. Subtract. | −30 |
| Divide ones. | 45 |
| Multiply. Subtract. | −45 |
| | 0 |

**Find the quotient.**

14. 54 ÷ 3    15. 60 ÷ 4    16. 108 ÷ 6

17. 999 ÷ 3    18. 250 ÷ 5    19. 505 ÷ 5

20. Is 488 ÷ 5 greater than or less than 100?

21. Is 310 ÷ 6 greater than or less than 50?

## Fractional Parts of Numbers
(Chapter 8)

What is $\frac{3}{4}$ of 12?

**Here's A Way!**

12 ÷ 4 = 3

$\frac{1}{4}$ of 12 = 3

$\frac{3}{4}$ of 12 = 3 × 3, or 9

**Find the fractional part.**

22. $\frac{2}{6}$ of 6    23. $\frac{1}{8}$ of 24    24. $\frac{4}{5}$ of 10

25. $\frac{9}{10}$ of 10    26. $\frac{2}{7}$ of 14    27. $\frac{5}{10}$ of 30

28. Which is greater, $\frac{1}{8}$ of 24 or $\frac{1}{6}$ of 24?

29. Which is greater, $\frac{1}{8}$ of 40 or $\frac{1}{9}$ of 36?

## Problem Solving

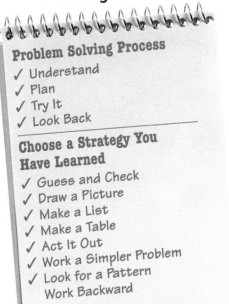

Problem Solving Process
✓ Understand
✓ Plan
✓ Try It
✓ Look Back

Choose a Strategy You Have Learned
✓ Guess and Check
✓ Draw a Picture
✓ Make a List
✓ Make a Table
✓ Act It Out
✓ Work a Simpler Problem
✓ Look for a Pattern
  Work Backward

**Choose any strategy you know to solve the problem. Show your work.**

30. Suppose a store in your neighborhood has a holiday sale. The store reduces the price of a toy by $\frac{1}{3}$ every 7 days until the price is below $10. The price of the toy starts at $27. In how many days will the toy cost less than $10?

31. I am a fraction in simplest form. The product of my numerator and 3 is equal to the product of my denominator and 2. Who am I?

# Weaving Fractions

**Art Connection** **With Your Group**

**P**eople all over the world use math to help them plan and create beautiful and useful designs. Weavers make their designs from cloth and wool. Furniture makers use leather and strips of cane.

You will use fractions to help you plan and "weave" a pattern. Use strips of paper of all different colors. You can also use fractions to describe your completed design.

## 1 Plan It

- As a group, choose the colors you would like to use. Decide what fraction of each color you want to appear in your work.
- Draw your design on graph paper.

## 2 Put It Together

- Cut sheets of colored paper into $\frac{1}{2}$ inch by 1 inch strips.
- Fold a large sheet of paper in half. From the fold, cut slits 1 inch apart. Stop 1 inch from the top. Unfold.
- Weave color strips through the slits to match the pattern you designed.

My favorite colors are green and purple, so I wanted to use lots of those colors in my weaving.

$\frac{1}{3}$ of my weaving is green.

## 3 Wrap It Up

- Work together to write a report about your weavings. Use fractions to describe how much of each color you used.
- How would you plan another weaving? How could you add and subtract fractions to change your design?

## 4 Discuss Your Results

- Have you covered all the points in Keep In Mind?
- How did other groups use fractions? Use fractions to describe which group used the most and least of each color.

**Internet**

> Visit the **Math Center** at **Houghton Mifflin Education Place.** http://www.eduplace.com

# Measurement and Time

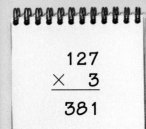
## Try This!

**H**ow can ordinary items help you take measurements? Follow these steps to use your shoe to find the length of your classroom in inches.

### What You'll Need

an inch ruler, paper, pencil

**1**

Measure the length of your shoe to the nearest inch.

②

Count the number of heel-to-toe steps it takes you to cross the room.

③

Multiply to find out about how long your classroom is from one side to the other in inches.

Why would someone with a different sized shoe still get the same number of inches in the classroom that you did?

My shoe = 9 inches
Classroom = 30 steps

$$
\begin{array}{r}
30 \\
\times 9 \\
\hline
\end{array}
$$

My shoe = 9 inches
Classroom = 30 steps
Classroom = 270 inches!

How long is your classroom in yards?

Ready to Go!

# LESSON 1

# Inch, Half Inch, and Quarter Inch

## Cooperative Learning Checklist

- ☐ Work alone.
- ☐ Work with a partner.
- ☑ Work with a group.

**S**uppose the length of an object is between whole inches. You can measure to the nearest **half inch** $\left(\frac{1}{2} \text{ in.}\right)$ or the nearest **quarter inch** $\left(\frac{1}{4} \text{ in.}\right)$.

### Getting Started

**What You'll Need:**
▶ inch ruler

**Vocabulary:**
inch
half inch
quarter inch
Glossary, p. 516

## Activity

- **With your group, find six items to measure.**
- **Make a chart like the one shown.**

| Item | Nearest inch | Nearest $\frac{1}{2}$ inch | Nearest $\frac{1}{4}$ inch |
|------|------|------|------|
| page | 9 | $8\frac{1}{2}$ | $8\frac{3}{4}$ |

### 1

- With your group, find six items, less than 12 in. long, to measure.
- Divide into two teams.
- Each team makes a chart to list the six items.

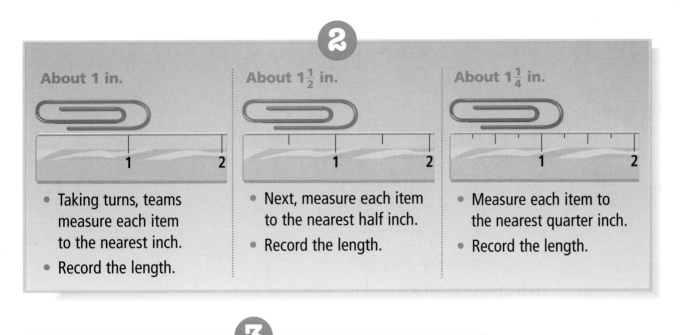

**②**

**About 1 in.**

• Taking turns, teams measure each item to the nearest inch.
• Record the length.

**About $1\frac{1}{2}$ in.**

• Next, measure each item to the nearest half inch.
• Record the length.

**About $1\frac{1}{4}$ in.**

• Measure each item to the nearest quarter inch.
• Record the length.

**③**

• The two teams compare their measurements.
• Which measurement is closer to the actual length of each item?

## Show What You Know!

**Estimation** Estimate the length of each object to the nearest inch. Then, measure to the nearest half inch and quarter inch.

1.

2.

3. Which of your estimates in exercises 1 and 2 was closest to the measured lengths?

**Use your ruler. Draw a line segment for each length.**

4. 5 in.　　5. $8\frac{1}{2}$ in.　　6. $13\frac{1}{4}$ in.　　7. $4\frac{1}{4}$ in.　　8. $6\frac{1}{2}$ in.

9. **Critical Thinking** Suppose you measure an object to the nearest quarter inch. Then, you measure it to the nearest inch. Is it possible to get the same result? Explain.

10. **Number Sense** If an object is measured to the nearest inch, half inch, and quarter inch, which is the most precise measurement? Explain your answer.

**More Practice Set 10.1, p. 504**

# Foot, Yard, and Mile

**A** **foot (ft)**, a **yard (yd)**, and a **mile (mi)** are customary units of measure.

**Getting Started**

Vocabulary:
equivalent
measures
Glossary, p. 516

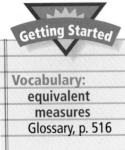

How long is a baseball bat? Suppose one classmate says it is 42 in. Another says it is 3 ft 6 in. You say it is $3\frac{1}{2}$ ft. All of you may be right. How can that be?

Knowing that 1 foot equals 12 inches can help you solve this problem.

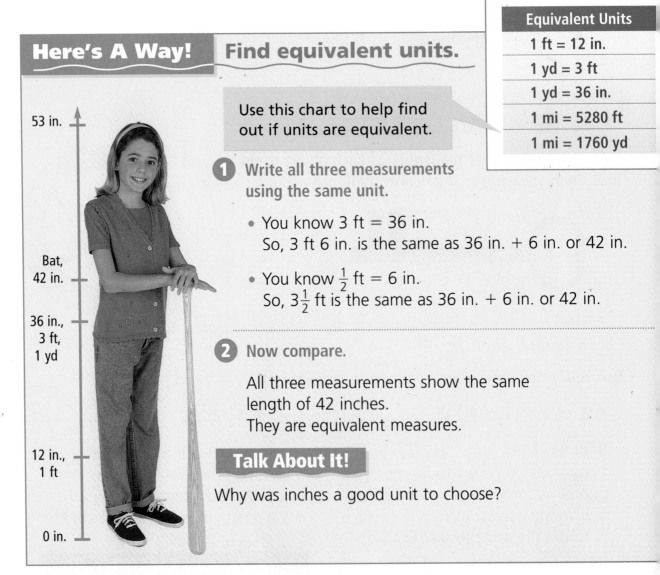

| Equivalent Units |
| --- |
| 1 ft = 12 in. |
| 1 yd = 3 ft |
| 1 yd = 36 in. |
| 1 mi = 5280 ft |
| 1 mi = 1760 yd |

**Here's A Way!** **Find equivalent units.**

Use this chart to help find out if units are equivalent.

**1** Write all three measurements using the same unit.

- You know 3 ft = 36 in.
  So, 3 ft 6 in. is the same as 36 in. + 6 in. or 42 in.

- You know $\frac{1}{2}$ ft = 6 in.
  So, $3\frac{1}{2}$ ft is the same as 36 in. + 6 in. or 42 in.

**2** Now compare.

All three measurements show the same length of 42 inches.
They are equivalent measures.

**Talk About It!**

Why was inches a good unit to choose?

53 in.

Bat, 42 in.

36 in., 3 ft, 1 yd

12 in., 1 ft

0 in.

## Show What You Know!

1. Explain two ways to find the number of inches in 5 ft.

**Write the letter of the better estimate of length.**

2. length of a bench
   a. 6 ft    b. 6 yd

3. length of your leg
   a. 2 in.    b. 2 ft

4. width of a bridge
   a. 50 mi    b. 50 ft

**Which measure would you use? Write *foot*, *yard*, or *mile*.**

5. your height

6. distance to the sun

7. width of a door

8. length of your desk

9. width of a car

10. height of a tree

11. **Critical Thinking** In exercises 5–10, explain why the unit of measure you chose makes sense to use.

## Work It Out!

**Choose and write the measure that is equivalent.**

12. 54 in.    13. 39 in.    14. 1 ft 4 in.

| 16 in. | $1\frac{1}{2}$ yd | 3 ft 3 in. |

**Complete the chart.**

| ft | 3 | 6 | 9 | 16. ? | 15 |
|----|---|---|---|-------|-----|
| yd | 1 | 2 | 15. ? | 4 | 17. ? |

18. **Number Sense** What fraction can you write to show what part of a foot is 1 inch? What part of a yard is 1 foot? Tell your reasoning.

19. **Critical Thinking** Explain how you could use a broken ruler, like this one, to measure the length of this baseball glove.

### Problem Solving

20. In baseball, the width of home plate is 17 in. Write the equivalent measurement in feet and inches.

21. When you hit a home run in baseball, you get to run around all the bases and score a run. If the distance between each base is 90 ft, how many yards do you run to score a home run? Explain how you got your answer.

**More Practice Set 10.2, p. 504**

# Perimeter

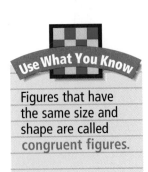

**Use What You Know**

Figures that have the same size and shape are called **congruent figures**.

**S**uppose you want to sew a border around a poncho like the one shown here. The poncho is 4 feet wide by 5 feet high. To find how long a strip you will have to cut for the border, you need to find the perimeter of the poncho.

The **perimeter** is the distance around a figure.

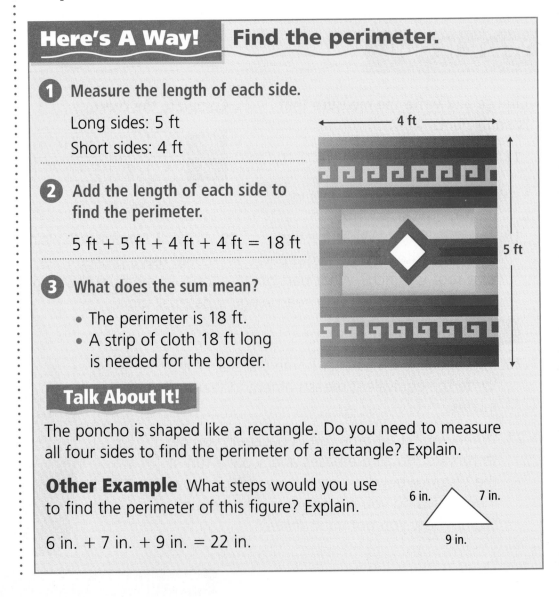

**Here's A Way!** | **Find the perimeter.**

**1** Measure the length of each side.

Long sides: 5 ft
Short sides: 4 ft

**2** Add the length of each side to find the perimeter.

5 ft + 5 ft + 4 ft + 4 ft = 18 ft

**3** What does the sum mean?

- The perimeter is 18 ft.
- A strip of cloth 18 ft long is needed for the border.

← 4 ft →

5 ft

**Talk About It!**

The poncho is shaped like a rectangle. Do you need to measure all four sides to find the perimeter of a rectangle? Explain.

**Other Example** What steps would you use to find the perimeter of this figure? Explain.

6 in.     7 in.

9 in.

6 in. + 7 in. + 9 in. = 22 in.

**Write the perimeter.**

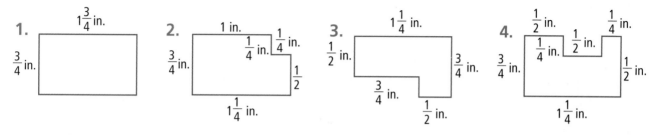

1.

2.

3.

4.

5. **Number Sense** Use a ruler to draw three different figures that have a perimeter of 1 ft.

6. **Critical Thinking** What steps can you use to find the perimeter of a square? Write a rule for finding the perimeter.

## Work It Out!

**Patterns** Draw the next two figures in the pattern. Describe the pattern. Then, complete the table.

1 in.  1 in. 1 in.  1 in. 1 in.

2 in.  2 in. 2 in.  2 in. 2 in.

3 in.  3 in. 3 in.  3 in. 3 in.

7. ?    8. ?

| Figure | Side Length | Perimeter |
|--------|-------------|-----------|
| a. | 1 in. | 5 in. |
| b. | 2 in. | 10 in. |
| c. | 3 in. | 9. ? |
| d. | 10. ? | 11. ? |
| e. | 12. ? | 13. ? |

14. **Patterns** Draw three squares. Draw the first with 2 in. sides, the second with 3 in. sides, and the third with 4 in. sides. Make a table like the one above. What do you notice about the perimeters? Describe the pattern.

15. **Create Your Own** Draw three congruent figures. Record the side lengths and the perimeter in a table.

16. **Problem Solving** Suppose you have a strip of cloth 19 ft long for trimming a poncho. Do you have enough material to trim a poncho that is 5 ft wide 5 ft high or one that is 6 ft wide and 3 ft high?

**Mixed Review** Order the numbers from least to greatest.

17. $\frac{2}{7}$ $\frac{5}{7}$ $\frac{4}{7}$    18. $9\frac{1}{2}$ in., $12\frac{1}{2}$ in., 1 ft.    19. $\frac{4}{9}$ $\frac{2}{3}$ $\frac{1}{9}$    20. $\frac{1}{2}$ $\frac{3}{8}$ $\frac{1}{8}$    21. $\frac{5}{6}$ $\frac{7}{12}$ $\frac{1}{6}$ $\frac{5}{12}$

**More Practice Set 10.3, p. 505**

# 4 Measurement Lab

Cooperative Learning
Checklist

☐ Work alone.
☐ Work with a partner.
☑ Work with a group.

**Getting Started**

**What You'll Need:**
▶ 12-inch ruler
▶ yardstick
▶ recording sheet
▶ art paper

**I**magine you are planning to rearrange your classroom. Before you draw a diagram of your plan, you need to measure the size of your classroom and the items in it.

**Activity**

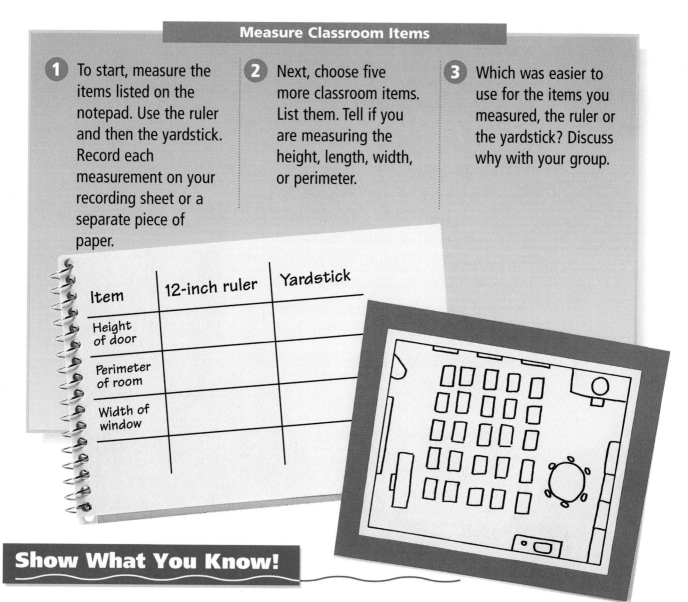

## Measure Classroom Items

**1** To start, measure the items listed on the notepad. Use the ruler and then the yardstick. Record each measurement on your recording sheet or a separate piece of paper.

**2** Next, choose five more classroom items. List them. Tell if you are measuring the height, length, width, or perimeter.

**3** Which was easier to use for the items you measured, the ruler or the yardstick? Discuss why with your group.

| Item | 12-inch ruler | Yardstick |
|---|---|---|
| Height of door | | |
| Perimeter of room | | |
| Width of window | | |

## Show What You Know!

**Use your recording sheet or copy and extend the chart above.**

1. Choose five more items in your classroom. First, estimate the measurement of each. Then, decide which tool is better for measuring each item. Record the actual measurement.

2. **Critical Thinking** How did you decide whether to use a ruler or a yardstick to measure an item?

3. When you used the 12-inch ruler, did you write your measurements in inches or in feet? Explain.

4. When you used the yardstick, which customary units did you use to label your answers—in., ft, or yd? Explain your answer.

5. **Create Your Own** With your group, draw a diagram to show how you would arrange your classroom. Record the actual measurements. Compare your diagram with other groups'.

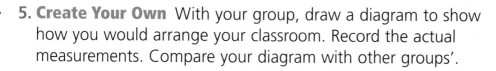

# Problem Solving
## Work Backward

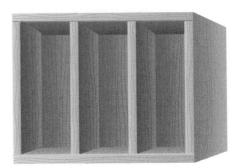

**Y**ou are planning to build a cabinet to fit inside a space that is 52 in. wide. Your cabinet will have 3 equal sections. There will be 2 boards dividing the sections and 1 board at either end. The wood you are using is 1 in. thick. How wide will each section be?

Use Work Backward to solve this problem.

## Here's A Way! Use Work Backward.

**1 Understand**

- How wide is the space that the cabinet has to fit inside?

- How wide is each of the dividing boards? Each of the end boards?

**2 Plan**

- Work backward to find out how wide each section will be.

**3 Try It**

- Subtract 1 in. for every dividing board and every end board.

- Why do you divide 48 in. by 3?

**4 Look Back**

- Each section is 16 in. wide.

- How did working brackward help you?

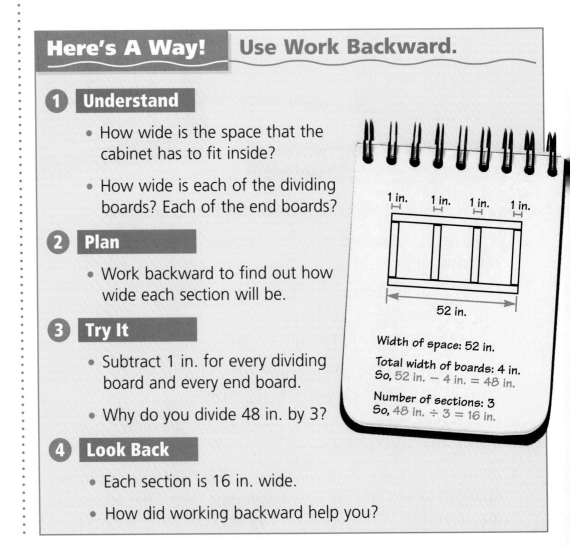

1 in.  1 in.  1 in.  1 in.

52 in.

Width of space: 52 in.

Total width of boards: 4 in.
So, 52 in. − 4 in. = 48 in.

Number of sections: 3
So, 48 in. ÷ 3 = 16 in.

**Use Work Backward to solve the problem.**

1. You find a 5-ft-long table to use as a desk. Your computer is 12 in. long and your printer is 13 in. long. You will use the rest of the table as workspace. How long will the workspace be?

2. **Critical Thinking** Could you fit 3 computers and 1 printer on the table? Explain why or why not.

## Work It Out!

**Use Work Backward or any other strategy to solve the problem.**

3. You build a door for a rectangular cabinet. The perimeter of the door is 12 ft. The width is 2 ft. What is the height of the door?

4. A store cuts the price of a CD player in half. Then it takes another $20 off. The new price is $49. What was the original price?

5. You and a friend use trim board to decorate cabinets. You cut off half of the board. Your friend cuts another 15 in. off the same board. The piece of board left is 20 in. long. How long was the original board?

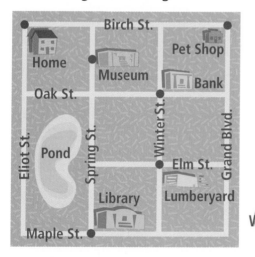

6. Rewrite these directions to show how you would return home, following the same route.
   - Go south on Eliot St. Turn left onto Maple St.
   - Go 2 blocks east on Maple St., and turn left onto Winter St.
   - Go 1 block north on Winter St. to the lumberyard.

7. Each figure is made up of 1-in. squares. What will be the perimeter of the next figure? Explain.

6 in.   10 in.   14 in.   18 in.

**Perimeters**

## Share Your Thinking

8. Which problems did you solve by using Work Backward?

9. How did you solve problem 7? Explain your strategy

# Customary Units of Capacity

## LESSON 6

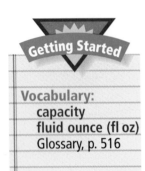

**Getting Started**

Vocabulary:
capacity
fluid ounce (fl oz)
Glossary, p. 516

**S**uppose you want to buy a quart of maple syrup. However, the store is out of quarts. What other containers of maple syrup can you buy that are equal to a quart of maple syrup?

You need to know how units of capacity are related. **Capacity** is the amount of liquid a container can hold.

gallon

quart

pint

cup

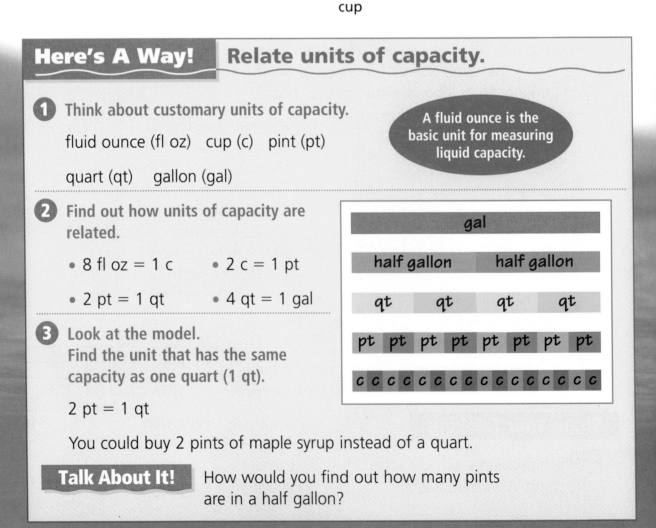

## Here's A Way! Relate units of capacity.

**1** Think about customary units of capacity.

fluid ounce (fl oz)   cup (c)   pint (pt)

quart (qt)   gallon (gal)

> A fluid ounce is the basic unit for measuring liquid capacity.

**2** Find out how units of capacity are related.

- 8 fl oz = 1 c
- 2 c = 1 pt
- 2 pt = 1 qt
- 4 qt = 1 gal

| gal | | | |
|---|---|---|---|
| half gallon | | half gallon | |
| qt | qt | qt | qt |
| pt | pt | pt | pt | pt | pt | pt | pt |
| c c c c c c c c c c c c c c c c |

**3** Look at the model. Find the unit that has the same capacity as one quart (1 qt).

2 pt = 1 qt

You could buy 2 pints of maple syrup instead of a quart.

**Talk About It!** How would you find out how many pints are in a half gallon?

## Show What You Know!

**Number Sense** Look at the model on page 348. Complete the table.

| Gallons | $\frac{1}{2}$ | 1 | 2 | 3 |
|---------|------|------|------|------|
| Quarts | 2 | 1. ? | 2. ? | 3. ? |
| Pints | 4. ? | 8 | 5. ? | 24 |
| Cups | 8 | 6. ? | 7. ? | 8. ? |

**Algebraic Reasoning** Write >, <, or = to make each statement true.

**9.** 8 cups ● 1 half gallon    **10.** 8 quarts ● 3 gallons    **11.** 16 cups ● 6 pints

## Work It Out!

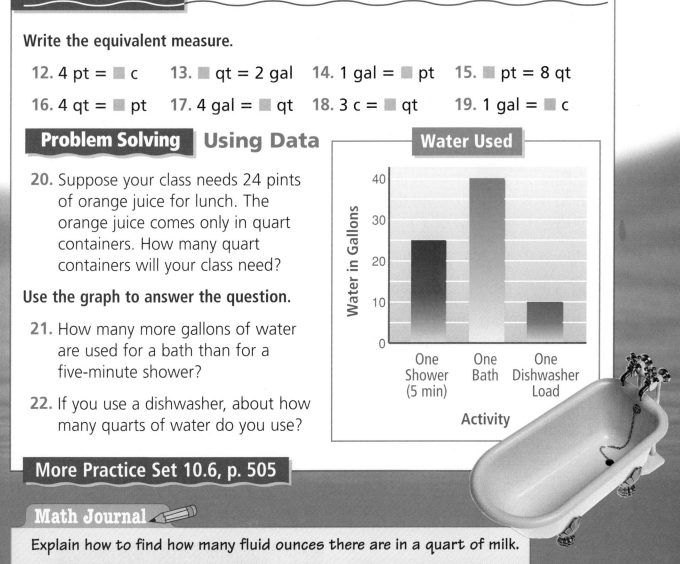

Write the equivalent measure.

**12.** 4 pt = ■ c    **13.** ■ qt = 2 gal    **14.** 1 gal = ■ pt    **15.** ■ pt = 8 qt

**16.** 4 qt = ■ pt    **17.** 4 gal = ■ qt    **18.** 3 c = ■ qt    **19.** 1 gal = ■ c

### Problem Solving Using Data

**20.** Suppose your class needs 24 pints of orange juice for lunch. The orange juice comes only in quart containers. How many quart containers will your class need?

Use the graph to answer the question.

**21.** How many more gallons of water are used for a bath than for a five-minute shower?

**22.** If you use a dishwasher, about how many quarts of water do you use?

**Water Used**

*Water in Gallons* — *Activity*: One Shower (5 min), One Bath, One Dishwasher Load

More Practice Set 10.6, p. 505

### Math Journal

Explain how to find how many fluid ounces there are in a quart of milk.

# LESSON 7

# Ounce, Pound, and Ton

1 pound

1 ounce

This small airplane weighs about 1 ton.

**O**unce (oz), pound (lb), and ton (T) are customary units of weight.

You can use the chart to write weights in equivalent units.

## Show What You Know!

| Equivalent Units |
| --- |
| 1 lb = 16 oz |
| 1 T = 2000 lb |

Write the letter of the better estimate of weight.

1. chicken
   a. 6 oz
   b. 6 lb

2. elephant
   a. 40 lb
   b. 4 T

3. tractor
   a. 1 T
   b. 100 lb

Choose the best unit for measuring. Write *oz*, *lb*, or *T*.

4. dog     5. coin     6. tomato     7. bus     8. car     9. desk

**Algebraic Reasoning** Make each statement true. Write >, <, or =.
Use the chart or use mental math.

10. 3 lb ● 42 oz   11. 4400 lb ● 3 T   12. 52 oz ● 5 lb   13. 4 T ● 8000 lb

14. **Critical Thinking** Suppose you need to mail a letter. You want to put the right amount of postage on it. Would you use ounces or pounds to find the weight of the letter?

**Calculator** Complete each statement.

15. 1 lb 3 oz = ■ oz     16. 10 lb 4 oz = ■ oz     17. 2 T 500 lb = ■ lb

**More Practice Set 10.7, p. 505**

# Midchapter Review

## for Pages 336–350

## Problem Solving

**Solve. Show your work.** (page 346)

1. Suppose you see a video game on sale for $25. The $25 price is $10 less than what the game cost during last week's half-price sale. How much did the game cost before last week's half-price sale?

## Concepts

**Choose the best unit for measuring.**
(pages 338, 340, 348, 350)

2. the weight of a person

3. the height of a building

4. the juice in a snack carton

5. the weight of a jet plane

6. the distance between two cities

**Find the answer.** (page 348)

7. What is the difference between an ounce and a fluid ounce?

| Units of Measurement |
| :---: |
| inch (in.) |
| foot (ft) |
| yard (yd) |
| mile (mi) |
| ounce (oz) |
| gallon (gal) |
| pound (lb) |
| ton (T) |

## Skills

**Write >, <or =.** (pages 344, 348)

8. 42 in. ● $1\frac{1}{2}$ yd

9. $2\frac{1}{2}$ ft ● 30 in.

10. 1 mi ● 4000 ft

11. 7 yd ● 300 in.

**Complete the statement.** (pages 344, 348, 350)

12. 16 fl oz = ■ qt

13. 3 gal = ■ c

14. 1 T = ■ lb

15. 40 oz = ■ lb

# Math *World*

**Throughout history, people have found different ways to measure time and weight.**

## Watching the Sun

In ancient times, Native Americans in the Southwest watched the sun. The sun's position in the sky told them the longest and shortest days of the year. Knowing these days helped them farm and plan ceremonies. Today, a sun watcher *(left)* stands on the edge of a canyon each morning. Day by day the rising sun gets closer to a rock column nearby. The day that the sun appears directly behind the column will be the shortest day of the year.

## History of Time

### Water clocks

Early Egyptians used bowls with marks on the inside to tell time. Water in the bowl dripped slowly out of a hole in the bottom. As the level of water got lower, it passed the marks, showing the time.

### Mechanical clocks

These clocks were first made in Europe and built of iron. A wheel moved weights to power the clock.

# Try This!

## BABYLONIAN UNITS OF WEIGHT

Babylonians first used standard weights. A standard weight is an object whose weight can be compared with the weights of other objects. A Babylonian unit of weight called the ma-nu was based on the weight of a date pit. The ma-nu was divided into 50 smaller units called shekels (SHEH kuhls). Follow these steps to make a balance, using 2 people counters to represent 1 shekel.

**1** Punch a hole in a paper cup near the rim. Punch another hole across from this hole. Put a 12-inch piece of string through both holes. Repeat this process for the other cup.

**2** Tie the cups to the ends of the coat hanger. Use tape to hold them in place.

**3** Tie a 12-inch piece of string to the top of a coat hanger. Hold the coat hanger level.

**4** Have a partner put an object into one cup. Then, add counters to the other cup to make the cups balance. Write the weight of your object using the Babylonian shekel.

## Pendulum clocks

A pendulum is a weight on a string. It moves back and forth at an even speed. The pendulum clock was much more accurate than earlier balance clocks.

## Respond

### Use your library . . .

to find other interesting objects that have been used in history as standard weights.

**Internet:**
Houghton Mifflin Education Place
Explore the Math Center at
http://www.eduplace.com

# Centimeter and Millimeter

**T**he ruler below shows **centimeters (cm)** and **millimeters (mm)**. There are 10 mm in 1 cm. These metric units are used to measure length.

## Activity

- Use a ruler that shows centimeters and millimeters.
- Find six items to measure that are shorter than your ruler.
- Make a chart like the one shown.

**Equivalent Units**

1 cm = 10 mm

| Items | Length to Nearest Centimeter | Length to Nearest Millimeter |
|---|---|---|

1

List the six items to be measured.

**2**

**About 4 cm.**

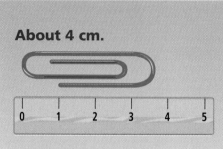

- Measure each item to the nearest centimeter.
- Record the length.

**About 37 mm.**

- Measure each item to the nearest millimeter.
- Record the length.

**3**

Compare measurements with your partner. Which measurement is closer to the actual length? How do you know?

## Show What You Know!

1. **Critical Thinking** Suppose you know the exact length of an object in centimeters. How can you find the length in millimeters without measuring?

**Estimation** First, estimate the length in centimeters. Then, measure.

2.

Silver jewelry

3.

Coin from Argentina

4.

Argentina

**Measure to the nearest centimeter. Then, write the measurement.**

5. length of your thumb

6. length of a pencil

7. length of a crayon

8. width of your math book

9. **Number Sense** Write your answers to exercises 5–8 in millimeters.

**More Practice Set 10.8, p. 506**

355

# Decimeter, Meter, and Kilometer

**Decimeter (dm), meter (m),** and **kilometer (km)** are metric units of length. Suppose you are in a relay race. Each team member runs a lap around the track. Together your laps total 1600 meters. Is this race more than or less than 2 kilometers?

Relay baton

You can use equivalent units of length to find out.

## Here's A Way!     Compare 1600 m to 2 km.

**1** Use the chart to find how many meters are in 1 km.

$$1 \text{ km} = 1000 \text{ m}$$

| km | 1 | 2 | 3 |
|----|------|------|------|
| m | 1000 | 2000 | 3000 |

**2** Use mental math. How many meters are in 2 km?

If 1 km = 1000 m, then 2 km = 2000 m.

You know that 1600 is less than 2000.

So, the relay race is less than 2 km.

| m | 1 | 2 | 3 |
|----|----|----|----|
| dm | 10 | 20 | 30 |

### Talk About It!

How could you use the charts to find the number of decimeters in 2 km?

1. **Critical Thinking** How are centimeters, decimeters, and meters related?

**Choose the better estimate.**

2. height of a book
   a. 15 m  b. 15 cm

3. length of a skateboard
   a. 1 m  b. 1 km

4. width of a chair
   a. 3 dm  b. 30 km

**Find equivalent measures.**

5. 20 dm = ■ m
6. ■ cm = 50 mm
7. ■ dm = 50 m
8. ■ km = 8000 m

9. Explain how you found the equivalent measure in exercise 6.

10. **Logical Reasoning** Name something that is about 1 dm.

11. **Number Sense** Which is a greater number, the length of your classroom in decimeters or in meters? Why?

## Work It Out!

**Choose the better estimate.**

12. length of a bicycle
    a. 2 km  b. 2 m

13. width of a classroom
    a. 70 m  b. 7 m

14. width of a door
    a. 1 dm  b. 1 m

**Find the equivalent measure.**

15. 8 dm = ■ cm
16. ■ m = 400 dm
17. ■ m = 2 km
18. ■ dm = 50 cm
19. 4000 m = ■ km
20. 9 m = ■ dm

### Problem Solving  Using Data

**Use the table to solve the exercise.**

21. How long does it take to jog 6000 m? How long does it take to walk the same distance?

| Kilometers | 1 | 2 | 3 | 4 | 5 | |
|---|---|---|---|---|---|---|
| Minutes to Walk | 15 | 30 | 45 | 60 | 75 | |
| Minutes to Jog | 6 | 12 | 18 | 24 | 30 | |

22. You jog for 24 minutes and walk for 45 minutes. How many more meters will you cover when you jog than when you walk?

23. **Estimation** Estimate the perimeter of your desk in centimeters. Write your estimate. Then, measure your desk. How close was your estimate?

**More Practice Set 10.9, p. 506**

# Metric Units of Capacity

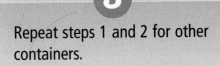

## LESSON 10

### Getting Started

**What You'll Need:**
- ► centimeter cubes
- ► small containers
- ► metric measuring cup
- ► recording sheet

**Vocabulary:**
- **milliliter (mL)**
- **liter (L)**
- Glossary, p. 516

**Milliliter (mL)** and **liter (L)** are metric units of capacity. There are 1000 mL in a liter.

A hollow centimeter cube holds 1 mL of water. You can use centimeter cubes to estimate how many milliliters will fill a container.

1 ml water

cm cube

### 1
**Use a small container.**

- Estimate how many milliliters the container holds. Record your estimate.
- Fill the container with centimeter cubes.
- Count the number of cubes you used. Record the number.
- Compare your estimate to the actual number of cubes you used.

### 2
**Find the actual capacity.**

- Use a metric measuring cup to find the actual capacity in milliliters.
- Compare the actual number of milliliters to the number of centimeter cubes you used in step 1.
- How close is your estimate?

### 3
Repeat steps 1 and 2 for other containers.

1. **Critical Thinking** How did the centimeter cubes help you estimate the capacity of the containers?

**Patterns** Complete the table. Describe any patterns you see.

| L | 1 | 2 | 2. ? | 4 | 3. ? |
|---|---|---|------|---|------|
| mL | 1000 | 4. ? | 3000 | 5. ? | 5000 |

**Estimation** Write the letter of the better estimate of capacity.

6. a bottle cap
   a. 3 mL  b. 3 L

7. a milk glass
   a. 150 mL  b. 2 L

8. a sand pail
   a. 5mL  b. 1 L

9. a can of beans
   a. 500 mL  b. 2 L

**Write the equivalent measure.**

10. 4 L = ■ mL

11. ■ mL = 7 L

12. 10 L = ■ mL

13. 5000 mL = ■ L

**Algebraic Reasoning** Make the statement true. Write >, <, or =.

14. 9 L ● 9 mL

15. 400 mL ● 4 L

16. 15 mL ● 15 L

17. 2 L ● 2000 mL

## Problem Solving Using Data

**Use the graph to answer the question.**

18. How many milliliters of water do you use to wash dishes by hand?

19. Do you think that you need to use 10 L of water to brush your teeth?

20. How many more milliliters of water does a dishwasher use than a person doing dishes by hand?

21. Write at least four facts you can read from the bar graph.

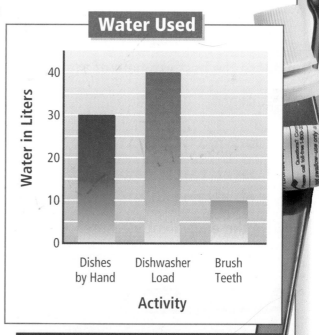

**Water Used**

Water in Liters

40
30
20
10
0

Dishes by Hand   Dishwasher Load   Brush Teeth

**Activity**

**More Practice Set 10.10, p. 507**

**Math Journal**

One container holds 20 L. Another container holds 2200 mL. Which container's capacity is greater? Explain.

# Gram and Kilogram

**G**ram (g) and **kilogram (kg)** are metric units of mass. A small photograph has a mass of about 1 gram. A camera has a mass of about 1 kilogram.

The equivalent units chart shows how grams and kilograms are related.

gram

kilogram

| Equivalent Units |
| --- |
| 1 kg = 1000 g |

## Show What You Know!

1. **Critical Thinking** Which customary unit of weight is closest to the mass of a photograph? An ounce? A pound? A ton?

**Choose the best estimate of the mass.**

2. pencil
   a. 2 kg
   b. 2 g

3. dog
   a. 1 kg
   b. 10 kg

4. bicycle
   a. 10 kg
   b. 10 g

5. rabbit
   a. 4 g
   b. 4 kg

6. polar bear
   a. 10 kg
   b. 325 kg

7. **Mental Math** How can you use mental math to find the number of grams in 10 kg?

**Write the equivalent measure.**

8. $1\frac{1}{2}$ kg = ■ g

9. 2 kg = ■ g

10. 500 g = ■ kg

11. ■ kg = 3000 g

### Problem Solving

12. If your camera is $2\frac{1}{2}$ kg, how many grams is it?

13. A small elevator has a 500-kg limit. These ten people are in line to enter in this order. Who is the last person allowed on the elevator?

| | |
| --- | --- |
| 1. Sam—50 kg | 6. Ned—80 kg |
| 2. Amy—50 kg | 7. Tracy—40 kg |
| 3. Jack—100 kg | 8. Raul—60 kg |
| 4. Larry—70 kg | 9. Peter—40 kg |
| 5. Mia—30 kg | 10. Julie—60 kg |

**More Practice Set 10.11, p. 507**

# Problem Solving

## Is the Answer Reasonable?

**S**uppose a classmate says that her cat's tail is 1 yd long. Is this measurement reasonable?

### You Decide

- Use a ruler to show how long 1 yd is.
- If a cat's tail is 1 yd long, how long would the entire cat be?
- Is your classmate's measurement reasonable? If not, what measurement might make more sense?

### Work It Out!

**Is the Answer Reasonable?**

**Ask Yourself:**

Did I answer the question?

Did I calculate correctly?

Is the answer labeled with the right units?

Does my answer need to be rounded to a whole number to make sense?

**Decide whether the measurement is reasonable. Explain your answer.**

1. A friend says that you can fit a 2-gal bottle of juice in your coat pocket.

2. Your cousin takes the bus to school because his house is 4 mi away.

3. Your teacher needs 3 people to help him carry a box, because it is so heavy. The box weighs 1000 g.

4. Your friend was very thirsty after the basketball game. She ran to the bench and drank 2 mL of water.

5. The back seat of your parents' car is 3 yd wide and 2 ft long.

6. A sign by a small bridge reads: "No trucks more than 5 tons can cross this bridge."

### Share Your Thinking

7. How do you decide if a measurement is reasonable?

8. When a measurement is not reasonable, how do you find one that makes more sense?

# 13 Temperature

Chicago, 32°F

Chicago, 90°F

**A** **thermometer** is a tool that measures temperature in degrees. Many thermometers have two temperature scales, **degrees Celsius (°C)** and **degrees Fahrenheit (°F)**. In Chicago, temperatures in December are about 32°F. If the temperature in Chicago were 32°C, would you go skiing or swimming?

## Here's A Way! Read a thermometer.

**1** Look at the Celsius scale on the thermometer.

- Notice that room temperature is 21°C.
- You know that room temperature is too warm for skiing.

**2** Find 32°C on the thermometer.

- You can see that it is higher than 21°C on the scale.
- This means that 32°C is warmer than 21°C.

Since 21°C is too warm for skiing, then 32°C is also too warm. So, swimming is the choice.

### Talk About It!

Which temperature is colder, 0°C or 0°F? Explain your reasoning.

°Fahrenheit | °Celsius

°F | °C

230° | 110°
220° |
212° → 210° ← 100° → 100°
200° | Water
190° | 90° Boils
180° | 80°
170° |
160° | 70°
150° |
140° | 60°
130° |
120° | 50° Normal
110° | Body
98.6° → 100° ← 40° Temperature
90° | 37°
80° |
70° → 70° ← 20° → 21°
60° | Room
50° | 10° Temperature
40° |
32° → 30° ← 0° → 0°
20° | Water
10° | -10° Freezes
0° |
-10° | -20°
-20° | -30°

**Write the letter of the better estimate of temperature.**

1. to swim outdoors
   a. 27°C  b. 27°F

2. to make a snowman
   a. 30°F  b. 30°C

3. to boil soup
   a. 100°C  b. 100°F

**Write the temperature in degrees Fahrenheit and degrees Celsius.**

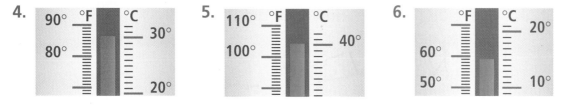

4. 90° °F  °C
   30°
   80°
   20°

5. 110° °F  °C
   40°
   100°

6. °F  °C
   20°
   60°
   50°  10°

7. **Critical Thinking** Describe the weather on a day when the temperature is 20°F.

## Work It Out!

8. **Critical Thinking** Which temperature is better for playing ice hockey outdoors, 28°F or 28°C? How do you know?

9. **Logical Reasoning** You know that it is 15° outside. But is it Celsius or Fahrenheit? You see icicles hanging from the roof. What scale are you using? Explain your thinking.

### Problem Solving  Using Data

10. In January is the temperature in Buenos Aires closer to 20°C or 30°C?

11. What is the temperature in July?

12. During which months could you go swimming in Buenos Aires? Do you go swimming during these same months?

13. **Critical Thinking** Would your classroom be warmer if you measured it in degrees Celsius rather than in degrees Fahrenheit? Explain your answer.

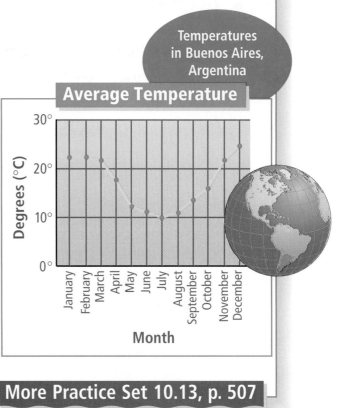

Temperatures in Buenos Aires, Argentina

**Average Temperature**

Degrees (°C)

Month

**More Practice Set 10.13, p. 507**

# Elapsed Time

SCHOOL BUS
74
74

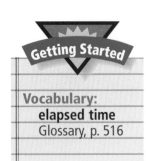

**Vocabulary:**
**elapsed time**
Glossary, p. 516

**S**uppose your class leaves at 9:15 A.M. for a trip to the Wildlife Habitat. You arrive at 11:23 A.M. How long did it take to get there?

You need to find the elapsed time to answer the question.

**Elapsed time** is the amount of time that has gone by.

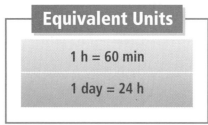

| Equivalent Units |
| :---: |
| 1 h = 60 min |
| 1 day = 24 h |

## Here's A Way!     Find the elapsed time.

Think of a clock.

**1** Find the number of hours from 9:15 A.M. to 11:15 A.M.

There are two hours from 9:15 A.M. to 11:15 A.M.

**2** Find the number of minutes from 11:15 A.M. to 11:23 A.M.

Count by 5's and 1's to find the minutes from 11:15 to 11:23. It is 8 minutes.

Your trip lasted 2 hours and 8 minutes.

### Talk About It!

• How do the clock faces help you picture the elapsed time?

• Can you think of another way to find how long the trip took? Explain your thinking.

**How much time has gone by? Write the answer.**

1.

2.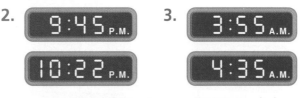

3.

4. Your class wants to take the habitat tour at 1:55 P.M. It is now 1:36 P.M. How many minutes are there until the tour begins?

5. **Number Sense** Suppose it is 10:15 A.M. What time will it be in 12 hours? In 24 hours? Explain your answer.

## Work It Out!

**Write the elapsed time. Count by 5's and 1's. Use a clock to help you.**

6. from 9:55 A.M. to 10:43 A.M.

7. from 3:25 P.M. to 4:06 P.M.

8. from 7:12 A.M. to 7:25 A.M.

9. from 2:40 P.M. to 3:43 P.M.

**Patterns** Copy and extend the pattern. Describe each pattern.

10. 3:35, 3:45, 3:55, ___, ___, ___

11. 1:30, 2:00, 2:30, ___, ___, ___

**Complete the table.**

| Days | 1 | 2 | 3 | 4 | 5 |
|------|---|---|---|---|---|
| Hours | 24 | 12.? | 72 | 13.? | 14.? |

### Problem Solving

15. Suppose it is 3:30 P.M. and your class is ready to leave the Wildlife Habitat. Your school bus, however, gets a flat tire. If it takes 55 minutes to fix the flat tire, at what time does your class finally leave?

16. Suppose your class has 35 minutes for lunch at the habitat's cafeteria.
    a. If lunch starts at 12:15 P.M., at what time will lunch end?
    b. If the film on tigers starts at 1:05 P.M., does your class have time to eat lunch first?

### Mixed Review    Add or subtract.

17. $\frac{1}{8} + \frac{3}{8}$

18. $3\frac{1}{2} + \frac{1}{2}$

19. $\frac{7}{12} - \frac{5}{12}$

20. $4\frac{1}{6} + 2\frac{4}{6}$

21. $7\frac{3}{5} - 2\frac{1}{5}$

**More Practice Set 10.14, p. 507**

# LESSON 15

# Problem Solving
## Using Work Backward and Other Strategies

### Getting Started

**What You'll Need:**
▶ calendar for March, April, and May
▶ recording sheet

**Problem Solving Process**
✓ Understand
✓ Plan
✓ Try It
✓ Look Back

**Choose a Strategy You Have Learned**
✓ Guess and Check
✓ Draw a Picture
✓ Make a List
✓ Make a Table
✓ Act It Out
✓ Work a Simpler Problem
✓ Look for a Pattern
✓ Work Backward

**S**tudents at your school are rehearsing a play. They want to print a program for the audience to read when the play is performed. But students need to find a way to pay for printing a program. Also, everything has to be done in time for the first performance.

### Schedule

| Task | Find businesses that will pay for advertisements. | Get the program ready for the printer. | Print the program. |
| --- | --- | --- | --- |
| Time Needed | 3 weeks | 1 week | 2 weeks |

**Y**ou and your friends offer to find businesses that will pay to advertise in the program. The programs must be ready 1 week before the play. The first performance of the play is the last Thursday in April. By what date must you and your friends start looking for businesses to buy advertisements?

- What problem needs to be solved?

- When must the programs be ready for the printer? How long before the first performance?

- What dates should you mark on a calendar? Why?

- Explain a strategy you can use to solve the problem. Then solve it.

**Use any strategy to solve the problem. Show your work.**

1. How many Saturday rehearsals can be held between March 1 and the day the play opens?

2. Students want to advertise the play in a weekly newspaper 3 times before the first performance. The paper comes out every Wednesday. Also, the paper must receive an advertisement 2 days before it comes out. On what date must students get their advertisement to the paper?

3. The newspaper advertisement will run 9 lines. The total cost of the advertisement is $27.00, including $1.35 tax. What is the cost for each line not including tax?

**Month: March**
| Sun. | Mon. | Tues. | Wed. | Thurs. | Fri. | Sat. |
|------|------|-------|------|--------|------|------|
|      |      |       |      |        |      |      |

**Month: April**
| Sun. | Mon. | Tues. | Wed. | Thurs. | Fri. | Sat. |
|------|------|-------|------|--------|------|------|
|      |      |       |      |        |      |      |

**Month: May**
| Sun. | Mon. | Tues. | Wed. | Thurs. | Fri. | Sat. |
|------|------|-------|------|--------|------|------|
|      |      |       |      |        |      |      |

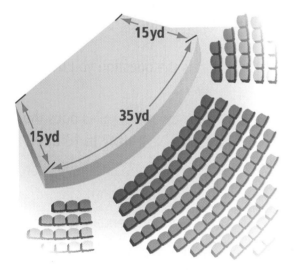

15 yd
35 yd
15 yd
15 yd

4. Students planning scenery for the play want to put a border of purple ribbon around the sides and front of the stage. The ribbon comes in rolls that are 12 yd long. How many rolls of ribbon will these students need to buy?

5. The school band will play 3 songs before each performance. Can the band play these songs in a different order for each of the play's 5 performances? Explain.

6. A group of 8 buys tickets at an average price of $4 per person. Explain how this is possible.

7. The play starts at 7:00 P.M. and ends at 8:45 P.M. There are 2 intermissions. One is 15 minutes long, and the other is 10 minutes long. How long is the play itself?

THE SECRET GARDEN — ADULTS $7.00
THE SECRET GARDEN — CHILDREN $3.00

## Share Your Thinking

8. Discuss problem 7 with a partner. Explain why you chose the strategy you used to solve it.

# Problem Solving
## Using Strategies

You can read more about hummingbirds in the pages of *Zoobooks*.

Alaska (U.S.)

Anchorage

Canada

*Pacific Ocean*

1438 mi

Vancouver

Seattle

679 mi

United States

San Francisco

347 mi

Los Angeles

1544 mi

**Mexico**

Mexico City

**E**very year rufous (ROO fuhs) hummingbirds fly from Mexico to Alaska and back to Mexico. On their way, they pass over Seattle.

**S**uppose a rufous hummingbird flies north over Seattle on April 1. The bird can fly about 30 mi in a day. Approximately where was it on February 1? Name the two cities it was flying between.

- What is the question you have to answer?
- About how many miles does the bird travel in 1 day? In 10 days?
- Where might the bird have been 10 days ago? 1 month ago?
- How might a calendar help you?
- Explain a strategy you can use to solve the problem. Then, solve it.

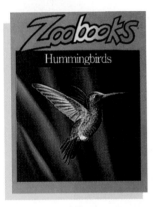

**Problem Solving Process**
✓ Understand
✓ Plan
✓ Try It
✓ Look Back

**Choose a Strategy You Have Learned**
✓ Guess and Check
✓ Draw a Picture
✓ Make a List
✓ Make a Table
✓ Act It Out
✓ Work a Simpler Problem
✓ Look for a Pattern
✓ Work Backward

## Work It Out!

**Use any strategy to solve each problem. Show your work.**

1. Suppose a young hummingbird makes its first flight on May 5. Around what date did the bird hatch? Explain your answer. Hint: Read the caption.

2. Together, the beak and tail of a hummingbird can make up $\frac{1}{2}$ of its total length. Suppose the length of the beak is $1\frac{1}{2}$ cm and the length of the tail is 3 cm. How long is the hummingbird?

When it is only 3 or 4 weeks old, a hummingbird is ready to leave its nest for good.

3. Look at the photograph on the left. Estimate how far it is from the top of the penny to the top of the bird's wing.

4. Hummingbirds can fly about 2400 ft in a minute. About how long would it take a hummingbird to fly across your classroom?

5. You and your friends are making food to put in hummingbird feeders. How many cups of sugar will you mix with 8 cups of water?

6. You have just completed a jigsaw puzzle. The puzzle is 12 in. by 18 in. You put a 1-in. frame around it. What is the perimeter of the inside of the frame? Of the outside of the frame?

Fill the feeder with one part sugar and four parts water.

## Share Your Thinking

7. Explain how you solved problem 6.

8. What problem solving strategies might be used by scientists who study birds? Explain.

# Chapter 10 Test

## for Pages 336–369

**Test-Taking Tips**
Do not spend too much time on one problem. If you are having trouble, skip the problem and go back to it later.

## Problem Solving

**Solve. Show your work.** (page 346)

1. After you wake up, it takes 15 minutes to get dressed for school. It takes a half-hour to eat breakfast, 20 minutes to walk to the school bus, and a half-hour to ride the bus. School starts at 9:00 A.M. By what time do you need to get out of bed to arrive at school 10 minutes early?

2. Suppose you leave home, walk north for three blocks, go east for two blocks, and then walk north again for three blocks. You arrive at the bus stop. Give directions for walking home from the bus stop.

## Concepts

**Do you need to find the perimeter to answer the question? Write *yes* or *no*.** (page 342)

3. How far would you jog if you ran around the outside of your school building three times?

4. How much water does your bathtub hold?

5. How much tape do you need to put a border around the classroom bulletin board?

6. How many rows of tomatoes should you plant in your garden?

**Choose the best metric units for measuring. Write *mL, mm, cm, m, km, g,* or *kg*.** (pages 354, 356, 358, 360)

7. the length of your pencil point

8. your height

9. the distance between two cities

10. the mass of a nail

**Estimate. Then measure the length to the nearest centimeter and to the nearest quarter inch.** (pages 338, 344, 354)

11.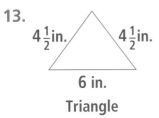
Estimate: __?__ cm
Measure: __?__ cm

12.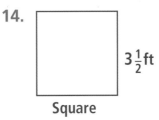
Estimate: __?__ in.
Measure: __?__ in.

**Find the perimeter.** (page 342)

13.
$4\frac{1}{2}$in.   $4\frac{1}{2}$in.
6 in.
Triangle

14.
$3\frac{1}{2}$ft
Square

**Copy and complete the statement.** (pages 340, 348, 350, 354, 356, 358, 360)

15. 30 kg = __?__ g

16. 2000 mL = 2 __?__

17. 3 __?__ = 9 ft

18. 2 qt = __?__ fl oz

19. 4 pt = __?__ gal

20. __?__ lb = 48 oz

21. 4 cm = 40 __?__

22. 2 km = __?__ dm

**Choose the letter of the better estimate.** (pages 362, 364)

23. the height of a bus     a. 3 m     b. 3 cm

24. outdoor temperature for swimming    a. 32°F     b. 32°C

25. travel time between an 8:15 A.M. departure and a 1:30 P.M. arrival
    a. 7 hours 15 minutes     b. 5 hours 15 minutes

## Performance Task

(page 362)

How would you show these average temperatures for Orlando, Florida on a graph?

January—70°F     April—81°F
February—72°F     May—87°F
March—76°F     June—89°F

• Explain how you labeled your graph.

**Keep In Mind . . .**
Your work will be evaluated on the following:
☑ A suitable graph
☑ Clear and correct labels
☑ Correct data
☑ Reasonable explanation

# Cumulative Review

## Equivalent Money Amounts
(Chapter 1)

Write the amount of money for 3 dollars, 3 quarters, and 2 dimes.

### Here's A Way!

Write a dollar sign. Use a decimal point to separate dollars and cents. $3.95

Write the amount of money.

**1.** 2 dollars, 10 quarters, 5 pennies

**2.** 10 nickels, 5 quarters

**3.** 1 nickel, 3 quarters, 5 dollars

Use mental math to find the value.

**4.** 10 dimes, 2 quarters, 2 nickels

**5.** 8 quarters, 5 dimes, 50 pennies

---

## Zeros in Subtraction (Chapter 2)
Find 105 − 29.

### Here's A Way!

Subtract.   $\overset{9\ 15}{10\,5}$   Check.   76
            − 29              + 29
             76               105

Find the difference. Show your work.

**6.** 302 − 37          **7.** 400 − 123

**8.** 1006 − 254        **9.** 5000 − 475

**10.** 500 − 199        **11.** $3.06 − $.97

---

## Quotients and Remainders
(Chapter 7)
Find 72 ÷ 5.

### Here's A Way!

Divide the tens.        14 R2
Multiply. Subtract.    5)72
Divide the ones.        −5
Multiply. Subtract.      22
Use an *R* to show      −20
the remainder.            2

So, 72 ÷ 5 is 14 R2.

Find the quotient and the remainder.

**12.** 75 ÷ 2          **13.** 13 ÷ 5

**14.** 26 ÷ 5          **15.** 100 ÷ 6

**16.** 336 ÷ 40        **17.** 435 ÷ 25

**18.** What multiplication fact helps you to find 26 ÷ 5?

## Fractions (Chapter 8)

Write $\frac{8}{10}$ in simplest form.

**Here's A Way!**

Find the common factor.  2
Divide both the numerator and the denominator by 2.

The simplest form of $\frac{8}{10}$ is $\frac{4}{5}$.

---

**Write the fraction in simplest form.**

19. $\frac{25}{100}$      20. $\frac{6}{36}$      21. $\frac{24}{27}$

22. $\frac{2}{10}$      23. $\frac{125}{125}$      24. $\frac{70}{350}$

25. How can you tell when a fraction is in simplest form?

---

## Adding and Subtracting Fractions
(Chapter 9)

Find $\frac{1}{4} + \frac{2}{4}$. Find $\frac{3}{8} - \frac{1}{4}$.

**Here's A Way!**

You can add like fractions.

$\frac{1}{4} + \frac{2}{4} = \frac{3}{4}$

Change unlike fractions to like fractions. $\frac{1}{4} = \frac{2}{8}$

Then subtract. $\frac{3}{8} - \frac{2}{8} = \frac{1}{8}$

---

**Add or subtract. Write the answer in simplest form.**

26. $\frac{1}{4} + \frac{1}{4}$      27. $\frac{5}{8} - \frac{1}{8}$      28. $\frac{5}{6} + \frac{3}{4}$

29. $\frac{3}{5} - \frac{1}{3}$      30. $\frac{15}{30} + \frac{14}{28}$      31. $\frac{9}{10} - \frac{4}{5}$

32. Do $\frac{3}{4}$ and $\frac{1}{4}$ have a difference of less than $\frac{1}{2}$? Explain your answer.

33. Do $\frac{6}{9}$ and $\frac{1}{9}$ have a difference of greater than $\frac{1}{3}$? Tell why.

---

## Problem Solving

**Problem Solving Process**
- ✓ Understand
- ✓ Plan
- ✓ Try It
- ✓ Look Back

**Choose a Strategy You Have Learned**
- ✓ Guess and Check
- ✓ Draw a Picture
- ✓ Make a List
- ✓ Make a Table
- ✓ Act It Out
- ✓ Work a Simpler Problem
- ✓ Look for a Pattern
- ✓ Work Backward

---

**Choose any strategy you know to solve the problem. Show your work.**

34. Suppose you walk one quarter of the way to school. You suddenly realize that you have forgotten your homework. It takes you 5 minutes to return home. Then you walk to school again at the same speed without stopping. What is the total time for your trip to school that morning?

35. Suppose there is an average of 7 minutes of commercials on TV each half hour. How many minutes of commercials are there from 7 A.M. to 11 P.M.?

# Amazing Animals

**Social Studies Connection**    **With Your Group**

**Y**ou are going to explore some amazing facts about animals. First you need to arrange data in ways that make sense to you. How many different ways can you arrange the data?

Organize the data into separate headings. Then make up questions for other groups to answer about it. Your group will answer questions on data organized by other groups.

Heights of Animals

20
15
10
5

Cat Kangaroo Crocodile

# Plan It

- Use the data in the table. Brainstorm ways to make the data clearer. For example, longest to shortest lifespans of the animals.
- Look at the headings to get ideas on how to rearrange the data. For example, you can make a chart, a table, a bar graph, or a pictograph.

## 2

# Put It Together

- Look at your new ways of presenting this data. Compare your results.
- Write down some questions to ask other students about your data.

1. Which animal is shortest?

2. How much bigger is the crocodile than the kangaroo?

| Animal | Height or Length | Weight (Pounds) | Life Span (Years) | Fastest Speed (Miles in 1 Hour) |
|---|---|---|---|---|
| Red Kangaroo | 5 feet | 200 | 7 – 10 | 30 |
| Blue Whale | 100 feet | 200000 | 45 | 22 |
| Bat | 12 inches | $\frac{1}{6} - \frac{2}{3}$ ounce | 10 – 25 | 15 |
| Hummingbird | 2 inches | 1 ounce | 2 | 60 |
| Nile Crocodile | 20 feet | 1650 | 70 – 100 | 29 |
| Cat | $2\frac{1}{2}$ feet | 6 – 20 | 13 | 30 |
| Bluefin Tuna | 11 – 16 feet | 1500 – 1800 | 20 | 65 |
| Cheetah | 7 feet | 110 – 140 | 7 | 70 |
| Emperor Penguin | 4 feet | 50 – 100 | 30 | $11\frac{1}{2}$ |

## 3

# Wrap It Up

- Share your data and your questions with other groups.
- Work together to answer the questions you get from other groups.

## 4

# Discuss Your Results

- Have you covered all the points in Keep In Mind?
- How did other groups organize the data? Tell which arrangement you liked the best.

**Internet**

> Visit the **Math Center** at **Houghton Mifflin Education Place.** http://www.eduplace.com

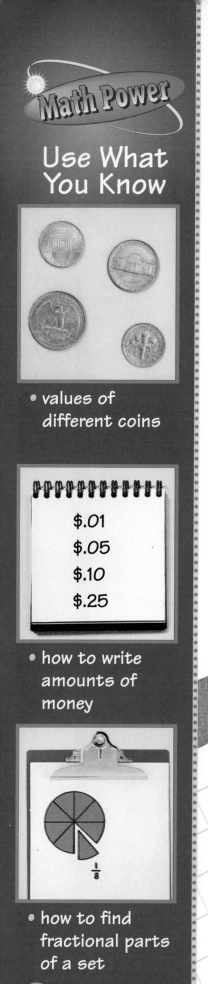

# Math Power

## Use What You Know

- values of different coins

$.01
$.05
$.10
$.25

- how to write amounts of money

$\frac{1}{8}$

- how to find fractional parts of a set

## CHAPTER 11

# Decimals

## Try This!

**D**id you know that coins represent fractions of, or parts of, a dollar? You can design your own dollar using different amounts of coins.

### What You'll Need

grid paper, 4 markers or crayons of different colors

### 1

Mark off part of your graph paper with 10 × 10 squares. The squares will stand for the 100 parts of a dollar.

**2**

Choose a color for each coin amount. Make a key to show the color you assign to each coin.

Key
☐ Penny
☐ Nickel
☐ Dime
☐ Quarter

**3**

Color in your dollar. Use at least one of each coin. If you use a 25¢ coin, you need to color 25 squares. Each square on the grid must be filled in.

On your dollar design, what does each one-hundredth square represent?

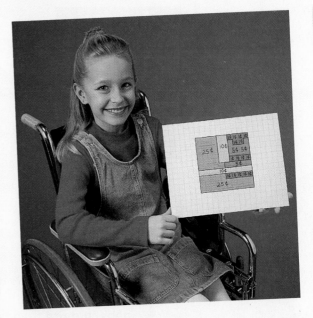

Write a fraction for the different coins you used in your dollar. How do you think decimals are related to fractions?

**Ready to Go!**

377

Work alone.

Work with a partner.

Work with a group.

## Tenths

**Getting Started**

**What You'll Need:**
► decimal models
► red crayons or pencils
► recording sheet

**O**ne way to show parts of a whole is to use fractions. Another way is to use decimals. This decimal model shows tenths. You can show tenths in words, fractions, or decimals.

1 of 10 sections is shaded.

| Words | one tenth |
|---|---|
| Fraction | $\frac{1}{10}$ |
| Decimal | 0.1 |

### Activity

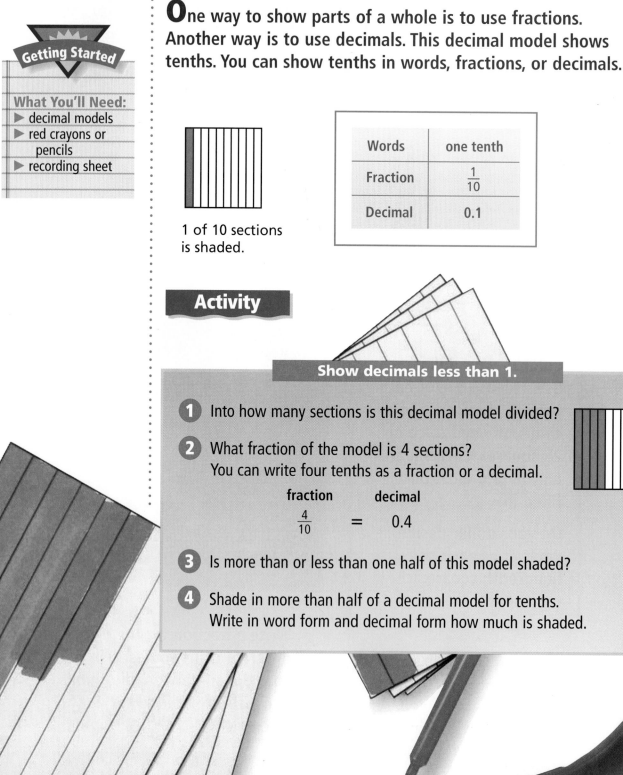

**Show decimals less than 1.**

1. Into how many sections is this decimal model divided?

2. What fraction of the model is 4 sections?
You can write four tenths as a fraction or a decimal.

fraction     decimal
$\frac{4}{10}$   =   0.4

3. Is more than or less than one half of this model shaded?

4. Shade in more than half of a decimal model for tenths.
Write in word form and decimal form how much is shaded.

**378** Chapter 11

## Shade, sort, and record.

1. Cut out 9 decimal models for tenths. Shade each model to make a set that shows 0.1 to 0.9.

2. Sort the models into groups that show less than one half shaded, exactly one half shaded, or more than one half shaded.

3. Record the tenths in words and decimals on your recording sheet or on a separate piece of paper.

## Show decimals greater than one.

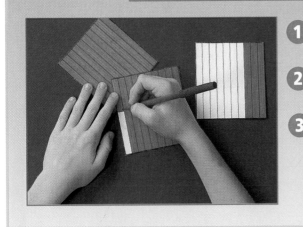

1. What number would you write for a tenths model that is completely shaded?

2. How many tenths models would you need to show 2.3? How would you shade them?

3. To say 2.3:
   First, say the whole number "2."
   Say "and" for the decimal point.
   Then, say "3 tenths" for the decimal.

## Show What You Know!

Use your recording sheet or draw decimal models. Color in whole squares and partial squares to show each of these amounts.

1. one and nine tenths
2. two and four tenths
3. 3.1
4. 1.3
5. 4.9

Write a decimal for each amount.

6. three and seven tenths
7. two and five tenths
8. seven and eight tenths

9. **Mental Math** Without drawing pictures, how can you tell that 2 is greater than 0.9?

10. **Critical Thinking** Explain how mixed numbers are like decimals that are greater than one. Use an example to explain your answer.

# LESSON 2

# Tenths and Hundredths

**Cooperative Learning**
**Checklist**

- ☑ Work alone.
- ☑ Work with a partner.
- ☐ Work with a group.

**Y**ou know that decimal models for tenths are divided into 10 equal parts. Decimal models for hundredths are divided into 100 equal parts. One hundredth is one of 100 equal parts. You can show hundredths in words, fractions, or decimals.

## Getting Started

**What You'll Need:**
- ▶ green and red crayons
- ▶ recording sheet
- ▶ 10 × 10 squared paper

**Vocabulary:**
**one hundredth**
Glossary, p. 516

## Activity

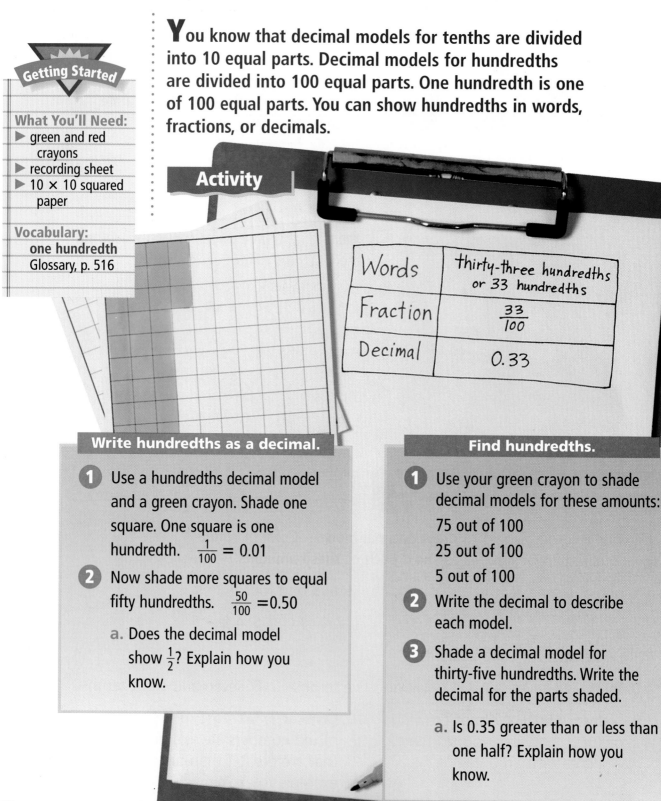

| Words | thirty-three hundredths or 33 hundredths |
|---|---|
| Fraction | $\frac{33}{100}$ |
| Decimal | 0.33 |

### Write hundredths as a decimal.

1. Use a hundredths decimal model and a green crayon. Shade one square. One square is one hundredth.  $\frac{1}{100} = 0.01$

2. Now shade more squares to equal fifty hundredths.  $\frac{50}{100} = 0.50$

   a. Does the decimal model show $\frac{1}{2}$? Explain how you know.

### Find hundredths.

1. Use your green crayon to shade decimal models for these amounts:

   75 out of 100

   25 out of 100

   5 out of 100

2. Write the decimal to describe each model.

3. Shade a decimal model for thirty-five hundredths. Write the decimal for the parts shaded.

   a. Is 0.35 greater than or less than one half? Explain how you know.

For exercises 1–4, use the recording sheet or a separate piece of paper to write the answer.

| Decimal | Greater or Less Than One Half |
|---------|-------------------------------|
| 0.75 |  |
| 0.25 |  |
| 0.95 |  |
| 0.45 |  |
| 0.50 |  |

1. Use a decimal model for each decimal in the chart. Is the shaded part greater than or less than $\frac{1}{2}$? Complete the chart.

2. The tenths decimal model and the hundredths decimal model, shown here, both have the same amount shaded. Draw two pairs of decimal models like these that show the same amount.

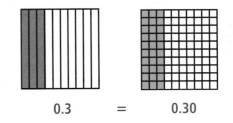

0.3    =    0.30

3. **Critical Thinking** Since 30 is greater than 3, why isn't 0.30 greater than 0.3?

4. Use decimal models for each pair of decimals in the chart. Then, use the models to help you complete the chart.

| Tenths Square | Hundredths Square | Compare |
|---------------|-------------------|---------|
| 0.6 | 0.25 | 0.6 > 0.25 |
| 0.5 | 0.05 | ? |
| 0.5 | 0.55 | ? |
| 0.3 | 0.30 | ? |
| 0.8 | 0.75 | ? |

**Number Sense** Each of these decimal models stand for one dollar. Write the amount of money shown by the shaded part. Use a decimal point and a dollar sign.

5.

6.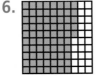

7.

381

# Place Value and Decimals

**Y**ou are mailing two packages. You know that one weighs 3.7 lb and that the other weighs 0.45 lb. What do these numbers mean? How do you read them?

You can use decimal models and a place-value chart to help you understand and read the numbers.

## Here's A Way!  Find the values of the digits.

**1** Show 3.7 with decimal models. Read the place-value chart.

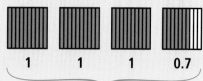

```
  1      1      1     0.7
         3.7
```

| Hundreds | Tens | Ones | | Tenths | Hundredths |
|---|---|---|---|---|---|
| 0 | 0 | 3 | . | 7 | 0 |

You say "3 and 7 tenths."

• The value of the digit 3 is 3 ones.
• The value of the digit 7 is 7 tenths.

**2** Show 0.45 with a decimal model. Read the place-value chart.

```
  0.45
```

| Hundreds | Tens | Ones | | Tenths | Hundredths |
|---|---|---|---|---|---|
| 0 | 0 | 0 | . | 4 | 5 |

You say "45 hundredths."

• The 0 shows there are no ones.
• The value of the digit 4 is 4 tenths.
• The value of the digit 5 is 5 hundredths.

**Talk About It!**  Look at the place-value charts. Does the value increase or decrease as you move from left to right? Explain your answer.

*EXPRESS*

**Write the decimal.**

1. 4 and 6 tenths          2. 32 hundredths          3. 3 dollars and 25 cents

**Number Sense  What is the value of the underlined digit?**

4. 24<u>7</u>.08          5. 196.<u>0</u>2          6. <u>4</u>3.36          7. 0.1<u>5</u>          8. 7<u>7</u>.37

**Write in words.**

9. 26.54          10. 16.09          11. 3.28          12. 4.1          13. 16.90

14. **Critical Thinking**  In exercise 13, is the decimal closer to 16 or to 17? Explain.

## Work It Out!

**Write a decimal to tell how much of the decimal model is shaded.**

15.          16.          17.          18.

**What does the digit 4 stand for in each number?**

19. 205.46          20. 49.05          21. 0.34          22. 34.90          23. 841.08

**Write the number in words.**

24. 58.08          25. 0.58          26. 5.80          27. 5.8          28. 50.58

**Patterns  Copy and write the missing numbers.**

29. 2.5, 2.6, ___, 2.8, ___, 3.0          30. 20.1, ___, 20.3, 20.4, ___

31. 1.48, 1.49, ___, 1.51, ___          32. 9.04, 9.05, ___, 9.07, ___

33. **Calculator**  Press [2] [+] [0] [.] [1] [=].
If you keep pressing [=] , your calculator will count by tenths.
Copy the number line. Use your calculator to fill in the missing numbers.

2.5  2.6  ▤  2.8  ▤  3.0  ▤  3.2  ▤  ▤  3.5  3.6  ▤  3.8  ▤  ▤  ▤  4.2  ▤  ▤  4.5

**More Practice Set 11.3, p. 508**

# Comparing Decimals

The scores for many Olympic events, like speed skating, are decimal numbers. Decimals are used because scores are reported using tenths and hundredths of seconds.

You can compare a decimal with tenths and a decimal with hundredths.

---

**Here's A Way!** **Compare 0.7 and 0.59.**

**Compare decimal models for hundredths.**
- Shade in 0.7 on one model.
- Shade in 0.59 on another model.
- Compare the models.

0.7          0.59

The hundredths model for 0.7 has more parts shaded.
So, 0.7 > 0.59.

---

**Compare digits.**
Look at the tenths place values.

0.7 ● 0.59 ➡️ Since 0.7 > 0.5, then 0.7 > 0.59.

**Talk About It!** How is comparing decimals like comparing whole numbers?

**Other Example** Some decimals have the same digit in the tenths place. For example, 0.79 and 0.70.

If the tenths digits are the same, compare the hundredths digits.

0.79 ● 0.70 ➡️ Since 9 > 0, then 0.79 > 0.70.

## Show What You Know!

**Copy and complete. Write >, <, or =.**

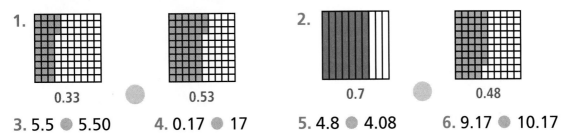

1. 0.33 ⬤ 0.53

2. 0.7 ⬤ 0.48

3. 5.5 ⬤ 5.50    4. 0.17 ⬤ 17    5. 4.8 ⬤ 4.08    6. 9.17 ⬤ 10.17

7. **Write About It** Describe how you could change the models for tenths and hundredths in exercise 2 to make the decimals equal. Make a drawing to explain your reasoning.

8. **Critical Thinking** Describe how you would compare 9.45 and 10.17? Explain your answer.

## Work It Out!

**Copy and complete. Write >, <, or =.**

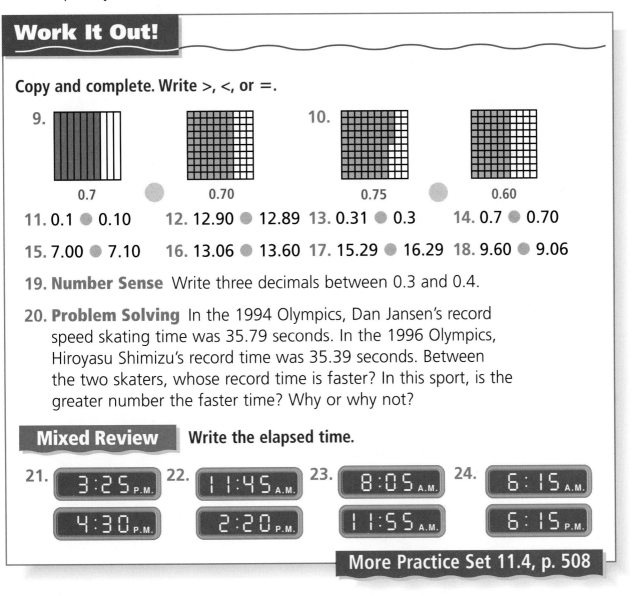

9. 0.7 ⬤ 0.70

10. 0.75 ⬤ 0.60

11. 0.1 ⬤ 0.10    12. 12.90 ⬤ 12.89    13. 0.31 ⬤ 0.3    14. 0.7 ⬤ 0.70

15. 7.00 ⬤ 7.10    16. 13.06 ⬤ 13.60    17. 15.29 ⬤ 16.29    18. 9.60 ⬤ 9.06

19. **Number Sense** Write three decimals between 0.3 and 0.4.

20. **Problem Solving** In the 1994 Olympics, Dan Jansen's record speed skating time was 35.79 seconds. In the 1996 Olympics, Hiroyasu Shimizu's record time was 35.39 seconds. Between the two skaters, whose record time is faster? In this sport, is the greater number the faster time? Why or why not?

**Mixed Review** Write the elapsed time.

21. 3:25 P.M.    22. 11:45 A.M.    23. 8:05 A.M.    24. 6:15 A.M.
    4:30 P.M.        2:20 P.M.          11:55 A.M.       6:15 P.M.

More Practice Set 11.4, p. 508

# Ordering Decimals

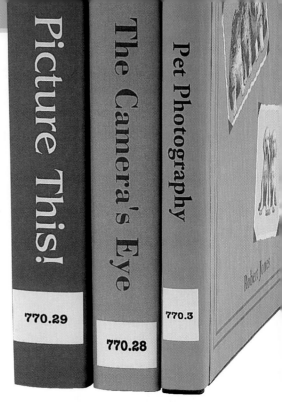

Picture This!

The Camera's Eye

Pet Photography

770.29

770.28

770.3

**M**ost libraries use the Dewey Decimal System to put books in order on the shelves. Each book is labeled with a decimal number and placed on the shelf in order from least to greatest.

To put these books in order, first compare the decimals.

---

## Here's A Way! Order from least to greatest.

**1** Line up the digits by place value.

770.29
770.28
770.30

770.3 = 770.30

**2** Compare the digits from left to right.

770.29
770.28
770.30

The first three digits are the same.

**3** Compare digits that are not the same in the tenths column.

770.29
770.28    3 > 2
770.30

770.3 is the greatest value.

**4** Compare digits that are not the same in the hundredths column.

770.29    9 > 8
770.28

770.29 is greater.

**5** Order the decimals from least to greatest.

770.28 < 770.29 < 770.3

So, the books ordered from least to greatest are 770.28, 770.29, and 770.3.

**Talk About It!** How is ordering decimals like ordering whole numbers?

**Other Examples** When dollar amounts are the same, compare the cents.
$3.52 > $3.30 because 52 cents > 30 cents.

## Show What You Know!

**Compare and order the decimals from least to greatest.**

1. 3.3, 3.88, 3.25

2. $1.40, $1.80, $1.08

3. 0.04, 0.4, 0.01

4. 24.89, 24.98, 24.9, 24.8

5. **Critical Thinking** Explain how you ordered the decimals in exercise 4.

**Patterns Copy and complete these number lines.**

6. 1.1   ?   1.3   1.4   ?

7. 1.05   ?   1.07   1.08   ?   ?   1.11

8. **Estimation** Estimate where 1.25 would be located on the number line in exercise 6. Then place 1.25 on your number line.

## Work It Out!

**Write the numbers in order from greatest to least.**

9. 12.34, 12.01, 12.45

10. 362.15, 362.1, 362.5

11. 13.2, 9.7, 10.0

12. 19.9, 19.99, 19.89, 19.98

13. 141.78, 141.08, 141.8, 141.88

14. 0.8, 0.08, 1.08, 0.18, 1.01

15. 100.1, 89.15, 104.13

16. 67, 67.3, 67.33, 67.03

17. **Algebraic Reasoning** The mystery number is a decimal in tenths between 4.3 and 4.8. Its digit in the tenths place is an even number. It is less than 4.72 and greater than 4.49. What is the mystery number?

**Critical Thinking Explain what is wrong with the reasoning.**

18. 0.3 < 0.21 because 3 < 21.

19. 2.6 < 2.18 because 26 < 218.

### Problem Solving

20. Three books on the shelf have the numbers 197.8, 197.85, and 197.91. The librarian has three more books to put on the shelf with the numbers 197.9, 197.82, and 197.86. How should all of these books be ordered on the shelf?

21. Four books are put in order by hundredths. If you look only at the digits after the decimal point, what four decimals in a row add up to 0.46? Use a calculator to help you.

**More Practice Set 11.5, p. 509**

# Problem Solving
## Look for a Pattern

Triangle 1          Triangle 2          Triangle 3

**L**ook at the triangles shown. The larger triangles are made of triangles the size of Triangle 1. Suppose the triangles continue to increase in size, following the same pattern. How can you find the perimeter for Triangle 4? For 5 and 6?

Looking for a pattern can help you solve this problem.

## Here's A Way!   Use Look for a Pattern.

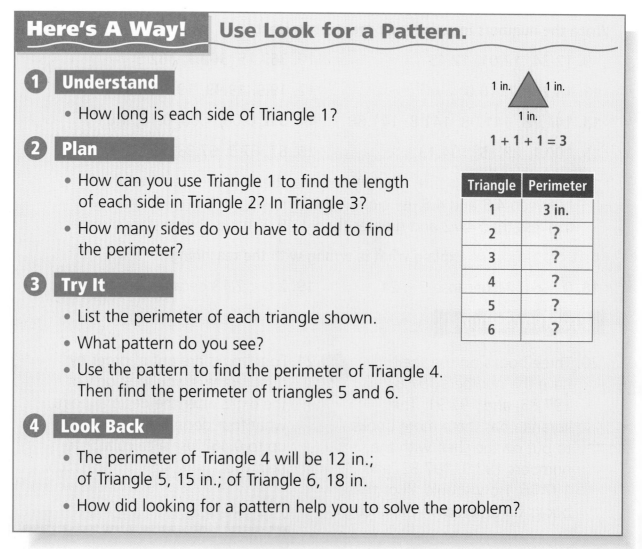

**1  Understand**

- How long is each side of Triangle 1?

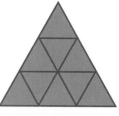

$$1 + 1 + 1 = 3$$

**2  Plan**

- How can you use Triangle 1 to find the length of each side in Triangle 2? In Triangle 3?
- How many sides do you have to add to find the perimeter?

| Triangle | Perimeter |
|----------|-----------|
| 1 | 3 in. |
| 2 | ? |
| 3 | ? |
| 4 | ? |
| 5 | ? |
| 6 | ? |

**3  Try It**

- List the perimeter of each triangle shown.
- What pattern do you see?
- Use the pattern to find the perimeter of Triangle 4. Then find the perimeter of triangles 5 and 6.

**4  Look Back**

- The perimeter of Triangle 4 will be 12 in.; of Triangle 5, 15 in.; of Triangle 6, 18 in.
- How did looking for a pattern help you to solve the problem?

**Use Look for a Pattern to solve the problem.**

1. Five squares are in a row. The first square is 2 cm on one side. The second square is 4 cm on one side. The third square is 8 cm on one side. If this doubling pattern continues, what is the perimeter of the fifth square?

2. **Critical Thinking** In problem 1, did you look for a pattern in the perimeter of each square or in the length of each side? Could you use either pattern to solve the problem?

## Work It Out!

**Use Look for a Pattern or any other strategy to solve the problem.**

3. List the next three decimals in the pattern shown.

4. During a 30-minute TV show, there are 4 commercial breaks. Each break shows 3 commercials. Each commercial runs 30 seconds. How long is the TV show itself?

5. Suppose you count backward. You start at 33. You count back 10 odd numbers. At what number do you stop?

6. Five racers finish 3 seconds apart. The first racer finishes in 12 seconds. What are the times for the other 4 racers?

7. The sum of two numbers is 68. Their difference is 22. What are the numbers?

8. Copy and continue this pattern to show what the 0.9 decimal square will be if this pattern continues.

9. **Create Your Own** Make up a pattern with decimals. See if a classmate can continue the pattern.

### Share Your Thinking

10. Which problems did you solve by looking for a pattern? How are these problems similar?

11. How can looking for a pattern keep you from having to draw a picture? Explain.

# Problem Solving
## Choose a Computation Method

**N**iagara Falls was formed about 10,000 years ago. Scientists predict it will last another 25,000 years. If this is true, how old will Niagara Falls be then?

| |
|---|
| **Choose a Computation Method** |
| **Ask Yourself:** |
| Do I need an exact answer or an estimate? |
| Should I use a model, paper and pencil, mental math, or a calculator? |
| What operation should I use? |

## You Decide

- Do you need to use a calculator, or can you do mental math to solve the problem?
- Decide which method you think would be better to use. Solve the problem. Explain why you chose the method you used.

## Work It Out!

**Use mental math or a calculator to solve the problem. Explain.**

1. A tour boat is one of the best ways to see Niagara Falls. There are 6 tour boats. Each boat makes 15 trips a day. How many trips in all are made to the falls each day?

2. Four tour boats can each carry 200 passengers. The fifth boat can carry 150 passengers, and the sixth boat can carry 175. If all 6 boats are full, how many passengers are there?

3. Niagara Falls is 184 ft high. A helicopter flies 800 ft above the base of the falls. How high is it above the top of the falls?

4. Part of Niagara Falls is called Horseshoe Falls. The edge of these falls moves back almost 4 ft each year. About how many feet have these falls moved back since you were born?

## Share Your Thinking

5. Which problems did you solve by using mental math? Explain what these problems have in common.

# Midchapter Review

## for Pages 376–390

**Solve. Show your work.** (page 388)

1. Suppose you have a picture that is 40 cm wide by 50 cm high. You plan to put a frame that is 10 cm wide all around it. What will the width and height of the outside of the frame be?

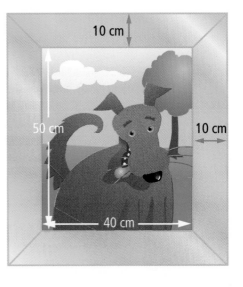

## Concepts

**Write the value of the digit in color for each decimal.** (pages 378, 380)

2. 0.4     3. 4.15     4. 1.07     5. 0.72     6. 0.72

7. The decimals 1.23 and 12.3 are made up of the same digits. Do the decimals have the same value? How can you tell?

8. Explain how to write $\frac{7}{10}$ and $\frac{7}{100}$ as decimals.

## Skills

**Write the decimal in standard form.** (pages 378, 380)

9. twelve and six hundredths

10. thirteen and thirteen hundredths

**Copy and complete. Write >, <, or =.** (page 384)

11. 1.50 ● 1.05                12. 0.4 ● 0.41

13. 5.5 ● 5.50                 14. 1.7 ● 0.98

**Write the decimals in order from least to greatest.** (page 386)

15. 0.1, 0.01, 0.11, 1.1        16. 12.4, 11.94, 12.04, 11.9

17. 0.19, 0.21, 0.09, 0.2       18. 21.5, 21.48, 20.98, 21.09

# Math *World*

Decimals are at the heart of the metric system, which is the world's most popular form of measurement.

## Going, Going, Gone Metric

Some countries use the metric system of measurement but still keep some customary measurements. Mexico

uses the metric system as well as an old measurement called the *pie* (PEE ay). A *pie* is $\frac{2}{100}$ of an inch less than 11 inches. The U.S. uses customary measurements, except for a few metric ones. A mile is a customary measurement; a kilometer is metric. Can you think of other examples?

## Dewey's Decimal System

Libraries that use the Dewey Decimal Classification System label their books with decimals. An American named Melvil Dewey created the system more than 100 years ago. Librarians assign every book a number based on its subject. Math books have numbers between 510 and 520. The subject of the book on the left is division.

513.214
H

## EARLY EUROPEAN DECIMALS

Today, there are two ways to separate the ones and tenths places in decimals. In the United States, we use a decimal point. People in parts of Europe use a decimal comma. Hundreds of years ago, people in Europe had other ways of writing decimals. Follow these steps to learn more about them.

**1** François Viete (vee ET) (1540–1603) was a French lawyer and mathematician. Viete sometimes wrote decimals with a short vertical line where we put the decimal point, like the problem on the right. Write the decimals 8.79 and 34.15 this way.

18|275

18 275

**2** Viete also wrote numbers with the decimal places underlined. Use this method to write 123.88 and 34.25.

**3** This is how the Flemish-Dutch mathematician Simon Stevin (1548–1620) would have written the number 354.72. What method do you think he used? Describe it to a friend, using your own example.

3 4 2 5 ⓪①②
Explanation: I used circled numbers to

3 5 4 7 2 ⓪①②

## Decimal Names

Computer software boxes have decimals on them to identify them. The first version is usually 1.0. Programs that are changed are renamed with a greater number. Tenths added to the number show that only small changes were made.

CHASE
VERSION
2.1.7

VERSION
3.0.1

4.0

### Respond

Work with a partner . . .
to find examples of the metric system being used in your school.

 **Internet:**
**Houghton Mifflin Education Place**
Explore the Math Center at
http://www.eduplace.com

## LESSON 8

# Using Rounding to Estimate

You can use a number line to help you round a decimal to the nearest whole number.

**Y**ou already know how to round whole numbers. You can use the same rules to round decimals.

Round decimals to the nearest whole number to estimate.

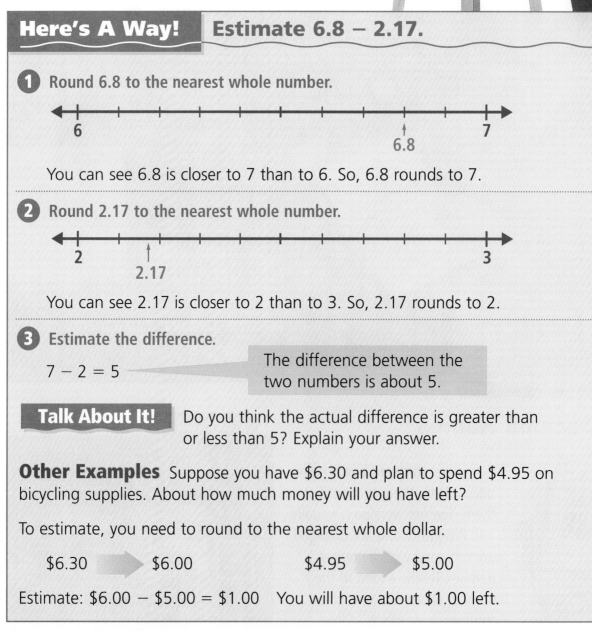

**Here's A Way!**    Estimate 6.8 − 2.17.

**1** Round 6.8 to the nearest whole number.

6                  ↑ 6.8        7

You can see 6.8 is closer to 7 than to 6. So, 6.8 rounds to 7.

**2** Round 2.17 to the nearest whole number.

2    ↑ 2.17                    3

You can see 2.17 is closer to 2 than to 3. So, 2.17 rounds to 2.

**3** Estimate the difference.

$7 - 2 = 5$

The difference between the two numbers is about 5.

**Talk About It!**   Do you think the actual difference is greater than or less than 5? Explain your answer.

**Other Examples**   Suppose you have $6.30 and plan to spend $4.95 on bicycling supplies. About how much money will you have left?

To estimate, you need to round to the nearest whole dollar.

$6.30   ➡   $6.00           $4.95   ➡   $5.00

Estimate: $6.00 − $5.00 = $1.00   You will have about $1.00 left.

Round to the nearest whole number. Draw a number line when it helps.

1. 3.9     2. 8.27     3. 16.39     4. 50.85     5. 89.51

Use rounding to estimate.

6.   6.2
  − 0.98

7.   4.6
  + 3.37

8.   9.46
  − 2.79

9.   $5.99
  + $6.99

10.   24.95
  − 15.6

11. **Critical Thinking** Is the exact answer to exercise 10 more than or less than your estimate? How do you know?

## Work It Out!

**Number Sense** What whole numbers are missing from the number line? Copy and complete.

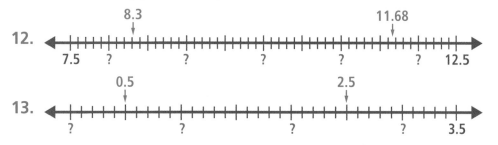

12.
             8.3                11.68
  7.5   ?      ?      ?      ?      ?  12.5

13.
      0.5            2.5
  ?      ?      ?      ?   3.5

Use rounding to estimate. Draw a number line when it helps.

14.   3.1
  + 2.88

15.   9.6
  − 3.82

16.   15.25
  − 2.3

17. 24.1 + 10.53     18. 5 − 1.3     19. 43.5 − 2.51

### Problem Solving

20. Suppose you plan to bicycle 92.28 miles on a two-day tour. If you plan to bicycle 50.16 miles on the first day, estimate how many miles you will bicycle on the second day.

21. Before leaving on the bicycle tour, you need to buy sun block, a headband, and a water bottle. You have $20. Will that be enough? Explain your answer.

| Item | Price |
| --- | --- |
| Sun Block | $6.89 |
| Headband | $3.39 |
| Water Bottle | $4.59 |

$4.59

$6.89

$3.39

More Practice Set 11.8 p. 509

# Adding Decimals

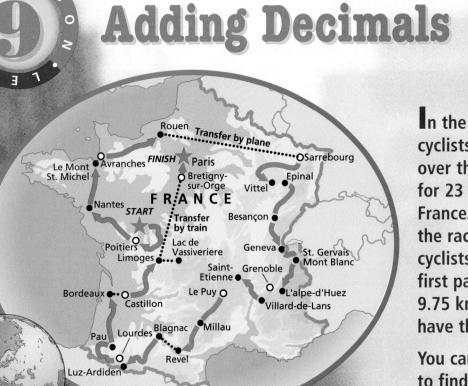

In the Tour de France, cyclists come from all over the world to race for 23 days throughout France. The first part of the race is 7.3 km. If the cyclists complete the first part and ride 9.75 km more, how far have they traveled?

You can add decimals to find the distance.

## Here's A Way! Add 7.3 km and 9.75 km.

**1** Estimate first to predict what the answer will be.

7.3 ➔ 7

9.75 ➔ 10

$$\begin{array}{r} 7 \\ + 10 \\ \hline 17 \end{array}$$

**2** Line up the digits by place value. Write zeros as necessary.

7.3 = 7.30

$$\begin{array}{r} 7.30 \\ + 9.75 \\ \hline \end{array}$$

**3** Add. Regroup if necessary. Write the decimal point in the sum.

$$\begin{array}{r} \overset{1}{7}.30 \\ + 9.75 \\ \hline 17.05 \end{array}$$

**4** The total distance is 17.05 km.

**Talk About It!** How does estimating the sum help you know if your answer is reasonable?

Estimate the answer. Record the estimate. Find the sum.

1.  7.5
    + 8.2

2.  4.56
    + 2.37

3.    5
    + 15.02

4.  16.16
    + 16.3

5.  $45.78
    + $5.62

6. 5.4 + 3.2 + 6

7. $132.34 + $46.16 + $.50

8. 108.7 + 65.46 + 3.04 + 2

9. $102.55 + $32.10 + $.04

10. **Critical Thinking** Why can you write the addend 0.5 as 0.50 and have the sum remain the same?

## Work It Out!

Find the sum.

11.  2.37
    + 5.61

12.  1
     1.1
   + 1.01

13.   0.5
      1.8
   + 30.2

14.   $.79
   + $3.29

15.  $4.57
     $2.99
   + $5.00

16. 0 + 0.6 + 78

17. 134.13 + 1 + 0.01

18. 40.09 + 0.01 + 21

19. $500 + $2.34 + $.25

**Estimation** Estimate. Is the sum greater than 10? Write *yes* or *no*.

20.  $4.79
   + $7.24

21.  6.43
   + 3.01

22.  4.29
   + 8.53

23.  $5.27
   + $3.89

24. **Calculator** Use your calculator to find the sums in exercises 20–23.

25. **Problem Solving** Suppose you are a cyclist in a race. The route is marked in four sections. Section 1 is 6.3 km. Section 2 is 10.25 km. Section 3 is 15.6 km. Section 4 is 12.50 km. How many kilometers is the race?

**Mixed Review**   Write the answer.

26. 9 × 507   27. 5)500   28. 3 × 689   29. 4)568   30. 7 × 246

More Practice Set 11.9, p. 509

# Subtracting Decimals

Cyclists from many countries travel to China to take part in a cycling race. On the last day, the course is 80.5 km. If a cyclist has 5.2 km to go, how far has he raced on that day?

You can subtract to find the answer.

## Here's A Way!  Find 80.5 km − 5.2 km.

**1** Estimate first.

$80.5 \Rightarrow 81$

$5.2 \Rightarrow 5$

$81 - 5 = 76$

**2** Line up place values and decimal points.

$$\begin{array}{r} 80.5 \\ -\ \ 5.2 \end{array}$$

**3** Subtract. Regroup if necessary.

$$\begin{array}{r} {\scriptstyle 7\,10} \\ 8\cancel{0}.5 \\ -\ \ 5.2 \\ \hline 75.3 \end{array}$$

The cyclist has traveled 75.3 km.

**Talk About It!**  When you subtract decimals, how can you check to see if your answer is reasonable?

**Other Examples** Sometimes the decimals you are subtracting do not have the same number of digits. For example, 42.8 − 26.53. Write zeros to make them equivalent decimals, and then subtract.

**1** Line up the digits by place value. Write zeros if necessary.

$$\begin{array}{r} 42.80 \\ -\ 26.53 \end{array}$$

Put a zero in the ones place.

**2** Subtract. Regroup if necessary.

$$\begin{array}{r} {\scriptstyle 3\ \ 12\ 7\ 10} \\ \cancel{4}\,2.\cancel{8}\,\cancel{0} \\ -\ 2\,6.5\,3 \\ \hline 1\,6.2\,7 \end{array}$$

**3** Check.

$$\begin{array}{r} 16.27 \\ +\ 26.53 \\ \hline 42.80 \end{array}$$

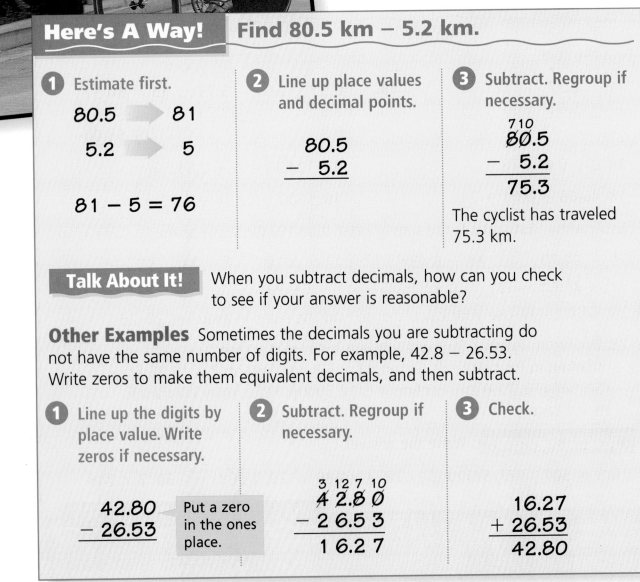

**Estimate. Record the estimate. Then write the difference.**

1.  7.8
  − 3.92

2.  13
  − 6.8

3.  44.32
  − 3.76

4.  4.2
  − 0.08

5.  71.4
  − 60.5

6. 0.84 − 0.7

7. 19.45 − 11.81

8. 12.11 − 7

9. 20.15 − 5.14

10. 6.35 − 4.2

11. 9.7 − 3.82

12. 25.06 − 12.01

13. 54.7 − 23.53

14. **Critical Thinking** How does knowing how to write equivalent decimals help you subtract hundredths from tenths?

## Work It Out!

**Estimate. Then write the difference.**

15.  0.91
  − 0.37

16.  42.99
  − 20.43

17.  22
  − 4.8

18.  18.04
  − 6

19.  12.6
  − 4

20. 17.81 − 4.65

21. 4.94 − 1.6

22. 38 − 17.1

23. 6.26 − 4.9

24. 5 − 0.89

25. 11.76 − 5.7

26. 18.75 − 9

27. 8.2 − 5.47

28. 4.9 − 3.5

### Problem Solving

29. Suppose you and a friend ride your bikes to a state park. You ride 5.7 mi each way to the state park and back. Your friend rides 7.2 mi each way to the state park and back. How much farther did your friend ride than you?

30. One women's bicycle race in the United States is 100.8 km long. Each lap is 16.8 km. Suppose a racer has two laps to go. How far has she already traveled?

More Practice Set 11.10, p. 510

### Math Journal

How are adding and subtracting decimals like adding and subtracting whole numbers?

# Adding and Subtracting Decimals

LESSON 11

**E**ach year cyclists ride from Tecate, Mexico, to Ensenada, Mexico. If the total distance of the race is 71.87 mi, what is the distance of part D of the race?

You can add and subtract to answer questions about the data.

## Here's A Way!  Add and subtract decimals.

### Add

Add to find the distance from part A through part C.

**1** Find on the map the distances for parts A, B, and C. List them.

Part A   17.5 mi
Part B   13.75 mi
Part C   16.88 mi

**2** Round to estimate the sum.

$18 + 14 + 17 = 49$

**3** Find the exact answer.

$17.5 + 13.75 + 16.88 = 48.13$

The distance from part A through part C is 48.13 mi.

### Subtract

Subtract to find the distance of part D.

**1** List the two distances that you know.

Total distance is 71.87 mi.
Part A through part C is 48.13 mi.

**2** Round to estimate the difference.

$72 - 48 = 24$

**3** Find the exact answer.

$71.87 - 48.13 = 23.74$

The distance of part D is 23.74 mi.

### Talk About It!

How does estimating help you know if the answer is reasonable?

Use a calculator or pencil and paper. Write the sum or the difference.

1.  3.2
   + 7.3

2.  9.66
   + 4

3.  7.4
   − 2.5

4.  $13
   − $6.80

5.  24.3
   − 14.2

**Mental Math** Find the sum or the difference.

6. 3.75 + 1.25      7. $10 − $2      8. 4.5 + 2 + 3.5      9. 7.35 − 0.25

10. **Critical Thinking** How were you able to use mental math to find the answer to exercise 7?

## Work It Out!

Write the sum or the difference. Circle the answers you find by using mental math.

11. 3.45 + 23.1      12. $4.50 − $1.50   13. 2.5 + 3.5      14. 21.5 + 0

15. 89.1 − 6         16. 15.9 − 0        17. 25.3 − 4.2     18. (1.25 + 2) − 3

Write the sum or the difference.

19.  42.99
    − 20.43

20.  10.42
    + 8.0

21.  27.4
    − 6.3

22.  $35
    − $5.25

23.  55.6
    + 30.4

24. **Critical Thinking** Explain how you can check to see if your answer is reasonable in exercise 23.

### Problem Solving

25. The route to Ensenada passes through mountains. Suppose it is 8.75 mi up the first mountain and 1.25 mi longer going down. What is the distance up and down the mountain?

26. Look at the map of the route on page 400. What is the difference in length between part D and part B of the route?

**More Practice Set 11.11, p. 510**

# Problem Solving
## Using Look for a Pattern and Other Strategies

**P**eople train for mountain bike races by cycling a certain distance every day. They ride up hills, over rocky paths, and across streams.

| Pedal Turns | Distance |
|:---:|:---:|
| 1 | 4.2 m |
| 2 | 8.4 m |
| 3 | 12.6 m |
| 4 | 16.8 m |

**Y**ou are riding a bicycle up a hill. You pedal all the way up without changing gears or changing your speed. It takes you $12\frac{1}{2}$ pedal turns to reach the top. How many meters have you gone?

- The table shows how far the bike goes each time you turn the pedal.

- How far will you go after 5 pedal turns? After 6 turns?

- Choose a strategy that can help solve the problem. Then solve it.

**Problem Solving Process**
- ✓ Understand
- ✓ Plan
- ✓ Try It
- ✓ Look Back

**Choose a Strategy You Have Learned**
- ✓ Guess and Check
- ✓ Draw a Picture
- ✓ Make a List
- ✓ Make a Table
- ✓ Act It Out
- ✓ Work a Simpler Problem
- ✓ Look for a Pattern
- ✓ Work Backward

## Work It Out!

**Use any strategy to solve the problem. Show your work.**

1. Is the total length of this bike course greater than or less than $\frac{1}{4}$ mi?

2. The distance around a different track is 0.3 mi. How many laps must you ride to travel more than 2 mi?

3. On a bicycle trip, you stop to rest after 6 mi. You have gone 0.75 of the way. How long is the entire trip?

4. You need a bike helmet. The one you want costs $27.87. You have $\frac{1}{3}$ of the money you need. How much more money do you need?

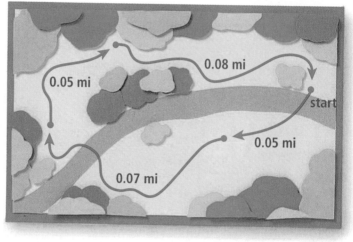

0.05 mi   0.08 mi

start

0.05 mi

0.07 mi

5. **Create Your Own** Design your own bike race course with four different sections. Make the course 0.3 mi from start to finish. Label the distance of each section.

6. Suppose the next figure is a half circle. If this pattern continues, draw the next two figures.

7. Suppose that each time you pedal, the rear sprocket wheel turns 2.75 times. How many times must you pedal for the rear sprocket wheel to turn more than 15 times?

8. A bike has 3 different sizes of front sprocket wheels. It also has 7 different sizes of rear sprocket wheels. How many different combinations are possible?

Front Sprocket Wheels

Rear Sprocket Wheels

### Share Your Thinking

9. Discuss problem 8 with a partner. What strategy did you each use?

# Problem Solving
## Using Strategies

You can read more about the Olympics in the pages of *Time* magazine.

**R**unners from all over the world compete every four years in the Summer Olympic Games. In 1996, the games were held in Atlanta, Georgia. There, runners set 13 new records.

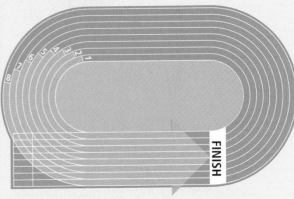

FINISH

**Problem Solving Process**
- ✓ Understand
- ✓ Plan
- ✓ Try It
- ✓ Look Back

**Choose a Strategy You Have Learned**
- ✓ Guess and Check
- ✓ Draw a Picture
- ✓ Make a List
- ✓ Make a Table
- ✓ Act It Out
- ✓ Work a Simpler Problem
- ✓ Look for a Pattern
- ✓ Work Backward

**F**or the 200-meter race, runners do not change lanes. They also do not start in a straight line. Almost all runners start ahead of another, and one starts last. Yet they all run the same distance. Can you explain how this is possible?

- Look at the diagram shown.
- Think about the distance around the outside of the track.
- Which lane has the longest distance? Which lane has the shortest distance?
- Explain a strategy that can help you to solve the problem. Then, solve it.

**Use any strategy to solve the problem. Show your work.**

1. One lap around an Olympic track is 400 m. How many laps would you need to run to complete a 10-kilometer race?

2. Two runners race once around a 400-meter track. One starts on the inside in Lane 1. The other starts in Lane 2. Who starts farther ahead?

3. In a relay race, team members take turns running. Teams have four members. If each member runs 800 m, how long is the entire race?

4. Suppose the U.S. relay team finishes 2 seconds before the Kenyans and 9 seconds before the Cubans. If the time for the Cubans is 8 minutes and 8 seconds, what were the other times?

### Men's 200–Meter Race: Top Five Runners

| Name | Record |
|------|--------|
| Michael Johnson | 19.32 seconds |
| Frank Fredericks | 19.68 seconds |
| Pietro Mennea | 19.72 seconds |
| Mike Marsh | 19.73 seconds |
| Carl Lewis | 19.75 seconds |

5. Michael Johnson set the record for the 200-meter race in 1996. Could he have run 400 meters in 38.64 seconds? Explain.

6. In 1996, Johnson broke his own record for the 200-meter race by about one third of a second. About how fast was his old record?

7. What if Johnson had a problem with his shoes in 1996? Suppose it took him 0.01 second longer to run each meter. Would he have beaten the record set by Frank Fredericks?

8. **Create Your Own** Write a problem about the Olympics. Use data on these pages or from magazine articles. Ask a friend to solve your problem.

Michael Johnson points to his 1996 world record.

### Share Your Thinking

9. What different strategies did you use to solve the problems in this lesson? Discuss them with a partner.

# Chapter 11 Test

## for Pages 376–405

**Test-Taking Tips**
When you look for patterns to solve problems, find how much greater or less each number is than the number before it.

## Problem Solving

**Solve. Show your work.** (pages 388, 402, 404)

**1.** Baseball posters sell for $1.50 in bin 1, $1.75 in bin 2, and $2.00 in bin 3. If the pattern continues, how much would you have to pay for a poster in bin 8?

**2.** Suppose the rainfall for January, February, and March added up to be the same amount as for April, May, and June. How much rain would have fallen from January to June?

| Total Rainfall | |
|---|---|
| April | 17.9 cm |
| May | 15.4 cm |
| June | 15.3 cm |

## Concepts

**Tell whether each decimal is less than $\frac{1}{2}$, between $\frac{1}{2}$ and 1, or more than 1.** (pages 378, 380)

**3.** 1.01　　　　**4.** 0.7　　　　**5.** 0.42　　　　**6.** 0.3

**What is the value of the digit in color?** (page 382)

**7.** 245.08　　　　**8.** 0.73　　　　**9.** 14.2

**Find the answers.** (pages 382, 394, 396, 398)

**10.** Can a decimal that has a 4 in the tenths place ever be less than a decimal that has a 3 in the hundredths place? Give an example to show why or why not.

**11.** Suppose you want to buy 3 pizzas. The pizzas cost $6.35 each. You have $15.78. How can you find out if you have enough money to buy 3 pizzas?

**12.** Explain how you would round 14.17 to the nearest whole number.

**13.** Is $3 a closer estimate than $4 for $.89 + $2.12? Why or why not?

**14.** How can you check to see whether 1.42 − 0.7 = 0.72?

Choose the correct sum or difference. Write *a*, *b*, *c*, or *d*. (pages 394, 396, 398, 400)

15. 32 − 24.76    a. 12.76    b. 6.24    c. 7.76    d. 7.24

16. 3.1 + 5.46 + 25    a. 61.46    b. 33.56    c. 38.47    d. 11.06

17. 121.11 + 32.4 + 0.07    a. 153.58    b. 154.48    c. 153.68    d. 154.58

18. 13.4 − 0.65    a. 12.85    b. 13.85    c. 12.75    d. 13.75

19. 103.01 − 98.8    a. 5.81    b. 4.21    c. 5.21    d. 4.81

Copy and complete. Write >, <, or =. (page 384)

20. 5.67 ● 5.76    21. 0.7 ● 0.70    22. 1.1 ● 1.09

Order from least to greatest. (page 386)

23. 0.3, 0.33, 0.13, 1.2    24. 1.17, 1.7, 1.1, 1.11    25. 0.98, 1.4, 1.98, 0.4

Estimate by rounding. (page 394)

26. 7.2 − 3.9    27. 12.98 + 0.87

28. 6 + 2.1 + 4.86    29. 9.75 − 4.1

## Performance Task

Many libraries use the Dewey Decimal System to put some books in order. With this system, librarians arrange books on a shelf by decimal number in least to greatest order. How would you order these books?

534.83    534.99    535.0    534.8    534.87    534.95    534.91

• Explain how you decided on the order.

# Cumulative Review

**Estimate Sums** (Chapter 2)
Estimate the sum of 231 and 463.

## Here's A Way!

Make a front-end estimate.

$200 + 400 = 600$

Adjust your estimate. Look for groups of about 100 in the other digits.

$600 + 100 = 700$

---

**Make a front-end estimate. Then adjust your estimate.**

1. $698 + 298$
2. $1450 + 8550$
3. $\$1.57 + \$4.43$
4. $\$25.00 + \$15.37$
5. $\$5.79 + \$1.99$
6. $\$3.42 + \$4.55$
7. $\$4.05 + \$3.69 + \$1.51$
8. For $1036 + 2202$, is your adjusted estimate greater than or less than the exact answer?

---

**Multiplication and Division Sentences** (Chapter 4)
Write a related division sentence for $2 \times 4 = 8$.

## Here's A Way!

Think of an array.

$2 \times 4 = 8$ or $8 \div 4 = 2$

---

**Find the missing number. Then, write a related multiplication or division sentence.**

9. $12 \div \blacksquare = 6$
10. $12 \times \blacksquare = 60$
11. $42 \div 7 = \blacksquare$
12. $10 \times 40 = \blacksquare$
13. $\blacksquare \times 14 = 28$
14. $5 \div 1 = \blacksquare$
15. $8 \times (4 + \blacksquare) = 40$
16. $5 = 50 \div (3 + \blacksquare)$

---

**Multiplying 3-Digit Numbers**
(Chapter 6)
Find $125 \times 4$.

## Here's A Way!

Multiply the ones. Regroup.
Multiply the tens. Add the regrouped tens.
Regroup.
Multiply the hundreds. Add the regrouped hundreds.

$$\begin{array}{r} \overset{1\,2}{125} \\ \times\quad 4 \\ \hline 500 \end{array}$$

---

**Find the answers.**

17. $123 \times 3$
18. $416 \times 5$
19. $101 \times 9$
20. $3 \times 333$
21. $2 \times 545$
22. $7 \times 362$
23. How many hundreds will be in the product of $202 \times 4$? Do you need to find the exact product to answer the question?

## Adding and Subtracting Mixed Numbers (Chapter 9)

Find $5\frac{7}{10} - 1\frac{3}{10}$.

**Here's A Way!**

Subtract the fractions. Then subtract the whole numbers.

$$\begin{array}{r} 5\frac{7}{10} \\ - 1\frac{3}{10} \\ \hline 4\frac{4}{10} \end{array}$$

Find the simplest form.

$4\frac{4}{10} = 4\frac{2}{5}$

Solve. Write the answer in simplest form.

24. $45\frac{2}{3} - 23\frac{1}{3}$

25. $10\frac{3}{16} - 7\frac{1}{16}$

26. $9\frac{3}{10} - 8\frac{1}{10}$

27. $4\frac{5}{8} + 2\frac{1}{8}$

28. $2\frac{3}{5} - 1\frac{1}{5}$

29. $3\frac{5}{12} - 2\frac{1}{12}$

30. $\begin{array}{r} 1\frac{1}{6} \\ + 2\frac{8}{6} \\ \hline \end{array}$

31. $\begin{array}{r} 6\frac{7}{12} \\ - 2\frac{5}{12} \\ \hline \end{array}$

## Equivalent Units (Chapter 10)

What are three other ways to write 1 yd 12 in.?

**Here's A Way!**

1 yd = 36 in. = 3 feet
1 ft = 12 in.
You can write 1 yd 12 in. as:
**1 yd 1 ft; 48 in.; or 4 ft**

Write two equivalent measurements.

32. 60 in.

33. 1 km

34. 3 m

35. 1 dm

36. 3 yd

37. 5280 ft

38. Which is greater, $2\frac{1}{2}$ yd or 5 ft?

39. Which is greater, 10 dm or 2 cm?

## Problem Solving

**Problem Solving Process**
✓ Understand
✓ Plan
✓ Try It
✓ Look Back

**Choose a Strategy You Have Learned**
✓ Guess and Check
✓ Draw a Picture
✓ Make a List
✓ Make a Table
✓ Act It Out
✓ Work a Simpler Problem
✓ Look for a Pattern
✓ Work Backward

Choose any strategy you know to solve the problem. Show your work.

40. How many nickels are in $100? How many dimes? How many quarters?

41. Suppose your sister earns $5.40 an hour at an after-school job. She begins work at 3:45 P.M. and ends work at 6:15 P.M. How much does she earn during that time?

## INVESTIGATION

# Classroom Olympics!

**Citizenship Connection**     **With Your Group**

**Keep In Mind . . .**

Your work will be evaluated on the following:

☑ Whether you add the decimals correctly

☑ How well you put together the information

☑ Whether your graph clearly shows the results

☑ How your group members divide tasks to plan your Olympics

**H**ave you ever wanted to participate in the Olympics? Here's your chance! You can design a set of Olympic events for you and your classmates to compete in. You will use a digital watch to time events the way judges do in the Olympics—using decimal points. Can you beat your own best time?

## Plan It

- Brainstorm a list of events you can play. Make sure all the events can be done by everyone. Think about the materials you have on hand to help you plan the events.
- Gather the materials you need for the events you chose.
- Divide into teams. Give your team a fun name.
- Choose a person who will act as timekeeper for your team.

## Put It Together

- Mark off the area in which you will do each event.
- Make a chart for your timekeeper to record each person's time for each event.

### The Dragons

| | Coin - Rolling | | B |
|---|---|---|---|
| | 1 | 2 | |
| Tom | | | |
| Mary | | | |
| Chun | | | |
| Pilar | | | |
| To | | | |

**Coin-Rolling  Build**

13.7 seconds

15.3 seconds

12.9 seconds

16.1 seconds
58.0 seconds

Average =
14.5 seconds

## Wrap It Up

- Play each game twice. Time and record each person's results for each event, in decimals.
- Add all your team's decimal results together for each event. Use a calculator to divide this number by the number of teammates to get the average.
- Decide how to show your results. For example, you could make a graph to compare all the teams' scores for one event.

## Discuss Your Results

- Have you covered all the points in Keep In Mind?
- Compare the first round of each event to the second round. Who improved the most?

**Internet**

> Visit the **Math Center** at **Houghton Mifflin Education Place.** http://www.eduplace.com

411

# Math Power

## Use What You Know

$$\begin{array}{r} 28 \\ \times\ 7 \\ \hline 196 \end{array}$$

- how to multiply by 1-digit numbers

$3 \times 10 = 30$

- how to use arrays to help you multiply

- product

- vocabulary

# Multiplying 2-Digit Numbers

## Try This!

**U**se place-value blocks and addition to help you multiply greater numbers. Follow the steps below to multiply 2-digit numbers.

### What You'll Need

place-value blocks in 100's, 10's and 1's

**1**

Start with an array that shows 10 × 10. Add place-value blocks to it until it shows 11 × 11. What is your product?

$$10 \times 10 =$$

$$11 \times 11 =$$

$$11 \times 12 =$$

$$12 \times 12 =$$

## 2

Build onto your array to make it show 11 × 12. What is your product? Build again so that it shows 12 × 12. What is the product now?

## 3

Now add to your array so that it shows 12 × 13. What is your product?

How does addition help you multiply greater numbers?

Estimate the product of 13 × 13. Then, build onto your array to check your estimation. How close were you?

**Ready to Go!**

# Mental Math: Using Patterns

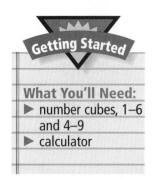

**Getting Started**

**What You'll Need:**
► number cubes, 1–6 and 4–9
► calculator

**U**se what you know about multiplying tens, hundreds, and thousands to find patterns when you multiply by a two-digit number.

## Rolling for Patterns!

**Activity**

**1**

Copy the chart. Then roll two number cubes.

• Write the digits you rolled in the first column.

### Multiplication Patterns

| Digits Rolled | Tens × Tens | Tens × Hundreds | Tens × Thousands |
|---|---|---|---|
| 3 and 7 | 30 × 70 | 30 × 700 | 30 × 7000 |
| | | | |

**2**

Use the digits to create a factor that is a multiple of 10 and another factor that is a multiple of 10, 100, and 1000. Use these to write 3 multiplication sentences. If you roll 3 and 7, you can make: 30 × 70, 30 × 700, and 30 × 7000.

- Roll the cubes at least 4 times to create 4 groups of factors.
- Record the factors.

**3**

Use your calculator to multiply the factors shown on your chart.

- Write the products.
- Look for patterns.

### Multiplication Patterns

| Digits Rolled | Tens × Tens | Tens × Hundreds | Tens × Thousands |
|---|---|---|---|
| 3 and 7 | 30 × 70 = 2100 | 30 × 700 = 21,000 | 30 × 7000 = 210,000 |
| 5 and 4 | 50 × 40 = 2000 | 50 × 400 = 20,000 | 50 × 4000 = 200,000 |
| | | | |
| | | | |

## Show What You Know!

1. Suppose you continue the multiplication pattern. What will 30 × 70,000 equal? What will 30 × 700,000 equal? Use mental math. Check your answers with a calculator.

2. How can knowing multiplication facts help you multiply multiples of 10, 100, and 1000?

3. **Write About It** Write a mental math rule for multiplying multiples of 10, 100, and 1000. Share your rule.

4. **Number Sense** Without multiplying, how can you decide whether 2,000,000 × 6,000,000 is equal to 4,000,000 × 3,000,000?

**Mental Math** Use mental math to find the product.

5. 40 × 7000   6. 40 × 700   7. 40 × 70   8. 60 × 80   9. 60 × 800

10. **Critical Thinking** How is adding multiples of 10 and 100 similar to multiplying multiples of 10 and 100? Use these examples.

50 + 40 = 90          20 × 30 = 600          300 + 700 = 1000

# Estimating Products

**Four squares**

In **front-end estimation**, the front digit stays the same.

| 26 | 348 |
|----|-----|
| ↓ | ↓ |
| 20 | 300 |

In **rounding**, the front digit may or may not change.

26 rounds to 30

348 rounds to 300

**Y**our class is making a mosaic. The mosaic will have 28 squares. Each square will have 32 triangles. So far, the class has cut out almost 600 triangles. Has your class cut out enough to make all the squares?

You can estimate to find out.

## Here's A Way! Estimate 28 × 32.

**1** Use front-end estimation to make a quick estimate.

$$28 \times 32$$
$$20 \times 30 = 600$$

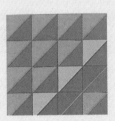

Since 28 is greater than 20, and 32 is greater than 30, 28 × 32 is greater than 600. So, 600 triangles is not enough to make 28 squares.

**2** Use rounding to estimate how many triangles are needed for the mosaic.

$$28 \times 32$$
$$30 \times 30 = 900$$

Your class will need to make about 900 triangles.

**Talk About It!** Multiply to find the exact number of triangles needed. Why do you think the rounded estimate is closer to the actual product?

Write the letter of the reasonable estimate.

**1.** 62 × $9.97
  a. $620
  b. $6200
  c. $62,000

**2.** 3 × 34
  a. 90
  b. 900
  c. 9000

**3.** 48 × 53
  a. 250
  b. 2500
  c. 25,000

**4.** 23 × 80
  a. 16
  b. 160
  c. 1600

**5.** 18 × 68
  a. 140
  b. 1400
  c. 14,000

Estimate the product. Describe the method you used.

**6.**  67 × 31

**7.**  $9.75 × 28

**8.**  46 × 47

**9.**  $5.69 × 19

**10.**  71 × 59

**11.** Is the actual product in exercise 8 greater than or less than 2500? Explain how you know.

Estimate the product. Describe the method you used.

**12.**  54 × 54

**13.**  $9.89 × 32

**14.**  628 × 4

**15.**  78 × 28

**16.** 12 × $10.25

**17.** 66 × 21

**18.** 5 × 220

**19.** 9 × $41.95

**Algebraic Reasoning** Estimate to compare. Write < or >.

**20.** 47 × 24 ● 38 × 31

**21.** 4 × 628 ● 4 × 432

**22.** 2 × $3.08 ● 12 × $4.98

**23.** 51 × 29 ● 49 × 37

### Problem Solving

Estimate to solve. Show your work.

**24.** Your class uses 22 sheets of paper to cover the bulletin board for a new display. About how many sheets of paper will your class use if you create 9 displays during the year?

**25.** A pad of colored paper has 120 sheets. If you use 37 sheets to make a classroom mosaic, about how many sheets are left?

**More Practice Set 12.2, p. 511**

# Multiplying by Multiples of Ten

**T**he secretary bird can fly, but it stays on the ground most of the time. It can walk up to 20 miles each day to find food. How many miles can a secretary bird walk in a year?

## Here's A Way!　Find 20 × 365.

**1** Multiply by the ones. Record the zero in the ones place.

```
  365
× 20
─────
    0
```

One years equals 365 days.

**2** Multiply by the tens. Regroup if necessary.

```
  1 1
  365
×  20
─────
 7300
```

A secretary bird can walk about 7300 miles.

### Talk About It!

- How do you know that 0 × 365 = 0?

- If one factor is a multiple of ten, will the ones digit of the product always be 0? Why or why not?

The secretary bird is more than 40 inches tall.

## Show What You Know!

**Estimation** If your estimate is greater than 1000, find the product.

1. 31
× 29

2. $111
× 50

3. 144
× 40

4. 144
× 20

5. $206
× 34

6. **Critical Thinking** How did you estimate the answer for exercise 1? Would you estimate 49 × 51 the same way? Explain.

**Algebraic Reasoning** Estimate to compare. Write < or >.

7. 49 × 40 ● 51 × 50
8. 21 × 40 ● 50 × 11
9. 321 × 30 ● 20 × 418

## Work It Out!

**Find the products.**

10. 20
× 36

11. 36
× 40

12. 36
× 60

13. 247
× 30

14. 247
× 60

15. 247
× 90

16. **Write About It** In exercises 10, 11, and 12, describe the pattern in the products. What pattern do you see in exercises 13, 14, and 15?

**Estimation** If the actual product will be greater than 5000, find the product.

17. 71
× 80

18. 33
× 80

19. 349
× 60

20. 78
× 30

21. 478
× 30

22. 45 × 20
23. 827 × 60
24. 349 × 40
25. 849 × 40
26. 91 × 90

27. **Problem Solving** A hummingbird can flap its wings 90 times each second. How many times can it flap its wings in 30 seconds? Estimate first, and then solve.

### Mixed Review

Copy and complete. Write >, <, or =.

28. 8.4 ● 8.39
29. 0.41 ● 0.32
30. $25\frac{2}{3}$ ● $2\frac{1}{8}$
31. 16.69 ● 17.69

**More Practice Set 12.3, p. 511**

419

# Problem Solving
## Using Work a Simpler Problem and Other Strategies

**Getting Started**

**What You'll Need:**
▶ grid paper
▶ ruler
▶ calculator

**P**eople are coming up with different ways to make cars go. Gasoline can do the job and so can electricity. One idea is to build solar-powered cars. These cars get their electricity from the sun.

**Problem Solving Process**
✓ Understand
✓ Plan
✓ Try It
✓ Look Back

**Choose a Strategy You Have Learned**
✓ Guess and Check
✓ Draw a Picture
✓ Make a List
✓ Make a Table
✓ Act It Out
✓ Work a Simpler Problem
✓ Look for a Pattern
✓ Work Backward

**Y**ou own a company that is building a solar car. Your solar car will have panels that change sunlight into electricity. The panels will be 30 cm by 40 cm. Each panel will be made up of squares that measure 10 cm on a side. How many of these squares will you need for 6 panels?

- What problem do you need to solve?
- What do you know about the size of 1 panel? Of 1 square?
- How many squares do you need to make one panel?
- How many panels do you need all together?
- Explain a strategy you can use to solve the problem. Then solve it.

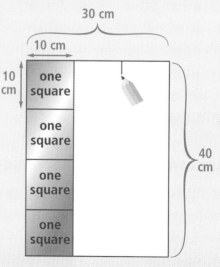

## Work It Out!

**Use any strategy to solve the problem. Show your work.**

1. Each solar panel needs a metal frame around it. You have a panel that is 30 cm × 40 cm. How many centimeters long will the frame be?

2. What is the cost of both the squares and the frame for a 30 cm × 40 cm solar panel?

3. a. You have $2275.00. What is the largest panel you could build?

   b. Will you have any money left over? How much?

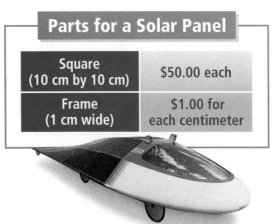

| Parts for a Solar Panel | |
|---|---|
| Square (10 cm by 10 cm) | $50.00 each |
| Frame (1 cm wide) | $1.00 for each centimeter |

4. Your company has two plans for a solar panel, as shown. Which plan will cost less to build? How much less? Include the cost of the frame.

5. The greater the area of a solar panel, the more electricity it makes. Which plan will make more electricity? Explain.

6. **Create Your Own** Design your own solar panel. How many squares did you use? Including the frame, how much will your panel cost?

7. How many more or fewer squares are in your plan than in Plan A?

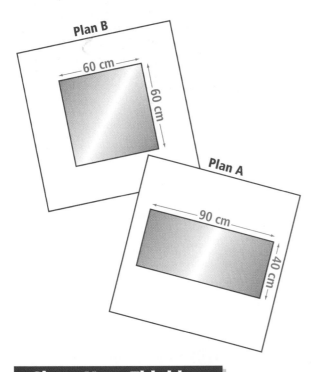

Plan B
60 cm
60 cm

Plan A
90 cm
40 cm

## Share Your Thinking

8. How did you solve problem 5? What did you need to know? Explain your answer.

9. What different strategies did you use to solve the problems in this lesson? Discuss them with a partner.

# Multiplying with Array Diagrams

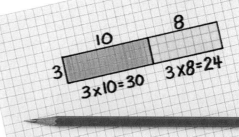

**Getting Started**

**What You'll Need:**
▶ grid paper

**Use What You Know**

An **array diagram** stands for an array of objects in equal rows.

When you label the sides of an array, the numbers are called **factors**. Remember that factors are the numbers you multiply to find a product.

**Y**ou have used array diagrams to find products like 3 × 18. An array diagram can also help you find 23 × 18.

## Here's A Way! Find 23 × 18.

**1** Draw an array diagram on grid paper. Label the tens and the ones for each factor.

**2** Find the product for each section of the array diagram.

**3** Add to find the total.

**200 + 160 + 30 + 24 = 414**

The product of 23 × 18 is 414.

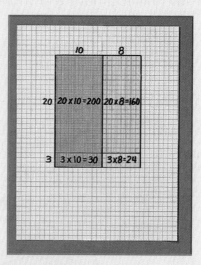

### Talk About It!

• Were you able to find the products for each section by using mental math? Why or why not?

• How is the array diagram for 23 × 18 similar to the array diagram for 3 × 18?

Draw an array diagram. Then write the product.

1. 11 × 88    2. 34 × 43    3. 13 × 27    4. 17 × 61    5. 29 × 52

Write the factors and product for the array diagram.

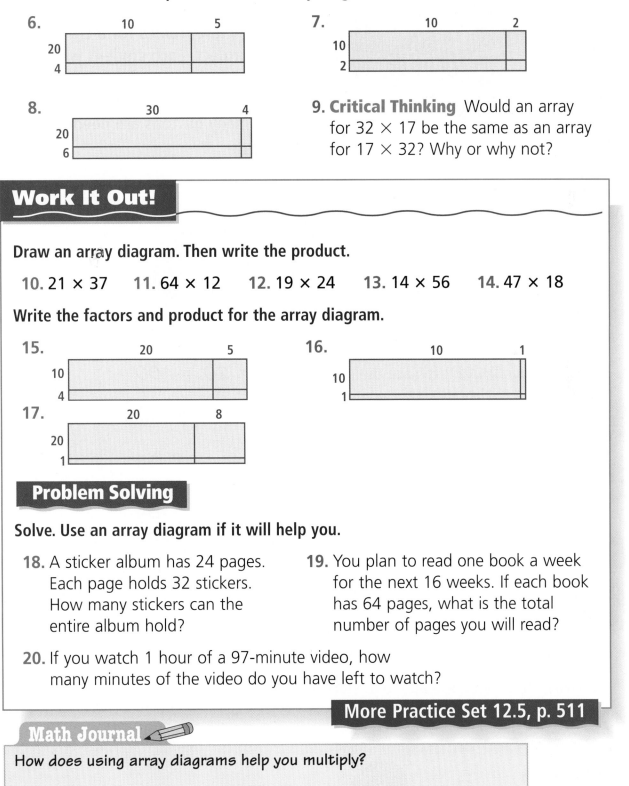

6.

| | 10 | 5 |
| 20 | | |
| 4 | | |

7.

| | 10 | 2 |
| 10 | | |
| 2 | | |

8.

| | 30 | 4 |
| 20 | | |
| 6 | | |

9. **Critical Thinking** Would an array for 32 × 17 be the same as an array for 17 × 32? Why or why not?

## Work It Out!

Draw an array diagram. Then write the product.

10. 21 × 37    11. 64 × 12    12. 19 × 24    13. 14 × 56    14. 47 × 18

Write the factors and product for the array diagram.

15.

| | 20 | 5 |
| 10 | | |
| 4 | | |

16.

| | 10 | 1 |
| 10 | | |
| 1 | | |

17.

| | 20 | 8 |
| 20 | | |
| 1 | | |

### Problem Solving

Solve. Use an array diagram if it will help you.

18. A sticker album has 24 pages. Each page holds 32 stickers. How many stickers can the entire album hold?

19. You plan to read one book a week for the next 16 weeks. If each book has 64 pages, what is the total number of pages you will read?

20. If you watch 1 hour of a 97-minute video, how many minutes of the video do you have left to watch?

**More Practice Set 12.5, p. 511**

**Math Journal**

How does using array diagrams help you multiply?

# Multiplying 2-Digit Numbers

**LESSON 6**

**Y**our class plans to make picture frames for a craft project. Each student will use 18 buttons to decorate a frame. If there are 23 students, how many buttons are needed?

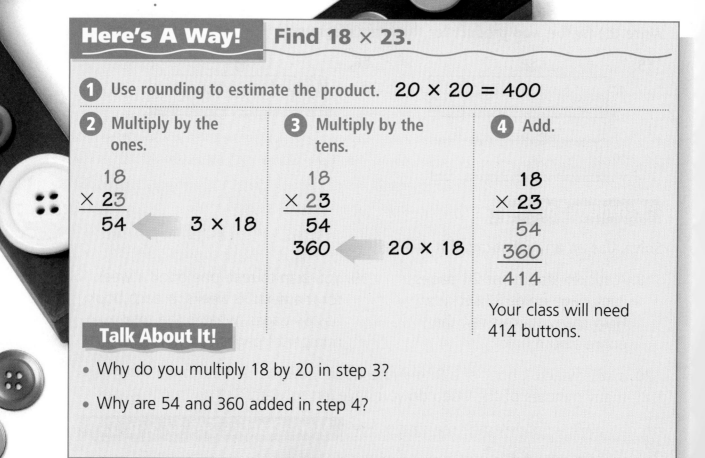

**Here's A Way!** Find 18 × 23.

**1** Use rounding to estimate the product. $20 \times 20 = 400$

**2** Multiply by the ones.

$$\begin{array}{r} 18 \\ \times\ 23 \\ \hline 54 \end{array}$$ ← 3 × 18

**3** Multiply by the tens.

$$\begin{array}{r} 18 \\ \times\ 23 \\ \hline 54 \\ 360 \end{array}$$ ← 20 × 18

**4** Add.

$$\begin{array}{r} 18 \\ \times\ 23 \\ \hline 54 \\ 360 \\ \hline 414 \end{array}$$

Your class will need 414 buttons.

**Talk About It!**

• Why do you multiply 18 by 20 in step 3?

• Why are 54 and 360 added in step 4?

# Show What You Know!

**Write the product.**

1.  47
    × 23

2.  25
    × 22

3.  32
    × 12

4.  13
    × 33

5.  51
    × 18

6. 33 × 35   7. 11 × 77   8. 55 × 65   9. 19 × 42   10. 49 × 81

# Work It Out!

**Write the product. Circle the product when you used mental math.**

11.  15
     × 22

12.  24
     × 28

13.  60
     × 20

14.  11
     × 19

15.  10
     × 70

16. 12 × 24   17. 14 × 54   18. 30 × 93   19. 27 × 45   20. 80 × 80

21. **Critical Thinking** How could you estimate to check whether your answers to exercises 16 through 20 make sense?

## Problem Solving

**Solve. Show your work.**

22. You want to decorate a jigsaw puzzle with a border. The puzzle is 24 inches wide and 18 inches long. How much border will you need to make?

**Puzzles**

A

18 in.

24 in.

B

24 in.

32 in.

23. Puzzle B is 32 inches wide and 24 inches long. Compare the areas of Puzzle A and Puzzle B. Which puzzle has the greater area? Explain how you know.

24. **Create Your Own** Write a problem in which you must multiply two 2-digit numbers to solve. Trade problems with a classmate. Check your answers.

## Mixed Review

**Write the answer.**

25.  42.34
    +  9.9

26.  76.7
   − 23.85

27.  53.09
   + 53.91

28.  60.5
   −  2.98

29.  $45.00
    −  4.50

More Practice Set 12.6, p. 512

# Problem Solving
## Logical Reasoning

**D**uring a craft project, your friend makes these statements:
  "Some wheels are red."
  "None of the shells are green."
  "All red pasta are bow ties."

**Are these statements true or false?**

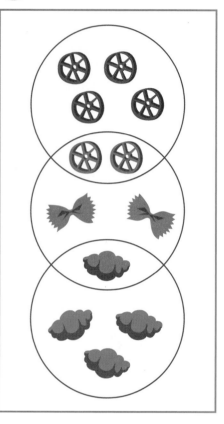

## You Decide

- Should you check each kind of pasta before deciding?
- Should you check each color before deciding?
- How do the circles help you to decide if a statement is true or false?

## Work It Out!

**Is the statement true or false? If false, rewrite the sentence to make it true.**

1. Some wheels are red.

2. Some shells are blue.

3. All shells are blue.

4. Some wheels are blue.

5. None of the green pasta are wheels.

6. Some of the red pasta are wheels.

7. **Create Your Own** Use *all*, *some*, or *none* to write one true and one false statement about the pasta.

## Share Your Thinking

8. What does it mean if a piece of pasta is inside two circles?

9. How would the picture change if you added a fourth kind of pasta? Explain.

# Midchapter Review

## for Pages 412–426

## Problem Solving

**Solve. Show your work.** (pages 420, 426)

**1.** You want to tile some walls of a room in a dollhouse. The room is 8 in. high. Each wall is 12 in. long. If each tile is 2 in. long and 2 in. wide, how many tiles will you need to tile one wall with no windows or doors? to tile three walls?

**2.** You decide instead to put a border around the top of the same room. The border print costs $.03 an inch. How much will it cost to put the border print along the top of 3 walls?

## Concepts

**Find the product. Write a multiplication fact that you can use.** (page 414)

**3.** $30 \times 700$      **4.** $400 \times 20$      **5.** $60 \times 300$

**Explain how to use estimation to decide if each product is greater than or less than 1000.** (page 416)

**6.** $64 \times 21$      **7.** $48 \times 19$      **8.** $215 \times 5$

**Write the factors and the product for the array diagram.** (page 422)

**9.**

| | 10 | 9 |
|---|---|---|
| 10 | $10 \times 10 = 100$ | $10 \times 9 = 90$ |
| 2 | $2 \times 10 = 20$ | $2 \times 9 = 18$ |

**10.**

| | 20 | 4 |
|---|---|---|
| 20 | $20 \times 20 = 400$ | $20 \times 4 = 80$ |
| 3 | $3 \times 20 = 60$ | $3 \times 4 = 12$ |

## Skills

**Use mental math to find the product.** (page 414)

**11.** $30 \times 800$      **12.** $400 \times 50$      **13.** $7 \times 7000$

**Estimate. Then write the exact product.** (pages 416, 418, 424)

**14.** $167 \times 30$      **15.** $723 \times 40$      **16.** $92 \times 70$

**17.** $54 \times 21$      **18.** $47 \times 36$      **19.** $12 \times 19$      **20.** $97 \times 85$

# Math World

Explore some slow and "lightning fast" ways to multiply. Find out the mathematical meaning of the Mayan calendar.

| | |
|---|---|
| I | 1 |
| V | 5 |
| X | 10 |
| L | 50 |
| C | 100 |
| D | 500 |
| M | 1,000 |

## Calculating Letters

It's easy to read a clock with Roman numerals once you know what the letters stand for. But can you imagine multiplying 2-digit numbers with Roman numerals? To multiply 108 by 24 (CVIII × XXIV), you would have to multiply each number in 108 by each number in 24, and add them together. This would take many separate multiplications and many more additions. To make calculating easier, the Romans used an abacus. An abacus is a device that uses beads to stand for numbers.

## Mayan Calendar Math

= KIN

One of the calendars used by the Maya had nine time periods. Each time period had its own symbol. The shortest period was the Kin, which equaled one day. The Maya's 360-day year was called Tun. This was the next longest period. After the Tun came the Katun, which equaled 20 Tun. How many days long was a Katun?

# Try This!

## INDIAN "LIGHTNING" MULTIPLICATION

The following method of multiplying two numbers was brought to Europe from India, probably in the 15th century. A European writer called it lightning multiplication because it was faster than the way most Europeans calculated. Do you agree? Follow these steps to find 34 × 57.

**1** Write the tens and ones in separate columns. Multiply the ones vertically. There are 28 ones. Write 8 and carry the 2.

**2** Multiply the tens and ones "crosswise." Add the products. Also, add the 2 from step 1. There are 43 tens. Write 3 and carry the 4.

**3** Multiply the tens from the original problem vertically to find the number of hundreds. Remember to add the number you carried over in step 3.

Try:     17 × 29     44 × 31

## Counting by 60

The ancient Sumerians (soo MAIR ee uns) used a base 60 system. The number words for 1 to 60 were formed like our base 10 system. But after 60, the number 60 became the base unit, instead of 10. From the number 60 on, counting was done by 60's.

### Respond

**Think about it . . .**

With a base 60 system like the Sumerians', how would people have expressed greater numbers?

Internet:
**Houghton Mifflin Education Place**
Explore the Math Center at
http://www.eduplace.com

# Multiplying 3-Digit Numbers

Boy among harvested roses, in Isparta, Turkey

Rose harvesters in Bulgaria

**D**id you know that it takes hundreds of thousands of flower petals to make one ounce of perfume?

On a flower farm, a worker can collect about 108 flower petals in 1 minute. How many petals can the worker collect in 15 minutes?

Multiply to find the product.

It's a good idea to estimate before multiplying.

108 rounds to 100

15 rounds to 20

100 × 20 = 2000

A worker can collect about 2000 petals in 15 minutes.

## Here's A Way! Find 15 × 108.

**1** Multiply by the ones.

```
  108
×  15
 540
```

```
  108
×   5
 540
```

**2** Multiply by the tens.

```
  108
×  15
 540
1080
```

```
  108
×  10
1080
```

**3** Add.

```
  108
×  15
 540
1080
1620
```

In 15 minutes, a worker can collect about 1620 flower petals.

### Talk About It!

Could you have estimated 15 × 108 by rounding just one factor? Explain. Why would your estimate be closer?

**Write the product.**

1. 104
× 12

2. 111
× 78

3. 372
× 34

4. 333
× 34

5. 125
× 40

6. 125
× 80

7. **Critical Thinking** How can the product in exercise 5 help you find the product in exercise 6?

## Work It Out!

**Estimation** If the estimate is greater than 10,000, find the exact product.

8. 401
× 31

9. 687
× 73

10. 232
× 23

11. 306
× 50

12. 865 × 65

13. 411 × 10

14. 907 × 71

15. 300 × 26

In exercises 16 through 19, find the product for *a*. Explain how to use the product for *a* to find the product for *b*.

16. a. 225 × 30
b. 225 × 60

17. a. 305 × 20
b. 305 × 40

18. a. 40 × 175
b. 80 × 175

19. a. 15 × 250
b. 30 × 250

### Problem Solving

20. The florist receives 50 orders for one dozen roses. A truck arrives with 35 buckets of roses. Each bucket has 20 roses. Will the florist have enough roses to fill the orders? Explain.

21. The garden center has a display of tulips. There are 18 rows of purple tulips and 12 rows of yellow tulips. Each row has 120 tulips. How many tulips are on display?

22. A flower shop has a two-day sale on lilies. If the shop sells 58 lilies on Tuesday and 79 lilies on Wednesday, how many lilies did the shop sell for those two days?

**More Practice Set 12.8, p. 512**

# Multiplying Money

**F**or a school festival, your class will string flowers to make Hawaiian leis (LAYZ). The order form shows the flowers needed. Find the total cost for the flowers.

| Quantity | Item No. | Type of Flower | Color | Unit Price | Total |
|----------|----------|----------------|-------|------------|-------|
| 12 dozen | CX-A | Carnations | Red | $.38 | |
| 12 dozen | GX-A | Ginger | White | $.47 | |
| 24 dozen | TX-B | Tuberoses | Yellow | $.19 | |

## Here's A Way! Use a calculator to find the cost.

**1** First, estimate the cost. Round the factors and multiply. Then, add to find the total.

$$12 \times 38¢ \rightarrow 10 \times 40¢ = \$4.00$$
$$12 \times 47¢ \rightarrow 10 \times 50¢ = \$5.00$$
$$24 \times 19¢ \rightarrow 20 \times 20¢ = \$4.00$$

$$\$4.00 + \$5.00 + \$4.00 = \$13.00$$

**2** Press these keys on the calculator to find the first product. (Remember: Calculators do not have a dollar sign.)

Now press the memory key (M+). This stores the product to be used later.

$$\boxed{1}\ \boxed{2}\ \boxed{\times}\ \boxed{.}\ \boxed{3}\ \boxed{8}\ \boxed{=}\ \boxed{M+}$$

M          4.56

**3** Press these keys to find the next product. Use the memory key to store the answer.

$$\boxed{1}\ \boxed{2}\ \boxed{\times}\ \boxed{.}\ \boxed{4}\ \boxed{7}\ \boxed{=}\ \boxed{M+}$$

M          5.64

**4** Press these keys to find the last product.

$$\boxed{2}\ \boxed{4}\ \boxed{\times}\ \boxed{.}\ \boxed{1}\ \boxed{9}\ \boxed{=}\ \boxed{M+}$$

M          4.56

**5** Now press the memory recall key (MRC) to find the sum of the stored products.

$$4.56 + 5.64 + 4.56$$

14.76

The flowers will cost $14.76.

**Talk About It!** How could you have found the cost without using the memory key?

# Show What You Know!

Make an estimate and record it. Write whether the actual product will be greater than or less than the estimate. Use a calculator to find the product.

1. $45.99
   × 18

2. $2.55
   × 37

3. $8.40
   × 12

4. $32.45
   × 22

5. $19.25
   × 11

6. **Critical Thinking** Suppose that the calculator shows 21175 for exercise 5. Is this answer reasonable? Why do you think the calculator might show this answer?

# Work It Out!

**Estimation** If the estimate is greater than $100, use a calculator to find the product.

7. $2.49
   × 28

8. $8.75
   × 61

9. $3.59
   × 15

10. $7.45
    × 21

11. $9.89
    × 18

12. $1.57
    × 38

13. $2.71
    × 63

14. $3.04
    × 32

15. $8.49
    × 87

16. $6.05
    × 46

## Problem Solving  Using Data

17. You have $10 to spend on flowers for the Hawaiian festival. What is the greatest number of carnations you can buy? What is the greatest number of ginger blossoms?

18. Suppose you want to order carnations and tuberoses. You have $20 to spend. How many of each flower will you buy? What colors will you order?

19. If you ordered 2 dozen of each flower in every color, what would be the total cost of your order?

| Flower | Color | Item No. | Price Per Dozen |
|--------|-------|----------|-----------------|
| Carnation | Red | CX-A | $0.38 |
| | Yellow | CX-B | $0.38 |
| | Pink | CX-C | $0.38 |
| Ginger | White | GX-A | $0.47 |
| | Yellow | GX-B | $0.47 |
| Tuberose | Red | TX-A | $0.19 |
| | Yellow | TX-B | $0.19 |
| | Purple | TX-C | $0.19 |
| Jasmine | Yellow | JX-A | $0.08 |
| | White | JX-B | $0.08 |

**More Practice Set 12.9, p. 512**

433

# LESSON 10 · Multiplying Three Factors

**O**ne package contains 6 sheets of stickers. Each sheet has 12 stickers on it. How many stickers will you have if you buy 15 packages?

## Here's A Way! Find 6 × 12 × 15.

You can find the total number by multiplying 6, 12, and 15 in any order.

| Multiply 12 by 6. Then multiply the product by 15. | Multiply 15 by 12. Then multiply the product by 6. | Multiply 6 by 15. Then multiply the product by 12. |
|---|---|---|
| $(6 \times 12) \times 15 =$ $72 \times 15 = 1080$ | $6 \times (12 \times 15) =$ $6 \times 180 = 1080$ | $(15 \times 6) \times 12 =$ $90 \times 12 = 1080$ |

**Talk About It!** What do these examples show about the order of factors in multiplication? What do they show about grouping factors in multiplication?

## Use What You Know

**Grouping Property**
If you change the grouping of the factors, the product remains the same.

**Order Property**
If you change the order of the factors, the product remains the same.

## Show What You Know!

Group the factors to multiply. Use parentheses.

1. 5 × 16 × 2    2. 4 × 16 × 25    3. 10 × 11 × 7

Group the factors. Then find the product.

4. 15 × 36 × 10    5. 22 × 8 × 40    6. 2 × 9 × 30

7. 23 × 76 × 0    8. 11 × 2 × 12    9. 17 × 4 × 5

10. **Mental Math** Which of exercises 4 through 9 could you solve using mental math? Explain.

## Work It Out!

**Show how you would group the factors to multiply.**

11. 5 × 12 × 8
12. 12 × 4 × 10
13. 11 × 5 × 13
14. 21 × 11 × 3

**Group the factors. Then find the product. Use mental math when you can.**

15. 18 × 8 × 13
16. 16 × 5 × 16
17. 7 × 23 × 12
18. 19 × 2 × 10

19. 45 × 15 × 0
20. 42 × 17 × 2
21. 4 × 54 × 14
22. 32 × 4 × 25

23. **Critical Thinking** Explain why you grouped exercise 20 the way you did.

**Patterns Complete the multiplication sentences. What pattern do you see in the factors and products?**

24. a. 3 × 12 × 15 = 540
    b. 6 × 12 × 15 = ▪
    c. 12 × 12 × 15 = ▪

25. a. 2 × 14 × 25 = 700
    b. 4 × 14 × 25 = ▪
    c. 8 × 14 × 25 = ▪

26. Copy and complete the multiplication magic square. Use three factors from the number box. Be sure that every row, column, and diagonal has the same product.

27. **Critical Thinking** How can you make a new multiplication magic square using the same numbers?

| Magic Square | | |
|---|---|---|
| ? | 4 | 18 |
| 36 | 6 | ? |
| 2 | ? | 12 |

| Number Box | | |
|---|---|---|
| 5 | 9 | 2 |
| 3 | 0 | 1 |

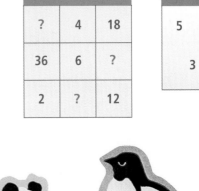

### Problem Solving Using Data

**Use the table to solve the problem.**

28. If you buy 10 packages of panda stickers and 10 packages of penguin stickers, how much money will you spend? How many stickers will you have?

29. Your teacher has $12 to spend on a month's supply of stickers. He wants to buy each kind of sticker. What combinations of packages can he buy? What is the total number of stickers for each combination?

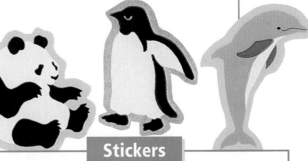

**Stickers**

| Animals | Stickers per Sheet | Sheets per Package | Cost per Package |
|---|---|---|---|
| Panda | 24 | 5 | $2.00 |
| Penguin | 18 | 10 | $4.00 |
| Dolphin | 12 | 12 | $3.00 |

**More Practice Set 12.10, p. 513**

# Problem Solving
## Using Strategies

You can read more about dragonflies in the pages of *Ranger Rick*.

**D**ragonflies have better eyesight than any other insect. Their eyes are made up of more than 20,000 parts. Each part is shaped like a hexagon.

**Problem Solving Process**

✓ Understand
✓ Plan
✓ Try It
✓ Look Back

**Choose a Strategy You Have Learned**

✓ Guess and Check
✓ Draw a Picture
✓ Make a List
✓ Make a Table
✓ Act It Out
✓ Work a Simpler Problem
✓ Look for a Pattern
✓ Work Backward

**H**exagons can fit together in a particular way. A single hexagon can be surrounded by a ring of equal-sized hexagons. The ring can be surrounded by a second ring, and then a third, and so on. Look at the diagram. How many hexagons will there be in the hundredth ring?

- Count the number of hexagons in each ring of the diagram.

- How many hexagons will there be in the fourth ring? In the fifth ring?

- Make a table to show the number of rings and the number of hexagons.

- Solve the problem. Explain the strategy you used.

## Work It Out!

**Use any strategy to solve the problem.**
**Show your work.**

1. Suppose an adult dragonfly eats
   600 insects each day. How many
   insects will it eat in 9 weeks?

2. Ancestors of the dragonfly had wings that
   measured 30 in. Now the wingspan is about $\frac{1}{5}$ of that.
   About how long is the wingspan of a dragonfly today?

3. A dragonfly can fly 40 miles in 1 hour. About how
   far can it fly in 15 minutes?

4. A dragonfly can see a moving insect up to 40 ft away.
   Suppose a dragonfly is at one end of a 75-ft porch. An insect
   is moving at the other end. How far onto the porch will the
   dragonfly have to fly before it sees the insect?

**Use the pictures or your own pattern blocks to answer the question.**

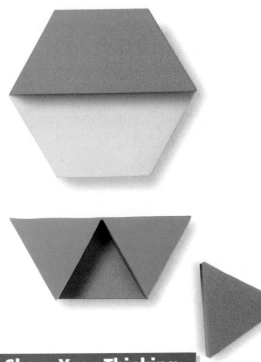

5. Two of the red shapes will entirely
   cover one hexagon. If you have
   29 red shapes, how many hexagons
   can you entirely cover?

6. Three triangles will cover one red
   shape. If you have 36 triangles, how
   many red shapes can you cover?

7. If 2 red shapes cover 1 hexagon,
   how many hexagons can you cover
   with 36 triangles?

8. If you have 23 red shapes and
   15 triangles, how many hexagons
   can you cover?

## Share Your Thinking

9. Choose a problem. Discuss it with a classmate. Did you
   both use the same strategy to solve it? Explain.

# Chapter 12 Test

## for Pages 412–437

## Problem Solving

**Solve. Show your work.** (pages 420, 436)

1. A row of dancers face east. Each dancer will make a quarter turn clockwise every second for exactly half a minute. What direction will the dancers face when the half minute is over?

2. A theater sign has 80 rows of 128 lights in each row. The lights in each row are red, blue, red, blue, red, blue, and so on. What fraction of the lights in the entire sign is red?

## Concepts

**Use the data on the chart. Write *true* or *false* for each statement.** (page 426)

3. Some students who are in band are also in orchestra.

4. None of the students in orchestra are in band.

5. All of the fourth graders are in band, orchestra, or both.

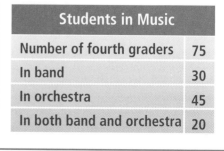

| Students in Music | |
|---|---|
| Number of fourth graders | 75 |
| In band | 30 |
| In orchestra | 45 |
| In both band and orchestra | 20 |

**Find the answer.** (pages 416, 418)

6. Should you use rounding or front-end estimation to find a closer estimate of $19 \times 29$? Tell why.

7. Will a front-end estimation for $37 \times 51$ be greater than or less than the exact product? How do you know?

8. Is $80 a closer estimate for $19.75 \times 8$ than $160? Why?

9. How can you use the product of $20 \times 24$ to find the product of $60 \times 24$?

10. How is an array diagram of $12 \times 8$ the same as an array diagram of $24 \times 4$? How is it different?

**Tell how you would group the factors. Explain your answer.** (page 434)

11. $2 \times 158 \times 5$

12. $4 \times 19 \times 25$

## Skills

Choose the answer that shows the products in the correct order. (page 414)

13. 70 × 80; 70 × 800; 70 × 8000
    a. 560,000; 56,000; 5600
    c. 5600; 56,000; 560,000
    b. 56,000; 5600; 560,000
    d. 5600; 560,000; 56,000

14. 20 × 50; 20 × 500; 20 × 5000
    a. 100,000; 1000; 10,000
    c. 10,000; 100,000; 1000
    b. 1000; 10,000; 100,000
    d. 100,000; 10,000; 1000

Choose the correct product. Write *a*, *b*, *c*, or *d*. (pages 418, 424, 430, 432, 434)

15. 13 × 11 × 5     a. 355     b. 625     c. 715     d. 500

16. 23 × 78     a. 1894     b. 1792     c. 1794     d. 1892

17. 207 × 17     a. 3549     b. 3649     c. 3509     d. 3519

18. $27.78 × 12     a. $33.36     b. $333.36     c. $3.36     d. $3336

19. 79 × 40     a. 316     b. 2860     c. 3160     d. 31,600

Copy and complete. Write > or <. (pages 418, 424)

20. 40 × 52 ● 30 × 76     21. 71 × 92 ● 61 × 78     22. 31 × 57 ● 28 × 89

Write the product. (pages 412, 418, 424, 430, 432)

23. 300 × 90     24. 20 × 89     25. 40 × 89     26. 504 × 23     27. 8 × $7.65

## Performance Task

(pages 416, 432)

Can you estimate possible earnings for each job?

| Part-Time Job | Earnings |
|---|---|
| Yard work for 20 weeks | $27 a week |
| Office helper for 15 weeks | $13 a week |
| Dog walking for 26 days | $5 a day |

• Which job will pay you the most? Which would you prefer and why?

# Cumulative Review

**Common Factors** (Chapter 4)

**What factors are common to 16 and 18?**

**Here's A Way!**

List all the factors of 16 and 18.

Factors of 16: 1, 2, 4, 8, 16
Factors of 18: 1, 2, 3, 6, 9, 18

The common factors are 1 and 2.

Find the common factors other than 1.

1. 6, 8, 12
2. 3, 9, 12
3. 10, 20, 30
4. 64, 48, 12
5. 10, 15, 25
6. 25, 60, 80

7. How many different pairs of factors does 12 have? What are they?

8. Suppose one number is a multiple of another. What do you know about the common factors of the two numbers?

---

**Turns** (Chapter 5)

**Which figures are turns of the shaded figure?**

**Here's A Way!**

a. b. c. d.

Figures c and d are turns of the shaded figure.

Choose the turns of the shaded figure.

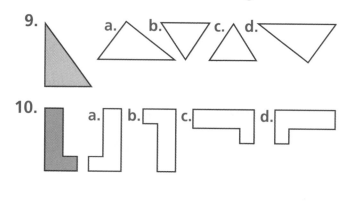

9. a. b. c. d.

10. a. b. c. d.

---

**Estimating Quotients** (Chapter 7)

**About how much is 98 ÷ 5?**

**Here's A Way!**

Use compatible numbers to estimate the quotient. What number is close to 98 and easily divisible by 5?
Since 100 ÷ 5 = 20, 98 ÷ 5 is about 20.

Estimate the quotient, using compatible numbers.

11. 331 ÷ 8
12. 375 ÷ 6
13. 415 ÷ 7
14. 219 ÷ 4
15. 97 ÷ 3
16. 189 ÷ 5

17. How many digits will be in the quotient of 610 ÷ 5?

18. How many digits will be in the quotient of 6100 ÷ 6?

## Adding Unlike Fractions (Chapter 9)

Find $\frac{1}{4} + \frac{5}{8}$.

**Here's A Way!**

Write an equivalent fraction for $\frac{1}{4}$.

$\frac{1}{4} = \frac{2}{8}$

Add the numerators.

$\frac{2}{8} + \frac{5}{8} = \frac{7}{8}$

**Solve. Write your answer in simplest form.**

19. $\frac{1}{12} + \frac{1}{4} + \frac{1}{6}$  20. $\frac{5}{12} + \frac{1}{3}$

21. $\frac{1}{8} + \frac{1}{4} + \frac{3}{8}$  22. $\frac{2}{5} + \frac{1}{10}$

23. $\frac{3}{15} + \frac{3}{5}$  24. $\frac{1}{8} + \frac{1}{2}$

---

## Elapsed Time (Chapter 10)

If you leave at 9:15 A.M. and return at 3:42 P.M., how long are you gone?

**Here's A Way!**

Find the number of hours.
9:15 A.M. to 3:15 P.M. = 6 hours
Find the number of minutes.
Count by 5's and 1's.
3:15 P.M. to 3:42 P.M. = 27 min
You will be gone 6 hours and 27 minutes.

**Find the elapsed time.**

25. from 2:15 P.M. to 7:20 P.M.

26. from 4:07 P.M. to 5:23 P.M.

27. from 8:46 A.M. to 1:09 P.M.

**Which time is longer?**

28. a. from 10:35 A.M. to 11:36 P.M.
    b. from 11:36 P.M. to 10:35 A.M.

29. a. from 1:22 A.M. to 9:17 P.M.
    b. from 9:17 P.M. to 1:22 A.M.

---

## Problem Solving

**Problem Solving Process**
✓ Understand
✓ Plan
✓ Try It
✓ Look Back

**Choose a Strategy You Have Learned**
✓ Guess and Check
✓ Draw a Picture
✓ Make a List
✓ Make a Table
✓ Act It Out
✓ Work a Simpler Problem
✓ Look for a Pattern
  Work Backward

Choose any strategy you know to solve the problem. Show your work.

30. How many hours are there from 9 A.M. on May 30 to 9 P.M. on June 2?

31. Suppose a rectangular rug measures 36 ft by 30 ft. Making only one cut, how can you cut the rug so that the longer side is twice as long as the shorter side?

# 12

INVESTIGATION

# Making Movies

**Media Connection**   **With Your Group**

A cartoon, or animated movie, is made up of single pictures called frames. One second of a cartoon contains 24 frames. When the frames are shown on a movie screen, the pictures seem to move. You and your group can plan your own two-minute animated movie.

Decide on a topic for your movie. Then decide how long each scene might last. Figure out how many drawings, or frames, you will need for each scene. Create a flip book showing part of the plan for your movie.

"THE CARROT STICK ESCAPE"

## 1

### Plan It

- Discuss subjects for your movie. Remember, it will only be 2 minutes long. Make a list of possible topics for the movie.
- List the scenes you want to show.
- Allow time to show the title. Also allow time for the ending credits—the names of the people who created the movie.

Film Name: The Carrot Stick Escape

| Scene | Title | Seconds | Drawings needed |
|-------|-------|---------|-----------------|
| 1 | Meet Mr. Carrot | 25 | 600 |
|  |  |  |  |

## 2

### Put It Together

- Remember that an animator needs 24 frames of drawings for every second of film.
- Calculate how many frames you need for each scene. Multiply the number of seconds for each scene by 24.
- Make a chart showing the number of scenes, frames, and seconds per frame, that you will need to create your film.

## 3

### Wrap It Up

- Design and draw a flip-book for one scene. Draw several pictures of an action taking place. For example, show a character bouncing to the top of a building. Suppose the scene contains 480 frames. It would last 20 seconds.
- Number your frames. Stack them with the lowest number on the bottom and the highest on top.
- Flip the pictures from bottom to top to see your movie in action.

## 4

### Discuss Your Results

- Have you covered all the points in Keep In Mind?
- Compare your flip book to the animated film you planned. How many drawings did you make for your scene? If you drew out as many as the actual movie needed, how large would your flip book be?

### Internet

> Visit the Math Center at **Houghton Mifflin Education Place.** http://www.eduplace.com

## Math Power

### Use What You Know

- how to use arrays to multiply

$$9 \quad 6 \quad 3$$
$$-3 \quad -3 \quad -3$$
$$\overline{6} \quad \overline{3} \quad \overline{0}$$

$$9 \div 3 = 3$$

- how to use repeated subtraction

$$3 \times 3 = 9$$

So,

$$9 \div 3 = 3$$

- how division and multiplication are related

# Dividing by 2-Digit Numbers

## Try This!

**W**hat if you have 275 pennies that you want to put in rolls, but you don't know how many wrappers you will need? You know that you can put 50 pennies into each wrapped roll. Dividing 275 by 50 will show you how many rolls you can make.

### What You'll Need

paper, pencil

**1**

Subtract 50 from 275. Write down the answer.

$$275$$
$$-\ 50$$

$$275 \atop {-\ 50} \atop \overline{225}} \quad {225 \atop {-\ 50}}$$

**2**

Subtract 50 from this answer. Continue to subtract in this way until you reach 0, or a number less than 50.

**3**

Count the number of problems you worked to find out the quotient of 275 ÷ 50. What is your remainder?

How many rolls of pennies can you make from 275?

How could you have estimated the quotient using multiplication to guide you?

**Ready to Go!**

445

# Mental Math: Using Patterns

**M**ental math can help you divide. You can use what you know about multiplication patterns to help you divide with multiples of 10, 100, 1000, and 10,000.

## Activity

**Getting Started**

**What You'll Need:**
▶ poster paper
▶ calculator

**Use What You Know**

You know how to use patterns to multiply.

$30 \times 2 = 60$

$30 \times 20 = 600$

$30 \times 200 = 6000$

$30 \times 2000 = 60,000$

**1**

Copy the chart shown below. Then find the missing numbers to complete it.

- Start with the 30's row. Find the number that belongs in the first empty box.

- Use patterns and mental math to help you divide or multiply.

- You can write a multiplication sentence with a missing factor. Or you can write a division sentence with a missing quotient.

$$30 \times \blacksquare = 120$$
$$120 \div 30 = \blacksquare$$

| ÷ or × | 120 | 240 | 360 | 1200 | 2400 | 3600 | 12,000 | 24,000 | 36,000 |
|--------|-----|-----|-----|------|------|------|--------|--------|--------|
| 30 | | | | | | | | | |
| 40 | | | | | | | | | |
| 60 | | | | | | | | | |

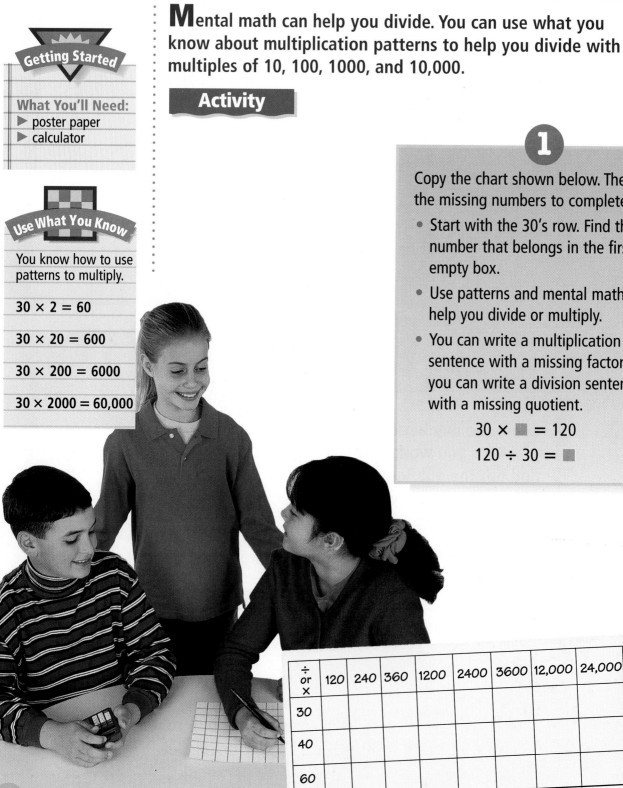

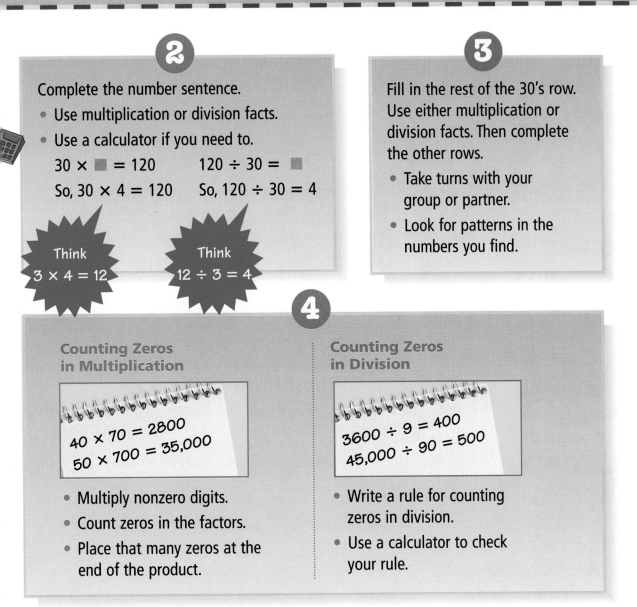

**2**

Complete the number sentence.

- Use multiplication or division facts.
- Use a calculator if you need to.

$30 \times \blacksquare = 120$    $120 \div 30 = \blacksquare$

So, $30 \times 4 = 120$    So, $120 \div 30 = 4$

Think
$3 \times 4 = 12$

Think
$12 \div 3 = 4$

**3**

Fill in the rest of the 30's row. Use either multiplication or division facts. Then complete the other rows.

- Take turns with your group or partner.
- Look for patterns in the numbers you find.

**4**

**Counting Zeros in Multiplication**

$40 \times 70 = 2800$
$50 \times 700 = 35,000$

- Multiply nonzero digits.
- Count zeros in the factors.
- Place that many zeros at the end of the product.

**Counting Zeros in Division**

$3600 \div 9 = 400$
$45,000 \div 90 = 500$

- Write a rule for counting zeros in division.
- Use a calculator to check your rule.

## Show What You Know!

Discuss each question and explain your answer.

1. **Critical Thinking** Did you need your calculator for the whole activity? Why or why not?

2. **Write About It** How are division patterns like multiplication patterns? How are they different?

Complete the number sentence.

3. $420 \div 7 = \blacksquare$

4. $4200 \div 70 = \blacksquare$

5. $4200 \div 700 = \blacksquare$

6. $300 \div 6 = \blacksquare$

7. $3000 \div 60 = \blacksquare$

8. $30,000 \div 6 = \blacksquare$

9. $50 \times 8 = \blacksquare$

10. $500 \times 80 = \blacksquare$

11. $500 \times 800 = \blacksquare$

**More Practice Set 13.1, p. 513**

# 2 Estimating Quotients

**B**rian Caldwell began sailing around the world alone at age 19. On the coast of Africa, he sailed from East London to Port Elizabeth, a distance of 152 miles. Suppose Brian sailed this distance in 32 hours. About how many miles did he sail each hour?

Compatible numbers can help you estimate.

*Brian Caldwell sails the boat that carried him around the world.*

**Use What You Know**

Compatible numbers are easy to work with because they divide evenly.
Examples: 4 and 2
32 and 8

## Here's A Way! Estimate 152 ÷ 32.

**1** Round to find compatible numbers.

152 ÷ 32

⬇

160 ÷ 40      150 ÷ 30

Think
16 ÷ 4

Think
15 ÷ 3

**2** Use the rounded numbers to divide.

160 ÷ 40 = 4

Think
16 ÷ 4 = 4

150 ÷ 30 = 5

Think
15 ÷ 3 = 5

So, the quotient of 152 ÷ 32 is between 4 and 5.

Brian sailed more than 4 miles each hour.

**Talk About It!** Will the exact quotient be closer to 4 or 5? Explain.

**Other Examples** About how long will it take Brian to go 1190 miles if he sails 54 miles a day? Estimate 1190 ÷ 54.

a. Round to find compatible numbers.
1200 ÷ 60
1000 ÷ 50

b. Estimate by dividing the rounded numbers.
1200 ÷ 60 = 20
1000 ÷ 50 = 20
The trip takes about 20 days.

## Show What You Know!

**Write the letters of the compatible numbers that help you estimate.**

1. 376 ÷ 43      a. 28 ÷ 4      b. 32 ÷ 4      c. 36 ÷ 4
2. 6750 ÷ 86      a. 56 ÷ 8      b. 64 ÷ 8      c. 72 ÷ 8

**Estimate the quotient.**

3. 247 ÷ 63      4. 387 ÷ 77      5. 6328 ÷ 73      6. 2741 ÷ 96      7. 7245 ÷ 84

8. **Critical Thinking** How can you use the rule for counting zeros in division to help you estimate quotients?

## Work It Out!

**Write the compatible numbers that help you estimate.**

9. 576 ÷ 98      10. 783 ÷ 85      11. 356 ÷ 72      12. 438 ÷ 73      13. 816 ÷ 89

**Estimate the quotient.**

14. 680 ÷ 26      15. 753 ÷ 42      16. 843 ÷ 22      17. 684 ÷ 63      18. 752 ÷ 25
19. 2750 ÷ 35      20. 4538 ÷ 47      21. 4750 ÷ 30      22. 8013 ÷ 48      23. 7700 ÷ 96

### Problem Solving   Using Data

24. Suppose Brian expected to sail 100 miles each day. How many days should it take him to sail from Hawaii to Vanuatu? How many more days should it take to reach Cocos Keeling?

25. Brian needed supplies while he was sailing. Suppose he bought supplies at all the places on the chart. At which place should he need to get the least amount of supplies? Explain.

**More Practice Set 13.2, p. 514**

### Parts of Brian's Route

| Place | Distance |
|---|---|
| Hawaii to Vanuatu | 2955 mi |
| Vanuatu to Cocos Keeling | 3824 mi |
| Cocos Keeling to Mauritius | 1999 mi |

Hawaii (huh WA ee)
Vanuatu (vah noo AH too)
Cocos Keeling (KOH kohs KEE ling)
Mauritius (maw RIHS uhs)

### Math Journal

How can estimating quotients help you divide?

# Problem Solving
## Make a Table

**S**uppose 9 babies are born every 2 seconds around the world. How many minutes would it take for 1350 babies to be born?

Make a table for the information you have. This strategy can help you solve problems such as these.

## Here's A Way! Use Make a Table.

### 1 Understand

• What happens every 2 seconds?

### 2 Plan

• How many groups of 2 seconds are there in a minute?

$$60 \div 2 = 30$$

• Find out how many babies are born every minute.

$$9 \times 30 = 270$$

• How can making a table help you solve the problem?

| Number of Babies Born | Minutes |
|---|---|
| 270 | 1 |
| 540 | 2 |
| 810 | ? |
| 1080 | ? |
| 1350 | ? |

### 3 Try It

• Make a table showing the number of minutes and the number of babies born.

• Complete the table to solve the problem.

### 4 Look Back

• It will take 5 minutes for 1350 babies to be born.

• How did making a table help you solve the problem?

## Show What You Know!

**Use Make a Table to solve the problem.**

1. You have 2 cases of baby food. There are 22 jars in each case. Suppose a baby eats 5 jars a day. But every second day, the baby needs an extra jar. How long will your supply last?

| Days | 1 | 2 | 3 | 4 | 5 |
|------|---|---|---|---|---|
| Jars | 5 | 11 | 16 | 22 | 27 |

2. **Critical Thinking** Could you have used a strategy other than Make a Table to solve problem 1? Explain.

## Work It Out!

**Use Make a Table or any other strategy to solve the problem.**

3. The world population increases by about 8 million people a month. How many months will it take for the world population to increase by 112 million? Explain your strategy.

4. Suppose an average of 12,100 babies are born in the U.S. every day in September. In every other month that year, about 11,400 babies are born a day. About how many more are born in September than in June?

5. A photographer charges $55 each year to photograph a baby once a year. Another photographer charges $100 for the first photo and then $15 every year after that. How long would you have to use the second photographer before saving money?

6. There are 10 rectangles in this diagram. Explain how you can find them.

7. You put 1 penny in a bank. The next day you put in 2 pennies and the next day 4 pennies. Following this pattern, on what day will the bank hold over $100?

### Share Your Thinking

8. Choose a problem you solved by making a table. How did you decide which numbers to use in the first column or row?

9. How are the Make a Table and Look for a Pattern strategies similar? How are they different?

451

# 1-Digit Quotients

You are about to enter a double-dutch competition. To break a record for speed jumping, suppose you have to jump 168 times in a minute. How many times would you have to jump in a second?

One minute equals 60 seconds. Divide 168 by 60 to find out.

## Here's A Way! Find 168 ÷ 60.

**Think**
$18 ÷ 6 = 3$

**1** Use compatible numbers to estimate.

$$168 ÷ 60 = \blacksquare \longrightarrow 180 ÷ 60 = 3$$

168 is less than 180. So the quotient will be less than 3.

**2** Regroup the hundreds and tens as ones. Then there will be enough ones to divide by 60.

$$60\overline{)168}$$

**Think**
168 ones

**3** Divide the ones. Multiply. Subtract. Write the remainder.

$$\begin{array}{r} 2 \text{ R48} \\ 60\overline{)168} \\ -120 \\ \hline 48 \end{array}$$

$60 × 2$

You would have to jump more than 2 steps each second to break the record.

## Talk About It!

Will the number of steps you have to jump each second be closer to 2 or to 3? Explain.

**Estimate first. Then divide.**

1. $19\overline{)84}$    2. $63\overline{)504}$    3. $46\overline{)92}$    4. $56\overline{)447}$    5. $18\overline{)73}$

6. $24\overline{)210}$    7. $76\overline{)76}$    8. $32\overline{)183}$    9. $47\overline{)329}$    10. $76\overline{)609}$

11. **Critical Thinking** What should you do if your remainder is greater than your divisor? Why?

## Work It Out!

**Estimate. If your estimate is greater than 5, find the exact answer.**

12. $49\overline{)95}$    13. $14\overline{)56}$    14. $82\overline{)536}$    15. $22\overline{)960}$    16. $76\overline{)547}$

17. $38\overline{)87}$    18. $56\overline{)365}$    19. $68\overline{)750}$    20. $25\overline{)220}$    21. $63\overline{)507}$

22. $288 \div 24$    23. $288 \div 48$    24. $288 \div 72$    25. $288 \div 32$    26. $288 \div 36$

27. **Number Sense** If $99 \div 17 = 5$ R14, what is $100 \div 17$?

**Patterns** Look for patterns to complete the set.

28. a. $1438 \div 28 = 51$ R10          29. a. $3472 \div 63 = 55$ R7
    b. $1439 \div 28 = 51$ R11              b. $3473 \div 63 = 55$ R8
    c. $1440 \div 28 = 51$ R12              c. $3474 \div 63 = 55$ R9
    d. ■ $\div 28 = $ ■ R■              d. ■ $\div 63 = $ ■ R■
    e. ■ $\div 28 = $ ■ R■              e. ■ $\div 63 = $ ■ R■

30. **Write About It** Look at exercises 28 and 29. What happens to the answer as the dividend becomes greater?

31. **Problem Solving** A carton holds 24 jump ropes. Suppose 200 ropes need to be packed in cartons. If all cartons are full except the last, how many jump ropes will be in the last carton? Explain.

**Mixed Review**    Write the answer.

32.  $\begin{array}{r} 46 \\ \times\ 16 \end{array}$    33.  $\begin{array}{r} 87 \\ \times\ 56 \end{array}$    34.  $\begin{array}{r} 491 \\ \times\ 60 \end{array}$    35. $\frac{1}{3} + \frac{5}{12}$    36. $\frac{14}{16} - \frac{5}{8}$

**More Practice Set 13.4, p. 514**

# 5

# 2-Digit Quotients

**M**ountain climbers are cleaning up trash from base camps on Mount Everest. Suppose 21 people carry 1281 pounds of trash down the mountain. Everyone carries the same amount. How many pounds does each person carry?

You can divide to find out.

Climbers leave behind tents, oxygen bottles, and other trash. Trash on Mount Everest may weigh 50 tons!

Trash is packed and weighed before it is carried away.

## Here's A Way!   Find 1281 ÷ 21.

**1** Estimate the quotient. Use compatible numbers.

$1281 \div 21 = \blacksquare$

$1200 \div 20 = 60$

$1400 \div 20 = 70$

Choose the numbers that will give you the best estimate. $1200 \div 20$ is closer to $1281 \div 21$. So the estimate of 60 is closer to the actual quotient.

**2** Divide the tens. Multiply. Then subtract.

$$
\begin{array}{r}
6 \\
21\overline{)1281} \\
-126 \\
\hline
21
\end{array}
$$

Think
128 tens ÷ 21

**3** Divide the ones. Multiply. Then subtract.

$$
\begin{array}{r}
61 \\
21\overline{)1281} \\
-126 \\
\hline
21 \\
-21 \\
\hline
0
\end{array}
$$

Each person carries 61 pounds of trash down the mountain.

**Talk About It!**
- How did you know where to place the first digit in the quotient?
- Do you need to add to check your answer? Explain.

## Show What You Know!

**Estimate. Then divide.**

1. $27\overline{)2098}$   2. $14\overline{)1176}$   3. $45\overline{)1484}$   4. $43\overline{)2259}$   5. $31\overline{)1364}$

6. $2132 \div 82$   7. $5092 \div 76$   8. $468 \div 36$   9. $4236 \div 65$   10. $6383 \div 79$

11. **Algebraic Reasoning** A 4-digit number is divided by a 2-digit number. Can the quotient be a 4-digit number? Explain.

## Work It Out!

**Estimate. If your estimate is greater than 10, find the exact answer.**

12. $19\overline{)152}$   13. $42\overline{)966}$   14. $25\overline{)425}$   15. $37\overline{)2170}$   16. $58\overline{)725}$

17. $525 \div 25$   18. $52 \div 24$   19. $927 \div 17$   20. $938 \div 29$   21. $375 \div 25$

**Patterns** Use the division sentences shown to answer the question.

22. If the pattern continues, what division sentence is next?

23. What pattern can you find in the divisors?

24. What pattern can you find in the quotients?

$$864 \div 12 = 72$$
$$864 \div 24 = 36$$
$$864 \div 48 = 18$$

## Problem Solving  Using Data

Use the chart to solve the problem.

25. Mount Everest is in the Himalayan mountain range. There are 5280 feet in a mile. About how many miles high is Everest?

26. A group is climbing Mount Kamet. Their base camp is 10,000 feet up the mountain. Suppose it takes them 12 days to climb from their camp to a place $\frac{2}{3}$ up the mountain. About how many feet did they climb each day?

### Some Himalayan Mountain Heights

| Mountain | Heights |
|---|---|
| Mount Everest | 29,028 ft |
| Mount Kailas | 22,027 ft |
| Mount Kamet | 25,447 ft |

Himalayan
(him uh LAY uhn)
Mount Everest (EV uhr ist)
Mount Kailas (kee LAS)
Mount Kamet (KUHM ayt)

### Mixed Review  Write the answer.

27. $\begin{array}{r} 46 \\ \times\ 29 \\ \hline \end{array}$   28. $\begin{array}{r} 24 \\ \times\ 9 \\ \hline \end{array}$   29. $\begin{array}{r} 53.42 \\ +\ 49.80 \\ \hline \end{array}$   30. $\begin{array}{r} 97.69 \\ -\ 6.89 \\ \hline \end{array}$

**More Practice Set 13.5, p. 514**

# Problem Solving
## Is the Answer Reasonable?

**T-SHIRTS $5.00**

**Y**ou are at a flea market with your friends, shopping for bargains. Someone is selling T-shirts. One of your friends points at the signs. "Look!" he says. "You can get twice as much for half the price!"

**Buy One, Get One Free!**

## Is the Answer Reasonable?

**Ask Yourself:**

Did I answer the question?

Did I calculate correctly?

Is the answer labeled with the right units?

Does my answer need to be rounded to a whole number to make sense?

## You Decide

- How much does one T-shirt cost?
- How much does each T-shirt cost if you get 2?
- Think about what your friend said. Is it reasonable? Explain.

## Work It Out!

**Decide whether the sentence in color is reasonable. Explain.**

1. A man is selling used books on an old picnic table. His prices are 3 books for $.99 or 12 books for $4. "The more you buy, the cheaper the price," he tells you.

2. Five pairs of dress-up shoes cost $4.25, and 10 pairs cost $8.50. You get twice the amount for twice the money, so the price for each pair is the same.

3. A woman is selling old clothes and jewelry by the pound. You can pick whatever you want and pay $.50 for 1 pound or $2.50 for 10 pounds. She tells you, "It's half price if you buy 10 pounds."

4. It is 12 miles to the flea market. It takes your father 20 minutes to drive you and your friends there. On the way home, the same trip takes 3 minutes longer. So your speed on the way home was greater.

## Share Your Thinking

5. How did you decide whether a statement was reasonable?

# Midchapter Review

## for Pages 444–456

## Problem Solving

Solve. Show your work. (pages 450, 456)

1. Your school's computer club has $85 to spend on disks. Two boxes of disks cost $5. How many boxes of disks can the computer club buy?

2. Suppose you decide to save some money every month. You save $5 in January. Then you decide to save $2 more each month than you did the month before. How much will you have saved by the end of October?

## Concepts

Write a multiplication or division fact that you can use to find each quotient. (page 446)

3. $2100 \div 70$        4. $400 \div 80$        5. $35,000 \div 700$

Explain how to use estimation to tell whether each quotient is between 6 and 7. (page 448)

6. $491 \div 61$        7. $246 \div 87$        8. $326 \div 49$

Is the answer reasonable? How can you tell without actually dividing? (page 454)

9. $567 \div 17$ is 32 R23        10. $421 \div 32$ is 103 R2

## Skills

Use patterns to find the quotient. (page 446)

11. $2400 \div 30$        12. $420 \div 7$        13. $540 \div 60$

Estimate first. Then divide. (pages 452, 454)

14. $21\overline{)95}$        15. $65\overline{)111}$        16. $45\overline{)247}$

17. $1578 \div 32$    18. $865 \div 50$    19. $2254 \div 24$    20. $4760 \div 84$

# Math World

Explore different ways of writing and solving long division problems. Learn how to keep track of goods the way the Aztecs would have.

## Spanish Long Division

768 ⌐32

Most students all over the world learn a similar method for solving division problems. In Spain, however, the way students learn division is a bit different from the method in your textbook. Spanish students write the divisor to the right of the dividend, like the problem above. Try solving some problems this way.

Spanish school children raise their hands in class.

## What's in a Name?

Did you know that when you work a division problem or other arithmetic problems, there is a name for it? A calculation like that is called an algorithm (AL gore ih them). We get this word from a famous Arab mathematician who lived from 680 to 750, named Al Khwarizmi (All HWOR is mee). He wrote a famous book about solving math problems. A few hundred years later, an Englishman translated it into Latin. He wrote Al Khwarizmi's name as *Algorithmus*.

# Try This!

The Aztecs kept records on parchment books called codices (COH duh sees). They used pictographs to record items paid to the government. To each pictograph they added symbols showing how many of that item was paid. Because they counted in 20s, they used small drawings for 20 and its multiples.

**1** First, plan a pictograph for 100 cocoa beans. Look at the symbols on the right. Which symbol makes sense for 100 cocoa beans? You can combine symbols or use the same symbol more than once.

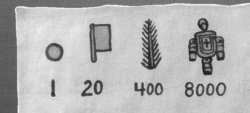

|  |  |  |  |
|---|---|---|---|
| 1 | 20 | 400 | 8000 |

**2** You know that 100 divided by 20 is 5. This tells you to add 5 flag symbols to your pictograph.

**3** Now show 125 cocoa beans.

**4** Create your own symbols and label the number amounts.

**Try:** 800 coats
200 jars of honey
1600 dishes

## Ironing Out Division

In the 10th century, some people used a method of division to solve problems called iron division. Iron division is no longer taught in schools, and it's a good thing. This method got its name because people thought it was like iron—extremely hard!

## Respond

**Think about it . . .**

From what you've learned about Aztec records, in what amounts do you think people paid for items?

**Internet:**
**Houghton Mifflin Education Place**
Explore the Math Center at
http://www.eduplace.com

459

# Using Division

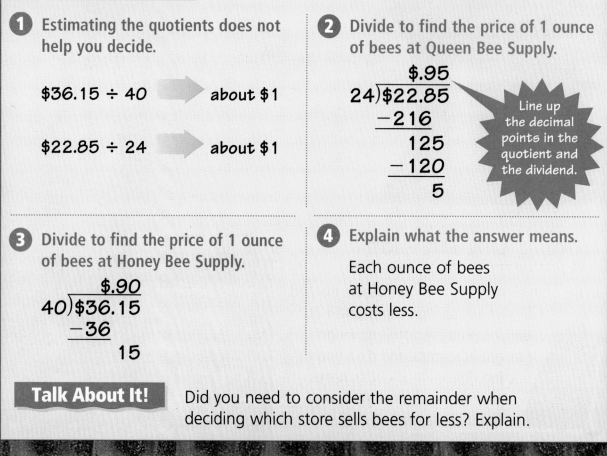

**A** farmer who raises bees to make honey needs to buy more bees. Two stores sell bees by the ounce. Honey Bee Supply sells 40 ounces of bees for $36.15. Queen Bee Supply sells 24 ounces of bees for $22.85. Which is the better buy?

Use division to find the price for each ounce at both stores.

People wear protective clothing to harvest honey.

---

## Here's A Way! Find $36.15 ÷ 40 and $22.85 ÷ 24.

**1** Estimating the quotients does not help you decide.

$36.15 ÷ 40 ➡ about $1

$22.85 ÷ 24 ➡ about $1

**2** Divide to find the price of 1 ounce of bees at Queen Bee Supply.

$$
\begin{array}{r}
\$.95 \\
24\overline{)\$22.85} \\
-216 \phantom{0}\\
\hline
125 \\
-120 \\
\hline
5
\end{array}
$$

Line up the decimal points in the quotient and the dividend.

**3** Divide to find the price of 1 ounce of bees at Honey Bee Supply.

$$
\begin{array}{r}
\$.90 \\
40\overline{)\$36.15} \\
-36 \phantom{00}\\
\hline
15
\end{array}
$$

**4** Explain what the answer means.

Each ounce of bees at Honey Bee Supply costs less.

---

**Talk About It!** Did you need to consider the remainder when deciding which store sells bees for less? Explain.

**Estimate. Then divide.**

1. $36.80 ÷ 40    2. $28.80 ÷ 72    3. $19.84 ÷ 32    4. $57.95 ÷ 95

5. Suppose Honey Bee Supply sells 62 ounces of bees for $52.75. Queen Bee Supply sells 43 ounces for $38.80. Which store has the better price? Explain how you decided.

6. **Critical Thinking** A bee farmer estimates that one store sells empty honey jars for less than $2 each. Another store charges more than $1 a jar. What should he do? Explain.

**Work It Out!**

**Estimate. Then divide.**

7. $59.04 ÷ 72    8. $65.52 ÷ 91    9. $35.52 ÷ 48    10. $10.60 ÷ 53

11. $74.82 ÷ 87    12. $81.84 ÷ 93    13. $25.53 ÷ 37    14. $42.48 ÷ 62

15. $94.10 ÷ 10    16. $54.40 ÷ 64    17. $35.50 ÷ 50    18. $63.75 ÷ 85

**Algebraic Reasoning Write >, <, or =.**

19. $14.28 ÷ 15 ⬤ $32.89 ÷ 26    20. $4.28 ÷ 12 ⬤ $7.50 ÷ 24

21. $43.92 ÷ 72 ⬤ $46.20 ÷ 42    22. $34.20 ÷ 18 ⬤ $32.30 ÷ 19

**Problem Solving** **Using Data**

**Honey Prices**

**Use the chart to solve the problem.**

23. Which kind of honey costs the least for each ounce?

24. Suppose a store has a sale on creamed honey. You can buy 2 jars for the price of 1. Which honey would now cost the least for each ounce?

25. A honey catalog charges $.08 an ounce for shipping and handling. You buy 16 ounces of clover honey and 48 ounces of wildflower honey. Will your bill be greater than $20? Explain.

| Honey | Size of Jar | Price |
|---|---|---|
| Clover Honey | 8 ounces | $1.36 |
| Wildflower Honey | 16 ounces | $2.40 |
| Creamed Honey | 12 ounces | $4.56 |

**More Practice Set 13.7, p. 514**

# Problem Solving
## Using Make a Table and Other Strategies

In the region around Boise, Idaho, the population has been growing quickly. People have been moving there from other states. The chart below shows about how many adults arrived each year from 1991 to 1995.

**IDAHO**
★Boise

### Problem Solving Process
✓ Understand
✓ Plan
✓ Try It
✓ Look Back

### Choose a Strategy You Have Learned
✓ Guess and Check
✓ Draw a Picture
✓ Make a List
✓ Make a Table
✓ Act It Out
✓ Work a Simpler Problem
✓ Look for a Pattern
✓ Work Backward

| Adults Arriving from Other States | | | | |
|------|------|------|------|------|
| 1991 | 1992 | 1993 | 1994 | 1995 |
| 5800 | 8100 | 9000 | 9100 | 8600 |

What if a new house was built for every 5 adults who moved to this region? Suppose that in 1991 and 1992 a new construction worker was hired for every 10 houses built. From 1993 to 1995, a new worker was hired for every 5 houses built. How many new workers were hired?

- What problem are you trying to solve?
- How many houses were built for the adults who moved there each year?
- How many new workers were needed each year?
- Explain a strategy you can use to solve the problem. Then solve it.

**Use any strategy to solve the problem. Show your work.**

1. The chart on page 462 shows the number of adults who moved to the Boise region. What if 1 child moved there for every 10 adults? How many children moved to the area?

2. Suppose that schools need 1 new teacher for every 20 new students. What if all the children who came to Boise were the right age for school? How many more teachers would these schools need by 1995?

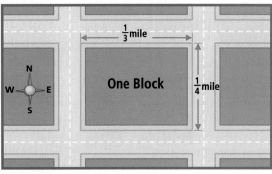

3. Your school is 3 blocks west and 4 blocks south from your house. How many miles do you have to walk to get to school?

4. You have a friend who lives 3 blocks farther west than you do. How many miles does your friend have to walk to school?

5. In Idaho, your basketball team wins $\frac{1}{2}$ of the first 8 games. There are 16 games altogether in the season. You need to win $\frac{3}{4}$ of them to qualify for a tournament. How many of the remaining games does your team need to win?

**Use the chart to answer the questions.**

| Driver's Licenses Issued to People from Other States, 1995 | | | | | | | | | | | |
|---|---|---|---|---|---|---|---|---|---|---|---|
| Jan. | Feb. | Mar. | Apr. | May | June | July | Aug. | Sep. | Oct. | Nov. | Dec. |
| 753 | 601 | 762 | 622 | 681 | 783 | 676 | 877 | 816 | 788 | 677 | 540 |

6. The chart shows how many people got Idaho driver's licenses in 1995. Was the average number of new licenses each month greater than 800? Explain.

7. What if you were in charge of taking the photographs for new Idaho driver's licenses? About how many pictures would you expect to take each day in April?

8. In which 3 months in a row were there a total of 2481 driver's licenses?

## Share Your Thinking

9. Suppose you were a member of a school board. What problem solving strategies might help you plan for the future? Explain.

# Problem Solving
## Using Strategies

**LESSON 9**

ZOONOOZ

**A** hippopotamus can be 15 feet long and weigh 8000 pounds. An animal this size needs a lot of food! In the wild, hippos eat grasses and other plants. The number of hippos that can live in a region depends on the amount of food there.

### Problem Solving Process
✓ Understand
✓ Plan
✓ Try It
✓ Look Back

### Choose a Strategy You Have Learned
✓ Guess and Check
✓ Draw a Picture
✓ Make a List
✓ Make a Table
✓ Act It Out
✓ Work a Simpler Problem
✓ Look for a Pattern
✓ Work Backward

**S**uppose the shaded region below is a park in Africa. This park has enough food so 25 hippos can live in every square mile. Suppose 125 hippos live in the park now. About how many more hippos could live there?

- How many hippos live in the park now?

- How can you use the grid to estimate the size of the park?

- How many hippos can live in each square mile?

- Explain a strategy that can help you to solve the problem. Then, solve it.

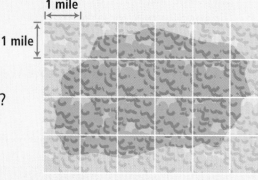

1 mile

1 mile

**Use any strategy to solve the problem. Show your work.**

| Hippo Weights | |
|---|---|
| Father | ? |
| Mother | 5940 lb |
| First Baby | 1465 lb |
| Second Baby | 429 lb |

1. The average weight of the 4 hippos in the chart is 3681 pounds. How much does the father weigh?

2. **Critical Thinking** What if the mother's weight was also left out of the chart? Could you have figured out the father's weight then? Explain why or why not.

3. The San Diego Zoo began building a new hippo exhibit in September 1994. It took workers 43 weeks to complete it. Suppose they worked 5 days a week for most of this time. For the last 8 weeks they worked 7 days a week. They also had 15 holidays. How many days did it take to build the exhibit?

4. Suppose that all the food has been eaten where the hippos are gathered. The nearest food is 3 miles away. If a hippo walks 4 miles in an hour, how many minutes will it take the hippo to reach the food?

5. You are designing a doorway for a hippo home. Hippos grow to different sizes, though usually in a range. How do you decide how big to make the doorway? Explain.

6. One day, a hippo ate $\frac{2}{3}$ of his food. The next day, he ate only $\frac{1}{2}$ of his food. The third day, he ate $\frac{1}{4}$. This is a pattern that repeats. How much will he eat on the fourth day?

7. Each week 4 hippos at a zoo eat a total of about 1680 pounds of food. About how much does each hippo eat every day?

8. In a zoo, hippos live in a much smaller area than they need in the wild. Why do these hippos need so little space? Hint: Think about food.

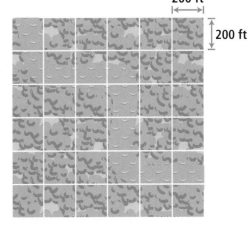

200 ft

200 ft

9. In the wild, a group of hippos needs at least 800 feet along the shore of a river. Suppose the living area for each hippo group is on one side of a river. Estimate how many groups could live along both sides of the river shown.

### Share Your Thinking

10. Which strategy did you use for problem 9? Discuss your strategy with a partner. How is this problem similar to the one on page 464? How is it different?

# Chapter 13 Test

## for Pages 444–465

**Test-Taking Tips**
If you have trouble solving a problem, try different strategies.

## Problem Solving

**Solve. Show your work.** (pages 450, 462, 464)

1. Suppose you jog 5 miles in an hour. How many minutes would it take you to jog to a store that is 3 miles away?

2. At your first visit to the gym, you exercise for 20 minutes. Every 3 visits after this, you increase the time by 10 minutes. After how many visits will your exercise increase to 1 hour?

## Concepts

**Tell if the statement is reasonable. Write *yes* or *no*.** (page 456, 460)

| Box of Cereal | Price |
|---|---|
| Jolly-O | 2 boxes for $3.99 |
| Muscle Mix | $2.79 each; buy one, get one free |
| Oats and Grains | 3 boxes for $10 |

3. Oats and Grains is the best buy.

4. The store takes in more money selling Jolly-O than Muscle Mix.

5. Jolly-O is the best buy if you can use only one box of cereal.

6. How could estimation help you answer problems 3–5?

**Write the multiplication fact you would use to help you divide the numbers mentally.** (page 446)

7. $5600 \div 70$                8. $300 \div 60$

**What compatible numbers do you need to estimate the quotients.** (page 448)

9. $7156 \div 87$          10. $427 \div 70$          11. $849 \div 27$

**Tell whether you would use multiplication or multiplication and addition to check the quotient. Explain your answer.** (page 454)

12. $474 \div 17$ is 27 R15     13. $768 \div 24 = 32$        14. $5365 \div 45$ is 119 R10

**Estimate. Tell which range is the most reasonable estimate for this quotient. Write *a, b, c,* or *d.* (page 448)**

15. 248 ÷ 8    a. 5–10    b. 10–20    c. 30–40    d. 100–200

16. 539 ÷ 51    a. 5–10    b. 10–20    c. 20–30    d. 100–200

**Estimate. Then choose the correct answer.**
**Write *a, b, c,* or *d.* (pages 448, 452, 454)**

17. 276 ÷ 70    a. 30 R66    b. 3 R66    c. 30 R76    d. 3 R76

18. 2687 ÷ 31    a. 86    b. 86 R21    c. 8 R21    d. 860 R21

19. $30.45 ÷ 15    a. $203    b. $20.30    c. $2.03    d. $2030

**Copy and complete. Write > or <. (page 448)**

20. 654 ÷ 32 ● 257 ÷ 23        21. 423 ÷ 821 ● 756 ÷ 9

22. 3454 ÷ 51 ● 4786 ÷ 94        23. 87 ÷ 32 ● 177 ÷ 9

**Divide. Circle the quotient if you used mental math. (pages 452, 454)**

24. 2178 ÷ 34        25. 2460 ÷ 30        26. 72,000 ÷ 800

## Performance Task

(page 456)

How can you use the chart to determine which container of peaches is the best buy?

### Prime Peaches

| Container Size | Small | Medium | Large | Jumbo |
|---|---|---|---|---|
| Number | 5 | 8 | 16 | 25 |
| Cost per Container | $1.25 | $1.80 | $2.20 | $3.75 |

**Keep In Mind . . .**

Your work will be evaluated on the following:

☑ Accurate data

☑ Accurate math

☑ Reasonableness of choice

☑ Clear explanation

• Explain why you made the choice you did.

# Cumulative Review

**Interpreting Data** (Chapter 3)
How many swimmers came to swim team practice last week?

**Here's A Way!**

Add the numbers to find the answer.
20 + 17 + 12 + 18 + 23 = 90

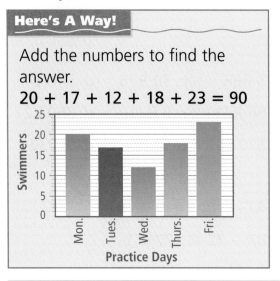

Use the bar graph to answer each question.

1. On which day was practice session most crowded? How do you know?

2. How many team members practiced on Thursday?

3. Which day had the fewest team members at practice?

4. How many more team members practiced on Tuesday than on Wednesday?

5. The swim team has 25 members. Did the whole team ever practice together?

---

**Ordering Fractions** (Chapter 8)
Order the fractions from least to greatest: $\frac{1}{3}$  $\frac{1}{4}$  $\frac{1}{2}$

**Here's A Way!**

Think of equivalent fractions.
$\frac{1}{3} = \frac{4}{12}$   $\frac{1}{4} = \frac{3}{12}$   $\frac{1}{2} = \frac{6}{12}$
Then, write the original fractions in order.   $\frac{1}{4}$  $\frac{1}{3}$  $\frac{1}{2}$

Order the fractions from least to greatest.

6. $\frac{3}{14}$  $\frac{3}{7}$  $\frac{2}{7}$     7. $\frac{5}{6}$  $\frac{7}{12}$  $\frac{1}{2}$     8. $\frac{7}{10}$  $\frac{11}{20}$  $\frac{4}{5}$

9. $\frac{3}{4}$  $\frac{11}{12}$  $\frac{5}{6}$     10. $\frac{5}{6}$  $\frac{13}{36}$  $\frac{5}{9}$     11. $\frac{23}{100}$  $\frac{4}{25}$  $\frac{19}{50}$

12. How did you find the order for exercise 11?

13. Are $\frac{1}{2}$  $\frac{1}{3}$  $\frac{1}{4}$  $\frac{1}{5}$  and $\frac{1}{6}$ in order from least to greatest or from greatest to least?

---

**Perimeter** (Chapter 10)
What is the perimeter of a hexagon with each side measuring 4 cm?

**Here's A Way!**

The hexagon has 6 equal sides. Multiply the side lengths.
6 × 4 cm = 24 cm

Find the perimeter.

14. a square with 3-in. sides

15. a pentagon with 10-m sides

16. a triangle with 5-ft sides

17. Explain how to find the perimeter of a rectangle.

## Writing Decimals (Chapter 11)

Write a decimal for three and four hundredths.

**Here's A Way!**

Write the number for each place.

3 ones and 0 tenths    4 hundredths

3    .    0    4

The decimal is 3.04.

Write as a decimal.

18. four and six tenths

19. sixteen and nine hundredths

20. twenty-five dollars and sixty-three cents

What does the highlighted digit represent?

21. 34.56      22. 7.03      23. 0.16

24. What whole number is closest to 0.9?

## Multiplying by Multiples of 10
(Chapter 12)

Find 16 × 1000.

**Here's A Way!**

16 × 1 = 16

To find 16 × 1000, write the same number of zeros in the product as there are in the factor.

16 × 1000 = 16,000

Find the product. Use mental math.

25. 14 × 10

26. 7 × 500

27. 43 × 2000

28. 452 × 20

29. 100 × 888

30. 10,000 × 453

## Problem Solving

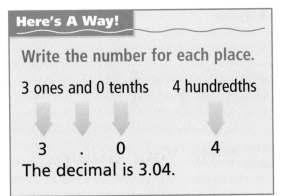

Problem Solving Process
✓ Understand
✓ Plan
✓ Try It
✓ Look Back

Choose a Strategy You Have Learned
✓ Guess and Check
✓ Draw a Picture
✓ Make a List
✓ Make a Table
✓ Act It Out
✓ Work a Simpler Problem
✓ Look for a Pattern
✓ Work Backward

Choose any strategy you know to solve the problem. Show your work.

31. Suppose 4 lb of apples cost $3.00. You can buy 16 oz of oranges for $1.00. Which fruit costs less for each pound? Justify your answer.

32. One teacher orders 8 bags of apples for the 35 children in the class. Each bag has 8 apples in it. Will there be enough for each child to have 2 apples? Explain your answer.

INVESTIGATION

# Earn To Learn!

**Consumer Connection** With Your Group

**I**s there something you would like to have in your classroom, such as a computer or art supplies? Your group will choose an item to buy, and then plan how you can raise the money.

After finding out how much the item you chose costs, brainstorm ways your group can earn money. Think about how much money to charge. Finally, make a poster to advertise your service or services.

## 1

### Plan It

- Think about items your class wants or needs. Find out the costs of each item. Check newspapers for store advertisements.
- Choose one or more items you want to buy. Decide on a total price.
- Think of ways you can earn money. Make a list of your ideas. Choose one way.

*SUPER SALE!*
*2-DAY HOME BEST BUYS*
START TOMORROW DURING OUR TOTAL HOME SALE

2 DAYS ONLY 59.99
8-Pc. Classic Set

2 DAYS ONLY 49.99
Tray Table Set or Wine Rack

2 DAYS ONLY 16.99
5-Pc. Place Setting

2 DAYS ONLY 14.99
Sheet Sets

Wish List: Computer
Price: $700.00
How to earn money?
 • Shovel snow
 • Weed gardens
 • Talent show !!
How much should tickets be?
 $5.00
How many should each person sell?
 $700 ÷ number of people in class

## 2

### Put It Together

- Think about how much you can charge for your service. Make sure your price is reasonable.
- Figure out how much each group and how much each person needs to earn so that the total money earned will meet the target goal.
- Think about how many customers each group will need to meet the goal.

## 4

### Discuss Your Results

- Have you covered all the points in Keep In Mind?
- Compare your goals and plans with those of other groups. What might you do differently?

**TALENT SHOW**
TO RAISE MONEY FOR CLASS COMPUTER

COME SEE
 — Orleans Jazz
 — Juggling/Comedy Acts
 — Dance Show

Tickets on Sale Now
Only $5.00

## 3

### Wrap It Up

- Make a poster advertising the service or services you will offer.
- Be sure to include a description of each service and the price.
- Decorate your poster so that it will get attention.

### Internet

> Visit the **Math Center** at **Houghton Mifflin Education Place.**
http://www.eduplace.com

## More Practice

**Set 1.3**   Use with pages 6–7. ······································

**Write the answer.**

1. 9 + 2        2. 6 + 8        3. 7 + 7        4. 5 + 9

5. 18 − 6       6. 22 − 11      7. 15 − 5       8. 9 − 6

9. 70 + 20 + 10      10. 15,000 − 5000      11. 600 + 800

12. 130 − 60         13. 9000 + 9000        14. 1200 − 800

**Set 1.5**   Use with pages 10–11. ·······························

**Write in standard form.**

1. three thousand, ten            2. 7000 + 500 + 400 + 7

3. four hundred twenty-five       4. 1000 + 600 + 9

**Write in words.**

5. 450                6. 500

7. 6910               8. 8322

9. 1244

**Write the value of the underlined digit.**

10. 5̲31            11. 2̲009            12. 32̲94

13. 932̲6           14. 5̲639

**Set 1.6**   Use with pages 12–13. ·······························

**Write the number that is halfway between each pair of numbers.**

1. 10, 30        2. 140, 180        3. 600, 800        4. 1000, 2000

**Write the number you estimate the arrow is pointing to.**

5.

6.

**Write in standard form.**

1. five hundred three thousand, sixty-one

2. nine hundred fifty-two thousand

3. six hundred thousand, seven

4. eighty-two thousand, twenty-nine

5. fifty thousand, one hundred five

6. one hundred thousand, seven hundred

7. three hundred thousand, forty-six

**Write in words.**

8. 871,072

9. 500,120

10. 120,000

**Write the value of the underlined digit.**

11. <u>7</u>99,031       12. 609,<u>4</u>14       13. 253,1<u>1</u>9       14. 716,947,<u>5</u>13

**Round to the nearest ten.**

| 1. 24 | 2. 61 | 3. 78 | 4. 57 | 5. 46 |
| 6. 44 | 7. 88 | 8. 16 | 9. 32 | 10. 93 |

**Round to the nearest hundred.**

| 11. 360 | 12. 874 | 13. 201 | 14. 619 | 15. 849 |
| 16. 178 | 17. 243 | 18. 514 | 19. 790 | 20. 496 |
| 21. 923 | 22. 371 | 23. 622 | 24. 488 | 25. 146 |

**Round to the nearest thousand.**

| 26. 6511 | 27. 8930 | 28. 4299 | 29. 1999 | 30. 3299 |
| 31. 2978 | 32. 5489 | 33. 7216 | 34. 9160 | 35. 6349 |

Write > or <.

1. 4329 ● 4339    2. 3566 ● 1566    3. 1763 ● 763    4. 9319 ● 7913

5. 9376 ● 4376    6. 7701 ● 7710    7. 2894 ● 2904    8. 7616 ● 7606

Write the numbers in order from the least to greatest.

9. 27,321; 67,100; 7672    10. 11,004; 8999; 10,004

11. 34,681; 3468; 43,681    12. 9807; 78,090; 4567

13. 29,061; 48,065; 2940    14. 33,471; 23,681; 54,970

Write the amount of money.

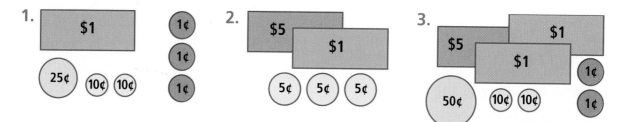

1. $1 1¢ 1¢ 25¢ 10¢ 10¢ 1¢

2. $5 $1 5¢ 5¢ 5¢

3. $5 $1 $1 $1 1¢ 50¢ 10¢ 10¢ 1¢

Find the pattern. Write the next three numbers.

4. 25¢, 35¢, 45¢, ■, ■, ■

5. $13, $15, $17, ■, ■, ■

6. $3.10, $3.20, $3.30, ■, ■, ■

7. 10¢, 15¢, 20¢, 25¢, ■, ■, ■

Write the amount, using the dollar sign and decimal point.

8. one dime more than twelve dollars

9. ten dollars less than eighty dollars and fifty cents

10. two nickels more than three quarters

**Write the least number of bills and coins you would receive as change.**

1. Cost of item: $0.79
   Cash given: $1.00

2. Cost of item: $4.43
   Cash given: $10.00

3. Cost of item: $13.03
   Cash given: $20.00

4. Cost of item: $12.85
   Cash given: $15.00

5. Cost of item: $1.19
   Cash given: $1.25

6. Cost of item: $18.98
   Cash given: $20.00

7. Cost of item: $0.51
   Cash given: $1.01

8. Cost of item: $21.70
   Cash given: $30.00

9. Cost of item: $36.10
   Cash given: $40.10

10. Cost of item: $4.51
    Cash given: $5.00

11. Cost of item: $89.01
    Cash given: $100.01

12. Cost of item: $0.58
    Cash given: $1.00

13. Cost of item: $44.95
    Cash given: $50.00

14. Cost of item: $9.01
    Cash given: $20.00

15. Cost of item: $3.67
    Cash given: $5.00

**Write the least number of pennies you could have.**

| | | | | |
|---|---|---|---|---|
| 1. $1.14 | 2. $6.56 | 3. $0.68 | 4. $0.79 | 5. $1.24 |
| 6. $2.32 | 7. $3.87 | 8. $1.98 | 9. $0.99 | 10. $1.51 |
| 11. $4.44 | 12. $0.91 | 13. $5.66 | 14. $2.72 | 15. $3.53 |

**Exchange each amount to get as many quarters as you can. Write the number of quarters.**

16. 100 pennies     17. 75 dimes          18. 100 nickels

19. $2.25     20. $4.75     21. $3.00     22. $1.50

23. $5.50     24. $6.25     25. $3.25     26. $2.00

27. $2.75     28. $6.00     29. $7.75     30. $4.25

**Copy and complete.**

1. $32 + 15 = \blacksquare + 32$

2. $27 + (51 + 49) = (\blacksquare + 51) + 49$

3. $322 - 0 = \blacksquare$

4. $17 - \blacksquare = 0$

5. $(\blacksquare + 500) + 9 = 64 + (500 + 9)$

6. $787 + \blacksquare = 787$

7. $92 + \blacksquare = 7 + 92$

8. $\blacksquare + 55 = 55 + 182$

9. $\blacksquare - 0 = 721$

10. $\blacksquare + 0 = 904$

11. $\blacksquare + 0 = 0 + 45$

12. $0 + 430 = \blacksquare$

13. $32 + 8 + 94 + 6 = (32 + \blacksquare) + (94 + 6)$

14. $(140 + \blacksquare) + 19 = 140 + (11 + 19)$

**Write the answer. Use mental math.**

| | | | | |
|---|---|---|---|---|
| 1. $17 + 4$ | 2. $4 + 57$ | 3. $5 + 48$ | 4. $98 + 3$ | 5. $27 + 8$ |
| 6. $63 + 5$ | 7. $45 + 6$ | 8. $51 + 9$ | 9. $34 - 5$ | 10. $25 - 7$ |
| 11. $42 - 3$ | 12. $65 - 8$ | 13. $75 - 7$ | 14. $56 - 6$ | 15. $38 - 7$ |
| 16. $72 - 4$ | 17. $32 + 9$ | 18. $84 - 5$ | 19. $19 + 9$ | 20. $41 - 4$ |

**Find the sum. Use mental math.**

| | | |
|---|---|---|
| 1. $65 + 10$ | 2. $30 + 75$ | 3. $25 + 45$ |
| 4. $55 + 55$ | 5. $225 + 225$ | 6. $650 + 250$ |
| 7. $305 + 125$ | 8. $415 + 115$ | 9. $2000 + 3500$ |
| 10. $1500 + 1500$ | 11. $2050 + 3050$ | 12. $4500 + 2500$ |
| 13. $15 + 20 + 25$ | 14. $30 + 65 + 5$ | 15. $10 + 45 + 55$ |
| 16. $13 + 12 + 19$ | 17. $88 + 80 + 82$ | 18. $28 + 25 + 30$ |

**Use with pages 54–55.** • • • • • • • • • • • • • • • • • • • • • • • • • • • • • •

1. List three number pairs in the the box with sums of about 100.

2. List three number pairs in box with sums of about 1000.

| 82 | | 56 | |
|----|----|----|----|
| | 23 | | 31 |
| 48 | | 67 | |

| 311 | | 240 | |
|----|----|----|----|
| | 715 | | 688 |
| 456 | | 542 | |

**Set 2.6** **Use with pages 56–57.** • • • • • • • • • • • • • • • • • • • • • • • • • • • •

**Find the sum.**

1.  93
  + 893

2.  56
  + 33

3.  $0.63
  + 0.93

4.  81
  + 64

5.  $0.99
  + 5.50

6.  $8.60
  + 5.09

7.  66
  + 919

8.  568
  + 47

9.  $0.98
  + 6.11

10.  344
  + 23

11.  839
  + 852

12.  72
  + 698

13.  $9.83
  + 8.93

14.  $6.09
  + 2.75

15.  167
  + 888

**Set 2.7** **Use with pages 58–59.** • • • • • • • • • • • • • • • • • • • • • • • • • • • •

**Find the sum.**

1.  808
  255
  + 551

2.  $60.22
  7.56
  + 46.69

3.  365
  9961
  + 1320

4.  895
  491
  + 471

5.  8013
  840
  + 845

6.  $0.94
  0.47
  0.27
  + 0.10

7.  7569
  96
  2184
  + 291

8.  5119
  7880
  9258
  + 8066

9.  918
  7341
  644
  + 32

10.  $8.18
  5.46
  9.87
  + 8.11

11. 58 + 47 + 40 + 65 + 71

12. $40.53 + $0.33 + $0.45 + $0.36 + $0.14

13. $0.16 + $0.95 + $0.63 + $0.89 + $0.42

14. 15 + 20 + 16 + 59 + 68

**Estimate by rounding to the greatest place.**

1. 29 + 53
2. 12 + 37
3. 19 + 38
4. $0.41 + $0.93
5. 282 + 197
6. 912 + 320
7. 693 + 196
8. 621 + 702
9. $1.12 + $3.98
10. $4.87 + $1.90
11. $0.68 + $0.24
12. $8.08 + $0.93
13. 1384 + 2009 + 1990
14. 4500 + 1010 + 5101
15. 1786 + 1209 + 1592

**Estimate by making a front-end estimate or by rounding.**

16. 521 + 304
17. 781 + 392
18. 279 + 430
19. 677 + 118 + 288
20. 813 + 833 + 198
21. 321 + 490 + 101
22. $1.01 + $0.21 + $0.98
23. $2.10 + $0.12 + $2.86
24. $0.79 + $0.89
25. 231 + 321
26. $89.01 + $27.95
27. $0.58 + $1.65
28. 44 + 95
29. 230 + 167 + 123
30. $9.02 + $1.99
31. $44.95 + $28.09
32. 23 + 89 + 17
33. 977 + 355

**Estimate. Use the method you like best.**

| 1. 787<br>− 592 | 2. 512<br>− 388 | 3. 410<br>− 108 | 4. 691<br>− 294 | 5. 996<br>− 389 |
| --- | --- | --- | --- | --- |
| 6. $12.04<br>− 10.06 | 7. $7.10<br>− 2.84 | 8. $9.09<br>− 4.86 | 9. $6.12<br>− 4.98 | 10. $25.94<br>− 21.11 |
| 11. 14,902<br>− 12,888 | 12. 35,673<br>− 11,124 | 13. 41,109<br>− 37,321 | 14. 28,684<br>− 19,694 | 15. 33,512<br>− 14,779 |

Use with pages 66–67. ••••••••••••••••••••••••••••••••

**Find the difference.**

| | | | | |
|---|---|---|---|---|
| 1. 39<br>− 16 | 2. 99<br>− 47 | 3. 62<br>− 21 | 4. $8.58<br>− 0.16 | 5. $1.55<br>− 0.49 |
| 6. 747<br>− 76 | 7. $7.87<br>− 0.78 | 8. 779<br>− 388 | 9. 499<br>− 82 | 10. $9.27<br>− 7.89 |
| 11. $7.24<br>− 3.42 | 12. 824<br>− 49 | 13. $92.67<br>− 43.10 | 14. $88.16<br>− 30.31 | 15. 6246<br>− 2989 |
| 16. 4331<br>− 2297 | 17. 6543<br>− 2651 | 18. $31.44<br>− 16.55 | 19. $78.78<br>− 19.95 | 20. 4321<br>− 1234 |

21. 7621 − 3004          22. 3985 − 492          23. $84.11 − $29.07

24. $35.52 − $16.99      25. 4226 − 3151         26. 6752 − 3877

Use with pages 70–71. ••••••••••••••••••••••••••••••••

**Find the difference.**

| | | | | |
|---|---|---|---|---|
| 1. 470<br>− 39 | 2. 607<br>− 24 | 3. 580<br>− 229 | 4. $3.05<br>− 1.64 | 5. $8.20<br>− 1.76 |
| 6. 505<br>− 329 | 7. 700<br>− 429 | 8. 6530<br>− 419 | 9. 8301<br>− 650 | 10. $50.50<br>− 3.72 |
| 11. 6009<br>− 3665 | 12. 4072<br>− 1154 | 13. 4660<br>− 297 | 14. $70.06<br>− 55.55 | 15. $80.00<br>− 32.22 |
| 16. 9260<br>− 8195 | 17. $94.83<br>− 10.29 | 18. $865.60<br>− 58.99 | 19. 60,700<br>− 120 | 20. 52,307<br>− 243 |

21. $4.10 − $2.56        22. 2070 − 853          23. 6470 − 350

24. 150 − 42             25. 33,800 − 2319       26. $59.60 − $2.27

**Write the answer.**

1.    9,388
   + 48,054

2.  $473.09
   +   78.52

3.   4215
   + 9093

4.   9,975
   + 14,034

5.  $58.83
   + 423.69

6.  $396.37
   −   30.55

7.   7065
   − 3526

8.   4328
   − 3782

9.   4957
   − 3640

10.  20,125
    −  9,268

11. 1397 − 776

12. $633.22 − $522.84

13. $968.44 − $283.99

14. $40.37 + $83.96

15. 90,450 + 84,090

16. 20,040 + 6,831

**Copy the chart. Use the data to complete it.**

1.

| Favorite Sport Survey | | |
| --- | --- | --- |
| **Sport** | **Tally** | **Total** |
| **Baseball** | //// | 4 |
| | | |
| | | |
| | | |

2. What is the least popular sport among the students?

3. How many students listed football as their favorite sport?

**Data: Students' Favorite Sport**

**Baseball:** Phil, Patrice, Alex, Marie

**Soccer:** Matt, Nancy, Jason

**Swimming:** Larry, Kim

**Football:** Barbara, Jim, Leonard, Stacey, Kyle

1. Copy and complete the table.

**Bundles of Magazines**

| Class | Tally | Total |
|---|---|---|
| Ms. Greene's | ‖‖‖ ‖‖‖ | 10 |
| Mr. Kiley's | ‖‖‖ | |
| Ms. Romero's | ‖‖‖ ‖‖‖ | |
| Mr. Stein's | ‖‖‖ ‖‖‖ ‖‖‖ | |

2. Copy and complete the bar graph.

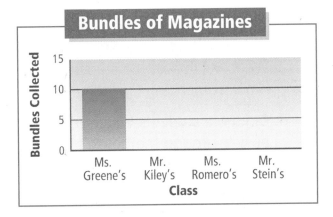

3. Which class collected the most bundles?

4. Which class or classes collected 10 bundles?

**Use the pictograph to answer each question.**

1. How many bicycles were sold in the first week?

2. Were more than 100 bicycles sold in the 4 weeks?

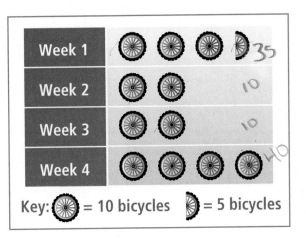

**Answer each question.**

1. On which day were sales lowest?

2. On which two days did the store sell the same number of books?

3. How many more books were sold on Wednesday than on Tuesday?

4. On which days were sales greater than 20?

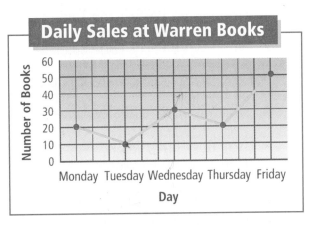

**Use the circle graph to answer each question.**

**What Students Did on Saturday Morning**

1. How many students were surveyed for the graph?

2. What fraction of the students did not visit friends?

3. Did more students watch television or help around the house?

4. How many more students worked on hobbies than watched television?

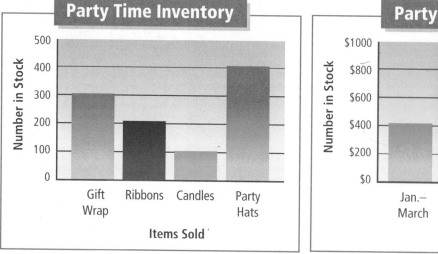

Helped Around the House → 4

Watched Television → 3

Visited Friends 15

Worked on Hobbies 8

**Use the graphs to answer each question.**

**Party Time Inventory**

Number in Stock: 500, 400, 300, 200, 100, 0

Gift Wrap, Ribbons, Candles, Party Hats

Items Sold

**Party Time Sales**

Number in Stock: $1000, $800, $600, $400, $200, $0

Jan.–March, April–June, July–Sept., Oct.–Dec.

Months

1. When were Party Time sales the highest?

2. When were Party Time sales $800 or more?

3. How many ribbons are in stock?

4. Which item does Party Time have the least number of in stock?

5. How much greater were sales from October to December than from January to March?

6. How many more party hats than candles are in stock?

**Use the picture to answer each question.**

1. What are the chances of picking a red marble from the jar?

2. What are the chances of picking a blue marble?

3. The chances of picking a green marble are the same as the chances of picking what other marble?

**Write the answer. Use mental math.**

| | | |
|---|---|---|
| 1. 22 + 29 | 2. 18 + 19 | 3. 65 + 39 |
| 4. 47 + 49 | 5. 12 + 59 | 6. 26 + 99 |
| 7. 44 + 69 | 8. 36 + 79 | 9. 77 + 9 |
| 10. 63 + 89 | 11. 58 + 19 | 12. 83 + 9 |
| 13. 33 + 49 | 14. 39 + 39 | 15. 71 + 29 |
| 16. 12 + 9 | 17. 49 + 29 | 18. 54 + 39 |
| 19. 49 + 49 | 20. 28 + 19 | 21. 57 − 49 |
| 22. 41 − 9 | 23. 38 − 29 | 24. 33 − 19 |
| 25. 65 − 39 | 26. 98 − 79 | 27. 76 − 19 |
| 28. 55 − 39 | 29. 88 − 69 | 30. 27 − 19 |
| 31. 66 − 9 | 32. 44 − 29 | 33. 72 − 59 |
| 34. 23 − 9 | 35. 82 − 49 | 36. 63 − 39 |
| 37. 77 − 59 | 38. 25 − 19 | 39. 58 − 9 |
| 40. 64 − 29 | 41. 32 − 19 | 42. 86 − 49 |

Write an addition sentence and a multiplication sentence for each.

1.    2.    3.

4.    5.    6.

Find the product.

| 1. | 2. | 3. | 4. | 5. | 6. | 7. |
|---|---|---|---|---|---|---|
| 5 | 10 | 7 | 3 | 8 | 7 | 5 |
| × 9 | × 2 | × 5 | × 5 | × 10 | × 10 | × 2 |

8. 4 × 5          9. 10 × 1          10. 5 × 0          11. 9 × 10

12. 0 × 10          13. 10 × 5          14. 8 × 5          15. 3 × 10

16. 1 × 5          17. 5 × 5          18. 10 × 4          19. 10 × 10

Write a division sentence for each multiplication sentence.

1. 8 × 2 = 16          2. 12 × 3 = 36          3. 4 × 8 = 32

4. 3 × 5 = 15          5. 6 × 7 = 42          6. 2 × 10 = 20

7. 6 × 3 = 18          8. 9 × 4 = 36          9. 7 × 2 = 14

10. 9 × 2 = 18          11. 5 × 4 = 20          12. 8 × 5 = 40

Divide. Use a related multiplication fact to help you.

13. 12 ÷ 3          14. 33 ÷ 11          15. 42 ÷ 6          16. 30 ÷ 5

17. 40 ÷ 4          18. 50 ÷ 10          19. 28 ÷ 7          20. 36 ÷ 3

21. 24 ÷ 6          22. 14 ÷ 2          23. 35 ÷ 5          24. 18 ÷ 9

**Use with pages 126–127.** •••••••••••••••••••••••••••••••••

**Find the quotient.**

1. $5\overline{)30}$     2. $5\overline{)20}$     3. $10\overline{)80}$     4. $5\overline{)15}$

5. $10\overline{)20}$     6. $45 \div 5$     7. $70 \div 10$     8. $100 \div 10$

9. $35 \div 5$     10. $50 \div 10$     11. $50 \div 5$     12. $40 \div 5$

13. $10 \div 10$     14. $10 \div 5$     15. $30 \div 10$     16. $5\overline{)5}$

17. $10\overline{)40}$     18. $10\overline{)60}$     19. $5\overline{)25}$     20. $10\overline{)90}$

**Use with pages 128–129.** •••••••••••••••••••••••••••••••

**Copy and complete the number sequence.**

1. $23 \times 8 = \blacksquare \times 23$     2. $344 \times 0 = \blacksquare$

3. $1898 \times \blacksquare = 1898$     4. $5 \times (\blacksquare \times 9) = 9 \times (5 \times 3)$

5. $\blacksquare \times 348 = 348 \times 45$     6. $\blacksquare \times 1492 = 0$

7. $1 \times 700 = \blacksquare$     8. $12 \times (4 \times 2) = \blacksquare \times (2 \times 12)$

9. $63 \times 24 \times 12 = 12 \times \blacksquare \times 24$     10. $\blacksquare \times 1 = 83$

11. $16 \div 16 = \blacksquare$     12. $\blacksquare \div 412 = 0$

13. $0 \div 420 = \blacksquare$     14. $819 \div \blacksquare = 819$

15. $758 \div \blacksquare = 758$     16. $\blacksquare \div 360 = 1$

17. $\blacksquare \div 280 = 0$     18. $\blacksquare \div 126 = 0$

19. $50 \div 50 = \blacksquare$     20. $75 \div \blacksquare = 1$

21. $\blacksquare \times 3 \times 14 = 3 \times 60 \times 14$     22. $778 \times 0 = \blacksquare$

23. $\blacksquare \times 1 = 45$     24. $(4 \times 8) \times 10 = 4 \times (10 \times \blacksquare)$

25. $315 \div \blacksquare = 315$     26. $0 \div 585 = \blacksquare$

27. $754 \div 754 = \blacksquare$     28. $62 \times \blacksquare = 8 \times 62$

Write the answer. Circle the answers you found using mental math.

| 1. 80<br>− 40 | 2. 428<br>− 319 | 3. 68<br>+ 4 | 4. 221<br>− 8 | 5. 23<br>42<br>+ 12 |
|---|---|---|---|---|
| 6. $4.10<br>+ 40.89 | 7. 73<br>− 18 | 8. 913<br>− 111 | 9. 47<br>+ 55 | 10. 675<br>− 119 |

Find the product.

| 1. $8 \times 5$ | 2. $3 \times 4$ | 3. $7 \times 4$ | 4. $9 \times 2$ |
|---|---|---|---|
| 5. $2 \times 2$ | 6. $4 \times 2$ | 7. $8 \times 6$ | 8. $8 \times 3$ |
| 9. $7 \times 8$ | 10. $2 \times 1$ | 11. $9 \times 2$ | 12. $6 \times 4$ |
| 13. $8 \times 8$ | 14. $6 \times 2$ | 15. $10 \times 4$ | 16. $4 \times 1$ |
| 17. $7 \times 2$ | 18. $8 \times 10$ | 19. $4 \times 8$ | 20. $2 \times 5$ |
| 21. $8 \times 2$ | 22. $5 \times 4$ | 23. $2 \times 3$ | 24. $4 \times 9$ |
| 25. $4 \times 4$ | 26. $8 \times 1$ | 27. $10 \times 2$ | 28. $9 \times 8$ |

Find the quotient.

| 1. $2\overline{)12}$ | 2. $4\overline{)8}$ | 3. $2\overline{)16}$ | 4. $8\overline{)72}$ |
|---|---|---|---|
| 5. $4\overline{)24}$ | 6. $2\overline{)14}$ | 7. $8\overline{)32}$ | 8. $2\overline{)8}$ |
| 9. $18 \div 2$ | 10. $20 \div 4$ | 11. $28 \div 4$ | 12. $56 \div 8$ |
| 13. $16 \div 4$ | 14. $4 \div 2$ | 15. $32 \div 4$ | 16. $10 \div 2$ |
| 17. $8\overline{)24}$ | 18. $8\overline{)40}$ | 19. $8\overline{)64}$ | 20. $8\overline{)8}$ |
| 21. $36 \div 4$ | 22. $2 \div 2$ | 23. $16 \div 8$ | 24. $12 \div 3$ |

**Write the answer.**

1. $6 \times 7$      2. $12 \div 6$      3. $3 \times 6$

4. $18 \div 3$      5. $42 \div 6$      6. $6 \times 10$

7. $5 \times 3$      8. $21 \div 3$      9. $1 \times 6$

10. $9 \times 6$      11. $24 \div 3$      12. $6 \div 3$

13. $5 \times 6$      14. $10 \times 3$      15. $3 \times 7$

16. $6 \div 6$      17. $6 \times 4$      18. $15 \div 3$

19. $27 \div 3$      20. $6 \times 6$      21. $30 \div 6$

22. $3 \times 2$      23. $54 \div 6$      24. $12 \div 3$

25. $8 \times 3$      26. $24 \div 6$      27. $3 \times 3$

28. $36 \div 6$      29. $3 \div 3$      30. $48 \div 6$

31. $3 \times 4$      32. $6 \times 2$      33. $60 \div 10$

**Write the answer.**

1. $4 \times 7$      2. $42 \div 7$      3. $9 \div 9$

4. $56 \div 7$      5. $10 \times 9$      6. $7 \times 7$

7. $7 \div 7$      8. $10 \times 7$      9. $45 \div 9$

10. $14 \div 7$      11. $18 \div 9$      12. $9 \times 9$

13. $35 \div 7$      14. $9 \times 7$      15. $49 \div 7$

16. $2 \times 7$      17. $5 \times 7$      18. $2 \times 9$

19. $63 \div 9$      20. $21 \div 7$      21. $72 \div 9$

22. $3 \times 7$      23. $6 \times 9$      24. $81 \div 9$

25. $9 \times 5$      26. $3 \times 9$      27. $8 \times 7$

28. $28 \div 7$      29. $27 \div 9$      30. $8 \times 9$

31. $36 \div 9$      32. $6 \times 7$      33. $90 \div 9$

**Find the quotient.**

1. 1000 ÷ 10       2. 240 ÷ 6       3. 5000 ÷ 5

4. 160 ÷ 2       5. 3200 ÷ 8       6. 10,000 ÷ 2

7. 360 ÷ 9       8. 2000 ÷ 4       9. 990 ÷ 3

10. 1600 ÷ 8       11. 450 ÷ 5       12. 210 ÷ 7

13. 28,000 ÷ 7       14. 8800 ÷ 4       15. 6000 ÷ 3

**Write the answer.**

16. 8 × 20       17. 120 ÷ 3       18. 3 × 900

19. 2220 ÷ 2       20. 4 × 6000       21. 810 ÷ 9

22. 2 × 80       23. 1400 ÷ 7       24. 5 × 500

25. 630 ÷ 3       26. 100 × 6       27. 12,000 ÷ 6

28. 70 × 7       29. 1500 ÷ 5       30. 9 × 7000

**Use the data to make a line plot. Then, use the line plot to solve each problem.**

| Number of Pets | | | | | |
|---|---|---|---|---|---|
| Keesha | 3 | Trevor | 4 | Luis | 0 |
| Bev | 2 | Jim | 1 | Jamal | 3 |
| Li | 0 | Sandy | 3 | Rob | 1 |

1. How many students do not have a pet?

2. Do more students have 1 pet or 2 pets?

3. What is the greatest number of pets that a student has?

4. How many more students have 3 pets than have 1 pet?

Tell which is a right angle.

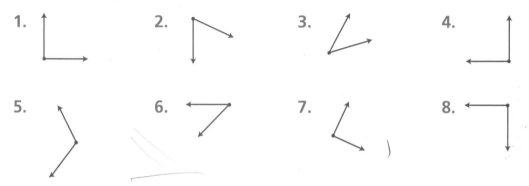

1.   2.   3.   4.

5.   6.   7.   8.

Tell how many right angles appear along the path from *A* to *B* in each drawing.

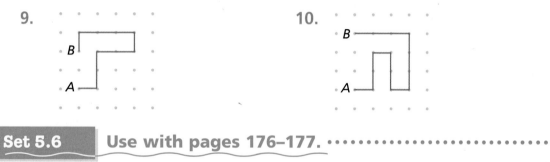

9.

10.

If the tracing is moved as shown by the slide arrow, does the tracing match the pattern? Write *yes* or *no*.

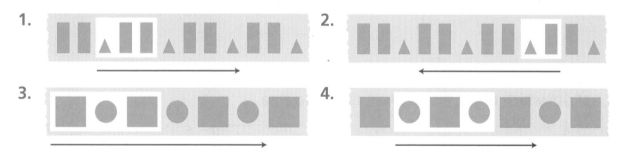

1.   2.

3.   4.

Copy the figure and slide arrow onto dot paper. Draw the slide for the slide arrow.

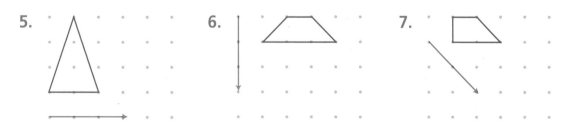

5.   6.   7.

**Set 5.7**  **Use with pages 178–179.** •••••••••••••••••••••••••••••••

Name the ordered pair for each of the following.

1. triangle
2. circle
3. star
4. diamond
5. rectangle
6. square

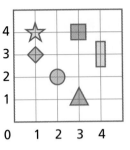

Copy the grid at the right onto squared paper. Join the points in order.

a. (1, 4)   b. (3, 2)   c. (6, 2)   d. (8, 4)

e. (1, 4)   f. (4, 4)   g. (4, 7)   h. (7, 4)

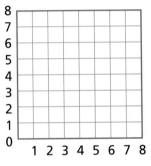

**Set 5.11**  **Use with pages 188–189.** •••••••••••••••••••••••••••••••

Give the area of each figure in square units.

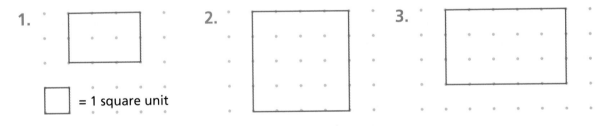

1.

☐ = 1 square unit

2.

3.

Write which of the figures have the same area.

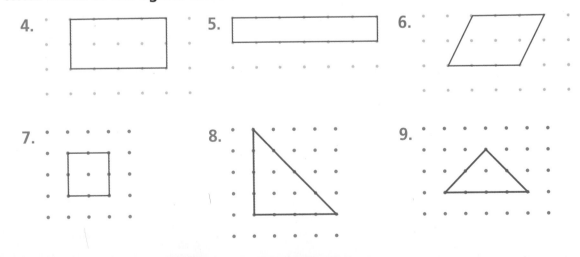

4.

5.

6.

7.

8.

9.

Trace each drawing below. Draw line segments to show each
single cube.

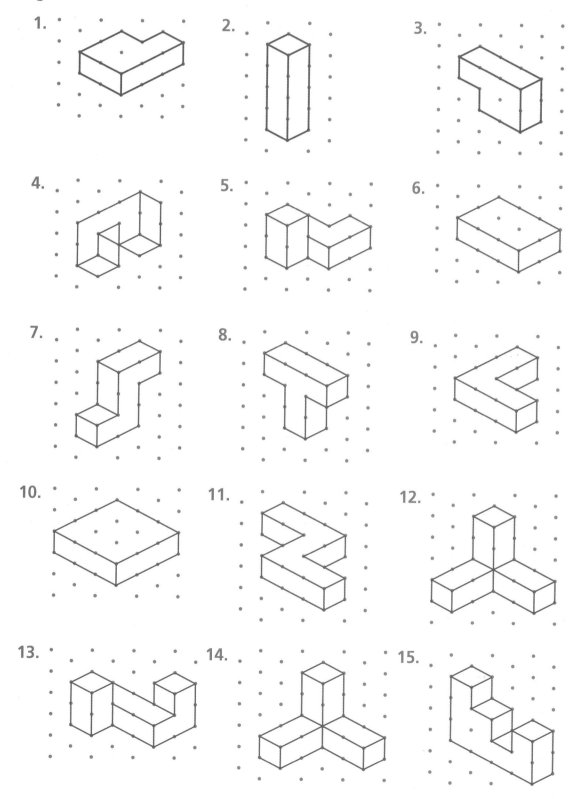

**Use with pages 208–209.**

**Estimate the product. Use front-end estimation.**

1. 77
   × 4

2. 839
   × 6

3. 4526
   × 5

4. 27
   × 9

5. $1.93
   × 3

6. 68
   × 4

7. 398
   × 5

8. 1854
   × 8

9. 2625
   × 9

10. $49.42
    × 2

11. 463
    × 7

**Estimate the product. Use rounding.**

12. 35
    × 9

13. 5978
    × 4

14. 666
    × 3

15. 756
    × 8

16. 82
    × 4

17. 612
    × 2

18. 4087
    × 6

19. 8080
    × 3

20. 753
    × 5

21. 4242
    × 3

22. 48
    × 9

23. 879
    × 4

24. 143
    × 9

25. 4294
    × 7

**Set 6.2** **Use with pages 210–211.**

**Write the product. Draw an array diagram to help you.**

1. 73
   × 4

2. 24
   × 6

3. 45
   × 5

4. 39
   × 3

5. 43
   × 7

6. 82
   × 2

7. 67
   × 8

8. 56
   × 9

9. 98
   × 2

10. 77
    × 3

11. 35
    × 4

12. 53
    × 5

13. 48
    × 3

14. 79
    × 5

15. 33
    × 8

16. 71
    × 6

17. 64
    × 2

18. 21
    × 7

19. 25
    × 9

20. 57
    × 2

**Use with pages 212–213.** ••••••••••••••••••••••••••••••••••••••••••

**Find the product.**

1. 87
   × 3

2. 52
   × 5

3. 65
   × 1

4. 88
   × 5

5. 58
   × 6

6. 94
   × 1

7. 3 × 77  8. 9 × 88  9. 8 × 69  10. 9 × 89

11. 81
    × 7

12. 42
    × 2

13. 94
    × 4

14. 16
    × 2

15. 38
    × 1

16. 18
    × 4

17. 8 × 86  18. 8 × 92  19. 9 × 22  20. 2 × 78

21. 72
    × 9

22. 57
    × 8

23. 33
    × 7

24. 85
    × 1

25. 91
    × 3

26. 91
    × 5

27. 4 × 73  28. 8 × 12  29. 4 × 39  30. 3 × 18

31. 6 × 91  32. 6 × 38  33. 9 × 25  34. 5 × 96

35. 34
    × 2

36. 88
    × 9

37. 77
    × 8

38. 69
    × 5

39. 14
    × 8

40. 44
    × 7

**Use with pages 214–215.** •••••••••••••••••••••••••••••••••••••••

**Find the product.**

1. 301
   × 5

2. 191
   × 3

3. 538
   × 9

4. 828
   × 2

5. 865
   × 2

6. 356
   × 5

7. 511
   × 7

8. 773
   × 5

9. 878
   × 4

10. 999
    × 6

11. 3 × 254  12. 5 × 763  13. 3 × 814  14. 9 × 182

15. 4 × 554  16. 6 × 207  17. 7 × 508  18. 2 × 891

**Estimate. Then, find the product.**

| | | | | |
|---|---|---|---|---|
| 1.  3577 <br> × 9 | 2.  9306 <br> × 7 | 3.  5418 <br> × 6 | 4.  5322 <br> × 4 | 5.  7215 <br> × 8 |
| 6.  2042 <br> × 9 | 7.  1528 <br> × 2 | 8.  8121 <br> × 7 | 9.  8697 <br> × 6 | 10.  4971 <br> × 4 |
| 11.  2096 <br> × 6 | 12.  5527 <br> × 4 | 13.  6531 <br> × 7 | 14.  7224 <br> × 2 | 15.  5668 <br> × 3 |
| 16.  5421 <br> × 5 | 17.  8585 <br> × 8 | 18.  7006 <br> × 9 | 19.  7216 <br> × 3 | 20.  9344 <br> × 4 |

21. 2 × 5329     22. 8 × 7138     23. 5 × 9188     24. 7 × 4635

25. 4 × 8425     26. 5 × 2021     27. 6 × 7648     28. 9 × 9828

**Estimate. Then, find the product. Use a calculator when your estimate is greater than $10.00.**

| | | |
|---|---|---|
| 1.  $8.02 <br> × 7 | 2.  $7.14 <br> × 9 | 3.  $1.12 <br> × 2 |
| 4.  $8.95 <br> × 1 | 5.  $4.14 <br> × 8 | 6.  $1.92 <br> × 8 |
| 7.  $4.95 <br> × 4 | 8.  $2.32 <br> × 7 | 9.  $4.56 <br> × 7 |
| 10.  $3.25 <br> × 5 | 11.  $19.95 <br> × 5 | 12.  $42.07 <br> × 7 |
| 13.  $30.09 <br> × 3 | 14.  $27.40 <br> × 9 | 15.  $83.55 <br> × 3 |

16. 2 × $ .12     17. 6 × $ .24     18. 9 × $ .49     19. 6 × $ .75

20. 6 × $27.06     21. 4 × $27.28     22. 8 × $52.18     23. 9 × $26.14

**Find the quotient and remainder.**

1. $9 \div 7$     2. $7 \div 2$     3. $25 \div 4$     4. $35 \div 6$     5. $36 \div 5$

6. $6\overline{)38}$     7. $3\overline{)16}$     8. $9\overline{)73}$     9. $9\overline{)67}$     10. $8\overline{)62}$

11. $36 \div 5$     12. $23 \div 3$     13. $67 \div 8$     14. $25 \div 3$     15. $33 \div 6$

16. $6\overline{)38}$     17. $8\overline{)29}$     18. $3\overline{)7}$     19. $5\overline{)23}$     20. $4\overline{)17}$

21. $20 \div 3$     22. $49 \div 5$     23. $18 \div 7$     24. $26 \div 8$     25. $44 \div 9$

26. $8\overline{)21}$     27. $2\overline{)7}$     28. $9\overline{)74}$     29. $8\overline{)66}$     30. $9\overline{)87}$

31. $71 \div 9$     32. $37 \div 4$     33. $50 \div 7$     34. $30 \div 7$     35. $45 \div 6$

36. $57 \div 9$     37. $41 \div 7$     38. $39 \div 4$     39. $29 \div 3$     40. $49 \div 5$

**Solve each problem. Decide what to do with each remainder.**

1. In gym class, no more than four students can stretch on a mat. Suppose your class has 27 students. How many mats will your class need for warm-ups?

2. The 27 students play soccer. Two teams of 11 players are needed. The remaining players will be substitutes. How many substitutes will each team have?

3. Your gym teacher has 25 soccer balls. She asks groups of students to practice a warm-up drill using 3 balls per group. How many groups of students will there be?

4. At the end of the week, the teacher gives each of the 27 students a fitness test that lasts 6 minutes. She tests one student at a time, while the rest of the students play a game. How many students can she test in a 55-minute class period? How many class periods will it take her to test all the students?

Estimate the quotient. Write the two multiples of 10 the estimate is between.

1. 5)489  2. 7)364  3. 4)236

4. 106 ÷ 5  5. 187 ÷ 6  6. 579 ÷ 9

7. 3)258  8. 6)349  9. 4)110

10. 100 ÷ 7  11. 222 ÷ 5  12. 593 ÷ 8

Estimate the quotient. Write the two multiples of 100 the estimate is between.

13. 4)746  14. 6)5294  15. 5)2678

16. 8)3803  17. 4)3492  18. 5)1890

19. 543 ÷ 3  20. 3645 ÷ 5  21. 269 ÷ 2

22. 880 ÷ 3  23. 6398 ÷ 8  24. 4655 ÷ 7

Estimate. Then, divide.

1. 7)88  2. 8)88  3. 3)48  4. 2)31  5. 4)56

6. 54 ÷ 2  7. 78 ÷ 3  8. 37 ÷ 2  9. 24 ÷ 2  10. 48 ÷ 2

11. 4)252  12. 9)398  13. 6)341  14. 7)118  15. 5)495

16. 279 ÷ 4  17. 641 ÷ 7  18. 484 ÷ 9  19. 481 ÷ 7  20. 390 ÷ 6

21. 2)177  22. 3)292  23. 4)317  24. 7)497  25. 6)416

26. 777 ÷ 8  27. 312 ÷ 4  28. 329 ÷ 7  29. 474 ÷ 8  30. 367 ÷ 4

**Use with pages 248–249.** ········································

**Divide.**

1. 550 ÷ 2

2. 595 ÷ 5

3. 953 ÷ 3

4. 1176 ÷ 4

5. 1342 ÷ 3

6. 4734 ÷ 5

7. 3608 ÷ 8

8. 7160 ÷ 8

9. 5346 ÷ 7

10. 4)2455

11. 4)1007

12. 6)690

13. 7)3969

14. 7)1584

15. 5)857

16. 2)644

17. 8)2269

18. 9)8711

19. 5)892

20. 3)791

21. 7)6869

**Use with pages 254–255.** ······································

**Divide.**

1. 832 ÷ 4

2. 840 ÷ 3

3. 943 ÷ 9

4. 1207 ÷ 6

5. 3015 ÷ 6

6. 1637 ÷ 8

7. 903 ÷ 5

8. 7240 ÷ 8

9. 4226 ÷ 7

10. 2)608

11. 4)682

12. 2)619

13. 6)644

14. 3)1820

15. 8)6452

16. 2)1204

17. 3)2250

18. 9)3154

19. 2)606

20. 3)540

21. 6)1207

22. 7)1428

23. 3)326

24. 2)1122

**Use with pages 260–261.** •••••••••••••••••••••••••••••••••

**Find the quotient.**

| | | | |
|---|---|---|---|
| 1. $3\overline{)\$\,.18}$ | 2. $5\overline{)\$\,.40}$ | 3. $8\overline{)\$\,.24}$ | 4. $9\overline{)\$\,.45}$ |
| 5. $3\overline{)\$\,.45}$ | 6. $2\overline{)\$\,.44}$ | 7. $3\overline{)\$\,.51}$ | 8. $5\overline{)\$\,.80}$ |
| 9. $5\overline{)\$1.40}$ | 10. $2\overline{)\$1.66}$ | 11. $8\overline{)\$3.76}$ | 12. $6\overline{)\$4.92}$ |
| 13. $4\overline{)\$7.12}$ | 14. $4\overline{)\$5.84}$ | 15. $6\overline{)\$9.24}$ | 16. $2\overline{)\$6.30}$ |

17. $\$14.13 \div 9$  18. $\$58.16 \div 8$  19. $\$12.74 \div 7$

20. $\$13.26 \div 6$  21. $\$27.86 \div 7$  22. $\$11.43 \div 3$

23. $\$12.80 \div 4$  24. $\$25.20 \div 6$  25. $\$29.08 \div 2$

26. $\$34.00 \div 5$  27. $\$17.68 \div 8$  28. $\$46.11 \div 3$

29. $\$61.20 \div 9$  30. $\$11.60 \div 4$  31. $\$23.50 \div 5$

32. $\$35.60 \div 4$  33. $\$49.60 \div 8$  34. $\$51.10 \div 7$

35. $\$\,.90 \div 3$  36. $\$46.20 \div 6$  37. $\$7.80 \div 2$

38. $\$51.30 \div 9$  39. $\$1.92 \div 4$  40. $\$14.50 \div 5$

**Use with pages 262–263.** •••••••••••••••••••••••••••••••

**Divide.**

1. $5\overline{)315}$  2. $4\overline{)276}$  3. $9\overline{)207}$  4. $6\overline{)211}$

5. $648 \div 8$  6. $523 \div 9$  7. $462 \div 7$

8. $2\overline{)982}$  9. $3\overline{)366}$  10. $5\overline{)845}$  11. $3\overline{)388}$

12. $896 \div 8$  13. $806 \div 3$  14. $710 \div 4$

15. $4\overline{)477}$  16. $2\overline{)271}$  17. $6\overline{)448}$  18. $4\overline{)358}$

19. $726 \div 7$  20. $108 \div 7$  21. $212 \div 5$

**Find the average.**

1. 4, 9, 8            2. 7, 7, 6, 4            3. 9, 5, 3, 4, 4

4. 19, 31, 13        5. 45, 90, 84, 21       6. 92, 15, 88, 70, 35

7. 315, 491          8. 112, 208, 211

9. 205, 210, 215, 220, 230      10. 1, 2, 5, 5, 9, 8

11. 22, 18, 32, 31, 10, 13      12. 310, 415, 502

**Write what fraction of each fraction model is shaded.**

1.   2.   3.

4.   5.   6.

**Match the fraction model with an equivalent fraction model.**

1.   2.   3.

a.   b.   c.

**Copy and complete to find the equivalent fraction.**

4. $\frac{3}{3} = \frac{\blacksquare}{12}$    5. $\frac{2}{5} = \frac{\blacksquare}{10}$    6. $\frac{2}{3} = \frac{\blacksquare}{6}$    7. $\frac{3}{4} = \frac{\blacksquare}{12}$

8. $\frac{1}{3} = \frac{\blacksquare}{6}$    9. $\frac{2}{4} = \frac{\blacksquare}{8}$    10. $\frac{4}{6} = \frac{\blacksquare}{12}$    11. $\frac{3}{5} = \frac{\blacksquare}{10}$

12. $\frac{1}{2} = \frac{\blacksquare}{6}$    13. $\frac{5}{6} = \frac{\blacksquare}{12}$    14. $\frac{1}{3} = \frac{\blacksquare}{12}$    15. $\frac{1}{2} = \frac{\blacksquare}{12}$

16. $\frac{1}{6} = \frac{\blacksquare}{12}$    17. $\frac{1}{4} = \frac{\blacksquare}{12}$    18. $\frac{4}{4} = \frac{\blacksquare}{8}$    19. $\frac{1}{5} = \frac{\blacksquare}{10}$

**Use with pages 284–285.** •••••••••••••••••••••••••••••••••••••••

**Copy and complete. Write >, <, or =.**

1. $\frac{3}{4}$ ● $\frac{2}{4}$  2. $\frac{3}{5}$ ● $\frac{4}{5}$  3. $\frac{1}{3}$ ● $\frac{5}{12}$  4. $\frac{6}{8}$ ● $\frac{7}{8}$  5. $\frac{3}{5}$ ● $\frac{6}{10}$

6. $\frac{1}{4}$ ● $\frac{1}{2}$  7. $\frac{7}{10}$ ● $\frac{4}{5}$  8. $\frac{3}{4}$ ● $\frac{8}{12}$  9. $\frac{2}{3}$ ● $\frac{3}{6}$  10. $\frac{2}{6}$ ● $\frac{5}{6}$

11. $\frac{1}{3}$ ● $\frac{3}{6}$  12. $\frac{4}{5}$ ● $\frac{2}{10}$  13. $\frac{4}{8}$ ● $\frac{1}{2}$  14. $\frac{3}{6}$ ● $\frac{1}{2}$  15. $\frac{3}{4}$ ● $\frac{1}{2}$

16. $\frac{3}{5}$ ● $\frac{5}{5}$  17. $\frac{5}{12}$ ● $\frac{2}{6}$  18. $\frac{5}{5}$ ● $\frac{10}{10}$  19. $\frac{7}{8}$ ● $\frac{3}{4}$  20. $\frac{1}{10}$ ● $\frac{4}{5}$

**Order the fractions from least to greatest.**

21. $\frac{3}{8}$ $\frac{7}{8}$ $\frac{2}{8}$  22. $\frac{3}{4}$ $\frac{1}{2}$ $\frac{1}{4}$  23. $\frac{3}{4}$ $\frac{1}{4}$ $\frac{5}{8}$

24. $\frac{2}{10}$ $\frac{3}{5}$ $\frac{4}{10}$  25. $\frac{1}{3}$ $\frac{2}{12}$ $\frac{8}{12}$  26. $\frac{3}{10}$ $\frac{7}{10}$ $\frac{1}{2}$

27. $\frac{7}{12}$ $\frac{3}{4}$ $\frac{2}{3}$  28. $\frac{1}{4}$ $\frac{1}{2}$ $\frac{3}{8}$  29. $\frac{1}{2}$ $\frac{5}{6}$ $\frac{2}{3}$

30. $\frac{3}{5}$ $\frac{1}{2}$ $\frac{7}{10}$ $\frac{1}{5}$  31. $\frac{2}{4}$ $\frac{3}{12}$ $\frac{1}{6}$ $\frac{2}{3}$  32. $\frac{3}{4}$ $\frac{5}{8}$ $\frac{3}{8}$ $\frac{1}{4}$

33. $\frac{1}{2}$ $\frac{3}{4}$ $\frac{1}{4}$ $\frac{1}{8}$  34. $\frac{2}{5}$ $\frac{5}{10}$ $\frac{3}{10}$ $\frac{1}{5}$  35. $\frac{5}{6}$ $\frac{4}{6}$ $\frac{5}{12}$ $\frac{2}{12}$

**Use with pages 292–293.** •••••••••••••••••••••••••••••••••••••••

**Write the answer.**

1. $\frac{1}{8}$ of 32  2. $\frac{1}{5}$ of 35  3. $\frac{2}{5}$ of 35  4. $\frac{1}{2}$ of 18  5. $\frac{1}{3}$ of 27

6. $\frac{1}{4}$ of $28  7. $\frac{1}{12}$ of 48  8. $\frac{1}{5}$ of 20 in.  9. $\frac{1}{10}$ of 60  10. $\frac{5}{10}$ of 16

11. $\frac{10}{10}$ of 10  12. $\frac{1}{4}$ of 12  13. $\frac{1}{6}$ of 54  14. $\frac{1}{5}$ of 5  15. $\frac{1}{3}$ of 30

16. $\frac{1}{8}$ of $40  17. $\frac{1}{12}$ of 36  18. $\frac{5}{12}$ of 36  19. $\frac{1}{6}$ of 24  20. $\frac{3}{6}$ of 24

21. $\frac{1}{6}$ of 48  22. $\frac{1}{5}$ of 25  23. $\frac{1}{12}$ of 24  24. $\frac{1}{3}$ of 9  25. $\frac{3}{4}$ of 8

How many fraction models are shaded? Write your answer as
a fraction and as a mixed number.

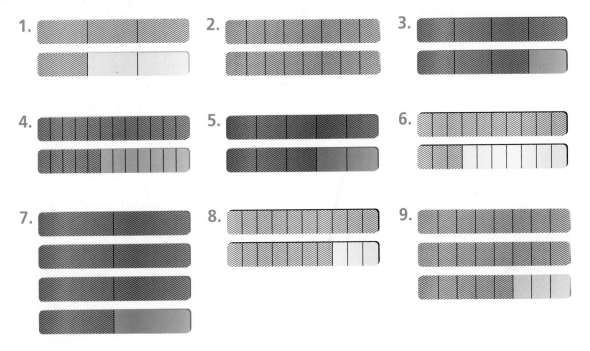

Write the answer.

1.  $\frac{4}{8}$ $+\frac{2}{8}$   2.  $\frac{3}{4}$ $-\frac{1}{4}$   3.  $\frac{2}{5}$ $+\frac{2}{5}$   4.  $\frac{2}{4}$ $+\frac{2}{4}$   5.  $\frac{5}{10}$ $+\frac{3}{10}$   6.  $\frac{5}{5}$ $-\frac{4}{5}$   7.  $\frac{3}{8}$ $-\frac{3}{8}$

8.  $\frac{8}{12}$ $-\frac{5}{12}$   9.  $\frac{3}{10}$ $+\frac{2}{10}$   10.  $\frac{9}{12}$ $-\frac{7}{12}$   11.  $\frac{1}{5}$ $+\frac{3}{5}$   12.  $\frac{6}{8}$ $-\frac{3}{8}$   13.  $\frac{2}{6}$ $+\frac{2}{6}$   14.  $\frac{4}{4}$ $-\frac{1}{4}$

15. $\frac{1}{8} + \frac{3}{8}$       16. $\frac{8}{8} - \frac{2}{8}$       17. $\frac{7}{12} + \frac{3}{12}$       18. $\frac{5}{6} - \frac{1}{6}$

19. $\frac{2}{3} + \frac{1}{3}$       20. $\frac{9}{12} - \frac{3}{12}$       21. $\frac{1}{2} - \frac{1}{2}$       22. $\frac{3}{10} + \frac{2}{10}$

23. $\frac{4}{5} - \frac{1}{5}$       24. $\frac{5}{6} - \frac{4}{6}$       25. $\frac{5}{12} + \frac{2}{12}$       26. $\frac{7}{10} - \frac{4}{10}$

**Solve each problem.**

1. You need $1\frac{1}{2}$ gallons of paint to paint a room. You have $\frac{3}{4}$ of a gallon. Do you have enough paint? Why or why not?

2. You started painting at 1:00 and finished the first wall at 1:45. What fraction of an hour did you spend on the first wall?

3. Your friend is making curtains for an art room. He needs $\frac{3}{5}$ of a yard of red and $\frac{2}{5}$ of a yard of blue fabric. How much fabric does he need in all?

4. You spent $\frac{1}{2}$ of $10 at the paint shop. Your friend spent $\frac{3}{4}$ of his $12. Who spent more?

**Use the map on page 314 to answer each question.**

1. What time is it in Texas?

2. What time is it in North Carolina?

3. If it is 6:00 P.M. in Colorado, what time is it in Kansas?

4. If it is 7:00 P.M. in Georgia, what time is it in Alabama?

5. Suppose you arrive in Arizona at 10:00 A.M., after a 6-hour flight from New York. What time did you leave New York?

6. Your cousin left Minnesota at 2:00 P.M. and arrived in Nevada at 5:00 P.M. How long was her flight?

**Write the sum. Use fraction models to help you.**

1. $\frac{2}{12}$ $+\frac{5}{6}$    2. $\frac{3}{8}$ $+\frac{1}{4}$    3. $\frac{2}{8}$ $+\frac{1}{2}$    4. $\frac{1}{10}$ $+\frac{1}{5}$    5. $\frac{2}{3}$ $+\frac{1}{12}$    6. $\frac{5}{10}$ $+\frac{1}{2}$    7. $\frac{1}{3}$ $+\frac{1}{12}$

8. $\frac{1}{12}$ $+\frac{2}{3}$    9. $\frac{3}{8}$ $+\frac{1}{2}$    10. $\frac{8}{10}$ $+\frac{1}{5}$    11. $\frac{3}{4}$ $+\frac{1}{12}$    12. $\frac{2}{8}$ $+\frac{1}{2}$    13. $\frac{3}{10}$ $+\frac{3}{5}$    14. $\frac{3}{8}$ $+\frac{2}{4}$

15. $\frac{1}{2} + \frac{1}{4}$    16. $\frac{3}{10} + \frac{2}{5}$    17. $\frac{5}{8} + \frac{1}{4}$    18. $\frac{1}{6} + \frac{5}{12}$

19. $\frac{5}{12} + \frac{1}{3}$    20. $\frac{7}{10} + \frac{1}{5}$    21. $\frac{1}{2} + \frac{1}{12}$    22. $\frac{1}{3} + \frac{1}{6}$

23. $\frac{2}{3} + \frac{1}{6}$    24. $\frac{7}{12} + \frac{1}{3}$    25. $\frac{1}{5} + \frac{3}{10}$    26. $\frac{2}{6} + \frac{2}{3}$

27. $\frac{1}{2} + \frac{3}{12}$    28. $\frac{2}{5} + \frac{1}{10}$    29. $\frac{3}{8} + \frac{1}{2}$    30. $\frac{1}{4} + \frac{1}{12}$

**Find the difference. Use fraction models to help you.**

1. $\frac{4}{8}$ $-\frac{4}{8}$    2. $\frac{10}{10}$ $-\frac{1}{10}$    3. $\frac{8}{12}$ $-\frac{1}{6}$    4. $\frac{4}{5}$ $-\frac{1}{10}$    5. $\frac{3}{10}$ $-\frac{1}{5}$    6. $\frac{1}{2}$ $-\frac{3}{8}$    7. $\frac{7}{8}$ $-\frac{1}{2}$

8. $\frac{3}{4}$ $-\frac{1}{12}$    9. $\frac{4}{5}$ $-\frac{3}{5}$    10. $\frac{5}{8}$ $-\frac{1}{4}$    11. $\frac{3}{5}$ $-\frac{3}{10}$    12. $\frac{3}{8}$ $-\frac{1}{5}$    13. $\frac{3}{8}$ $-\frac{1}{4}$    14. $\frac{3}{4}$ $-\frac{3}{8}$

15. $\frac{7}{8} - \frac{3}{4}$    16. $\frac{1}{2} - \frac{1}{4}$    17. $\frac{3}{4} - \frac{4}{12}$    18. $\frac{1}{3} - \frac{3}{12}$

19. $\frac{4}{6} - \frac{1}{3}$    20. $\frac{3}{8} - \frac{1}{4}$    21. $\frac{9}{10} - \frac{2}{5}$    22. $\frac{6}{8} - \frac{1}{4}$

23. $\frac{1}{6} - \frac{1}{12}$    24. $\frac{1}{2} - \frac{3}{6}$    25. $\frac{2}{3} - \frac{7}{12}$    26. $\frac{2}{3} - \frac{2}{6}$

**Use with pages 322–323.** ••••••••••••••••••••••••••••••••••

**Write the answer.**

1. $6\frac{1}{3}$
$+ 1\frac{1}{3}$

2. $3\frac{2}{8}$
$+ \frac{2}{8}$

3. $7\frac{1}{2}$
$- 6$

4. $6$
$+ \frac{3}{8}$

5. $3\frac{1}{8}$
$- 2\frac{1}{8}$

6. $2\frac{3}{12}$
$+ 4\frac{6}{12}$

7. $1\frac{7}{8}$
$- \frac{1}{3}$

8. $3\frac{2}{5}$
$- 3\frac{2}{5}$

9. $4\frac{9}{12}$
$- 1\frac{1}{12}$

10. $5\frac{5}{8}$
$- 3\frac{1}{8}$

11. $1\frac{1}{4} + 2$

12. $3\frac{3}{4} - 2\frac{3}{4}$

13. $1\frac{7}{8} - \frac{3}{8}$

14. $2\frac{2}{10} + \frac{1}{10}$

15. $7\frac{1}{3} + 2$

16. $4\frac{3}{12} + 3\frac{1}{12}$

17. $9\frac{2}{10} - 2\frac{1}{10}$

18. $8\frac{5}{6} - \frac{1}{6}$

19. $1\frac{6}{8} - 1\frac{6}{8}$

20. $3\frac{6}{12} + 2\frac{1}{12}$

21. $1\frac{8}{12} - 1\frac{3}{12}$

22. $7\frac{5}{6} - \frac{1}{6}$

**Use with pages 338–339.** ••••••••••••••••••••••••••••••••

**Measure the length to the nearest quarter inch.**

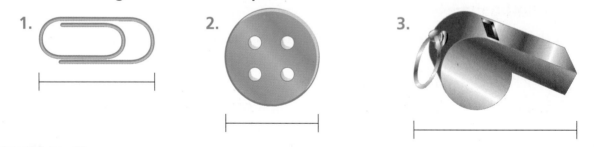

1.    2.    3.

**Use with pages 340–341.** ••••••••••••••••••••••••••••••••

**Which unit would you use to measure each item? Write *foot*, *yard*, or *mile*.**

1. height of a table

2. width of a garden

3. distance across a parking lot

4. distance to Cuba

5. length of a driveway

6. depth of a pool

7. distance of a marathon

8. height of a fire escape

9. distance around a car

10. mail carrier's route

11. distance you can throw a ball

12. width of a checkers board

**Use with pages 342–343.** • • • • • • • • • • • • • • • • • • • • • • • • • • • • • • •

**Find the perimeter.**

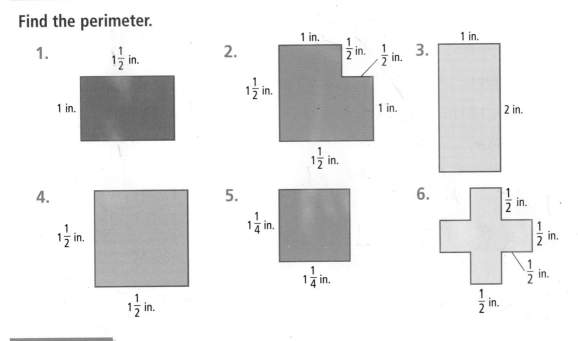

1. $1\frac{1}{2}$ in.  1 in.

2. 1 in.  $\frac{1}{2}$ in.  $\frac{1}{2}$ in.  $1\frac{1}{2}$ in.  1 in.  $1\frac{1}{2}$ in.

3. 1 in.  2 in.

4. $1\frac{1}{2}$ in.  $1\frac{1}{2}$ in.

5. $1\frac{1}{4}$ in.  $1\frac{1}{4}$ in.

6. $\frac{1}{2}$ in.  $\frac{1}{2}$ in.  $\frac{1}{2}$ in.  $\frac{1}{2}$ in.

**Set 10.6**   **Use with pages 348–349.** • • • • • • • • • • • • • • • • • • • • • • • • • • • • •

**Make each statement true. Write >, <, or =.**

1. 1 half-gallon ● 4 cups
2. 1 gallon ● 3 quarts
3. 3 quarts ● 8 pints
4. 2 quarts ● 1 half gallon
5. 16 cups ● 1 gallon
6. 4 cups ● 1 pint
7. 3 gallons ● 14 quarts
8. 5 pints ● 18 cups
9. 32 fl oz ● 2 pints
10. 2 cups ● 12 fl oz
11. 3 gallons ● 25 pints
12. 32 fl oz ● 3 cups
13. 4 quarts ● 128 fl oz
14. 6 pints ● 1 half gallon
15. 16 cups ● 4 quarts
16. 128 fl oz ● 1 half gallon

**Set 10.7**   **Use with page 350.** • • • • • • • • • • • • • • • • • • • • • • • • • • • • • • •

**Make each statement true. Write >, <, or =.**

1. 2 lb ● 36 oz
2. 2 T ● 3600 lb
3. 50 oz ● 5 lb
4. 4000 lb ● 2 T
5. 64 oz ● 4 lb
6. 10 lb ● 160 oz
7. 14 oz ● 1 lb
8. 25 oz ● 3 lb
9. 4 T ● 6000 lb

Measure the length to the nearest centimeter.

1. ⊢————————⊣    2. ⊢————————————⊣    3. ⊢——⊣

Write in millimeters.

4. 6 cm    5. 14 cm    6. 2 cm    7. 7 cm    8. 12 cm    9. 10 cm    10. 8 cm

Find the perimeter.

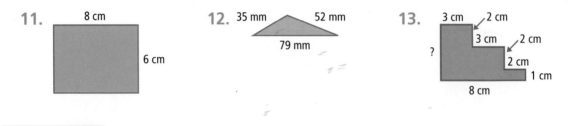

11.    8 cm    12. 35 mm ╱╲ 52 mm    13.    3 cm ╱ 2 cm
       6 cm        79 mm                   3 cm ╱ 2 cm
                                        ?          2 cm
                                                      1 cm
                                              8 cm

Copy and complete. Make a table or use mental math.

1. 3 dm = ■ cm        2. 4000 m = ■ km        3. 700 cm = ■ m

4. 400 cm = ■ m       5. 20 cm = ■ dm         6. 6 km = ■ m

Choose the better estimate.

7. the width of your thumbnail        a. 1 mm        b. 10 mm

8. the height of a paper cup          a. 1 dm        b. 10 dm

9. the length of a paper clip         a. 3 mm        b. 30 mm

10. the height of a giraffe           a. 5 m         b. 50 m

Choose the unit you would use to measure the capacity of each item.

1. a vitamin bottle              a. liters        b. milliliters

2. a baby's spoon                a. liters        b. milliliters

3. a washing machine             a. liters        b. milliliters

4. a bottle of cough medicine    a. liters        b. milliliters

**Set 10.11**   Use with page 360.

**Copy and complete. Make a table or use mental math.**

1. 3kg = ■ g           2. 7000 g = ■ kg           3. ■ kg = 500 g

**Choose the better estimate.**

4. the mass of a nickel
   a. 50 g           b. 5 kg

5. the mass of a baseball bat
   a. 1 kg           b. 1 g

6. the mass of a basketball
   a. 6 g            b. 600 g

7. the mass of a polar bear
   a. 30 kg          b. 300 kg

**Set 10.13**   Use with pages 362–363.

**Write the temperature.**

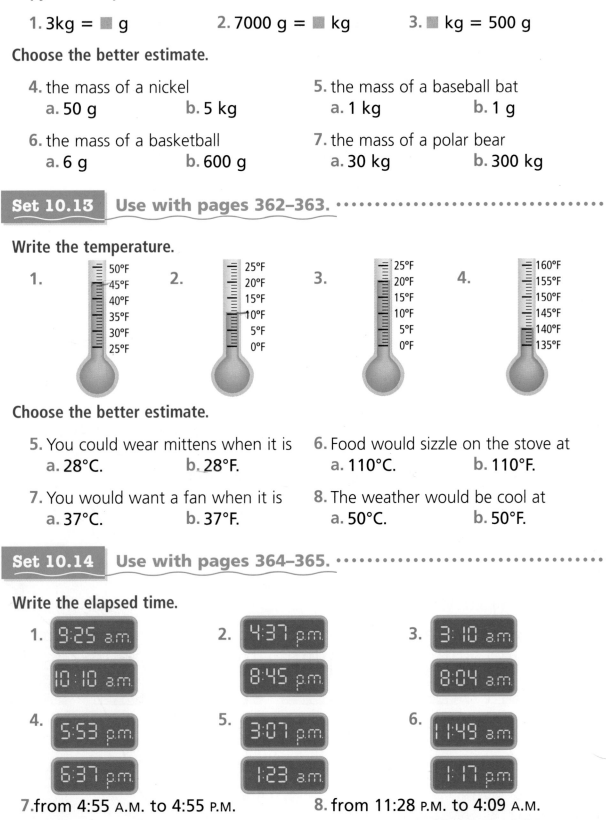

1.   2.   3.   4.

**Choose the better estimate.**

5. You could wear mittens when it is
   a. 28°C.          b. 28°F.

6. Food would sizzle on the stove at
   a. 110°C.         b. 110°F.

7. You would want a fan when it is
   a. 37°C.          b. 37°F.

8. The weather would be cool at
   a. 50°C.          b. 50°F.

**Set 10.14**   Use with pages 364–365.

**Write the elapsed time.**

1. 9:25 a.m.
   10:10 a.m.

2. 4:37 p.m.
   8:45 p.m.

3. 3:10 a.m.
   8:04 a.m.

4. 5:53 p.m.
   6:37 p.m.

5. 3:07 p.m.
   1:23 a.m.

6. 11:49 a.m.
   1:17 p.m.

7. from 4:55 A.M. to 4:55 P.M.

8. from 11:28 P.M. to 4:09 A.M.

**Write the decimal.**

1. three tenths

2. two and nine tenths

3. seven hundredths

4. nine tenths

5. five and two tenths

6. four and six hundredths

**What does the underlined digit stand for?**

7. 21.<u>4</u>

8. 0.1<u>2</u>

9. <u>5</u>.2

10. <u>4</u>0.8

11. 13.6<u>4</u>

12. 18.<u>6</u>

13. <u>6</u>8.3

14. 3.2<u>5</u>

15. 19.0<u>8</u>

16. 4<u>6</u>.9

**Write in words.**

17. 0.4

18. 7.03

19. 20.2

20. 0.53

21. 14.6

22. 20.01

23. 0.7

24. 0.29

25. 8.15

26. 9.6

**Write the decimal.**

27. $\frac{9}{100}$

28. two and eleven hundredths

29. $21\frac{17}{100}$

30. $39\frac{4}{10}$

31. $18\frac{16}{100}$

32. $\frac{37}{100}$

33. $5\frac{2}{10}$

34. $40\frac{8}{100}$

35. nine and ninety-nine hundredths

36. one and forty hundredths

37. four and twelve hundredths

38. six tenths

**Copy and complete. Write >, <, or =.**

1.

2.

3.

4. 7.76 ● 7.80

5. 63.42 ● 63.24

6. $14.05 ● $14.50

7. 4.4 ● 4.40

8. $.70 ● $.70

9. 0.6 ● 0.59

**Write the numbers in order from least to greatest.**

1. 3.02; 3.20; 3.0

2. $57.23; $57.13; $57.20

3. 9.5; 9.89; 9.7

4. 26.5; 25.98; 26.01; 26

5. 40.8; 40.56; 40.09; 40.3

6. 14.8; 13.9; 14; 14.6

7. $32.05; $32.01; $32.10

8. 22.12; 22.06; 22.16; 21.99

9. 0.96; 0.87; 0.69; 0.78

10. $66.53; $65.89; $66.98; $66.82

11. 7.19; 7.04; 7.14; 7; 7.21

**Round to the nearest whole number. Draw a number line to help you.**

1. 6.3     2. 8.6     3. 4.2     4. 2.9     5. 2.7

6. $4.12     7. $3.66     8. $1.10     9. $6.98     10. $4.49

**Use rounding to estimate. Draw a number line to help you.**

11. 4.9 − 1.9     12. 8.48 + 9.16     13. 4.46 + 1.29     14. 7.7 − 2.4

15. $9.12 + $9.85     16. $4.22 − $1.88     17. $8.86 + $4.19     18. $6.35 − $4.13

**Find the sum.**

1.  
0.23  
0.7  
+ 6.2

2.  
68.57  
0.47  
+ 85.76

3.  
0.5  
+ 7.7

4.  
0.45 mi  
+ 0.4 mi

5.  
1  
0.69  
+ 1.8

6. 0.6 + 0.52 + 6.57     7. $36.36 + $2.30     8. 0.28 + 5.1

9. $7.28 + $.41     10. 61.6 + 0.3

11. 2.4 cm + 5.2 cm     12. $88 + $.08

13. 7.7 in. + 71.4 in. + 5.6 in.     14. 0.75 + 0.52 + 0.4

15.  
0  
0.2  
+ 5.2

16.  
$.55  
+ .20

17.  
0.89  
0.03  
+ 0.87

18.  
0.4  
0.2  
+ 7.6

19.  
8.77  
+ 0.4

**Use with pages 398–399.** •••••••••••••••••••••••••••••••••••••••••

**Find the difference.**

| 1. | 0.3 | 2. | 0.53 m | 3. | 0.6 | 4. | 6.4 | 5. | $47.60 |
|---|---|---|---|---|---|---|---|---|---|
| | − 0 | | − 0.47 m | | − 0.53 | | − 3.6 | | − 6.00 |

6. 5 − 0.79          7. 3.32 − 0.5          8. 9.3 mL − 8 mL

9. 6.5 − 6          10. 69.3 − 0.22          11. 52.7 − 0.29

12. $99.92 − $72          13. 7.48 − 0          14. 0.18 − 0.1

| 15. | 7.07 | 16. | 2.4 | 17. | 8.7 km | 18. | 0.2 | 19. | 3.5 |
|---|---|---|---|---|---|---|---|---|---|
| | − 0.97 | | − 0.13 | | − 6.37 km | | − 0.15 | | − 3.1 |

**Use with pages 400–401.** ••••••••••••••••••••••••••••••••••••••••

**Estimate. Use any method you wish.**

| 1. | $8.12 | 2. | $7.98 | 3. | $4.21 | 4. | $8.18 |
|---|---|---|---|---|---|---|---|
| | 2.03 | | 5.18 | | 6.18 | | 4.02 |
| | + 2.10 | | + 5.20 | | + 6.81 | | + 2.12 |

| 5. | $9.45 | 6. | $3.80 | 7. | $7.14 | 8. | $6.36 |
|---|---|---|---|---|---|---|---|
| | 1.27 | | 5.65 | | 2.20 | | 4.72 |
| | 2.23 | | 3.42 | | 4.79 | | 2.69 |
| | + 4.51 | | + 1.23 | | + 1.81 | | + 2.28 |

**Use with pages 414–415.** ••••••••••••••••••••••••••••••••••••••••

**Use mental math. Write the answer.**

1. 5 × 30          2. 7 × 70          3. 4 × 20          4. 8 × 50

5. 30 × 60          6. 40 × 90          7. 20 × 80          8. 60 × 70

9. 50 × 400          10. 70 × 500          11. 30 × 900          12. 80 × 300

13. 20 × 5000          14. 40 × 2000          15. 50 × 6000          16. 70 × 4000

17. 500 + 800          18. 300 + 400          19. 700 + 700          20. 200 + 900

**Estimate. Use any method you wish.**

| 1.   73 | 2.   88 | 3.   47 | 4.   31 | 5.   29 |
|---|---|---|---|---|
| × 21 | × 32 | × 48 | × 63 | × 19 |

| 6.   498 | 7.   706 | 8.   382 | 9.   417 | 10.   288 |
|---|---|---|---|---|
| ×   9 | ×   4 | ×   5 | ×   3 | ×   7 |

| 11.  $1.96 | 12.  $3.05 | 13.  $8.94 | 14.  $2.79 | 15.  $4.21 |
|---|---|---|---|---|
| ×   29 | ×   41 | ×   32 | ×   58 | ×   63 |

**Find the product.**

| 1.   79 | 2.   31 | 3.   13 | 4.   17 | 5.   21 |
|---|---|---|---|---|
| × 50 | × 90 | × 70 | × 90 | × 20 |

| 6.   191 | 7.   170 | 8.   156 | 9.   841 | 10.   496 |
|---|---|---|---|---|
| ×  80 | ×  80 | ×  30 | ×  70 | ×  10 |

11. 40 × 30             12. 60 × 78             13. 80 × 851

14. 80 × 804            15. 40 × 142            16. 90 × 225

**Write the product. Use an array diagram to help you multiply.**

| 1.   87 | 2.   85 | 3.   64 | 4.   22 | 5.   94 | 6.   32 |
|---|---|---|---|---|---|
| × 93 | × 74 | × 77 | × 41 | × 99 | × 64 |

7. 63 × 68             8. 36 × 27             9. 66 × 63

10. 17 × 29            11. 68 × 36            12. 37 × 31

| 13.   52 | 14.   97 | 15.   21 | 16.   45 | 17.   82 | 18.   63 |
|---|---|---|---|---|---|
| × 67 | × 85 | × 69 | × 17 | × 18 | × 42 |

**Find the product.**

1. 81
   × 92

2. 35
   × 69

3. 11 pt
   × 53

4. 11
   × 34

5. 94
   × 79

6. 24 in.
   × 52

7. 13 × 79

8. 82 × 45

9. 23 × 81 lb

10. 54 × 47

11. 69 × 77

12. 56 × 11

13. 42 m
    × 11

14. 89
    × 65

15. 69
    × 35

16. 51
    × 95

17. 87
    × 42

18. 21
    × 76

**Set 12.8**  Use with pages 430–431. • • • • • • • • • • • • • • • • • • • • • • • • • • •

**Find the product.**

1. 144
   × 11

2. 582
   × 71

3. 138
   × 59

4. 954 yd
   × 89

5. 182
   × 31

6. 64 × 651 yd

7. 14 × 239

8. 86 × 923 oz

9. 44 × 725

10. 11 × 804

11. 14 × 855

12. 387
    × 38

13. 383
    × 64

14. 805
    × 36

15. 362
    × 97

16. 415
    × 11

**Set 12.9**  Use with pages 432–433. • • • • • • • • • • • • • • • • • • • • • • • • • • •

**Find the product.**

1. $ .11
   × 53

2. $ .81
   × 95

3. $ .16
   × 44

4. $ .42
   × 44

5. $ .98
   × 43

6. 67 × $.89

7. 66 × $.55

8. 29 × $.44

9. 79 × $6.24

10. 25 × $1.51

11. 69 × $5.51

12. $1.81
    × 38

13. $8.57
    × 75

14. $7.96
    × 41

15. $6.97
    × 68

16. $9.71
    × 44

**Write the product.**

1. 87 × 3 × 89
2. 5 × 85 × 29
3. 81 × 12 × 7
4. 42 × 37 × 2
5. 49 × 8 × 78
6. 6 × 22 × 67
7. 2 × 38 × 22
8. 83 × 45 × 3
9. 14 × 8 × 88
10. 6 × 41 × 17
11. 27 × 7 × 95
12. 74 × 1 × 44
13. 28 × 59 × 5
14. 6 × 91 × 38
15. 38 × 36 × 3
16. 92 × 7 × 26
17. 79 × 28 × 6
18. 6 × 84 × 14
19. 68 × 8 × 17
20. 67 × 6 × 11
21. 7 × 25 × 32

**Write the letter of the correct quotient.**

1. 400 ÷ 80    a. 5    b. 50    c. 500
2. 1600 ÷ 4    a. 4    b. 40    c. 400
3. 3600 ÷ 90    a. 4    b. 40    c. 400
4. 6400 ÷ 80    a. 8    b. 80    c. 800

**Write the quotient. Use mental math.**

5. 800 ÷ 40
6. 280 ÷ 70
7. 200 ÷ 50
8. 360 ÷ 4
9. 1800 ÷ 3
10. 7200 ÷ 80
11. 2500 ÷ 50
12. 5400 ÷ 60
13. 6300 ÷ 700
14. 2400 ÷ 4
15. 8100 ÷ 9
16. 4900 ÷ 700
17. 3600 ÷ 600
18. 3000 ÷ 5
19. 4200 ÷ 60

**Write the missing factor. Use mental math.**

20. 30 × ■ = 210
21. ■ × 60 = 2400
22. 500 × ■ = 1500
23. ■ × 40 = 2000
24. 60 × ■ = 1200
25. 900 × ■ = 2700
26. 30 × ■ = 2100
27. ■ × 5 = 500
28. ■ × 3 = 900

**Set 13.2** Use with pages 448–449. •••••••••••••••••••••••••••••••••••

Estimate the quotient. Write the two multiples of 10 the estimate is between.

1. 32)1682
2. 38)792
3. 67)4934
4. 44)600

5. 790 ÷ 22
6. 5243 ÷ 66
7. 2043 ÷ 25
8. 2578 ÷ 42

9. 23)790
10. 19)534
11. 21)930
12. 63)3276

**Set 13.4** Use with pages 452–453. •••••••••••••••••••••••••••••••••••

Divide.

1. 51)98
2. 15)80
3. 17)42
4. 27)45
5. 14)52

6. 65 ÷ 13
7. 81 ÷ 11
8. 66 ÷ 32

9. 78)488
10. 14)126
11. 98)686
12. 93)129
13. 53)109

**Set 13.5** Use with pages 454–455. •••••••••••••••••••••••••••••••••••

Divide.

1. 47)517
2. 11)808
3. 49)751
4. 49)659
5. 14)266

6. 45)718
7. 22)601
8. 49)703
9. 16)730
10. 72)792

11. 753 ÷ 24
12. 292 ÷ 16
13. 396 ÷ 12

14. 778 ÷ 62
15. 763 ÷ 22
16. 990 ÷ 45

**Set 13.7** Use with pages 460–461. •••••••••••••••••••••••••••••••••••

Divide.

1. 26)66
2. 27)80
3. 25)75
4. 15)51

5. 83 ÷ 59
6. 84 ÷ 21
7. 70 ÷ 11

8. 37)255
9. 85)425
10. 77)154
11. 93)129

# Table of Measures

The charts on this page show common measures. Check the glossary and index to find out more about each measure.

## Customary Measures

**Length**
1 foot (ft) = 12 inches (in.)
1 yard (yd) = 3 feet
1 yard = 36 inches
1 mile (mi) = 5280 feet
1 mile = 1760 yards

**Liquid**
1 cup (c) = 8 fluid ounces (fl oz)
1 pint (pt) = 2 cups
1 quart (qt) = 2 pints
1 gallon (gal) = 4 quarts

**Weight**
1 pound (lb) = 16 ounces (oz)
1 ton (T) = 2000 pounds

## Metric Measures

**Length**
1 centimeter (cm) = 10 millimeters (mm)
1 decimeter (dm) = 10 centimeters
1 meter (m) = 10 decimeters
1 meter = 100 centimeters
1 kilometer (km) = 1000 meters

**Liquid**
1 liter (L) = 1000 milliliters (mL)

**Mass**
1 kilogram (kg) = 1000 grams (g)

## Time

**Time**
1 minute (min) = 60 seconds (s)
1 hour (h) = 60 minutes
1 day (d) = 24 hours
1 week (wk) = 7 days
1 year (yr) = 12 months (mo)
1 year = 52 weeks

# Glossary

**addend** A number added.
Example: $5 + 9 = 14$

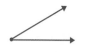

addends

**adjusted estimation** When estimating with digits in the greatest place does not help solve the problem, then look at digits in the next place.

**A.M.** The hours from 12:00 midnight to 12:00 noon.

**angle** A figure that is formed when two lines, or rays, meet.

**area** A measure of how much surface is covered by a figure.

**array** An arrangement of objects in equal rows.

**array diagram** A simpler way to show an array.

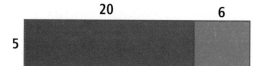

**average** The quotient found by dividing the sum of a group of numbers by the number of addends.
Example: The average of 2, 4, 1, 5 is $12 \div 4$, or 3.

**bar graph** A graph using bars of different lengths to show and compare information.

**capacity** The amount a container can hold.

**Celcius** The metric temperature scale.

**centimeter (cm)** A metric unit of length; 100 centimeters equals 1 meter.

**centimeter ruler** A ruler marked in centimeters.

**circle** A closed figure in which every point is the same distance from the center.

**circle graph** A graph that shows a total amount divided into parts.

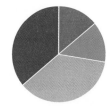

**closed figure** A figure with an inside and an outside.

**common factor** A number that is a factor of two or more numbers.
Example: 1, 2, 3, 6 are common factors of 18 and 24.

**common multiple** A number that is a multiple of two or more numbers.
Example: 6, 12, 24, 30 are common multiples of 2 and 3.

**compatible numbers** Numbers that are easy to work with and divide easily.
Example: 3 and 12 are compatible numbers.

**cone** A solid that has a circular base and comes to a point.

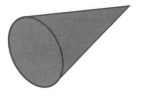

**congruent** Having the same size and shape.

**congruent figures** Figures that are the same size and shape.

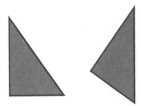

**cube** A solid that has 6 square faces the same size.

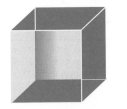

**cup (c)** A customary unit of capacity; 2 cups equal 1 pint.

**customary system** The measurement system that uses foot, quart, pound, and degrees Fahrenheit.

**cylinder** A solid that has parallel, congruent circular bases.

············· **D** ·············

**data** Information or facts.

**day** A 24-hour period.

**decimal** A number with one or more digits to the right of a decimal point.
Example:   1.4   2.03   0.569

**decimal point (.)** A symbol used to separate dollars and cents in money amounts; a symbol used to separate ones and tenths in decimals.
Example:   $1.50 3.2

⬆ ⬆

decimal points

**decimeter (dm)** A metric unit of length; 1 decimeter equals 10 centimeters.

**degree (°)** A unit for measuring temperature.

517

**degree Celsius (°C)** The metric unit for measuring temperature.

**degree Fahrenheit (°F)** The customary unit for measuring temperature.

**denominator** The number written below the bar in a fraction.

Example: $\frac{1}{4}$ ⟵ denominator

**diameter** A line of symmetry of a circle.

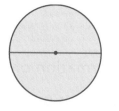

**difference** The answer in a subtraction problem.
Example: $12 - 5 = 7$

difference

**digit** Any one of the ten number symbols 0, 1, 2, 3, 4, 5, 6, 7, 8, or 9.

**dividend** The number that is divided in a division problem.
Example: $36 \div 9 = 4$

dividend

**divisor** The number by which the dividend is divided in a division problem.
Example: $36 \div 9 = 4$

divisor

**divisible** When a number is capable of being divided into equal parts without a remainder.

**dollar sign ($)** A symbol written before a number to show dollars in money amounts.
Example: $1.50

dollar sign

········· **E** ·········

**edge** The segment where two faces of a solid figure meet.

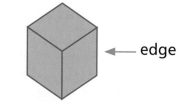
edge

**elapsed time** Time that has gone by.

**endpoint** The point at the end of a line segment.
Example:

endpoints

**equivalent fractions** Two or more fractions that name the same amount.

Example: $\frac{6}{8}$ and $\frac{3}{4}$ are equivalent fractions.

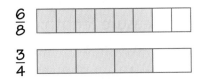

**equivalent measures** Measures that have the same amount.
Example: 42 inches = 3 feet 6 inches = $3\frac{1}{2}$ feet

**estimate** A number close to an exact amount. An estimate tells about how much.

**even number** A whole number that is a multiple of 2. Even numbers end in 0, 2, 4, 6, or 8. The numbers 56 and 48 are even.

**expanded form** A number written as the sum of the values of the digits.
Example: The number 2469 can be written as 2000 + 400 + 60 + 9 (number form) or 2 thousands + 4 hundreds + 6 tens + 9 ones (short word form).

·············· **F** ··············

**face** A flat surface of a solid.

face

**factors** The numbers used in a multiplication problem.

Example: $2 \times 9 = 18$

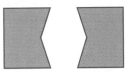

factors

**Fahrenheit** The customary temperature scale.

**flip** A move that makes a figure face in the opposite direction.

**fluid ounce (fl oz)** The basic unit for measuring liquid capacity; 16 fluid ounces equal 1 pint.

**foot (ft)** A customary unit of length; 1 foot equals 12 inches.

**fraction** A number that names a part of a whole or a part of a group.

Examples: $\frac{1}{2}$  $\frac{1}{3}$  $\frac{3}{4}$

**front-end estimation** An estimate made by looking at the digits in the greatest place value to find about how much.

·············· **G** ··············

**gallon (gal)** A customary unit of capacity; 1 gallon equals 4 quarts

**gram (g)** A metric unit of mass (weight).

**grid** Line segments that crisscross to form evenly space squares.

**grouping property of addition** When the grouping of addends is changed, the sum remains the same.
Example:  (2 + 4) + 6 = 12
           2 + (4 + 6) = 12

**grouping property of multiplication** When the grouping of factors is changed, the product remains the same.
Example:  (1 × 2) × 5 = 10
           1 × (2 × 5) = 10

**half inch** The halfway point of an inch.

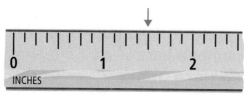

**half turn** A turn that causes a figure to point in a different direction.

**hexagon** A polygon with 6 sides.

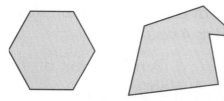

**hour** A unit of time; 1 hour equals 60 minutes.

**inch (in.)** A customary unit used to measure length; 12 inches equal 1 foot.

**inch ruler** A measuring tool marked in inches.

**kilogram (kg)** A metric unit of mass (weight); 1 kilogram equals 1000 grams.

**kilometer (km)** A metric unit of length; 1 kilometer equals 1000 meters.

**line** A path that goes on and on in both directions.

**line graph** A graph that uses a line to show changes over a period of time.

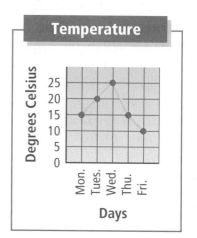

**line of symmetry** A line that divides a figure into two matching parts.

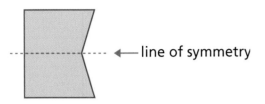
← line of symmetry

**line plot** A diagram showing data on a number line.

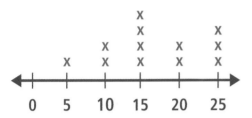

**line segment** Part of a line having two endpoints.

A |————————————| B

**liter (L)** The metric unit of capacity; 1 liter equals 1000 milliliters.

**mass** The amount of matter in an object.

**mean** The average of a set of numbers, found by adding numbers in the set and dividing by the number of addends.

**median** The number that falls exactly in the middle when a set of numbers is arranged in order from least to greatest.

**meter (m)** A metric unit of length; 1 meter equals 100 centimeters.

**metric system** The measurement system that uses meter, liter, gram, and degrees Celsius.

**mile (mi)** A customary unit of length; 1 mile equals 5280 feet.

**milliliter (mL)** A metric unit of capacity; 1000 milliliters equal 1 liter.

**millimeter (mm)** A metric unit of length; 10 millimeters equal 1 centimeter.

**million** 1000 thousands or 10 hundred thousands; the number after 999,999 is one million (1,000,000).

**minute (min)** A unit of time; 60 seconds equal 1 minute.

**mixed number** A number that has a whole number part and a fraction part.
Example: $2\frac{1}{6}$

**multiple** A product of two whole numbers.
Example:  $4 \times 2 = 8$
The number 8 is a multiple of 4 and of 2.

**multiplication property of one** If any factor is multiplied by one, the product is the same as that factor.
Example:
$4 \times 1 = 4$  $1 \times 51 = 51$

**multiplication property of zero** If any factor is multiplied by zero, the product is zero.
Examples: $7 \times 0 = 0$
$0 \times 238 = 0$

**net** A flat pattern that folds into a solid.

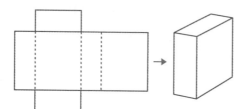

**numerator** The number written above the bar in a fraction.

Example: $\frac{1}{6}$ ← numerator

**odd number** A whole number that is not a multiple of 2. Odd numbers end in 1, 3, 5, 7, or 9. The numbers 67 and 493 are odd numbers.

**one hundredth** One of 100 equal parts; $\frac{1}{100}$ or 0.01.

**one tenth** One of 10 equal parts; $\frac{1}{10}$ or 0.10.

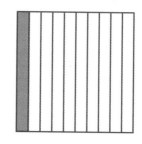

**ordered pair** A pair of numbers or letters that names a point on a grid.

**order property of addition** When the order of two addends is changed, the sum remains the same.
Examples:
$4 + 1 = 5$  $62 + 34 = 96$
$1 + 4 = 5$  $34 + 62 = 96$

**order property of multiplication** When the order of the factors is changed, the product remains the same.
Examples:
$3 \times 5 = 15$  $2 \times 117 = 234$
$5 \times 3 = 15$  $117 \times 2 = 234$

**ounce (oz)** A customary measure of weight; 16 ounces equal 1 pound.

**parallel lines** Lines that are always the same distance apart.

**parentheses ( )** Used in number sentences to show what part of a problem to solve first.

**pentagon** A polygon with 5 sides.
Examples:

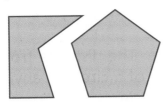

**perimeter** The distance around a figure. The perimeter of this rectangle is 12 cm.

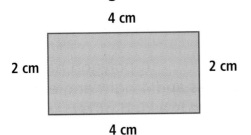

**perpendicular** When two lines or line segments cross to form right angles.

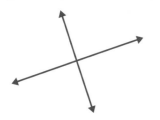

**pictograph** A graph that uses pictures to stand for data.

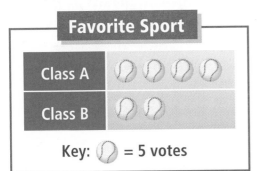

**pint (pt)** A customary unit of capacity; 2 pints equal 1 quart.

**place value** The value of a position in a number.
Example: In 7943, the digit 7 is in the thousands place.

| Thousands | Hundreds | Tens | Ones |
|-----------|----------|------|------|
| 7 | 9 | 4 | 3 |

**P.M.** The hours from 12:00 noon to 12:00 midnight.

**point** An exact place or position in space, represented by a dot.

**polygon** A closed figure made up of line segments with three or more sides.

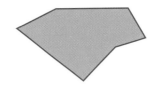

**pound (lb)** A customary unit of weight; 1 pound equals 16 ounces.

**prediction** Something that is guessed in advance, based on previous experience.

**prism** A figure that is named for the shape of its two parallel bases.

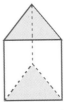

**probability** The chance that an event will occur.

**product** The answer in a multiplication problem.
Example: $5 \times 3 = 15$

product

**pyramid** A solid having a polygon for a base with all other faces triangular and sharing a common vertex.

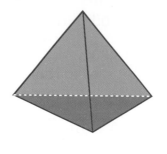

**quadrilateral** A four-sided figure.

**quart (qt)** A customary unit of capacity; 4 quarts equal 1 gallon.

**quarter** Name for 25¢, one fourth, or $\frac{1}{4}$.

**quarter inch** One fourth of an inch.

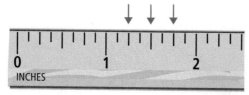

**quotient** The answer in a division problem.
Example: $36 \div 9 = 4$

quotient

**radius** The distance from the center of a circle to any point on a circle.

6 cm

**rectangle** A polygon having 4 sides and 4 right angles. A square is a kind of rectangle.

**rectangular array** An arrangement of objects in equal rows.
Example: $3 \times 14$

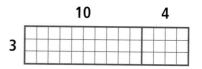

**rectangular prism** A prism having 6 rectangular faces.

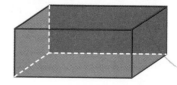

524

**remainder** The number left over in a division problem when the dividend is not divisible by the divisor. Example:

$$9\overline{)38} \quad 4\ R2$$

**right angle** A quarter turn.

**Roman numerals** Symbols used for numbers by the Roman people long ago. I, V, X, L, D, C, and M are Roman numerals.

**rounded number** A number expressed to the nearest ten, hundred, thousand, and so on. 436 rounded to the nearest ten is 440.

···········  Ⓢ  ···········

**second** A unit of time; 60 seconds equal 1 minute.

**side** A line segment forming part of a figure.

**similar figures** Figures that have the same shape but not necessarily the same size.

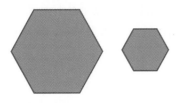

**simplest form** A fraction whose numerator and denominator have no common factor greater than 1. Example: $\frac{2}{3}$ is the simplest form of $\frac{8}{12}$.

**slide** A motion in which every point of a figure moves the same distance in the same direction.

**slide arrow** An arrow that shows the distance and direction to slide a figure.

**solid** A figure in space that is named by its shape.

**sphere** A solid having the shape of a ball.

**square** A polygon with 4 right angles and 4 equal sides.

**square centimeter (sq cm)** A metric unit used to measure area.

**square inch (sq in.)** A customary unit used to measure area.

**standard form** The usual, or common, way of writing a number, using digits.
Example: The standard form of twenty-seven is 27.

**sum** The answer in an addition problem.
Example: 5 + 4 = 9

sum

**survey** A way to collect data by asking questions of many people.

**temperature** A measure of how hot or cold something is.

**thermometer** An instrument that measures temperature.

**ton (T)** A customary unit of mass (weight); 1 ton equals 2000 pounds.

**triangle** A polygon with 3 sides and 3 vertices.

**turn** The rotation of a figure around a point.

**value** In 324, the 2 is in the tens place. Its value is 20.

**vertex** The corner point of an angle, a closed plane figure, or a solid.

**vertices** More than one vertex.

vertex

**volume** The number of cubic units that could fit inside a container or a solid.

**whole number** Any of the numbers 0, 1, 2, 3, 4, 5, and so on.

**yard (yd)** A customary unit of length; 1 yard equals 3 feet.

**yardstick** A ruler marked in inches and feet, that is one yard long.

**zero property of addition** The sum of zero and one addend is the addend.
Examples: 4.9 + 0 = 4.9
0 + 6.7 = 6.7

**zero property of multiplication** The product of any factor and zero is zero.
Example: 4 × 0 = 0

# Acknowledgments

For each of the selections listed below, grateful acknowledgment is made for permission to reprint copyrighted material as follows:

Cover of *Kids Discover: Explorers* magazine, 1996 issue. Reprinted by permission of Kids Discover.

Cover of *Kids Discover: Solar System* magazine, 1996 issue. Reprinted by permission of Kids Discover.

Cover of *Kids Discover: Tornadoes* magazine, June/July 1996 issue. Reprinted by permission of Kids Discover.

Cover of *National Geographic* magazine, September 1990 issue. Reprinted by permission of National Geographic Society.

Cover of *Outside* magazine, April 1996 issue. Reprinted by permission from *Outside* magazine. Copyright ©1996, Mariah Media Publications.

Cover of *Ranger Rick* magazine. Reprinted from the May 1993 issue of *Ranger Rick* magazine, with the permission of the publisher, National Wildlife Federation. Copyright ©1993 by NWF.

Cover of *Ranger Rick* magazine. Reprinted from the September 1996 issue of *Ranger Rick* magazine, with the permission of the publisher, National Wildlife Federation. Copyright ©1996 by NWF.

Cover of *Time* magazine, August 12, 1996 issue. Reprinted by permission of Time, Inc.

Cover of *U.S. News & World Report* magazine, July 15, 1996 issue. Reprinted by permission of U.S. News & World Report Inc.

Cover of *Zoobooks* magazine, March 1996 issue. Reprinted by permission of Wildlife Education, Ltd.

Cover of *Zoonooz* magazine, February 1995 issue. Reprinted by permission of Zoological Society of San Diego.

*Decimal Squares, Fraction Bars,* and *Tower of Bars* were created by Professor Albert C. Bennett, Jr., and are registered trademarks of Scott Resources. They are used by permission of Scott Resources. All rights reserved.